Mephistopheles

Other books by Jeffrey Burton Russell:

Dissent and Reform in the Early Middle Ages (1965)
Medieval Civilization (1968)
A History of Medieval Christianity: Prophecy and Order (1968)
Religious Dissent in the Middle Ages (1971)
Witchcraft in the Middle Ages (1972)
*The Devil: Perceptions of Evil from Antiquity to Primitive
   Christianity* (1977)
A History of Witchcraft: Sorcerers, Heretics, Pagans (1980)
Medieval Heresies: A Bibliography (with C. T. Berkhout) (1981)
Satan: The Early Christian Tradition (1981)
Lucifer: The Devil in the Middle Ages (1984)
*The Prince of Darkness: Radical Evil
   and the Power of Good in History* (1988)

Mephistopheles

The Devil in the Modern World

JEFFREY BURTON RUSSELL

Cornell University Press

ITHACA AND LONDON

First published 1986 by Cornell University Press.
Second printing 1988.
First published, Cornell Paperbacks, 1990.

International Standard Book Number 0-8014-1808-9 (cloth)
International Standard Book Number 0-8014-9718-3 (paper)
Library of Congress Catalog Card Number 86-47648

Printed in the United States of America

*Librarians: Library of Congress cataloging information
appears on the last page of the book.*

To
Jack Vizzard and Sally Fitzgerald
And in Honor of
W. A. Mozart and Flannery O'Connor
whose joy
is the antidote for evil

Contents

Illustrations

Preface

In writing this book and the earlier volumes of this series, I have pursued the idea of the Devil in the Judeo-Christian-Muslim context because these are the religious traditions that originated and developed the idea. They have faced the problem most squarely because it emerges most sharply in these monotheist religions, in which the existence of evil contrasts with the idea of a single good and omnipotent God. I have pursued the idea in Christianity particularly, partly because of my own cultural and linguistic areas of knowledge, and partly because Christianity and the philosophical traditions arising out of Christian culture have been most explicit in formulating and confronting the problem of evil. I have followed no denominational course nor adhered to any orthodoxy other than the desire to pursue the truth as openly and as broadly as possible.

In this series, *The Devil* took the subject from the earliest times through the period of the New Testament; *Satan* covered early Christianity through the fifth century; *Lucifer* dealt with the Middle Ages. This volume treats the period from the Reformation to the present. Whereas the first three volumes showed the development of a degree of consensus, even in detail, about the concept of the Devil, the fourth volume shows a fragmentation of the tradition. Its title reflects this fragmentation, for the name Mephistopheles was invented in the sixteenth century for the figure of the Devil in the Faust legend, which eventually led Western literature into such untraditional views as Goethe's in his decidedly unchristian *Faust*.

The split between Protestant and Catholic in the Reformation began the process of fragmentation, but because Protestantism originally followed the Catholic tradition of diabology, serious splitting in the concept is visible only from the end of the seventeenth century. At that time, the discrediting of the witch craze helped to discredit the idea of the Devil as well, and in the eighteenth century the rationalist philosophies of the Enlightenment undermined the epistemological foundations of Christian tradition and further weakened diabology. By the end of the eighteenth century most educated people (including Christians) were ready to dismiss the idea altogether. Just at that time, however, Romanticism revived the Devil as a powerful and ambivalent symbol: the Romantic Devil personified noble rebellion against autocracy or served at least as an ambivalent representative of both liberty and selfishness. Toward the end of the nineteenth century, the Devil was quite a popular figure in literature, art, and music, usually as an ironic metaphor for the corruption and foolishness of humanity. The horrors of twentieth-century genocide and war have revived serious philosophical concern with radical evil, and the Devil is once again a serious issue for modern theology.

Except in a few sections, I have discussed only works that I can read in the original languages, because in such a delicate field as the history of concepts translations can lose essential points as well as nuances. All translations, except where otherwise noted, are mine. Throughout I have used the term "diabology" to refer to the theory of the Devil. Strictly speaking, the term would be "diabolology" (Greek *diabolos* + *logos*), but this is unfamiliar, pedantic, and extremely difficult to pronounce, so I have modernized it.

In the two decades that I have been exploring and reflecting upon this subject, my views have continued to develop. One learns to know that one cannot know and that in the end all that is left is the desire to know, for wisdom is greater than knowledge, and greater than wisdom is love.

I am deeply grateful to those who have been particularly helpful with this volume: Stuart Atkins, Carl Berkhout, Richard Comstock, Kara Enroth, Robert Erickson, Alberto Ferreiro, Sally Fitzgerald, Abraham Friesen, David Griffin, Robert Griffin, Eloise Hay, Richard Helgerson, Walter Kaufmann, Henry Ansgar Kelly, Gerald Larson, Leonard Marsak, Pamela Morgan, J. Sears McGee, Michael O'Connell, Norman Ravitch, Cheryl Riggs, Diana Russell, Jack Vizzard, and Michael Whitacre. I also thank the Research Committee and the Interlibrary Loan Department of the University of California, Santa Barbara.

JEFFREY BURTON RUSSELL

Santa Barbara, California

Abbreviations

DEVIL: Jeffrey B. Russell, *The Devil: Perceptions of Evil from Antiquity to Primitive Christianity*. Ithaca, 1977.

LUCIFER: Jeffrey B. Russell, *Lucifer: The Devil in the Middle Ages*. Ithaca, 1984.

SATAN: Jeffrey B. Russell, *Satan: The Early Christian Tradition*. Ithaca, 1981.

Mephistopheles

I would open my heart, if not my intellect (for that is beyond me) to the whole circle of truth.

JOHN HENRY NEWMAN

More than in the Devil, I am interested in the indications of Grace.

FLANNERY O'CONNOR

1 *Evil*

The Devil is the best-known symbol of radical evil. The existence of radical evil is clear to anyone not blinded by current relativism. On the world level it expresses itself in the willingness to put the entire planet at nuclear risk. At present, with arsenals of nuclear weapons estimated at seventy times the quantity needed to kill every living vertebrate on earth, we are stubbornly making preparations for a war that will profit no individual, nation, or ideology but will condemn thousands of millions to a horrible death. What force urges us down a path that is daily more dangerous? To whose advantage is the nuclear destruction of the planet? Only that force which from the beginning has with infinite cruelty and malice willed the destruction of the cosmos. If we are to avoid nuclear war, we must confront radical evil squarely.

On the individual level radical evil expresses itself in actions of unfathomable cruelty. The closest we get to the reality of evil is our own direct experience of evil in ourselves and in others. Perhaps only sociopaths lack this direct intuition. On November 14, 1984, UPI reported:

Cynthia Palmer, 29, and her live-in boyfriend, John Lane, 36, pleaded innocent to burning to death Mrs. Palmer's 4-year-old daughter in an oven. The two, who told neighbors shortly before their arrest that they were "cooking Lucifer," were arraigned Tuesday in Androscoggin County [Maine] Superior court. They were arrested Oct. 27 at their Auburn tenement apartment. Angela Palmer was found stuffed in the electric oven. The door was jammed shut with a chair.

I have consistently defined evil in two categories. The first is passive evil, the suffering that a sentient being feels. Suffering is the conscious sense of fear, dread, terror, agony, depression, or despair that may accompany pain or the threat or memory of pain. The second is active evil, the willingness of a responsible sentient being to inflict suffering upon a fellow sentient being. Traditionally, evil has been divided into three categories: (1) metaphysical evil, the lack of perfection inherent in any created world; (2) natural evil, the suffering that comes from "acts of nature" such as cancers and tornadoes; (3) moral evil, the deliberate willingness to inflict suffering. We are primarily concerned with moral evil, though in a sense the categories overlap, for if God exists, he is ultimately responsible for natural evil.

The radical nature of evil appears in the examples above. The suffering of the child in the oven is a suffering of absolute intensity; the suffering of billions of creatures in a nuclear war projects that one absolute suffering upon an entire planet. The more intense is one's love for this planet and its creatures, the greater is one's agony over the evil that twists it. Sensitivity to evil is sensitivity born of love.

The Devil is the symbol of radical evil. But does he exist, and in what sense?

The key to the question is *in what sense*. The first thing is to know what line of approach to the existence of the Devil we are taking. This question of how we know seems unfamiliar because we have been brought up to imagine that something is either "real" or "not real," as if there were only one valid world view, only one way to look at things, only one approach to truth. Given the overwhelming prestige of natural science during the past century, we usually go on to assume that the only approach to truth is through natural science. In our society this assumption is so broadly fixed that it seems to be "common sense." But philosophers and scientists know that there are multiple truth systems, multiple approaches to reality. Science is one such approach. But science is, like all other approaches, a construct of the human mind, shifting in time and based upon undemonstrable assumptions of faith. There is no possible scientific proof of the bases of science, no proof of the "external, objective world out there, uninfluenced by human consciousness. . . . The quantitativeness of physics does not guarantee an objective physical world and . . . there is no meaningful boundary—indeed no real difference—between the subjective and objective approaches to things."[1]

This is in no way to detract from science, which has constructed the

1. R. S. Jones, *Physics as Metaphor* (Minneapolis, 1982), pp. 49, 171.

most impressive and dramatic system in human experience. But science has its limits, and beyond those limits there are, like other galaxies, other truth systems. These systems are not without resemblances to science, but their modes of thought are quite different: among them are history, myth, poetry, theology, art, and analytical psychology. Other truth systems have existed in the human past; still more may exist in future; we can only guess what thought structures exist among other intelligent beings.

It is therefore possible to demonstrate a truth in one system that cannot be demonstrated in another. Art cannot demonstrate the components of sulfuric acid; science cannot judge the beauty of a Grecian urn. What is "true" in one system may not make sense in another. What is "real" in one system may not even be "real" in another.

This does not mean that there is no truth at all. It does not mean that any statement about sulfuric acid is as good as any other or that any judgment of the beauty of an urn is as good as any other. The truth is never simple, and any effort to make it so fails. This applies not least to the simplistic view that "everything is relative." The truth is difficult to get at; it is dynamic rather than static; and it exists in the tension between the knower and that which is known. We cannot ever grasp ultimate truth, but we can point toward that truth by engaging ourselves, by thinking clearly, and by not muddling categories.

Does the Devil exist? The answer is not simple, and it must not be muddled. Nothing can be known "absolutely," "in itself." This is the first step in understanding anything at all. We know only one thing directly and absolutely, and that is that "something is thinking." Everything else, including your own existence as an individual entity, is understood only in terms of that thinking. You perceive an elm tree, yet you do not know the elm tree in itself but only your thought of the tree, a thought formed by your sense impressions filtered through your brain and then assimilated into the mental structures that you have learned. Nothing guarantees that these processes produce a perception that corresponds to the reality of the tree itself. It is likely (though not certain) that some degree of correspondence exists, but the reality of the tree is so complex and multifaceted that your idea can at best encompass only a tiny fraction of its reality.

Of course, we make our way around the world as if our ideas do have some correspondence with reality, and this is quite proper, for we would not have survived or evolved if they did not. Relativism doesn't work. It remains more probable that the tree is a growing plant than

Felix Labisse, *Asmodée, Balaam, et Astaroth machinant la possession de Soeur Jeanne des Anges* (Asmodeus, Balaam, and Ashtaroth planning the possession of Sister Jeanne of the Angels), 1975. Oil on canvas. Courtesy of Galerie Isy Brachot, Brussels.

that it is a spaceship. However, both of these categories are already scientific. It is perfectly plausible that in addition to being an elm tree of a certain variety, shape, and mass the tree is also a "totem" or a "symbol of beauty" or "the tree on which John Smith was hanged"—all of which are statements about the tree that may be valid in truth structures other than the scientific. Consider how different the tree would seem to you if you had seen trees only at night, or if you had been blind from birth, or if you had seen trees only from a jetliner at forty thousand feet. Consider how differently a tree must be perceived by a dog, a woodpecker, a needle-borer, and an inhabitant of a planet of Vega. Vastly different senses, vastly different brain structures, vastly different mental structures: these guarantee vastly different perceptions of what the tree is.

Knowing this leads to an understanding that every thought system is limited and precarious. The truth is not encapsulated in any system but is that toward which the variety of truth systems converge, and the only truth we can ever achieve lies in the dynamics of the search, the intentionality of the mind toward truth. A tree is a plant; a tree is a sign of the beauty of the cosmos; a tree is a totem; a tree is raw material for a telephone pole; a tree is a historical monument. These are not mutually exclusive statements; they are different kinds of valid statements about the reality of the tree.

Thus there can be no one answer to the question of whether the Devil exists. The fact that most people today dismiss the idea as old-fashioned, even "disproved," is the result of a muddle in which science is called on to pass judgment in matters unrelated to science. The existence of the Devil cannot be meaningfully approached by science, because science is by definition restricted to investigating the physical and can say nothing about the spiritual. Further, the question of evil is a question of moral value, and science again by definition cannot discover moral values. Finally, moral evil is a matter of free choice rather than of cause and effect, and science cannot investigate truly freewill decisions, which by definition have no causes.

Many people today seem to believe that a question that cannot be investigated by science cannot be investigated at all. Confident that the only reality is material and that there is nothing real that science cannot investigate, they dismiss the idea of the Devil as meaningless. Now it is certainly true that the Devil cannot exist in a scientific sense. But he can exist in a theological sense, in a mythological sense, in a psychological sense, and in a historical sense; and these approaches are, like science, capable of fixing a course on truth.

This book is a historical treatment of the Devil. History at its best opens our minds to unfamiliar modes of thought rather than mining the past for data to fit our own preconceptions. It avoids the odd assumption that the predominant world view of our own time is somehow forever true. But modern historians finds themselves in a dilemma. On the one hand, they are drawn toward materialism. On the other hand, and more powerfully, they are drawn toward relativism, and that relativism, oddly, also leads them to accept materialism, since that is the most common viewpoint of the late twentieth century and is the basis for most of the new methodological vogues: it is "where the action is." Materialist history has produced much that is of value, but it also suffers from limitations, the first of which is that there is no compelling philosophical reason to assume the priority of materialism over idealism.[2] Ultimate reality is, in other words, at least as likely to be "idea" as "matter." In considering the Devil, materialist historians begin with the knowledge that the Devil does not exist scientifically and then slide into the assumptions that the Devil therefore does not exist historically; that the idea is outdated by science and therefore silly; that there is no point of studying it in itself; and that its only use lies in helping them understand the "mentalities" that produced it—mentalities formed by the material, social conditions that materialist historians take to be the only realities.

This sort of dilemma can be avoided by taking a more idealist tack. Idealist historians realize that their own world view and that of their contemporaries is as precarious as those of the past; they are therefore willing to learn from the world views of other cultures; and they believe that ideas are important in themselves, affecting material conditions as well as being affected by them, and having a life and meaning of their own. The idea of the Devil is an important concept in understanding the nature of evil, and as such it points toward the truth. The Devil exists historically as a long-lived and immensely influential concept aimed at the truth about evil.[3]

2. S. Toulmin, *Human Understanding*, 3 vols. (Princeton, 1972–), vol. 1, p. 49, speaks of the relativity of "all . . . types of concepts—including even our most fundamental scientific ideas." Jones notes (p. 63) that "universal authority may be claimed for an abstract, timeless system of 'rational standards' only if it has first been shown on what foundation that universal and unqualified authority rests; but no formal scheme can, by itself, prove its own authority." The idea that the materialist, positivist, scientistic world view has been proved is an illusion.

3. A convincing defense of the history of ideas is F. Oakley, *Omnipotence, Covenant, and Order* (Ithaca, 1984), pp. 15–40.

In aiming at the truth, we obtain knowledge—not of noumena (things in themselves) but of phenomena, human conceptions of noumena. The elm tree in itself is a noumenon and unknowable; your idea of the tree is a phenomenon, and it is knowable. Phenomena are not merely subjective or relative, for they are formed in the tension between your mind and senses and the tree in itself. Phenomena are collective as well as individual. The collective phenomenon of elm tree is a concept of elm tree that many people share; it is verifiable, understandable, and describable. The phenomenon of tree is not identical among individuals, nor is the collective phenomenon of tree identical among groups and societies. The phenomenon of tree is quite different to an Iroquois, an ancient Canaanite, and an Oregon lumberman. Phenomena such as "tree" are changeable, but because they are rooted in an external reality, their changeability is less pronounced than that of phenomena rooted in human constructions alone. What humans have created, they can change substantially. "The Constitution," for example, is a phenomenon that has changed substantially with time. The brake on change on "the Constitution" is not so much observation of external reality as observation of tradition. What "the Constitution" is is governed by the tradition of what it is. "Tree" can be defined scientifically as well as historically, but the only effective way to define "the Constitution" is historically, by describing its tradition.

"The Devil" is best investigated by history, which does not make the faith assumptions of theology yet can, unlike science, address the phenomenon directly. Since the history of the Devil embraces other modes of knowing the Devil, such as theology, mythology, and literature, it is superior to all other approaches in that it includes them all. The Devil is therefore best defined in terms of his history.

The "history of the Devil" does not mean the history of the Devil-in-himself, which would be impossible. It means the history of the phenomenon, the history of the concept of the Devil. This concept has changed through time. The Devil has had four fundamentally different modes: (1) a principle independent of God; (2) an aspect of God; (3) a created being, a fallen angel; (4) a symbol of human evil. These variations, different though they are, have participated in shaping a tradition, a tradition that over the millennia gradually extrudes and excludes some views while retaining others. As the tradition moves along, it does not necessarily get better—in the sense that a 1687 view of the Devil would be better than a 1387 view—but it does get fuller; and as the tradition becomes richer, it approaches truth. The closest we can get to the truth about the Devil is the examination of the tradition as a whole.

As the Protestant Reformation was beginning, the concept of the Devil had been refined over fifteen hundred years, and though it still contained a number of inconsistencies, it had achieved a consensus that was both wide and deep. That consensus continued throughout the Reformation, spanning the gap between Catholic and Protestant. By the end of the seventeenth century, however, it had begun to come apart, opening up to a wide and diverse set of new ideas and values. That is the story of this book, which begins now with the Reformation of the sixteenth century.

2   *The Reformed Devil*

The sixteenth century spans the difference between the time of Luther and the time of Shakespeare. It was a period that witnessed a profound shift in the center of gravity of perceptions of evil, from the world of spirits to the world of humanity. The Reformation of the sixteenth century produced a divergence in theology between Protestant and Catholic, a divergence that was narrow at first but widened rapidly, eventually encouraging the growth of the non-Christian and secular views that have come to dominate Western society.

The Reformation, a complex set of events, can be divided broadly into three main sectors: the "magisterial Reformation" of the learned, relatively conservative Protestant leaders Martin Luther (1483–1546), John Calvin (1509–1564), and Huldrich Zwingli (1484–1535); the Radical Reformation of the Anabaptists, Unitarians, and Thomas Muntzer (1489–1525); and the Catholic Reformation typified by the career of Ignatius Loyola (1491–1556) and by the Ecumenical Council of Trent (1545–1563). These movements were also tied (whether in accord or discord) with the growth of humanist scholarship typified by Desiderius Erasmus (1466?–1536). The beginning of the Reformation is by convention dated October 31, 1517, when Luther issued his ninety-five theses. Luther was excommunicated on January 3, 1521; the *Protest* of the German Lutheran nobles at the Diet of Speier in 1529 produced the term "Protestant." The religious wars that proceeded from the schism continued until the Treaty of Westphalia in 1648. Such were a few of the landmark events of the most important period in the history of Christianity and Western thought since the age of Constantine.[1]

1. On the Reformation in general, see S. Ozment, *The Age of Reform, 1250–1550* (New Haven, 1980); L. Spitz, *The Protestant Reformation, 1517–1559* (New York, 1985).

The diabological assumptions of the sixteenth century continued to be for the most part essentially traditional, even medieval. Witchcraft, Luther, Calvin, the Catholic Reformation, the mystics, and pre-Faustian literature all continued the old ways of perceiving the Devil. The sharpest turn in the history of diabology came not with the Reformation but with the Enlightenment of the eighteenth century. Reformation thought, both Catholic and Protestant, was continuous with that of the Middle Ages: Luther, Calvin, and even Zwingli were all in the Aristotelian, scholastic, Augustinian mode that had characterized Western thought for a millennium. Whereas two radically different world views—those of hermetic magic and material science—were beginning to emerge and challenge the whole traditional Christian system, the Reformation debate focused narrowly on competing views within the old Augustinian-Aristotelian tradition.

Many streams of late medieval thought flowed freely into Reformation channels. Nominalism, especially the Ockhamism of Gabriel Biel (1425?–1495), continued its great influence. Nominalism, the "modern way" of the fourteenth and fifteenth centuries, nurtured both the free-will side and the predestinarian side of the debate about human responsibility. Ockhamism emphasized the utter freedom of both God and man. On the one hand it affirmed the utter freedom and hence the omnipotence of God, but on the other hand it stressed the freedom of the human individual. The extreme defenders of free will, such as Biel, had argued that sincere moral effort and good works could earn grace and that free moral cooperation with grace could earn rewards. Against this Luther reacted angrily, and in general both Catholic and Protestant reformers agreed that grace was a free gift of God that could not be earned in any way. The debates of the sixteenth and seventeenth centuries were focused on the somewhat more narrow questions of whether grace was extended to all and whether, once it was extended, one was free to resist it. The tendency of most theology in those centuries was predestinarian, but both Catholics and Protestants remained "practical Pelagians," preachers of free will in the pulpit, for few dared to tell congregations that their salvation or damnation had been eternally decreed.

Nominalist skepticism about the ability of logic to reach the truth about God engendered a number of other ideas prominent in Reformation thinking. One was fideism, an emphasis upon faith over reason; closely related to fideism was the emphasis upon revealed, biblical religion over rational discourse. These two tendencies became the passwords of the Reformation: *sola fides; sola scriptura*—faith alone and scripture alone. Such ideas reinforced the anticlericalism that arose in part from corruptions of the church (though these have been exaggerated), in part from medieval anticlerical movements such as fifteenth-century Hussitism, and in part from the inference from *sola fides* and *sola scriptura* that an authority structure of bishops and priests might be dispensable. Skepticism about the wide claims of the papacy had been lively since the conciliar movement of the fifteenth century. Nominalism also encouraged mysticism, which was at its height from the fourteenth through the seventeenth century and produced some of its most outstanding examples in the Lutheran Jakob Boehme and the Catholics Teresa of Avila and John of the Cross.

Underneath this generally conservative traditionalism a radical shift in world view was slowly being prepared by deep social changes. The growth of towns and the middle class encouraged the growth of literacy far beyond the priesthood, and this meant that the middle classes could now read and interpret the Bible on their own; more important, it meant that increasing numbers of literate people focused their attention on the concerns of the secular world: making money, building businesses, raising families. Added to these developments was the rise of the secular nation-state with its concerns for state power and international influence. A gradual turning of attention from the other world to this world followed naturally.

Humanism spread from Italy into the north in the sixteenth century, bringing with it the beginnings of skeptical, critical, and secular thought. The nominalist division between faith and intellect encouraged the growth of empirical, material science. Another emerging world view was hermetic magic, which for a century sustained a vigorous and sophisticated competition with science. Until a few decades ago hermetic magic was misunderstood, muddled with witchcraft, and thought to be an ignorant product of the lower forms of Aristotelianism. Magic is so tied in our minds to childish stories, stage conjurors, and sloppy, anything-may-happen fantasies that it is difficult to grasp how sophisticated a structure of thought Renaissance magic was. The underlying idea that the cosmos is a unity whose every part influences every other part in a vast system of "sympathies" means that no part of the cosmos is isolated from any other part. Stars, minerals, plants, and the human body and mind all interact in ways that are often hidden (occult) but are nonetheless regular, rational, and discoverable.[2]

2. On magic, see F. Yates, *The Occult Philosophy in the Elizabethan Age* (London, 1979).

Neither the scientific nor the hermetic view of the world had much room for the Devil. Yet Satan, far from being ready to retire, reached his height of power just at the moment when the intellectual structures supporting him were beginning to shake. The theology of Luther and the rise of the witch craze both encouraged belief in the Devil. And no one seemed aware that three radically divergent world views—Aristotelian Christianity, hermetic magic, and material science—were in conflict. It was like a collision of galaxies, an interpenetration on so vast a scale that an individual scarcely noticed it. The result was an inevitable confusion of terms, one of the worst of which was the confusion of magic and witchcraft. Some sixteenth-century intellectuals did make an attempt to distinguish "natural magic" (hermetic, intellectual magic) from "profane magic" (vulgar witchcraft and sorcery), but many intellectuals of the conservative, Aristotelian camp either ignorantly or deliberately confused the two in order to discredit the magicians. Jean Bodin, the Aristotelian author of *De la démonomanie des sorciers* (1580), though well aware of the distinction, did not scruple to link the magicians with the witches. When the magical world view was defeated, partly owing to this unfair connection, science emerged unscathed above the rubble of both Aristotelianism and magic.

The witch craze had roots in the Middle Ages, but its ugly maturity occurred in the sixteenth and seventeenth centuries. According to the Christian theology of that era, witches were people who had formally given themselves to the Devil by making a pact with him: in return for their service, Satan rewarded them with magical powers, which they used for evil purposes. They rendered people impotent or sterile, they blighted crops, they caused diseases, they dried up cattle. In short, any natural disaster could be blamed on them. Demonic obsession and possession, mental illness, and radical shifts of mood or behavior were also laid at their door. They formally renounced Christ and worshiped the Devil. They met at night, often flying to their "sabbat" on brooms, fences, or animals or simply levitating through the air. They held incestuous orgies. They kidnapped and sacrificed Christian babies, eating their flesh in parody of holy communion or rendering their fat for use in ointments and poisons. Witches were to be found all over Europe, in every neighborhood, all linked in one great conspiracy under the generalship of Satan against the Christian community.

Such a conspiracy never existed, yet papal pronouncements, Catholic councils, Protestant synods, inquistorial tribunals, secular courts, and leading scholars all repeatedly proclaimed its reality. Millions were sus-

Hans Baldung Grien, *Hexenszene* (The Witches), 1514. Aided by their familiar demons in the form of animals, the witches prepare to set off for the sabbat. Ink drawing on paper. Courtesy of Graphische Sammlung Albertina, Vienna.

pected, tortured, or threatened with torture; probably more than a hundred thousand were executed. The craze reached full spate with Innocent VIII's publication of the bull *Summis desiderantes affectibus*, which was included by the inquisitors Sprenger and Institoris as a preface to their *Malleus maleficarum* (1486), a book that had enormous influence. The craze continued until the end of the seventeenth century.

The witch craze moved against many of the intellectual currents of the time: nominalist skepticism, hermetic magic, and humanism. But it was encouraged by Aristotelian scholars as a defense against the competing ideas of magic and science. For the most part it was an invention of the elite, gradually spreading down through pulpit and courtroom to the people, who accepted it greedily as an explanation for their own troubles. It varied in intensity in time and place and was exacerbated by local disasters and social tensions (its intensity may even be correlated with outbreaks of ergot poisoning in crops). It was certainly aggravated by the religious and political tensions of the Reformation. And it was both cause and result of the revival of the idea of the Devil, who had been flagging but now returned to his kingdom in full pomp and regalia.[3]

Aside from witchcraft, the Protestant Reformation itself was the most important element in the revival of the Devil. The Protestant emphasis upon *sola scriptura*—the Bible as the only source of authority—meant a due regard for New Testament teaching on Satan. Because of their fear of witchcraft, the reformers went further; despite their enthusiasm for pruning out of tradition any growths that they considered not to be rooted in scripture, they uncritically accepted virtually the entire tradition of medieval diabology. In the long run, the Protestant emphasis upon the absolute sovereignty of God and the refusal to believe that any being could interpose between man and God may have promoted skepticism about Satan's power, but if so, it took almost two centuries to do so.

Protestant concern about the Devil was, on the whole, stronger than Catholic. Luther's theology, Lutheran "Devil books," and Protestant plays and poems all made the Devil's powers greater and wider than at any time since the first few centuries of Christianity. Part of the reason

---

3. On witchcraft, see B. Easlea, *Witch Hunting, Magic and the New Philosophy* (Brighton, Sussex, 1980); J. B. Russell, *A History of Witchcraft* (London, 1980).

may have been the removal by the Protestants of such structures as exorcism and private confession, through which beliefs in the Devil could be contained or controlled. More important was the temptation to enlist the Devil in the propaganda battle against religious opponents. For Protestant pastors the pope was the Antichrist; John Bale, Protestant Bishop of Ossory (1495–1563), told how Satan in the form of a hermit boasted that "we religious" and contemplatives never study the Bible and claimed the pope as a good friend who was helping him against true Christianity.

In Catholic exorcisms, on the other hand, the demons were reported to praise Protestant doctrines as they fled screaming from the bodies of their victims. The religious tensions, culminating in wars, between Catholics and Protestants and among varieties of Protestants promoted the sense that the Devil was lurking everywhere.

Another important reason for the growth of Satan's power in the sixteenth century may have been the turning inward of the Christian conscience, found not only in Protestantism but in the new introspective character of Catholicism typified by Ignatius Loyola. Earlier ages had seen the Devil's opponent as God, Christ, or the whole Christian community. If attacked by Satan, you could at least feel part of a great army upon whose hosts you could call for aid. But now it was you versus the Devil; you alone, the individual, who had the responsibility for fending him off. No one denied that the grace of Christ protected the faithful, but the new introspection placed upon the individual the burden of examining his soul for signs of a weak faith that would invite the Devil in. Bishop Bale observed that the true Christian's challenge was to examine his own soul for any signs of weakness, insincerity, lukewarmness, or lack of faith and charity; these would be the marks of the Devil's power. Medieval Christianity offered a kind of analog in the struggle of the individual saint against Satan, but a saint was a person of unusual strength, a hero, an "athlete of God," whose enormous faith shielded him and allowed him to rout his enemy triumphantly. But now there was no shining saint armed with the buckler and sword of glory, only the solitary Christian, alone in his closet with his Bible, pondering his sins, unsure of his faith, fearful of the power of temptation.

Against biology, against the social nature of mankind, against Paul's mystical body of Christ, against the practice of the early Christian community, against centuries of Christian tradition, this individualistic emphasis on self-reliance and competition left the Christian naked on a

MALLEVS
MALEFICARVM,
MALEFICAS ET EARVM
haeresim frameâ conterens,

EX VARIIS AVCTORIBVS COMPILATVS,
& in quatuor Tomos iustè distributus,

*QVORVM DVO PRIORES VANAS DÆMONVM
versutias, prastigiosas eorum delusiones, superstitiosas Strigimagarum
caeremonias, horrendos etiam cum illis congressus; exactam denique
tam pestiferá sectá disquisitionem, & punitionem complectuntur.
Tertius praxim Exorcistarum ad Dæmonum, & Strigimagarum male-
ficia de Christi fidelibus pellenda; Quartus verò Artem Doctrinalem,
Benedictionalem, & Exorcismalem continet.*

TOMVS PRIMVS.
Iudices Auctorum, copiaxm, rerúmque non desunt,

Editio novissima, infinitis penè mendis expurgata ; cuique accessit Fuga
Dæmonum & Complementum artis exorcisticæ.

Ve sint mulier, in quibus Pythonicus, vel divinationis fuerit spiritus, morte moriatur ;
Leuitici cap. 10.

LVGDVNI,
Sumptibus CLAVDII BOVRGEAT, sub signo Mercurij Galli.

M. DC. LXIX.
CVM PRIVILEGIO REGIS.

The title page of the *Malleus maleficarum*, "The Hammer of the Witches," by the inquisitors Sprenger and Institoris. This edition appeared in 1669, a testimony to its long popularity: originally published in 1486, it was the most influential book in launching the long witch craze.

black heath at night, exposed to the winter winds of evil. No wonder the literary heroes of the age were Faust, standing alone at the midnight crossroads with Mephistopheles, and Macbeth alone on the blasted heath with the three witches. Isolation provoked terror, terror an exaggerated view of the Devil's power.[4]

The period that saw a vast increase in the Devil's powers also witnessed the beginnings of overt skepticism. The world views of nominalism, humanism, hermetic magic, and science had little room for Satan. Moreover, the heightened terror brought on by introspective individualism must have provoked in many hearts an intense psychological reaction against belief in the evil powers; the fearsome excesses of witchcraft and religious strife caused others to doubt. Aconcio, an Italian Protestant, wrote that the Devil did his deadliest work in inciting Christians against one another; he called for toleration of all Christians (except, of course, Catholics and Unitarians).[5] In 1563 Johann Wier expressed skepticism about witchcraft and diabolism in his book *On Magic*; Michel de Montaigne (1533–1592) argued that the existence of witchcraft was surely not firmly enough established to justify killing people; but such views would be rare among intellectuals for another century. Intellectual skepticism was outdone by the stout incredulity of the practical layman: Keith Thomas reports that Brian Walker of Durham announced, "I do not believe there is either God or Devil, neither will I believe in anything but what I see."

The response of believers to such skepticism was *"nullus diabolus nullus redemptor"* (no Devil, no redeemer). Believers suspected that if the Devil, the second best-known figure in Christianity, could be excised from the Christian tradition, then any other figure might be eliminated as well. If Christ did not come to save us from the power of the Devil, as the New Testament said, then perhaps he did not save us at all. The replacement of a world view in which God and the Devil fit coherently by one in which they did not meant that the existence of God would ultimately be questioned as well as that of the Devil; the process has only taken a bit longer with God.[6]

---

4. On the power of the Devil in the art of the age, see B. Bamberger, *Fallen Angels* (Philadelphia, 1952); H. Bekker, "The Lucifer Motif in the German Drama of the Sixteenth Century," *Monatshefte für deutsche Sprache und Literatur*, 51 (1959), 237–247; H. Vatter, *The Devil in English Literature* (Bern, 1978). On John Bale, see Vatter, pp. 108–113, and D. P. Walker, *Unclean Spirits* (Philadelphia, 1981).

5. G. Aconcio, *Stratagematum Satanae libri VIII*, 1565 (Florence, 1946).

6. A.-E. Buchrucker, "Die Bedeutung des Teufels für die Theologie Luthers: Nul-

The old world view of Augustine and the scholastics was still vigorously alive in the thought of Luther (1483–1546), who devoted more of his theology and personal concern to the Devil than anyone had done since the desert fathers.[7] Luther planned to attend law school but was terrified by a lightning storm into making a pledge to God; he entered the house of the Augustinian canons at Erfurt in 1505. At Erfurt and then at Wittenberg he studied Aristotle, Biel, and the nominalist *via moderna;* he came later to reject Aristotle but never abandoned many of the assumptions of nominalist scholasticism. In 1513 Pope Leo X proclaimed the sale of indulgences, and Luther, a professor of scripture at Wittenberg since 1511, began to question the direction the church had taken; he was also suffering deep and painful scruples about his worthiness to be a priest. About 1515 he had an experience of personal conversion, in which he was convinced that good works and efforts are of no value without grace and that *sola fides,* faith alone, could open us to salvation. He issued his ninety-five theses in 1517 and by the next year was already referring to the papacy as a monster. At the time of his Leipzig disputation with John Eck in 1519, Luther adopted *sola scriptura,* claiming to base his beliefs on the Bible alone and rejecting the additional authority of tradition, popes, and councils. In 1520 the pope condemned the professor, who retorted, "I regard the see of Rome as possessed by Satan and as the throne of Antichrist" (WA 6.595–612). The next year he was formally excommunicated; efforts by moderates to effect a reconciliation failed; and the schism began.

The theology of Luther, the most prolific Christian writer of all time, is topical and allusive like Augustine's rather than systematic like Aquinas' or Calvin's. It owes much to medieval theology (especially nominalism), to mysticism, and above all to Luther's own psychology, expressed in his deep devotion to the Bible. It was also shaped by debates with other theologians. Few Christian writers have been as polemical as Luther; like Augustine's, his views must be understood in terms of his response to those with whom he (often violently) disagreed. For Luther

lus diabolus—nullus Redemptor," *Theologische Zeitschrift,* 29 (1973), 385–399; K. Thomas, *Religion and the Decline of Magic* (New York, 1971), pp. 170, 469.

7. On Luther, see H. Oberman, *Luther: Mensch zwischen Gott und Teufel,* 2d ed. (Berlin, 1983); J. M. Todd, *Luther: A Life* (New York, 1982). I use the following standard abbreviations for Luther's works: WA—Weimar Ausgabe (Kritische Gesamtausgabe), *Werke,* 61 vols. (Weimar, 1883); WAT—Weimar Ausgabe (Kritische Gesamtausgabe), *Tischreden,* 6 vols. (Weimar, 1883); WAB—Weimar Ausgabe (Kritische Gesamtausgabe), *Briefwechsel,* 17 vols. (Weimar, 1883).

the only valid bases for thought were faith and the Bible (WA 10/3.208–209). Next to the Bible his chief source was Augustine, but he contrasted his "true" Augustine to the Augustinian scholastics, who, he believed, had overextended the range of reason. Reason gets us nowhere without grace, and grace teaches us best when we read the Bible in the light of our faith. Reason must be used only in its proper sphere, which is as an aid to understanding the truth that we have already learned from faith and the Bible.

The absolute omnipotence of God and its corollary, predestination, were also fundamental to Luther. In 1525 he wrote *De servo arbitrio, The Unfree Will*, in refutation of Erasmus' *De libero arbitrio* (1524). In this work, in his catechism of 1529, and elsewhere in his writing, Luther embraced absolute predestination, maintaining that anything else was an illogical, almost blasphemous limitation on the sovereign will of God. "Therefore," he said, "we must go to extremes, deny free will altogether, and ascribe everything to God" (WA 18.755). A human being has no power at all to achieve his own salvation; he is always in the power of God or else under the power of Satan, to whom God gives authority over the wicked. God chooses those whom he saves and turns the others over to the Devil. Christ did not die for all but only for the elect.[8] In boldly grasping the nettle of predestination, Luther was aware of its pricks: if the cosmos is so closely determined, what is the need of sacraments, sermons, or the incarnation itself? He was unable to resolve those difficulties, but he was never willing to allow any limitation whatever on the power of God. In this he was again a faithful nominalist, but except Calvin, perhaps no Christian theologian before or since has been so unflinchingly consistent in affirming the total omnipotence of God.

Omnipotence, Luther believed, is twofold. First, God has natural omnipotence; that is, he is the originator of the cosmos and as such is absolutely free to make the cosmos exactly as he chooses. Everything in the cosmos *is* because he wills it to be; if he did not choose it, it would not exist. Second, God has theological omnipotence; he is not only the remote but also the immediate cause of everything that is. This is no absent God but one who has every mote in the universe in his immedi-

---

8. WA 18.635; 17/1.47–48; 56.182: "Deus vult me obligari et omnes, et tamen non dat gratiam, nisi cui velit, nec vult omnibus, sed electionem in illis sibi reservat." On Luther's predestination, see L. Urban, "Was Luther a Thoroughgoing Determinist?" *Journal of Theological Studies*, 22 (1971), 113–137; F. Brosché, *Luther on Predestination* (Stockholm, 1978), p. 121; and E. Winter, *Erasmus-Luther Discourse on Free Will* (New York, 1961).

ate gaze. God never lets the reins fall from his hand; he directs heaven and earth, hell, the Devil, and all creatures. God would be ridiculous if he were not in charge of everything or if anything were done without his power (WA 12.587; 18.718). Where the great theologians of the past, Augustine and Aquinas, had nominally affirmed free will while describing a cosmos that was in fact predestined, Luther specifically denied that free will was compatible with God's omnipotence. Whatever is, is from God; nothing is done without the natural and theological will of God.

In such a cosmos, God is both remotely and immediately responsible for evil. Even Luther blinked at this point, distinguishing between two aspects of God and contrasting the just, stern, and apparently cruel face of God with the kind, merciful, and loving face of God, which we can know only through the revelation of Christ. There is only one God, but we limited mortals seem to see him as a double figure, willing both good and evil. Since evil is, it must be the will of God. Yet God also wills the good against the evil. Thus it can be said that God wills evil; God wills good; God does not will evil; God does not will good.[9] To our limited understanding, some things appear good and others evil, but ultimately all evils are good, since all that God does is good (WA 1.75; 18.708; 31/1.447). We often cannot grasp God's motivations. Evils, for example, may be punishment for our sins (WA 3.223–224). God is also responsible for hardening of hearts and for *Anfechtung*.[10] *Anfechtung* is a combination of trials, testing, doubt, despair, terror, and desolation. It is sent to us by both God and the Devil. *Anfechtung* takes advantage of our every doubt, our every fear, our every scruple. It can destroy anyone not fully fortified by faith.[11]

God is thus composed of apparent antinomies, an idea that Luther took from the mystics. God is wrath, and God is love. God is repudiation, and God is grace. God is law, and God is mercy. God wills wickedness and hates the wicked. The natural, unaided reason cannot

9. WA 56.187. Cf. WAT 2.10; WA 18.709: "Hic vides Deum, cum in malis et per malos operatur, mala quidem fieri, Deum tamen non posse male facere, licet mala per malos faciat, quia ipse bonus male facere non potest, malis tamen instrumenti utitur."

10. WAT 2.20: "Gott liebet die Anfechtungen und ist ihnen gram. Lieb hat er sie, wenn sie uns zu dem Gebet reizen und treiben; gram ist er ihnen aber, wenn wir dadurch verzweifeln" (God likes and hates Anfechtung. He likes it when it impels us to prayer but hates it when it causes us to despair).

11. WA 15.451; 16.140; 40/2.414–418; 42.110. See H. Obendiek, *Der Teufel bei Martin Luther* (Berlin, 1931), pp. 193–201; Brosché, pp. 67, 137–140.

penetrate this mystery; without grace we see God as stupid, imprudent, terrifying, or cruel (WA 16.142). Since our notions of good and evil are different from and infinitely inferior to God's, we cannot always grasp the good in his purposes. We perceive God as having a double will, willing both good and evil. We see God as willing evil and sin, yet with the will that he reveals to us in Christ, he wills the good. In fact this apparent double will is one united will that we cannot understand (WA 18.550). Beneath the apparent antinomies, God is pure goodness and love. Though God hides under the mask of the Devil, the goodness, power, and mercy of God cannot be understood by metaphysics but only by experience.[12] The will of God is present in all evil, even in hell, turning all evil to ultimate good (WA 6.127; 13.591). Luther clearly and courageously saw that this hard doctrine was a corollary of the absolute omnipotence of God.

The hidden, stern will of God can appear to be the Devil's will.[13] Though Luther verged on saying that the Devil was the manifestation of one side of God, he refrained from doing so, for the Devil's will is only *apparently* the same as God's will; while the Devil and God may will the same thing, their purpose is never the same. Yet the Devil is God's tool, if not his arm. The Devil would not exist if God had not created him; the Devil would not be evil if God had not willed him to be evil; the Devil could not work evil if God did not allow him to do so. In any evil event—an *Anfechtung*, for example—both the Devil and God are active. *Anfechtung* comes from the Devil—and from God. The difference is in motive. Whereas God has an ultimately benevolent purpose in every act, the Devil's aim is always to destroy. One's unaided intellect is unable to tell the difference between God and Devil in any situation, but grace and faith provide the discernment through which one can distinguish the hand of God from the hand of Satan (WA 5.387; 11.24; 15.451; 40/2.13).

The Devil is God's tool, like a pruning hook or a hoe that he uses to cultivate his garden. The hoe takes pleasure in destroying the weeds for its own purpose, but it can never move out of God's hands or weed where he does not wish, or thwart his purpose of building a beautiful garden (WA 16.203; 18.709; 45.638–639). Thus the Devil always does God's work. When a pastor was murdered in 1527, Luther felt it and

---

12. WA 36.428–430; 40.2/417–420; 44.429; Brosché, p. 116.
13. WA 17/2.13; 41.675: "Er stelt sich ut Teufel"; 43.229–232; R. Bainton, *Here I Stand* (New York, 1950), p. 179; Buchrucker, p. 399.

pondered it deeply. It was the work of an evil person; the evil person was the Devil's tool; but the Devil was God's tool. Luther suggested that God's providence might use the murder to encourage others to become devoted pastors like Pastor George. The murder was committed through God's gracious and paternal order as well as through the Devil's raging hatred. How else could it be in a cosmos where God guides the motion of every atom and the course of every star?[14] All evils come from both the Devil and God, but the Devil wills the evil in them and God wills the good that comes out of them. "God incites the Devil to evil, but he does not do evil himself."[15] Since God turns Satan's every effort to the good, God does good not in spite of the Devil but in and through the Devil, and God is himself present in the Devil (WA 15.644; 18.709; 40/3.519). The good that God wills in an event is his own work (*opus proprium*); the evil that God wills through Satan is God's *opus alienum*. When God's *Anfechtung* afflicted Job, for example, God's *opus alienum* was the temptation of Job, but his *opus proprium* was the strengthening of Job's faith. If there were no evil and no Devil, then virtue would wither for lack of challenge (WA 40/2.417).

The knowledge that God works through the Devil may tempt us to hopelessness and horror; unaided by grace, we would doubt God's own goodness. But the mercy of God in the incarnation of Christ shows us the *Deus revelatus*, the revealed God, who is the God of mercy and love. Through Christ's love we can understand that in all the apparent harshness of the world, God's loving presence and purpose are never absent.[16]

Anyone who defends the absolute omnipotence of God is obliged to take a position similar to Luther's. If all is from God, then evil and the Devil are from God. But this unflinching monism does not lead to acquiescence in evil. Though the Devil does evil under God's command, God also hates the evil and wishes us to fight against it. God struggles mightily against Satan, with every human heart as the battleground and every human soul as ally or opponent.

In a cosmos ruled by absolute omnipotence, the individual human has no freedom. He or she is subject to the will either of God or of Satan. The soul, said Luther, is like a horse: when God rides it, it goes where

14. WA 23.402–431, esp. 424–425: "Durch Gotts gnedige und veterliche ordnung, und durchs teuffels wüetigen hass."

15. WA 16.143: "Deus incitat diabolum ad malum, sed non facit malum."

16. WA 39/1.249–250, 426–427; 41.675. See also H.-M. Barth, *Der Teufel und Jesus Christus in der Theologie Martin Luthers* (Göttingen, 1967), pp. 201–202.

God chooses; when the Devil rides it, it goes where the Devil chooses. The two riders dispute the mount between themselves, but the horse has no choice; it obeys whoever is in the saddle.[17]

Luther felt this struggle intensely within his own soul. His diabology came not only from scripture and tradition but also from personal experience. As Heiko Oberman puts it, "Sein Leben war Kampf gegen den Teufel (his whole life was a war against Satan)." This is no exaggeration. Luther's world view was that each individual, and humanity in general, was caught in a tension between Christ and the Devil. Luther experienced both directly and could not dispense with the Devil without calling into question both Christ and the very tension that he experienced so deeply. Like the desert fathers and the medieval saints, Luther felt that the Devil attacks more intensely as one advances in faith. He reported that the Devil attempted to deter him from God's work in every possible way: through temptations, distractions, and even physical manifestations. He rattled around behind Luther's stove; at the Wartburg castle he pelted nuts at the roof and rolled casks down the stairwell; at the Coburg he appeared to Luther in the form of a serpent and the form of a star; he grunted audibly like a pig; he disputed with Luther like a scholastic; he emitted stenches; he sometimes lodged in Luther's bowels and was closely associated in the Reformer's mind with feces and flatus. Satan's eagerness for Luther's soul kept him so close that he "slept with Luther more than Katie (Luther's wife)." Oberman suggests that Luther's concern about the Devil was fixed in childhood by his mother, neighbors, and teachers. His association of the Devil with feces was intense, but it seems less the product of an obsessive personality when one understands that such associations were part of a long medieval tradition. It had something to do with the Reformer's chronic constipation, no doubt, but also to do with tradition, with his desire to communicate forcefully with the common people on a concrete level, and with his tendency to invective. It also, Oberman suggests, has a theological justification. The human body is the temple of God, yet it is frail and ridiculous, excretion being perhaps its most absurd function. Luther contrasts the divinity of the human body, which Jesus had dignified, with its ridiculous aspects, which Satan apes and mocks to

17. WA 18.635, 709. This famous image, which Calvin also used, is derived from Pseudo-Augustine, *Hypomnesticon* (c. A.D. 435), *Patrologia Latina*, 45.1632, and ultimately from Ps. 73:22. See A. Adam, "Die Herkunft des Lutherwortes vom menschlichen Willen als Reittier Gottes," *Luther-Jahrbuch*, 29 (1962), 25–33; Oberman, pp. 232–234. The evil person has no choice but to do evil, for evil is what he is: WA 18.709.

our shame.[18] Luther felt that the Devil was trying to block his efforts to serve God and that if he gave up those efforts, Satan would leave him alone (WA 32.121; 40/2.172; WAB 4.288).

Luther's account of the Devil's role in the history of the cosmos is virtually identical with that of medieval tradition. Lucifer was created good, the highest of the angels, but he chose to betray his creator. His motives were pride, which led him to presume to imitate God, and envy of humankind, because God's choice to become a man rather than an angel set human nature over angelic nature.[19] He was thrust out of heaven; eager for revenge, he corrupted Adam and Eve; as a result of their original sin, God gave humanity over to him and made him lord of this world (WA 12.394; 13.89; 19.644). Having us in his power, he daily afflicts us; he is responsible for all natural evils such as storms, diseases, and mental depressions (WA 36.564; 37.152–153; 43.64). Worse, he is constantly at our side tempting us to sin. The first cause of evil, he is the cause of every individual sin as well, encouraging individuals to despair and nations to warfare.[20] He assigns an individual demon to encourage each individual vice, and he and his demons can appear anywhere and in whatever form they choose, even that of Christ himself.[21] All human sinners are servants of the Devil.[22]

18. WAT 1.153, 232–233, 244–245, 289: "Er schlefft vil mer bey mir denn meine Ketha"; 2.306; 6.215–219; 5.328–329; WA 16.435; Oberman, pp. 108–114, 163–166, 260–285, 304–307.

19. WA 1.269; 15.473; 25.456; 37.286; 40/2.138–140; 41.488; 42.18.62; 43.3. There are two traditional variations on Lucifer's envy of humanity: first, that it arose at our creation because God made us in his own image; second, that it arose when it was known in heaven that God would take on human nature as Christ. The latter scenario created several difficulties: if Satan had known that the inevitable result of his fall would be the incarnation and his defeat at the hands of Christ, would he have rebelled? And, if he had not rebelled, the incarnation might not have been necessary. Milton attempted to straighten this out in *Paradise Lost*. But Milton differed with Luther in another major respect: Luther did not believe in a war in heaven at the beginning of the world; rather, he interpreted Revelation 12 as referring to the struggle of the early Christians against their persecutors. For Luther, the Devil was hurled from heaven—as in the medieval mystery plays—by the simple fiat of God. See S. P. Revard, *The War in Heaven* (Ithaca, 1980), p. 109.

20. WA 9.638; 16.435; 18.659; 32.176; 42.414; WAT 1.506–511.

21. Various beings, including birds, apes, giants, goats, snakes, and wolves: WAT 1.153, 511; 2.358; 4.687; 5.150; WA 14.434: "diabolus semper simia Dei"; 34/1.311; 50.644–647. The Devil feigns to be Christ: WA 40/2.13. See A. Adam, "Der Teufel als Gottes Affe: Vorgeschichte eines Lutherwortes," *Luther Jahrbuch*, 28 (1961), 104–109.

22. Luther was influenced by Sebastian Brandt's *Narrenschiff* (1494), in which humans are portrayed as fools sailing in a ship manned by a crew of follies, vices, or demons.

Goya, *El Gran Cabron*: the Devil in the form of a goat is presiding at a witches' sabbat. Mural transferred to canvas, 1821–1822. Courtesy of the Prado Museum, Madrid.

Satan's power over us is shattered by the incarnation of Jesus Christ.[23] Before Christ's advent, Satan had been sure of his power over us, and when Christ came he was enraged, because he knew that the Lord would destroy him.[24] The Devil tried to stop Christ from the very beginning of his ministry, tempting him as soon as he went out into the desert after his baptism.[25] But God made Christ an obstructor against the great obstructor, and Christ struck Satan blow after telling blow: in his incarnation, in his miracles, in his preaching, and in his passion. The Devil plotted the passion in unthinking rage against Christ, and God used it to overthrow the Devil, the proof being Christ's resurrection.[26] The world, the flesh, and the Devil still remain to tempt us, but they have no more power over us. One little word—the name of the Savior—can fell them. Christ's defeat of the Devil is renewed again and again and culminates at the last judgment. Until then, the kingdom of Christ is in constant opposition to the kingdom of the Devil, which is the kingdom of this world. The kingdom of God consists of those who follow Christ; it is characterized by grace, revelation, devotion to the Bible, and faith. The kingdom of this world is characterized by sin, reliance upon law, and trust in reason. The invisible church, the Christian community with Christ as its head, is in the kingdom of heaven; but the visible church, with its corruptions, is in the kingdom of this world. There is no neutral ground; everyone lives in one kingdom or the other.[27]

The Devil still has power in the world because so many choose to follow him. Some make deliberate pact with him: Luther was no skeptic of witchcraft; through prayer, he himself saved a student at Wittenberg who had made the formal renunciation of Christ. All sinners serve in the Devil's army, as do pagans, heretics, Catholics, monks, Turks, and

23. Luther's emphasis upon the shattering of Satan's power by Christ helped revive the assumptions of ransom theory, which had been out of favor since the twelfth century. See LUCIFER, pp. 104–106, 168–180; WA 7.596; 20.343; 27.109; 28.607: "Redemptionem non possem laudare, nisi Satanam et hostes eius meminero"; 28.607.

24. WA 13.467; 15.460; 16.97; 17/2.220; 29.80; 40/2.21; 44.756; 45.505; 50.270.

25. WA 17/1.64; 28.404; 32.14–15; 40/2.495.

26. WA 9.598; 17/1.69; 20.316, 327, 360; 29.253; 34/1.225; 36.58; 37.22, 50; 40/1.276: "Est unus qui vocatur Christus, est diabolus diabolorum, infernus infernorum, occidit mihi legem, diabolum, mortem, et te conculcat"; 40/1.279: "Christus est diabolus contra meum diabolum"; 57C.128.

27. WA 17/2.106, 217; 18.743; 31/1.178; 32.341; 42.229; 44.754. For the identity of this world with the Devil, see WAB 8.353.

radical Protestants. The pope is the Antichrist himself.[28] Luther's view
that the whole world was in tension between God and the Devil did not
permit him to see ecclesiastical disputes as matters of honest disagreement or even politics; they were always aspects of the great cosmic war.

The Devil's power remains "as big as the world, as wide as the world,
and he extends from heaven down into hell," yet "the evil spirit has not
a hairbreadth more power over us than God's goodness permits."[29]
Christ puts a great arsenal of weaponry against the Devil at the disposal
of Christians, including baptism, the Bible, preaching, the sacraments,
and song.[30] Luther's best-known contribution to popular diabology is
his famous hymn, "A Mighty Fortress Is Our God," whose main point
is Christ's defeat of Satan:

> A mighty fortress is our God,
> A good weapon and defense;
> He helps us in every need
> That befalls us.
> The old, evil enemy
> Is determined to get us;
> He makes his cruel plans
> With great might and cruel cunning;
> Nothing on earth is like him. . . .
> But if the whole world were full of devils
> Eager to swallow us,
> We would not fear,
> For we should still be saved.
> The prince of this world,
> No matter how fierce he claims to be,
> Can do us no harm;
> His power is under judgment;
> One little word can fell him.[31]

28. WAB 2.293: "Papa est Christi adversarius et apostolus diaboli." For Luther on
"papists," see WA 8.477–563; 51.287–288. On radicals, WA 23.112; 26.161; 28.5;
40/2.355: "papistae nobis inimici, sed Scwermeri sunt voll Teufel." On Turks, WA
30/2.81–197; 37.50. On monks, WA 8.503. On heretics in general, WA 5.164: "hoc iam
esset non theologissare, sed diabologissare"; 5.202; 17/2.221; 18.134, 764; 19.498;
32.330; 37.19; 40/1.35; 46.499: "hinc multae haereses ortae, der Teufel fat allzeit sein
spiel." Some heretics are possessed by the Devil: WA 18.194; Karlstadt was possessed by
"eyns rachgyrigen teuffels": WA 49.102; 51.498.

29. WA 9.589; 15.460; 17/1.46–47; 23.70; WAT 2.527.

30. On baptism, see WA 19.537–541; 30/1.212–222. On the Bible, WA 9.638;
18.659; 30/1.127–129, 146. On preaching on the gospel, WA 28.289.

31. The original words can be found in Gustav Roskov, *Geschichte des Teufels* (Leipzig,
1869), vol. 2, p. 475:

Our every defense against Satan rests upon the power of Jesus Christ. With that power, the Protestant Reformation itself is a mighty defense.[32]

Luther also used more direct means. He exorcized his student Johann Schlaginhaufen himself.[33] He also marshaled cheerfulness, laughter, boisterousness, bawdiness, scorn, insults, obscenity, and farts—everything active, assertive, earthy, and good-humored—to fend off the *Anfechtungen* and depressions on which the evil one thrives; one of his best defenses against the Devil was to go to bed with Katie.[34] In the end of time, the Devil will be finally and completely destroyed, along with those mortals foolish enough to follow him. God will have no more need of him, for the elect will all have entered into the Kingdom of God, from which the Evil One and his servants are forever excluded (WA 26.509).

Luther's ideas were both effect and cause of the deeply shifting religious mentality of his day. Popular movements of reform and lay piety

---

Ein feste Burg ist unser Gott
Ein gute Wehr und Waffen,
Er hilft uns frei aus aller Noth
Die uns itzt hat betroffen.
Der alt böse Feind
Mit Ernst er's izt meint,
Gross Macht und viel List
Sein grausam Rüstzeug ist,
Auf Erd ist nicht seines Gleichen. . . .
Und wenn die Welt voll Teufel wär
Und wollt uns gar verschlingen,
So fürchten wir uns nicht so sehr
Es soll uns doch gelingen.
Der Fürst dieser Welt
So saur er sich stellt,
Thut er uns doch nicht,
Das macht er ist gericht
Ein Wörtlein kann ihn fällen.

See also E. Hirsch, "Das Wörtlein, das den Teufel fällen kann," in Hirsch, *Lutherstudien*, 2 vols. (Gütersloh, 1954), vol. 2, pp. 93–98.

32. On the church, see WA 30/1.190; 44.793; 46.500. On the Reformation, see WA 39/1.489; 44.398, 447.

33. WAT 1.483–484; 2.19–20, 28–31, 131–132.

34. WAT 1.233: "Die besten kempff, die ich mit yhm gehabt hab, hab ich in meynem bett gehabt an meiner Kethen seyten." See K. Roos, *The Devil in 16th Century German Literature* (Frankfurt, 1972), p. 18, for a list of Luther's insults of the Devil, including *Junker Teufel, schwarze Tausenkünstler, Kuckuck, Mönder, Bösewicht, Ketzer,* and *Rottengeist.* Luther drew enthusiastically upon folklore with its myriad of insulting names for demons.

had begun to sweep Germany in the fifteenth century; in the sixteenth, the prodigious eloquence and energy of Luther transformed those currents into a new religious orientation. Luther's followers, Philipp Melanchthon and a host of others, spread the Reformer's views; his translation of the Bible into German was received with such wide enthusiasm that it became from that time on the standard of educated German; his ideas were debated in sermons, popular books, and catechisms.

The catechisms—some written to help the clergy instruct the laity, others directly for the laity—provide a view of what the faithful were expected to believe. Catechetical books did not exist before the fifteenth century, when they were first used as moral guides for penitents preparing for confession; the invention of printing encouraged their widespread use. The idea was expanded to include instructions for children and those preparing for confirmation, and they were quickly adopted by Protestants as well as Catholics. Dietrich Kolde's *Christenspiegel* of 1470 was the first printed German catechism; Luther wrote a catechism for children in 1508–1509, and his influential greater and smaller catechisms in 1529; his follower Melanchthon composed a children's catechism in 1540–1543.[35] The catechisms were backed up by formal confessions of faith: Catholic at the Council of Trent; Protestant in the Augsburg Confession, the Thirty-nine Articles, and the Westminster Confession.

The place of the Devil in these documents is secure but seldom salient. His existence, his influence, and his threat to Christians and Christianity are never discounted. In the catechism of Canisius, for example, Satan appears 67 times, Jesus only 63. The clearest statements are found in Luther's Greater Catechism of 1529, in which the Reformer discusses the Evil One in relation to the Lord's Prayer, the Creed, baptism, and the Eucharist.[36] Still, attention to the Devil was never recommended, and the calm with which he was approached in the catechisms, even at the height of the witch craze, indicates that—secure though his existence was in scripture and tradition—he was never considered a safe or proper focus of Christian attention. The Christian was asked to turn his gaze away from the shadow and toward the light of the Lord.

---

35. See Luther's *Kleine Katechismus*, WA 30/1.239–425, and *Grosse Katechismus*, WA 30/1.123–238.

36. WA 30/1.186, 197, 202–213, 232. See also J. Delumeau, *Catholics between Luther and Voltaire* (London, 1977), p. 173.

John Calvin, the second leader of the Protestant Reformation, studied humanities, law, and theology and came into contact with Lutheran ideas in the 1520s. In the early 1530s he underwent a conversion to Protestantism and from 1536 to 1541 became a leader of the Reformation at Geneva and Strasbourg, where he was influenced by Martin Bucer. His *Institutes of the Christian Religion*, a precise, rational statement of the evangelical position, was both a statement of his own beliefs and a political effort to stop Francis I from prosecuting the Evangelicals. More methodical, logical, and ordered than Luther's works, Calvin's *Institutes* became the basis for what came to be known as Reformed or Evangelical Christianity.[37]

Calvin enthusiastically subscribed to the principles of faith alone and scripture alone. Since human nature was completely deformed at the time of original sin, natural reason is unable to obtain any truth at all without the illumination of faith, and natural morality can only sin without the aid of grace. True knowledge comes from the Bible, which the Holy Spirit interprets for those whom faith has saved. Calvin agreed with Luther's view of the total omnipotence of God. God is in complete control of every element of the cosmos. No fate, fortune, chance, or freedom limits this complete sovereignty. This means that God is responsible for evil. Why God ordains evil is a mystery that we are not permitted to unravel. Yet, Calvin insisted, God has only one united will; though he seems to our limited intelligence to do both good and evil, he always works for the ultimate good. Cold and compelling logic led Calvin to deny that God could be said merely to permit evil; God not only permits but actively wills evil, as when "he turned Pharaoh over to Satan to be confirmed in the obstinacy of his breast." In every evil human act, three forces are working together: the human will to sin, the Devil's will to evil, and God's will to the ultimate good. In every evil person both Satan and the Lord are at work, each for his own purpose.[38]

Calvin's doctrine of double predestination flowed directly and logically from this doctrine of absolute omnipotence. Occasionally, Calvin affirmed free will, but what he meant by free will was freedom from bondage to sin, a freedom obtained by grace, which leaves us free to be

37. The *Institutes* (*Christianae religionis institutio*) were first published in 1536, with a second edition in 1539, a third in 1543, and a fourth in 1559; the first edition in French appeared in 1541. I use the 1559 edition. The Commentaries cited below may be found in *Ioanni Calvini opera quae supersunt omnia*, 59 vols. (Berlin, 1863–1900), vols. 45–55.

38. *Inst.* 1.14.1–19; 1.17.5; 1.18.1; 2.4.2–5; Comm. on Matt. 6:13.

our true selves. We have no power to refuse grace. Those whom God chooses cannot refuse him, and those whom God does not choose have no way to be saved. The gift of grace inevitably engenders faith. Predestination is "God's eternal order by virtue of which he decrees in himself what, according to his will, is to happen to every individual human being. . . . To some, eternal life is assigned; to others, eternal damnation. Accordingly, then, as the individual is created for the one or the other goal, he is . . . predestined to life or to death."[39] Calvin admitted that this was a "horrible doctrine" (*decretum horribile*) but asserted that it is necessary because "no one can deny that God foreknew the future final fate of man before he created him, and that he foreknew it because he ordained it by his own decree" (*Inst.* 3.2.57).

Calvin outlined the doctrine as follows: God chooses the elect before the foundation of the world; he chooses those to be rejected and damned (*reprobi*) before the foundation of the world, and these are delivered unreservedly to the Devil (Comm. on John 13:27). Thus Adam's fall was ordained before the creation of the world. That all humans fell in Adam and Eve is clear from 1 Cor. 5:22 and Rom. 5:18. But though Calvin enthusiastically endorsed Paul in affirming the unity of all humanity in Adam, he rejected the unity of all humanity in Christ, the second Adam. For Christ did not come to save everyone, but only those whom God has chosen in all eternity. It is a mystery why Christ does not save us all, but that he does not is obvious from two things: that sinners abound, and that God has the absolute freedom and power to grant or withhold grace regardless of merit. Since nothing can place any limits on God, it is inconceivable that anything could exist or occur that God has not ordained. Double predestination was a courageous and consistent deduction from absolute omnipotence, but it seems to have entailed a limitation of God's mercy, if not his justice, and also to have eliminated the point of the incarnation, since God can save and damn by eternal decree (*Inst.* 3.23.5).

The Devil's role in Calvin's scheme was similar to his role in Luther's. Calvin began by firmly rejecting the skeptical view that angels and demons are only ideas in human minds (*Inst.* 1.14.19). But though Calvin granted the Devil as much theoretical power as Luther did, he did not give him nearly as much attention. In this he was more con-

---

39. *Inst.* 3.21.5. Cf. 2.5; 3.21.7; 3.22.11; 3.23.5; Comm. on John 8:34, 13:27. For Calvin's use of the image of the human will as a beast ridden by God or the Devil, see *Inst.* 2.4.1.

sistent than his German colleague. Luther's intense personal experience of Satan caused him, against his own strict monism, to attribute to the Devil huge force in the world. Calvin's ideas of Satan were drawn from theology more than from experience; in consequence, he ascribed to the Devil a narrower scope: Satan is completely regulated by God and cannot even conceive of any evil that God does not expressly assign him. He is simply the executor of God's judgments: "To carry out his judgments through Satan as the minister of his wrath, God destines men's purposes as he pleases, arouses their wills, and strengthens their endeavors."[40]

Recognizing that the Bible offers few particulars on the fall and activities of Satan, Calvin insisted that it was inappropriate to explore these questions in detail.[41] When he did discuss Satan, however, he gave him almost all his medieval attributes: Satan has physical and spiritual powers; he is responsible for tempting humanity to original sin and to individual sins; he is the cause of heresy, popery, and witchcraft. His power over humans is at God's pleasure, though over the elect that power is only nominal, but it is also God's pleasure to destroy that power through the saving act of Christ, whose chief purpose is the destruction of Satan's kingdom. Christ is in no way a ransom paid to the Devil; rather, he crushes the Devil as God destroys any tool with which he has finished. Evil persists after the incarnation also by God's will; Christ's victory over Satan is full, but its complete "manifestation is properly said to be delayed until the last day," at which time Satan will be annihilated (Comm. on Luke 19:12). The persistence of sin after Christ's passion is no more astounding than its existence beforehand, for the effects of Christ's saving mission extend equally in all directions in time and space. It is an eternal action on the part of God, which saves those before as well as after Christ.[42]

40. *Inst.* 2.4.3. Cf. 1.14.14–19; 1.16.1–2; 1.17.8–9; Comm. on 2 Cor. 12:17; Comm. on Matt. 12:29; Comm. on Isa. 10:26; Comm. on John 3:2; Comm. on Acts 19:13; Comm. on Deut. 18:10. On Calvin and the Devil, see P. F. Jensen, "Calvin and Witchcraft," *Reformed Theological Review*, 34 (1975), 76–86; O. Pfister, *Calvins Eingreifen in die Hexer- und Hexenprozesse von Peney 1545 nach seiner Bedeutung für Geschichte und Gegenwart* (Zurich, 1947).

41. *Inst.* 1.14.13–16; Comm. on 2 Pet. 2:4.

42. Comm. on Luke 1:68. On the Devil in general, see *Inst.* 1.14.13–18; 2.5.1; Comm. on Gen. 3:1–3; Comm. on Isa. 36:10; Comm. on Matt. 25:41–43, 27:11; Comm. on John 3:17, 6:15, 8:44; Comm. on 1 John 3:8; Comm. on 1 Pet. 5:8; Comm. on 2 Pet. 2:4. On the Devil's powers, see Comm. on Isa. 13:21, 24:14; Comm. on Matt. 12:22; Comm. on Luke 4:33, 13:10. On the Devil as responsible for witchcraft and popery, see Comm. on John 7:41. For Satan's limited power over the elect, see Comm. on Acts 12:23. For

The diabology of Zwingli and of the radical reformers, such as Muntzer and the Anabaptists, was not much different from that of Luther and Calvin except for a tendency to universalism—belief in the salvation of all, including the fallen angels—and some skepticism about the existence of a personal Devil. At a synod of 1550 in Venice, the unorthodox Italian Anabaptists denied the existence of the Devil and of hell, as well as the existence of angels, the virgin birth, and the divinity of Christ. This antitrinitarianism, a forerunner of Enlightenment Deism, was an early trump against belief in Satan, but both Protestants and Catholics took such harsh measures against its skepticism that it was scarcely heard.[43]

The Catholic Reformation and the Protestant Reformation are now understood as two parts of a general movement of reform. However, deep differences pitted their adherents against one another, the result being that many ideas on both sides tended to be formulated and hardened in opposition to the other. Still, this opposition had a number of constructive aspects: the critical study of the history of theology and the church, increasing concern for the instruction of the laity, and a reevaluation of the structure of the church.

The systematic theology of the Catholic Reformation tended to revert to medieval realism. Nominalism and Augustinianism were largely set aside in favor of a revived systematic realism associated primarily with Jesuits such as Ignatius Loyola, Robert Bellarmine (1542–1621), and Francisco Suarez (1548–1617). The teachings of Thomas Aquinas (1225–1274) were revived and elevated, as Thomism, almost to the realm of dogmatic truth. As the papacy—in response to the Protestant threat—consolidated its control over that part of the church that remained Catholic, Rome became a center of Catholic theology for the first time, and theology and papal authority came to be closely melded. The new Thomism offered little new theology, devoting itself to refining details of the scholastic system in the conviction that reason, based on revelation and aided by God's grace, could construct an objectively true view of the cosmos. The virtue of the approach is that it preserved

---

Satan's power crushed by Christ, *Inst.* 2.8.15; 2.16.7; 2.11.15; Comm. on Isa. 59:19; Comm. on Luke 10:18; Comm. on Eph. 4:8; Comm. on Heb. 2:14. On Satan and original sin, *Inst.* 1.14.18; 2.1–5; Comm. on 1 Cor. 12:2; Comm. on Gen. 3:15, 8.21; Comm. on Amos 5:15; Comm. on John 13:27. Like Luther, Calvin had no place for the war in heaven; for Calvin the only biblical texts relating to the fall of Lucifer were 2 Pet. 2–4, Jude 6, and Luke 10.8. See Revard, p. 109.

43. On Zwingli, see G. R. Potter, *Zwingli* (Cambridge, 1976). On the radicals, see G. H. Williams, *The Radical Reformation* (Philadelphia, 1962), esp. pp. 202, 562.

the valuable insights of medieval theology; its drawback was that its rigidity precluded openness to new ideas and approaches, thus rejecting what was constructive, along with what was destructive, in modern thought. Protestantism came to have the opposite set of virtues and defects: it lost many insights by rejecting tradition too vigorously; it was open to new currents of thought but sometimes embraced novelties too swiftly and uncritically. The relative openness of Protestantism meant that new ideas on diabology appeared more frequently in Protestant circles, while Catholicism held to scholasticism until the late twentieth century. The influential Carmelite anthology entitled *Satan*, published in 1948, was the last important book on the Devil arising from the old Thomism.[44]

In the context of rising papal authority and Thomist revival, the Council of Trent met in a number of sessions between 1545 and 1563 and set a tacit seal upon the Thomist view of the Devil and demons. Modern Catholic theologians, respectful of councils yet eager to expunge diabology from theology, have tended to evade the issue. On the one hand, only two ecumenical councils—Fourth Lateran (1215) and Trent—made explicit statements about the Devil. On the other, virtually all Christian theologians, popes, and councils from the beginning of the church into the present century have assumed his existence and power. Trent made no statement affirming the Devil's existence only because no one was challenging it; further, three of its decrees define aspects of the Devil's activities: session 3, *Decreta de symbolo fidei* (February 4, 1546), citing Eph. 6:12, takes the Devil's existence for granted; session 5, *Decretum de peccato originali* (June 17, 1546), chapter one, affirms the Devil's power over us as a result of original sin and blames him for the existence of old and new heresies, including Protestantism; session 14, *De extrema unctione* (November 5, 1551), chapter nine, describes the cleverness of the Devil in his efforts to lead us away from the faith.[45]

44. Bruno de Jésus-Marie, ed., *Satan* (Paris, 1948).

45. Sess. 5, ch. 1: As a result of original sin we are "sub ejus potestate, qui mortis deinde habuit imperium, hoc est diaboli" (Heb. 2:14); this session also refers to "serpens ille antiquus, humani generis non solum nova, sed etiam vetera dissidia perpetuus hostis." Sess. 14, ch. 9: "Nam etsi adversarius noster occasiones per omnem vitam quaerat et captet, ut devorare animas nostras quoquo modo possit: nullum tamen tempus est, quo vehementius, ille omnes suae versutiae nervos intendat ad perdendos nos penitus, et a fiducia etiam, si possit, divinae misericordiae deturbandos, quam cum impendere nobis exitum vitae perspicit." For the decrees of Trent, see H. H. Schroeder, *Canons and Decrees of the Council of Trent* (St. Louis, 1941).

The Devil also held his accustomed place in the view of contemplatives or mystics. Contemplative Christianity is intensely unitive, characterized by a strong sense of the presence of God everywhere and by its emphasis upon leading a life of prayer directed toward union with God. For the mystics, whatever blocks the progress of the soul and the cosmos toward union with God is the Devil's work. The closer you come to that goal, the more the Devil strives to divert you; for this reason, mystics often have intense and immediate experiences with the Devil. Their deep introspection makes them acutely aware of the power of evil tendencies within the soul. The most influential sixteenth-century contemplatives were the Carmelites Teresa of Avila and John of the Cross, the Lutheran Jakob Boehme, and the founder of the Society of Jesus (Jesuits), Ignatius Loyola.

Loyola, who proposed systematic rules for spiritual training, was sharply conscious that the deadly enemy of humanity works to divert all Christians from their proper goal of serving Christ in order to make them his own servants instead. From his fiery throne he sends out his demons to every part of the world. No one at any time is ever free from the temptations suggested by these eager demons. The Devil seeks to convince us that worldly pleasures and sensual delights will make us happy. Often we are deluded into yielding, but the results are always the same: anxiety, sadness, and desolation. Satan seems sometimes to console us, but whatever good he purports to offer is really only for his own evil designs, never for our welfare. Ignatius refined the psychological insights of the desert fathers on the discernment of spirits. If we are pointed toward God, the action of a good spirit in our hearts will always promote peace, joy, hope, faith, charity, tears of repentance and love, and elevation of mind, while the action of an evil spirit will bring upset, depression, concern for worldly things, and aridity of soul. However, if we are steeped in habitual sin and pointed away from God, the action of a good spirit calling us to repentance will seem harsh, while the action of an evil spirit, lulling us into a false peace with our evil lives, will seem pleasant and easy. To discern good from evil, therefore, we need to understand our own basic orientation as well as the effect of the spirits themselves. All the Devil's powers and wiles, great though they are, yield immediately when confronted with the superior strength of Jesus Christ. Ignatius offers a way to defeat the Devil that is, he says, invariably effective: steadfast faith in Christ.[46]

46. "The General Examination of Conscience," week 2, day 4: Meditation on two

For the Lutheran mystic Jakob Boehme (1575–1624) both good and evil emanate from God. The cosmos is oriented toward God when it maintains the two in balance. But to ignore the light and focus on the darkness is to upset the cosmic harmony. Lucifer, the greatest angel, combined the two qualities in his nature, but he freely chose to unbalance the world by seeking the darkness only. He seeks to twist the world that God has made and so enters into our "center," the ground of being of our souls, where he uses all his craft to bend us away from integration and harmony. But so long as the soul remains in "resigned humility just as a fountain depends on its source, ceaselessly drawing and drinking the waters that flow forth from God," it will be safe and at peace.[47]

The great contemplatives Teresa of Avila (1515–1582) and John of the Cross (1542–1591) were deeply involved in the reform of the Carmelite order. Teresa is best known for her discussion of the grades of prayer through which the soul that is focused upon the love of God passes before reaching the "central mansion" of the soul, where Christ lives. Teresa distinguished sharply between the essence of mysticism, which is loving contemplation of God infused by God's own love and grace, and the tangential phenomena that may accompany the contemplative life: visions, audible sensations, ecstasy (Teresa preferred the terms "suspension" or "rapture"), levitation, and stigmata. Such phenomena can easily be manipulated by Satan to his own ends; Satan may create illusions of such things in order to corrupt the gullible; even when they come from God, the Devil may twist them by making us proud of them or by causing us to care for them more than for the real experience of God that they accompany. John warned of avarice for spiritual gifts. The purpose of the contemplative life, he said, is not to obtain spiritual favors but to give up one's will and one's desire to God.[48]

---

stewards; and "Rules for the Discernment of Spirits," both in *Spiritual Exercises*. See Ignatius Loyola, *Obras completas*, ed. Ignacio Iparriguirre (Madrid, 1952). On Ignatius see H. Boehmer, *Ignatius von Loyola* (Stuttgart, 1941); H. Rahner, *Ignatius the Theologian* (New York, 1968); H. Rahner, *The Spirituality of St. Ignatius Loyola* (Chicago, 1953).

47. Jakob Boehme, *Der Weg zu Christo*, in W. E. Peuckert, *Jacob Boehme sämtliche Schriften*, 11 vols. (Stuttgart, 1955–1961), vol. 4 (1957), the Fourth Treatise, 30; see the Fourth Treatise, 1–30; the Fifth, 8; the Eighth, 1–22; the Ninth, 43–63. Boehme wrote "The Way to Christ", in 1622; cf. his "Aurora" (1612), "The Three Principles of the Divine Essence" (1619), and *Mysterium magnum* (1624). On Boehme, see A. Liem, *Jacob Boehme: Insights into the Challenge of Evil* (Wallingford, Pa., 1977); C. Musès, *Illumination on Jacob Boehme* (New York, 1951).

48. See Santa Teresa de Jesús, *Obras completas*, 2d ed. ed. E. de la Madre de Dios

Although Teresa warned against taking the Devil too seriously and advised that his powers should be despised (*tener en poco*), both she and John perceived Satan as always and everywhere active against all Christians, especially the contemplatives, whom he seeks at all costs to block from their goal of union with God. Though he is always powerless against the defense that Christ raises up in a faithful soul, at the least sign of weakness he rushes in with suggestions that seem reasonable and good at the moment but yield only confusion, aridity, or disgust. His temptations are ingeniously diverse: he encourages self-righteousness and false humility and discourages us from prayer; he causes us to feel guilty for having received God's grace and to labor under the impossible burden of trying to earn it; he makes us ill-tempered toward others; he creates illusions and distractions in the intellect; he inspires the doubt and fear that the understanding we are granted in contemplation is illusion. Sometimes we feel that we have lost control of our souls, as if demons were tossing them back and forth like balls. Sometimes we feel that we are making no progress, but even when the boat is becalmed, God is secretly stirring in the sails and moving us along.

Against those who are not discouraged by such temptations, Satan makes direct and visible assaults. He repeatedly visited Teresa, usually in invisible form: she would feel his presence as the manifestation of the living lie, deceit, and hypocrisy. Sometimes he appeared visibly: he perched in repulsive shape on her left hand; his body exuded a flame that cast no shadow; with a hideous mouth he warned her that though she had escaped him hitherto, he would have her yet. When she made the sign of the cross, he disappeared, only to reappear again shortly. She finally banished him by sprinkling holy water on him: thereafter, she always recommended holy water as the most effective physical sign of grace in repulsing the Devil. The Devil frequently beat her, shaking her body with invisible blows. She had visions of battles between angels and demons and of the torments of hell.

The writings of Teresa and John, like those of Luther, indicate the powerful hold that traditional diabology had upon sixteenth-century

---

(Madrid, 1967), *Camino de perfeccion, Moradas del castillo interior,* and esp. *Libro de la vida,* chs. 12–13, 26, 30–32. On Teresa, see S. Clissold, *St. Teresa of Avila* (London, 1979); M. Lépée, "St. Teresa of Jesus and the Devil," in Bruno de Jésus-Marie, pp. 97–102. See also Juan de la Cruz, *Obras,* ed. D. Silverio de Santa Teresa (Burgos, 1931), esp. *Subida del Monte Carmelo* and *Noche oscura.* On John, see Crisógono de Jesús Sacramentado, *The Life of St. John of the Cross* (London, 1958); L. Cristiani, *St. John of the Cross* (New York, 1962); A. Cugno, *Saint John of the Cross: Reflections on Mystical Experience* (New York, 1982).

thought. They also pose a problem for modern historians, for they cannot be dismissed as uncritical medieval hagiography or legendary accretions. They are autobiographical accounts written by those who had the experiences themselves. What were the experiences really? Modern viewpoints such as depth psychology provide us with new angles and new questions, but no one mode of thought, new or old, should be supposed to exhaust the truth, and any interpretation that dismisses Teresa's own perceptions of the phenomena is unsophisticated and reductionist.

The graphic arts continued the late medieval iconography of Satan, but Hieronymus Bosch (d. 1516) and his followers, such as Pieter Brueghel the Elder (d. 1569), transformed and extended it. Bosch's iconography corresponded closely to the traditional Christian view, but it introduced a complex and varied symbolism open to interpretation on a number of levels, and he shifted the focus of evil from the demonic to the human. The gloating faces that rejoice in Christ's suffering in *Ecee Homo*, *Christ before Pilate*, and *Christ Carrying the Cross* are examples in art of what Shakespeare would accomplish in poetry: the transference of demonic qualities to human beings. The gloaters are human, but they have crossed into the realm of the totally evil. The grotesqueness that characterizes Bosch's art serves the specific function of portraying the deformity of evil. The confused, twisted faces of demons and demonic humans are contrasted with the serene face of *Christ Bearing the Cross*.[49]

Sixteenth-century literary diabology may be divided roughly into pre-Faustian literature, the Faust legend, and post-Faustian literature. One widely popular genre was the *Teufelsbücher* ("Devil books"), written primarily by Lutheran pastors in simple language for the edification of the Protestant laity. Flourishing from about 1545 to the early seventeenth century, they appeared in a number of formats: treatises, compendia, letters, poems, and dramas. Each book was characterized by its discussion of a particular vice and its special demons. Behind the demons of dressing, eating, drinking, cursing, hunting, dancing, theatergoing, and other worldly concerns stood the Devil, an intensely powerful figure acting everywhere and always, deluding the individual

49. On Bosch and Bruegel see L. Baldass, *Hieronymus Bosch*, 2d ed. (Vienna, 1959); W. S. Gibson, *Bruegel* (New York, 1977); S. Orienti, *Hieronymus Bosch* (New York, 1979); J. Wirth, "La démonologie de Bosch," in *Diables et diableries* (Geneva, 1977), pp. 71–85. Other influential paintings were Lorenzo Lotto's *Saint Michael Driving Out the Devil* (1554–1556), and the famous *Ritter, Tod, und Teufel* of Albrecht Dürer (1471–1528).

Hieronymus Bosch (1450–1516), *Christ Carrying the Cross*, detail. The faces of the people mocking Christ have been demonized. Oil on wood. Courtesy of the Musée des Beaux-Arts, Ghent.

conscience and sowing discord in families, parishes, nations, and international affairs.[50]

Under the influence of Luther and the witch craze, and because of the harsh religious tensions of the era, sixteenth-century literature tended to take the Devil more seriously than that of the previous centuries.[51] Though some works carry on the light, satirical late medieval tradition and some even express skepticism about witches, others are earnest treatises on the worship that witches render their evil master.

A favorite genre was the epic poem or play portraying the fall of the angels and the glorious victory of Christ (or Michael) over the evil angels at the beginning of the world. This war in heaven, for which there is no clear Biblical warrant, had been assumed by a number of medieval writers on the basis of their reading of Revelation 12. However, the idea seldom appeared in the mystery dramas of the late Middle Ages, and it was specifically rejected by Luther and Calvin. Yet its inherent drama

50. On the Teufelsbücher see K. L. Roos, *The Devil in 16th Century German Literature: The Teufelsbücher* (Frankfurt, 1972). Many of the Teufelsbücher were compiled by the publisher Sigmund Feyerabend in the *Theatrum diabolorum* (Frankfurt, 1569; 2d ed., 1575; 3rd ed., 1587).

51. The most important pre-Faustian works and post-Faustian works not showing the influence of Faust are the publication in 1473 of the German translation of Jacobus de Theramo's *Belial;* the *Malleus maleficarum* of Sprenger and Institoris, 1486; Federico Frezzi, *Il Quadriregio* (1481); Baptista Mantuan, *Georgius* (1507); Bernard of Como, *Tractatus de strigis* (1508); Johann Trithemius, *Liber octo quaestionum* (1508); Martin of Arles, *Tractatus de superstitione* (1510); Marco Girolamo Vida, *Chrstiados Libri VI* (1527); Hans Sachs, *Tragedia von Schöpfung, fal, und austreibung Ade aus dem Paradeyss* (c. 1530); Thomas Kirchmeyer (Naogeorgus), *Pammachus* (1538); Valten Voith, *Ein schön lieblich Spiel von den herrlichen Ursprung* (1538); Hieronymus Ziegler, *Protoplastus* (1545); Naogeorgus, *Satyrae* (1550); Jacob Ruff, *Adam und Heva* (1550); Johann Wier, Weyer, or Wierus, *On Magic* (1563); Aconcio, *Strategematum Satanae Libri VIII* (1565); Clemens Stephani, *Geistliche Action, wie man des Teufels Listen und Eingeben furnehmlich in Sterbens-Stund und Zeiten entfliehen soll* (1568); Antonio Alfano, *La battaglia celeste tra Michele e Lucifero* (1568); Guillaume de Bartas, *La Sepmaine* (1578); Jean Bodin, *De la démonomanie des sorciers* (1580); Torquato Tasso, *Gerusalemme liberata* (1581); De Bartas, *La Seconde semaine* and *Hexameriad* (1584); Erasmo di Valvasone, *L'Angeleida* (1590); Jacques Auguste de Thou, *Parabata vinctus, sive triumphus Christi* (1595); Edmund Spenser, *An Hymne to Heavenly Love* (1596); Spenser, *The Faerie Queene* (1589–1596); Nicholas Remi, *Demonolatriae libri tres* (1595); Martin del Rio, *Disquisitio magicarum libri sex* (1595); Hugo de Groot (Grotius), *Adamus Exul* (1601); Friedrich Taubmann, *Bellum angelicum* (1604); Gasparo Murtola, *Della creatione del mundo* (1608); Pierre de Lancre, *Tableau de l'inconstance* (1605); Giambattista Marini, *La Strage degli innocenti* (1610); Giambattista Andreini, *L'Adamo* (1613); Thomas Adams, *The Blacke Devill or the Apostate* (1615); Giovandomenico Peri, *La guerra angelica* (c. 1612); William Alexander, *Doomsday* (1614); Alfonso de Acevedo, *De la creación del mundo* (1615); Thomas Peyton, *The Glass of Time* (1620); Odorico Valmanara, *Daemonomachiae* (1623); Phineas Fletcher, *The Locusts or Appolyonists* (1627).

and its suitability to elegant classical martial imagery made it irresistible to the many poets and playwrights of the sixteenth and seventeenth centuries who sought to adapt the conventions of such classical epics as the *Iliad* and the *Aeneid* to Christian myth. In their magnificent battle scenes, Christ or his surrogate Michael are epic heroes locked in deadly combat with Satan, whose characteristics are sometimes drawn in part from the classical hero's adversary, such as Aeneas' enemy Turnus.

These epics also contained scenes, reminiscent of the medieval mysteries, of the council that the Devil holds in hell after he and his comrades have been thrust down out of heaven. Sometimes these epics lend themselves to polemic: in Naogeorgus' *Pammachus*, the pope leads the powers of hell in battle array against the armies of Christ captained by Luther. Grotius' influential play *Adamus exul* depicts a Lucifer who hates God, whom he calls the "savage Thunderer," for having expelled him from the joys of heaven. Lucifer, aware that he cannot dislodge the Almighty from his throne, plans in revenge to ruin the creature that God has made in his own image. If he can corrupt Adam and Eve, they will join him in the miseries of hell. After failing with Adam, he solicits Eve successfully with eloquent flattery; Adam then joins his wife out of loyalty and love. Satan rejoices, savoring the suffering that humanity must henceforth endure. Grotius provides an early hint of what would become a motif of the Romantics, seeing his Satan from within and encouraging the audience to grasp the Devil's feelings and motives. Grotius' Satan longs for freedom, regretting his chains, and crying out that it is better not to be at all than to be unfree.

The voice of satire, like that of skepticism, was faint in the early part of the century, with the great exceptions of Nicolo Machiavelli (1469–1527) and François Rabelais (1494?–1553). Rabelais's *Gargantua et Pantagruel* was the first major work to present demonic figures who are both sympathetic and even justified in their rebellion. The giant Gargantua and his son Pantagruel (whose name is derived from Arnoul Gréban's medieval mystery play) are comic, secularized demons.[52] The most interesting character is Panurge, whose name, "doer of all things,"

---

52. N. Machiavelli, "Belfagor," in A. Gilbert, ed., *Machiavelli: The Chief Works and Others* (Durham, N.C., 1965), pp. 869–877; F. Rabelais, *Les cinq livres*, 2 vols. (Paris, 1552). See E. M. Duval, "Pantagruel's Genealogy and the Redemptive Design of Rabelais' Pantagruel," *Publications of the Modern Language Association*, 99 (1984), 162–178; R. Griffin, "The Devil and Panurge," *Studi francesi*, 47/48 (1972), 329–336; R. C. La Charité, "Devildom and Rabelais' Pantagruel," *French Review*, 49 (1975), 42–50. On Gréban, see LUCIFER, ch. 9.

suggests the multifaceted personality of the Devil. Like the traditional Devil, Panurge shifts his appearance, costume, voice, and manner to fit the situation. He had been a student at Toledo, a city known as a center of hermetic magic, and there he had worked with the "rector of the faculty of diabology, the Reverend Father Picatris."[53] Panurge is the prototype of the worldly Mephistopheles in the Faust literature of the eighteenth and nineteenth centuries: tall, handsome, elegant, and of noble lineage, though the observant could discern his demonic origins in his pallor, his blemishes, and his great age of over three hundred years.

The figure of Faust is—after Christ, Mary, and the Devil—the single most popular character in the history of Western Christian culture. Plays, paintings, poems, novels, operas, cantatas, and films from the sixteenth to the present century have featured Faust and his demonic companion Mephistopheles. If the legend of Don Juan, closely bound to that of Faust, is included—with all its manifestations from Mozart's *Don Giovanni* to Shaw's *Don Juan in Hell*—the story is a leitmotif of Western art for half a millennium.[54]

The legend of Faust is based on the life of a historical person, a philosophy and theology student who, after obtaining a degree in philosophy, turned to hermetic magic and then degenerated into casting horoscopes and predicting the future for money. A number of influential people seem to have been impressed by his wit; others recognized him as a charlatan. The historical identity of this person is not firmly established.[55] The earliest source is Trithemius, who wrote in 1507; Luther and his followers seem to have been chiefly responsible for turning the historical person into a legendary figure. Luther, who despised hermetic magic as a vain and prideful attempt to grasp divine knowledge through the intellect, hastened to link all magic with witchcraft. If a person practices magic, Luther reasoned, he can do so only with the help of the Devil. The first attested link of Faust with the Devil dates from about 1540, and the first mention of his pact with the Devil

53. This figure is derived from Picatrix, the name of a historical author of a treatise on magic. See L. Thorndike, *A History of Magic and Experimental Science*, 8 vols. (New York, 1923–1958), vol. 2, pp. 813–821.

54. On the Faust legend, see A. Dabezies, *Le Mythe de Faust* (Paris, 1972); J. W. Smeed, *Faust in Literature* (London, 1975).

55. He may have been born c. 1478–1480; it is not even sure that his family name was Faust, for Faustus (Latin "fortunate") may have been an assumed classical name such as was common among the Renaissance humanists, and one theory identifies him with a student named Georg Helmstetter. It is as Faustus that he first appears in the sources, and the earliest give his name as Georg, not Johann.

as late as about 1580. The more extraordinary the feats that legend ascribed to Faustus, the more assuredly Lutherans proclaimed that he was in league with Satan. Once this basic assumption was made, Faustus could be linked with the ancient tradition of pact going back to Simon Magus, Theophilus, Cyprian and Joanna, and witchcraft.[56]

In the 1540s, Luther's disciple Melanchthon wrote an account of Faustus' life allegedly based upon personal acquaintance but already heavily colored by bias, and many early accounts were by Lutherans, including Johannes Gast, Johannes Manlius, and Wolfgang Bütner. The first book devoted entirely to Faust was a mixture of legend and fantasy published by Johann Spiess in 1587 under the title of *Historia von Dr. Johann Faustus*. The Spiess version became known as the "Faustbook" and went into numerous translations and editions all over Europe.[57]

The Faustbook tells how Faustus, abandoning philosophy, turns to magic. Given the antischolastic bias of the Protestant Reformation, it was natural that the Faustbook should make the figure of the man who sells his soul to Satan a scholar: Faust desires to obtain knowledge by his own efforts rather than to receive it by grace. This individualistic rebellion ties Faust's sin to the original sin of humanity (Adam and Eve's theft of the forbidden fruit of the tree of knowledge) and to pride (the original sin of Satan himself). It is the prototype of the Romantic and modern revolt against authority. In order to master magical lore, Faustus determines to call up the Devil. Going to a crossroads at night, he inscribes magical circles and characters upon the ground and invokes a spirit (*Gaist*) by the name of Beelzebub. Here the author deliberately mixes magic and witchcraft, the traditional signs and symbols of her-

---

56. See LUCIFER, pp. 80–84.

57. A number of more or less independent versions of the Faustbook appeared in manuscript and print in the 1580s and 1590s, but it was the 1587 version that became standard. It was probably first translated into English in 1587 or 1588, as Marlowe's play was written in 1588 or 1589, but the first extant translation is dated 1592. It was translated into Dutch in 1592 and French in 1598. For the German Faustbook, see H. G. Haile, ed., *Das Faustbuch nach der Wolfenbüttler Handschrift* (Berlin, 1963); H. Wiemken, ed., *Doctor Fausti Weheklag: Die Volksbücher von D. Johann Faust und Christoph Wagner* (Bremen, 1961). The original edition of the English translation is by H. Logeman in *Recueil des travaux de l'Université de Gand*, 24 (1900), and is readily accessible in the edition by W. Rose, *The Historie of the Damnable Life and Deserved Death of Doctor John Faustus* (Notre Dame, 1963). Similar stories of magic and pact abounded in the sixteenth century: for example, the tale of Mariken van Nieumeghen, who submitted to Satan sexually in return for instruction in magic (L. De Bruyn, *Woman and the Devil in Sixteenth-Century Literature* [Tisbury, Wilts., 1979], p. 3).

This sixteenth-century engraving shows a pre-Goethean conception of Dr. Faustus.

metic magic with the witchlike invocation of an evil spirit. The spirit appears, taking the form of a dragon, a fiery globe, a fiery man, and finally a greyfriar. This shapeshifting identifies the spirit with the traditional Devil, and the figure of the greyfriar identifies him with monkery and popery, the Devil's chief tools on earth. The spirit explains to Faustus that he is a member of a great hierarchy whose prince is Lucifer. Though himself a potentate in hell, he is only the servant of this great prince, whose express permission he needs before he can agree to serve the scholar.[58]

The spirit's name, here spelled Mephostophiles, first appears in the title of chapter four and in the text in chapter five. The 1587 Faustbook is the first attested appearance of this name of the Devil. It is not a traditional Judeo-Christian or folkloric name but a brand new coinage by a Renaissance humanist drawing upon Greek, Latin, and possibly Hebrew elements. Both the originator and his intentions are unknown, so the derivation of the name is uncertain. The chief elements are the Greek *mē*, "not"; *phōs, photos*, "light"; and *philos*, "lover"—yielding "he who is not a lover of light," an ironic parody of *Lucifer*, "lightbearer." The ending *philos* was changed to *philēs* to conform to normal Greek usage, as in Aristoteles, Hades, or Aristophanes, though Shakespeare still used the Latinized form of *philos* in his "Mephistophilus" in *The Merry Wives of Windsor*. *Mephost-* seems to have been changed to *Mephist-* by attraction to the Latin *mephitis*, "pungent, sulfurous, stinking." The Hebrew word *tophel*, "liar," is another possible element, though the form Mephis*tophel*es is actually Goethean, not sixteenth-century.[59] That the name is a purely modern invention of uncertain origins makes it an elegant symbol of the modern Devil with his many novel and diverse forms.

58. The spirit explains that Lucifer is emperor of hell, which is divided into five kingdoms: the East, ruled by Lucifer himself; the North, ruled by Beelzebub; the South, by Belial; the West, by Astaroth; the center, by Phlegethon. The influence of humanism and the blending of hermetic and witch traditions appear in the introduction of the classical figure Phlegethon into the midst of the traditional Judeo-Christian demons.

59. Bachtold-Stäubli, *Handwörterbuch des deutschen Aberglaubens*, 11 vols. (Berlin-Leipzig, 1927–1942), vol. 6, cols. 174–182, gives a variety of possible though seemingly fanciful Hebrew roots. A possible metathesis may have occurred from *Mephotosphiles* to *Mephostophiles*, but the former is unattested. The *Passauer Höllenzwang*, approximately contemporary with the Faustbook, uses *Mephistophiel* as well as *Mephistophiles*, indicating a possible sensitivity to the fact that Hebrew angels' names usually end in *-el* ("lord"). A. Oehlke, "Zum Namen Mephistopheles," *Goethejahrbuch*, 34 (1913), 198–199, suggested the combination of the Biblical names Mephiboseth and Ahitophel (2 Sam. 4:4, 15:12).

Mephistopheles goes to Lucifer and obtains permission to serve Faustus if the scholar will promise to give himself up body and soul to the prince of hell. Faustus makes a written pact in blood, denies Christ, and promises to be an enemy of the Christian people. Though this pact was modeled on that of the medieval Theophilus, its more immediate and specific model was the pact attributed to contemporary witches. Theophilus gave up his soul in exchange for being returned to his lost honors and offices, but it was the witches who were believed to promise to do whatever harm they could to the Christian community. In 1587, during the height of the witch craze, the story of pact would have made it plain to all that the magician Faust was involved with witchcraft. The written pact supposedly found in Faustus' house when he died granted him twenty-four years of freedom, at the end of which time the Devil would come to claim him.

Contented with the arrangements (for a while), Faust bids Mephistopheles take on the form of a Franciscan friar whenever he appears, another unsubtle bit of anti-Catholic propaganda. In response to Faust's eager queries about the nature of hell, Mephisto explains that Lucifer had originally been a seraph and proceeds to treat him to a perfectly traditional account of the fall of the angels.[60] Mephisto describes hell as filthy, sulfurous, fiery, stinking, and misty—in short, mephitic—and he goes on at Faustus' request to lead the scholar on a tour of hell.[61] Horrifed by hell, Faustus contemplates repentance, but Mephistopheles assures him that that is impossible. What can I do to escape? the scholar asks. The spirit replies: Be humble and glorify God. But, he adds, this is something you have never done. Well, then, Faust pleads, what can I do *now* to escape? Mephisto quashes him: it is too late. To his original sin of pride and his original folly, Faustus adds the final and unforgivable sin of despair. He can make his escape only by throwing himself upon the mercy of God; this is what saved Theophilus. But Faustus refuses: when it comes to the crunch, he prefers eternal torment and separation from God to any kind of submission. A great irony lies in wait for him, for he does not realize that his refusal to submit to God subjects him to a crueler lord.

After his tour of hell, Faustus' original desire for knowledge and

60. The author was as confused about Lucifer's rank as the medieval theologians: ch. 10 calls him a seraph; ch. 13, a cherub.

61. Here he meets Beelzebub and the other traditional higher demons as well as such classical and newfangled demons as Chamagusta, Dythycan, Brachus, and Anobis. The tour of hell derives from the medieval narratives of journeys to the other world.

power is transmuted into adolescent fantasies of lust and domination. Here the author drew perhaps too enthusiastically upon the popular legends that had sprung up around the figure of Faust, yet the stories do serve the serious purpose of showing the degradation of one who delivers himself to evil—rather like Milton's Satan, who begins as prince of hell and ends as a hissing viper. Faust journeys to Rome to feast at the pope's palace, jam-packed (of course) with whores and drunkards, and he shows his contempt for the pontiff by whistling in his face (possibly a bowdlerization, given Luther's interest in other kinds of wind); the bluff English translation simply has Faustus striking the pope's face. Then Faustus journeys on to Constantinople, where, pretending to be the Prophet Muhammad, he obtains access to the sultan's seraglio. He wanders Europe selling his horoscopes and other magic to emperors, bishops, professors, and draftsmen. Some of his exploits are Rabelaisian: he devours a bale of hay; he summons up Helen of Troy and satisfies his lust with her, but she turns out to be a succubus.

As his twenty-four years near their conclusion, Faustus several times again contemplates repentance, each time rejecting it and once even signing a pact confirming the sale of his soul. At last, as the hour draws near, he summons his colleagues and students and recounts the entire story, warning them against sin, temptation, evil companions, and the wiles of the Devil. He seems momentarily to hope that this act of piety may earn him the mercy that Lucifer would carry off only his body and spare his soul. But realizing that such hopes are vain, Faustus yields to despair. At midnight the students feel a great wind arise and shake the house; they hear a hissing noise and Faustus screaming for help. Then all is silent. Next morning they find his strangely mutilated body thrown upon the dungheap (one version has his head turned front to back).

Faust transforms the ancient Theophilus legend into a fable for the nearly modern world. First, the story is homocentric. In the medieval tales, the tension is between the Devil and Christ, or the Virgin, or another saint; in Theophilus, the Virgin appears and does the Devil down by ripping up the contract before Satan can claim his victim. But in Faust, the tension is between Devil and man: Faustus creates his own predicament and must get himself out of it if he can; he does not think it an option to throw himself upon the mercy of God.

Second, this homocentrism is closely tied to individualism. Given the Protestant emphasis upon the lonely struggle of each person isolated in combat with spiritual powers, Faustus has no recourse to a community or a communion of saints. He does not even think of confession or the Eucharist, and the Lutheran author certainly wanted no Blessed Virgin intervening to save him.

Third, the story is pessimistic. In the medieval legends, the sinner repented and was saved; here he finds only the stark wages of sin: the individual turns away from God and, once having sinned, hardens his heart against repentance. In this there is more than a touch of pre-destination and even fatalism. The story thus becomes a source and a vehicle for modern pessimism; like the horror films of our own century, it shows the real power of evil while ignoring the power of good.

Fourth, the story reveals a Protestant and modern ambivalence toward knowledge. Faustus' original sin is the prideful desire to obtain knowledge for its own sake and for the sake of the power it gives. Protestantism, drawing upon medieval nominalism and mysticism, insisted that the soul unaided by grace cannot obtain any true knowledge; the search for knowledge for the use one may make of it is an illusion and a sin. This rather ironically ended by producing a tension between Christianity on the one hand and science and scholarship on the other; the modern view, of course, is that knowledge is primarily important for its use in promoting human comfort, secondarily for its own sake, and certainly not for the glory of God. The division between these two points of view has deformed Western thought for centuries.

Fifth, the character of Mephistopheles begins a transformation of the Devil's character: he is at least a little sympathetic with his victim, and he shows some small signs of introspection, including a hint of regret for his own rebellion. The internalization and humanization of Satan's character became a main theme in the post-Faustian literature of the late sixteenth and seventeenth centuries.

The first great literary expression of the Faust legend was the *Doctor Faustus* of Christopher Marlowe (1564–1593), probably written in 1588 or 1589.[62] Marlowe's plot follows the Faustbook closely. The jarring dissonances between the scenes in which Marlowe's sublime poetry is heard and those dominated by clowning have led some critics to argue that Marlowe must have had a collaborator. This may be true, but the dissonances of the play only reflect those of the original Faustbook and have, moreover, the dramatic function of emphasizing ironically the degeneration of Faustus from a scholar thirsty for knowledge to a

---

62. The best edition of Marlowe's *Doctor Faustus*, giving both the 1604 and the 1616 texts, is W. Greg, *Doctor Faustus 1604–1616* (Oxford, 1950). I cite the 1616 text.

clownish trickster. Faustus' first sin is pride: in the beginning he imagines that he can manipulate Mephistopheles to fulfill his own immoderate ambitions:

> By him, I'le be great Emperour of the world,
> And make a bridge, through the moving Aire
> To passe the Ocean: with a band of men
> I'le joyne the Hils that bind the *Affrick* shore,
> And make that Country, continent to Spaine,
> And both contributary to my Crowne. [1.3.329]

Soon Mephisto, using flattery, false promises, and threats, gains the upper hand. Faust begins to grasp the enormity of the situation when Mephisto shows him hell, but now he succumbs to his last and fatal sin, despair. He refuses to believe that Christ can save him, because he knows that repentance entails renouncing the power he has gained and is enjoying too much: "I do repent; and yet I do despair" (5.1.184). In the end, the Devil drags him off shrieking; his limbs are torn asunder, and his students find his mutilated body the following morning.

Faustus is a traditional Christian play making the moral statement that lust for worldly fame and power leads to destruction.[63] Mephistopheles is, as Dorothy Sayers remarks, a "spiritual lunatic, but like many lunatics, he is extremely plausible and cunning."[64] But Marlowe adds psychological depth to this traditional view of the Devil's character. Mephisto is not entirely evil, for he regrets his loss of felicity; moody and introspective, he is far from the stupid, clowning Devil of the medieval stage and in some ways prefigures the Romantic Satan. Aware of his fate, he deeply regrets it:

> Hell hath no limits, nor is circumscrib'd,
> In one selfe place: but where we are is hell,
> And where hell is there we must ever be.
> And to be short, when all the world dissolves,
> And every creature shall be purifi'd,
> All places shall be hell that are not heaven. [2.1.513]

63. Too much has been made of Marlowe's skepticism. He was rebellious and unorthodox, but nothing indicates that he did not take God and the Devil seriously, at least at the time he wrote *Faustus*.

64. D. Sayers, "The Faust-Legend and the Idea of the Devil," *Publications of the English Goethe Society*, n.s. 15 (1945), 7.

Where God is, is reality. All else, Mephisto knows, is illusion, nothingness: "Why this is hell nor am I out of it" (1.3.300). The individual
Christian is responsible for his own fate: the Devil does not need to
tempt Faustus; overcome by his own pride and desire, Faustus takes the
initiative. Mephisto is not even a contributing cause to his ruin but
merely a tool that Faustus uses to effect his sin, and Mephisto's later
domination of his soul is a domination that he freely grants. This is not
the medieval struggle between Christ and Satan but a modern man's
deliberate ruin of his own life.

The Devil is a serious figure in a number of other works of the period,
but by the end of the century two contrary tendencies had asserted
themselves: a revival of the comic Devil, and a shift of the focus of evil
from the Devil to the human personality. Ben Jonson's *The Devil Is an
Ass* (1616) depicts a completely comic Satan, and the horrifying plays of
John Webster, *The White Devil* (c. 1608) and *The Duchess of Malfi* (c.
1614), present the demonic as arising from the human personality.[65]

In the work of William Shakespeare (1564–1616), the Devil never
appears in his own form, though spirits often make a direct appearance.
The spirits are sometimes evil, as the witches in *Macbeth* (1606); sometimes portentous and ambiguous, as Hamlet's father (1603); sometimes
numinous, as in *A Midsummer's Night's Dream* (1595); and sometimes
comic, as the false faeries of *The Merry Wives of Windsor* (1600). But the
burden of evil and terror in Shakespeare lies far less in demonic spirits
than in demonic humans, humans who have an appetite for evil for its
own sake: Aaron in *Titus Andronicus* (1594), Richard III (1594), Iago in
Othello (1604), Macbeth and Lady Macbeth, and Goneril, Edmund, and
Regan in *King Lear* (1606).[66]

Even Shakespeare's heroes betray traces of the demonic. Hamlet re-

---

65. Robert Greene's treatment of Satan in *Friar Bacon and Friar Bungay* (1594) is also
comic. Other influential treatments of evil are Barnabe Barnes' *The Devil's Charter* (1607),
Thomas Adams' *The Blacke Devill or The Apostate* (1615), John Webster's *The Devil's Law
Case* (1623), and Thomas Middleton's *The Changeling* (1623).

66. I use *The Complete Works of William Shakespeare*, ed. John Dover Wilson (Cambridge, 1980). In the huge Shakespeare bibliography the following offer particularly
helpful treatments of evil, villainy, and the demonic: C. N. Coe, *Demi-Devils: The Character of Shakespeare's Villains* (New York, 1963); L. W. Cushman, *The Devil and the Vice in
the English Dramatic Literature before Shakespeare* (Halle, 1900); G. W. Knight, "Macbeth
and the Nature of Evil," *Hibbert Journal*, 28 (1930), 328–342; E. Prosser, *Hamlet and
Revenge*, 2d ed., (Stanford, 1971); B. Spivack, *Shakespeare and the Allegory of Evil* (New
York, 1958); C. Spivack, *The Comedy of Evil on Shakespeare's Stage* (Rutherford, N.J.,
1978).

jects love and compassion; Lear, consumed with self-pity, rails against the cosmos; Othello indulges his jealousy in childish tests of affection that block him from perceiving true love; Leontes in *The Winter's Tale* (1609), deluded by jealousy, imprisons his wife and attempts to kill the man he falsely suspects of being her lover. The great dramatist instinctively felt that to his age evil was more convincing in human than in spirit form. Yet the evil in Shakespeare's characters often transcends the boundaries of normal human sin and vice. Shakespeare sensed in the human heart a desire for evil for evil's sake, an evil transcending our conscious errors and failings. In this respect, at least, he believed in the Devil.

In *Titus Andronicus*, Aaron, the "chief architect and plotter of these woes" (5.3.122), is called "the incarnate devil" (5.1.40), and his own words betray a malice transcending human motivation:

> O, how this villainy
> Doth fat me with the very thought of it!
> Let fools do good, and fair men call for grace,
> Aaron will have his soul black like his face. [3.1.203–206]

He murders with a cruel jest on his lips: slaying the Nurse, he sneers, "Wheak, wheak! So cries a pig preparèd to the spit" (4.2.146–147). He boasts of his crimes—"Hell, let my deeds be witness to my worth" (5.1.103)—and he refuses to repent:

> I am no baby, I, that with base prayers
> I should repent the evils I have done.
> Ten thousand worse than ever yet I did
> Would I perform if I might have my will.
> If one good deed in all my life I did,
> I do repent it from my very soul. [5.3.185–190; cf. 5.1.123–150]

These are not the words of a Faustus who seeks satisfaction of his human desires and then cringes at the price he must pay. They are not even the words of a Mephistopheles doing evil in the service of Satan but mourning his lost beatitude. They are the words of Satan and bear the marks of the same boasting hardness that Milton would place in the Devil's mouth in hell. The only human motivation of Aaron's behavior is his racial blackness, which he feels as a deformity; he is bitter at being formed differently from his companions. But his resentment of his blackness, like Lucifer's resentment of being created inferior to God, is the vain, irrational hatred of the world as it is. His resentment is a mere excuse, for there can be no sufficient cause of the motion of a free will. Aaron freely chooses evil for the sake of evil.

Richard III is another villain beyond villainy, a character whose unremitting malice Shakespeare maintains through three plays (*2 Henry VI, 3 Henry VI,* and *Richard III*). Richard's hunchback, like Aaron's blackness, is a sign and an ostensible motivation of his evil:

> Then, since the heavens have shaped my body so,
> Let hell make crooked my mind to answer it.
> I have no brother, I am like no brother;
> And this word "love," which greybeards call divine,
> Be resident in men like one another
> And not in me: I am myself alone. [*3 Henry VI*, 5.6.78–83]

Richard's disfigurement, like Aaron's, is excuse more than motivation: the desire for evil for its own sake is ingrained in his nature. His words, full of despair, self-pity, isolation, and resolute malice, are Satanic. "I am determined to prove a villain," he asserts coldly (*Richard III*, 1.1.30; 5.3.190–195). Like Satan, he is a liar and a murderer from the beginning. He sneers at virtue and displays his evil nature with cold, sardonic humor. In the end he is damned by his explicit refusal to hope or to trust:

> I shall despair. There is no creature loves me;
> And if I die, no soul will pity me:
> Nay, wherefore should they, since that I myself
> Find in myself no pity to myself. [*Richard III*, 5.3.200–203][67]

Angelo in *Measure for Measure* (1604) is too human in his motivations to be entirely demonic, yet he has sensed, as Claudio remarks, that "our natures do pursue, / Like rats that ravin down their proper bane, / A thirsty evil, and when we drink, we die." I am what I am; I shall be damned; I wish neither mercy nor pity; I shall remain myself, locked in myself for all eternity: this message of Shakespeare's villains is an old one, and its lines were first written in hell.

In his late tragedies—*Hamlet, Othello, Lear,* and *Macbeth*—Shakespeare shows an increasing concern with radical evil and with the de-

---

67. See also *3 Henry VI* 5.6.57–58; *Richard III* 1.1.14–41, 118–120; 1.2.104–109; 2.2.107–111; 3.1.94; 5.5.194–202.

monic. Hamlet is no demon, and his anguish is understandable: his uncle has murdered his father; his mother has married the murderer; his old friends from Wittenberg have been paid to kill him. Yet once he opens himself to revenge, the Devil enters and gradually shapes him to his own purpose. Hamlet plots murder; he sends away the loving Ophelia to madness and suicide; he dispatches the kindly if bungling Polonius with a quick sword thrust and a cruel jest; he plans the ruin and humiliation of his mother, who in spite of her sins still loves him. He rejects the opportunity of executing Claudius when he finds the king at prayer repenting his sins, lest death in a moment of repentance should lead the king to salvation; Hamlet prefers to lose God a soul than to lose the full savor of his revenge. When in the end he dies, he dies in combat with Laertes, a decent man who is attempting to avenge his sister Ophelia.

The key to the play, which critics and producers have usually tried to fit into the wrong door, is the alleged ghost of Hamlet's father, whose brooding presence darkens the whole first act and indeed the entire play. For the ghost is not so much a ghost as a demon or the Devil himself.[68] The most meaningful way to address the question of what the ghost really is is to ask what Shakespeare intended him to be and what function he fulfills in the play. Clearly, Shakespeare's primary intent is that the ghost should appear ambiguous to the audience, to the characters, and especially to Hamlet. From the moment they see the ghost at the very outset of the play, the characters are unsure what to make of him. Is he a ghost, or is he a demon? Shakespeare fully intended the ambiguity to remain.

Whether the supposed ghost is really a demon depends first upon whether the play is pagan or Christian in flavor. Marcellus puts the apparition into a clearly Christian context (1.1.157–164), discussing the season of Advent, which is so full of grace that no evil spirit dare walk abroad; but Horatio puts it into a pagan context (1.1.112–125), referring to the ghosts of classical Roman tradition. As the play can be read either in terms of Greek tragedy and fatal flaw or in terms of Christian sin and guilt, this initial ambiguity must remain. To the extent that we follow Marcellus' Christian context—and the education and assumptions of

---

68. I had independently identified the ghost with the Devil before reading Prosser's *Hamlet and Revenge* and was delighted to find confirmation of my own views with additional details. What appears here is a conflation of my own and Prosser's evidence. For a learned description of spirits almost contemporary with Shakespeare, see Robert Burton (1576–1640), *Anatomie of Melancholie*, pt. 1.2, mem. 1, subsect. 2.

Shakespeare's audience and of Shakespeare himself remained basically Christian—we need to weigh ghost against demon in Christian terms. Much labor has been lost in discussing the distinctions between Catholic and Protestant demonology, some critics claiming that Hamlet's ghost is Catholic because Catholics believed in purgatory while Protestants rejected it. It is true that the ghost announces that he has come from purgatory—though in scarcely orthodox terms—but the main problem with the argument is that there was no significant difference between Catholic and Protestant teaching on ghosts. Most theologians rejected the possibility of ghosts, though some, including Gregory the Great, had argued that dead souls might appear to living people in dreams or visions. The standard view was that a "ghost" was more likely a demon or the Devil taking on human form. Superstition about ghosts continued, and ghost stories persisted in Christian Europe into Shakespeare's time, but ghosts were never a coherent part of Christian theology. Naturally, Shakespeare's audiences were not on the whole theologically sophisticated, but most would have known the presumption that an apparition was a demon rather than a ghost.

The characters themselves react with the same presumption; they are much more inclined to believe the specter to be a demon. Horatio addresses it first:

> What art thou that usurpst this time of night,
> Together with that fair and warlike form
> In which the majesty of buried Denmark
> Did sometimes march? by heaven I charge thee, speak! [1.1.46–49]

Horatio reports it to Hamlet as "a figure *like* your father" (1.2.199), and before he sees it himself, Hamlet is unsure and suspicious: "If it assume / my noble father's person, / I'll speak to it though hell itself should gape" (1.2.244–245). When he sees it, he is bold to address it, but his mind is by no means settled.

> Be thou a spirit of health or a goblin damn'd,
> Bring with thee airs from heaven or blasts from hell,
> Be thy intents wicked or charitable,
> Thou comest in such a questionable shape
> That I will speak to thee. [1.4.40–44]

And immediately Hamlet makes his decision, a fatal one: "I'll call thee Hamlet, king, father, royal Dane" (1.4.44–45). Horatio is terrified and warns the prince: what if it should take you to the summit of the battlements and there "assume some other horrible form" that will drive you mad? (1.4.72). But Hamlet has made his fatal act of faith in the thing, a tragically mistaken act of discernment that will lead him to ruin. He continues to harbor doubts:

> The spirit that I have seen
> May be a devil, and the devil hath power
> T'assume a pleasing shape, yea, or perhaps
> Out of my weakness and my melancholy,
> As he is very potent with such spirits,
> Abuses me to damn me. [2.2.612–617]

He proceeds to plan the play to "catch the conscience of the king" and learns that the ghost has spoken true and that his uncle really is his father's murderer. What he fails to recall is that the Devil knows very well how to speak the truth in order to gain the destruction of souls, and here the Devil is hungry for Claudius' and Gertrude's souls as well as Hamlet's.

The function of the ghost's ambivalence is clear. He must be ambivalent enough to fool the audience because he must be ambivalent enough to fool Hamlet. Were the ghost clearly identifiable as Satan to the audience and the other characters, Hamlet's uncertainty and his failure in discernment would be unconvincing and unsympathetic. The Devil has got to be convincing enough as ghost to deceive Hamlet and, by the way, to make the point that he may deceive every human being, including the audience, as well.

Shakespeare's first intent, then, was to maintain the ghost's ambivalence. His second intent was to have us understand that the ghost really is the Devil so that we may be moved by Hamlet's terrible mistake and so that we may understand its consequences. Shakespeare knew that the audience's presumption would be that the ghost is really a demon; he also offers clear indications that the presumption is correct. The thing appears at midnight in a deserted, precipitous, and dangerous place. When Horatio uses the name of heaven to charge it to speak, it immediately stalks away. When it appears the second time, it disappears at cockcrow (1.1.139), and Horatio describes its reaction to the herald of dawn: "It started like a guilty thing / Upon a fearful summons" (1.1.148–149; cf. 1.2.217–218). Its countenance is troubled and "very pale" (1.2.233). Marcellus' speech (1.1.157–164) links it to evil spirits who cannot walk by day or in the holy season of Advent. The apparition announces that it is from purgatory, but on no account would one expect the Devil to tell the truth when doing so is to his disadvantage. Like Ivan Karamazov's Satan centuries later, the Devil denies his existence for his own purposes. The ghost is envious, jealous, conceited, and arrogant, and its description of the crimes of Claudius and Gertrude is full of coarseness and fury (1.5.42–91). It speaks no word of love to Hamlet; that the dead king's only advice to his son is to press for revenge is the clearest evidence of deceit, for a soul in purgatory is a soul that is saved and focused on the love of God; on no account could such a soul demand revenge. To make the point almost crudely clear to the audience, Shakespeare has the ghost speak to Hamlet and Horatio from beneath the stage, the place where demons dwell. He bids them swear—Horatio secrecy and Hamlet revenge. No saved soul would ever demand such oaths, or indeed any oaths at all. The ghost keeps shifting its position under the stage (the Devil is the most notorious of shifters), and Hamlet jests oddly in calling it a mole and a "pioner" digging tunnels in the earth (1.5.102–181). Shakespeare does everything but tell us directly that the ghost is the Devil; he does not tell us directly because he wants us to share the doubt and so understand Hamlet's own difficulty in making an accurate act of discernment.

Discernment is the key. The center of any act of discernment is based upon the knowledge that a good tree bears good fruit and an evil tree evil fruit. If the fruit be evil, the tree cannot be good. Hamlet should have been able to tell that a spirit who speaks grossly and demands revenge is not from God but the Devil. Yet he concludes, with damnable weakness, that "it is an honest ghost" (1.5.138). We are prepared for Hamlet to make just such an error, for his soliloquy in Act 1, Scene 2 has revealed that he was already obsessed by rage at his mother and uncle and that his soul was open to ready deception by an evil spirit. Naturally, the Devil disguises himself under a fair form and offers us rags and tatters of goodness so that we will not see the true shape beneath. The ghost cautions Hamlet, with apparent compassion, "Taint not thy mind, nor let thy soul contrive / Against thy mother aught" (1.5.86–87). But this comes after the ghost has already tainted Hamlet's mind with graphic pictures of lust and murder, and the notion that Hamlet could kill his uncle without contriving anything against his uncle's wife is patent absurdity. Hamlet's own hatred has opened the door of his soul to evil, and the Devil freely enters. It is under the Devil's guidance, then, that Hamlet proceeds with his vengeful scheme.

Increasingly cold and cruel, he destroys Ophelia, Laertes, and Polonius as well as the guilty Claudius and Gertrude. It is true that Hamlet asks pardon of Laertes, and in that may lie some hope for his tormented soul, but the hope of Denmark (and the cosmos Denmark represents) lies not in Hamlet's plots but in the advent of a new king who can dispel the dark shadow of the old king brooding on the battlements. Again, discernment is the key. For if we can understand Hamlet's evil choice to accept the apparition as his father's ghost, we are also in a position to know better than Hamlet, for we know what the ultimate results of that choice are. Hamlet and Horatio are to some degree entitled to doubts, but the audience is not. The course of action that the specter urged led to death, destruction, and the ruin of innocents. The specter was not the ghost of King Hamlet or of any human being.

In *Othello*, Shakespeare's engagement with evil deepens. Iago is on the borderline between the human and the diabolical. He has the semblance of human motive in his envy of Cassio, whom Othello has appointed lieutenant instead of him (1.1.8), and he later claims, though without conviction, that Othello has cuckolded him and that in retaliation he lusts for Desdemona himself (1.3.386; 2.1.289–315).[69] These motives are rationalizations for a deep and disinterested hatred. Even the first motive is only, like Aaron's blackness and Richard's deformity, an excuse masking Iago's free choice of absolute evil. In *Othello*, of course, Shakespeare inverts the colors and makes his villain white and his hero black. Ironically, Iago refers to Othello as a devil (1.192), but later it becomes clear which of the two is from hell. Othello, having at last discovered Iago's treachery, tries to kill him. "I look down at his feet," says Othello, expecting cloven hooves, "but that's a fable. If that thou be'st a devil, I cannot kill thee." And Iago replies, "I bleed sir, but not killed" (5.2.288–290).

Iago's destruction of Othello, Desdemona, Cassio, Roderigo, and Emilia, with the harm he does to the Venetian state, draws not one sigh of human remorse from him. He is implacable:

> I have't. It is engendered. Hell and night
> Must bring this monstrous birth to the world's light.
>
>   .   .   .

---

69. Desdemona's name seems to derive, appropriately, from the Greek *deisdaimonia:* "dread of spirits."

> Divinity of hell!
> When devils will the blackest sins put on,
> They do suggest at first with heavenly shows,
> As I do now. . . .
> So will I turn her virtue into pitch,
> And out of her own goodness make the net
> That shall enmesh them all. [1.3.403–404; 2.3.345–348, 355–357]

In Act 3, Othello and Iago kneel together in an odd rite in which Othello vows vengeance against Desdemona, while Iago in return offers his services of "wit, hands, and heart." The scene represents a kind of pact, with Othello as Faust and Iago as Mephisto. It is also an exchange of vows in hideous parody of the marriage vows that the two have determined to destroy (3.3.462–481).[70] Iago is more hardened in evil than Mephistopheles, and his fundamental crimes are those of Lucifer himself: pride, treason to his lord, temptation of the innocent, lack of repentance, and above all the lie. "My lord," he assures Othello, "you know I love you" (3.3.119).

The evil of Edmund, Goneril, and Regan in *Lear* is not less or less gratuitous. Edmund's excuse is his illegitimacy. Because he is a bastard, he deceives his father, Gloucester, into believing his brother Edgar a traitor. Edgar is driven into banishment; Gloucester, his eyes dug out by Cornwall, is sent to wander the earth blind.[71] Edmund plots against his own allies, seeks to seduce Regan, and tries to lure Goneril from her husband, Albany. Bastardy cannot account for such liberality of evil; a transcendent evil thrusts its way through the thin membrane of excuse. Edmund exclaims:

> A credulous father! and a brother noble
> Whose nature is so far from doing harms
> That he suspects none; on whose foolish honesty
> My practices ride easy! I see the business.
> Let me, if not by birth, have lands by wit;
> All with me's meet that I can fashion fit. [1.2.187–192]

70. I am grateful to Professor Michael O'Connell for suggesting the significance of this scene to me.

71. When Edgar wanders about disguised as mad "Tom," he recites the names of demons—Flibbertigibbet, Hobbibidence, Mahu, Modo, Obidicut, and Smulkin—derived from exorcisms by the Jesuit William Weston in 1585–1586 (*Lear* 3.4; 4.1). Shakespeare learned this from Samuel Harsnett's *Declaration of Egregious Popish Impostures* (London, 1603). I thank Professor O'Connell for this information, too.

Edmund's betrayal of his father and brother mirrors the two queens' betrayal of their father and sister, and they lack even Edmund's motivation. Goneril's husband Albany is not deceived as to what he has in a wife:

> See thyself, devil!
> Proper deformity shows not in the fiend
> So horrid as in woman. . . .
> Howe'er thou art a fiend,
> A woman's shape doth shield thee.

To which Goneril replies with the sneer that evil reserves for the good: "Marry, your manhood! mew!" (4.2.60–68).

Macbeth is set in a dark, misty world of evil and illusion, and some of the most successful productions—such as Laird Williamson's in 1983—surround or interpenetrate the action with lurking demonic spirits urging ruin. The supernatural shrouds the play from the beginning: the three witches are the first characters on the stage, and the demonic dominates the whole play. Macbeth himself is no demon, and his motives are human. A weak man, he is ambitious and dominated by an unflinchingly ambitious wife, whose own villainy, despair, and ruin (5.3–4) are dramatically subordinate to her husband's. Lady Macbeth, the witches, and the demonic all blend into a pitiless flood of transcendent evil that overwhelms Duncan, Lady Macduff and her children, and the whole wretched realm. It is an evil flood that sweeps Macbeth along to his doom. Like Faustus, Macbeth is caught up by his initial pride and ambition; once engaged by sin he cannot disengage; he tries ineffectively to check himself and to repent, but he is urged back to his crime by Lady Macbeth, as Faustus is by Mephistopheles (5.3.22–28). Macbeth's final sin, like that of Faustus, is despair as his first was pride (5.3.22–28). The gray "Tomorrow and tomorrow" speech (5.5.19–28) is the perfect expression of that dull, uncaring despair and sense of meaninglessness which is the state of mind to which Satan most likes to bring us. The world that God the poet has constructed is, for Macbeth and Satan alike, "A tale told by an idiot, full of sound and fury, / Signifying nothing" (5.4.19–28).

In the end, a certain heroic grandeur rests on Macbeth as he stands alone, abandoned, in his ruined castle, deserted by his courtiers and warriors, betrayed by the witches, and hunted by his mortal enemy. "I will not yield," he tells Macduff, and our hearts rise to his courage. But this is not heroism; it is the desperate defiance of a ruined soul. "Lay on, Macduff, / And damned be him that first cries, 'Hold, enough'" (5.8.33–34). The irony of these, Macbeth's last lines, is that they are the perfect inversion of the truth: Macbeth is damned precisely because he never does cry, "Hold, enough." Like Faustus and like Milton's Satan, Macbeth has made evil so much a part of his nature that he cannot put an end to it without ending himself. He has become simply an extension of that transcendent evil. The Williamson production of *Macbeth* ended with the usurper's severed head facing for all eternity the head of Satan displayed by the witches. The miasma of darkness, evil, and unreality that shrouds Scotland, like that which shrouds Hamlet's Denmark, is burned away by the advent of a new king.

The sixteenth century, beginning with Luther and ending with Shakespeare, witnessed a great change in the concept of the Devil and evil. Shakespeare's villains allow transcendent evil to work in them, sometimes to overwhelm them, but they are not demons themselves. The theater in which good struggles against evil is no longer the halls of heaven or the pit of hell: it is the human heart. And not so much the heart of the Christian community as the heart of the individual standing alone with his God—and his Satan. The rise of bourgeois, competitive society encouraged the individualism of Protestant theology and of hermetic magic. Belief in witchcraft and belief in the Devil remained strong in Shakespeare's day, but the world view that underlay such beliefs had been shaken. Over subsequent centuries, that world view would not fall, but it would gradually subside. That Satan's evil would be internalized and located in the human heart may be appropriate, for we can know nothing of Satan in himself, and all that we say about the Devil we say out of the experience of our own hearts. Shakespeare made his villains in the image of Satan, but Satan had originally been made in the image of human villains. For more than a millennium evil had been projected upon an angelic power; now evil was refracted back upon humanity. Yet the transcendent power of evil, which Shakespeare understood so directly and intuitively, remains.

3 The Devil between Two Worlds

The conflict between the traditional Christian world view and a rational philosophy based on materialism continued in the seventeenth century and ended with the victory of materialism. This victory was neither sudden nor complete. Although the erosion of the traditional, scholastic world view was apparent to the intellectual leaders of the England of Charles II (1660–1685) and the France of Louis XIV (1643–1715), another two centuries elapsed before it was plain to all. Still, the latent skepticism about the Devil that only a few hardy souls dared express in 1600 had by 1700 become part of that treasury of unspoken commonsense assumptions which any society holds (rightly or wrongly) at a given time. The decline of the Devil and hell was brought about by a number of developments, including the rise of science after 1660, disgust with the religious wars of 1618–1648 on the Continent and 1640–1660 in England, and a longing for a calm, rational view of the cosmos. In Protestantism, belief in predestination diminished in favor of a broad, tolerant, sunny Arminianism in which the majestic God of Luther and Calvin was replaced by a vaguely benevolent and remote deity.

One of the most important reasons for the decline of Satan was the decline of the witch craze. Witchcraft took a steep downturn in the mid-seventeenth century, as people wearied of being terrified—terrified of the threatening presence of hostile spirits, and terrified of prosecution. Suspicion of and prosecution for witchcraft had become so widespread in some areas as to touch even the governing elites. When the elite themselves began to be threatened, they willingly lent their influence to the process of educating the populace in the new orthodoxy of skepticism. Once this occurred, the theoretical arguments against belief in witchcraft began to prosper. Protestants, who had been slow to extend their criticism of medieval religion to witchcraft, belatedly realized that there was no scriptural basis for belief in diabolical sorcery. Theologians also began to fear that the figure of the Devil had become so prominent as to create the danger of making him seem practically independent of God.[1] Reginald Scot, whose *Discoverie of Witchcraft* (1584) was many times reprinted in the seventeenth century, argued vehemently against the excesses of demonology represented by witchcraft. Scot was no positivist or scientific materialist; he wrote in the context of the old world view and himself believed in Satan. But, he observed, many of the biblical references to demons are figures of speech, and Christianity neither requires nor should tolerate the superstition that we are constantly under attack by evil spirits. Another view, increasingly common among both Protestants and Catholics by the end of the century, was that although the reality of demonic possession at the time of Christ was confirmed by the New Testament, nothing in the Bible obliges us to believe that any possessions have taken place since the apostolic period.

This moderate skepticism was at first overwhelmed by impassioned defenses of witch beliefs such as those of King James VI of Scotland, *Daemonologie* (1597), and Matthew Hopkins, *Discoverie of Witches* (1647), the latter a self-serving document seeking to justify the author's calling as a professional witchfinder. Later in the century, learned and reasonable defenses of witch beliefs continued to appear, such as Joseph Glanvill's *Some Philosophical Considerations Touching Witches and Witchcraft* (1666) and his revised and expanded *Sadducismus triumphatus* (1681). Glanvill, an open-minded latitudinarian who believed in the compatibility of science and religion, questioned all kinds of dogmatism— including that of the rationalists—and opposed the materialist reductionism of Thomas Hobbes. Glanvill therefore refused to dismiss belief in the Devil and pleaded for open-minded investigation of reports of demons. The *Treatise Proving Spirits, Witches, and Supernatural Operations* (1672) of Meric Casaubon approved the rise of empiricism but cautioned lest science end by slighting spiritual matters, and it called upon empirical, historical evidence to defend belief in nonmaterial entities.

Eventually, however, skepticism prevailed. John Webster's *Displaying of Supposed Witchcraft* (1677) took a thoroughly skeptical position, and in 1691 Balthasar Bekker, a Dutch pastor, published *De betoverte wereld,*

---

1. K. M. Briggs, *Pale Hecate's Team* (London, 1962), p. 151.

Joseph Glanvill's *Sadducismus triumphatus* (1681) was one of the last scholarly defenses of belief in witchcraft. The frontispiece illustrates a number of standard assumptions about sorcery.

"The Enchanted World," which affirmed that all beliefs about the Devil and evil angels are derived from paganism, from false interpretations of the Bible influenced by Manicheans, from perverted Catholic tradition, and from Protestant failure to discard these patent falsehoods. Bekker did much to weaken the enchanted world, and the final blows to the intellectual defense of witchcraft were dealt by Francis Hutchinson's *Historical Essay concerning Witchcraft* in 1718, by which time he was preaching to an audience already largely converted.

In the 1660s and 1670s the notion that demons might be nothing more than symbols of human evil began to spread. By 1700 the belief that God and the Devil are always busy in the affairs of this world had yielded to the conviction that their intervention is rare. Increasing religious skepticism was capped by philosophical, rationalist skepticism of the kind represented by Hobbes, René Descartes, and John Locke, who observed that the existence of incorporeal spirits cannot be demonstrated. Cannot be, that is, in a world view using their assumptions: the new materialists were as dogmatic as the old idealists in their insistence that their own undemonstrable assumptions were the only correct ones. Perhaps the chief fault of the new skepticism was that it was not skeptical enough: it did not face the precariousness of its own premises.

The growing skepticism encountered two kinds of resistance. One was simply the force of momentum: people do not quickly change their beliefs. This was true in law as well as in theology, and Robert Mandrou has described the considerable courage it took for judges to admit that the vast and complex body of precedent gathered by their forebears in the matter of witchcraft was all worthless.[2] The second was a conscious and concerted reaction on the part of traditional Christians to a view that they (correctly) saw as undermining the bases of their faith. An English Puritan, Richard Greenham, anticipated Baudelaire's famous epigram by declaring that "it is a policy of the Devil to persuade us that there is no Devil."[3] The passion of those writers defending demonology and witchcraft was not a bizarre sign of mental instability: it was a reasonable (if misplaced) defense of the traditional world view, for they saw that a doctrine questioning the existence of purely spiritual beings could, and would, move from skepticism about the existence of the Devil to skepticism about the existence of God himself.

Seventeenth-century skeptics as a whole did not urge a move from Christianity to atheism or even to mechanistic Deism. Rather, they

2. R. Mandrou, *Magistrats et sorciers en France au XVIIe siècle* (Paris, 1980).
3. Quoted in K. Thomas, *Religion and the Decline of Magic* (New York, 1971), p. 476.

represent an intermediate stage characterized by a defense of Christianity on rational metaphysical lines. The Jesuits, carefully separating the supernatural from the natural order, defended the use of both science and metaphysics, each in its proper sphere. The principles of Gottfried Wilhelm Leibniz (1646–1716) were still essentially metaphysical and scholastic. Knowledge, Leibniz argued, was based on natural reason; revelation provides knowledge beyond the reaches of natural reason, but that revelation must then be subjected to reason. The difference between the new rationalists and the medieval scholastics was that the former shifted the weight of their faith far more toward reason than revelation, to the extent that the Christian scheme of salvation gradually receded into the background. Some of the rationalists went much further, denying the epistemological independence of Christian theology and attempting to interpret Christianity in terms of a natural reason based upon materialist assumptions. Three logical stages (which overlapped chronologically) occurred in this process. First, Christian theology is assumed to explain all phenomena; second, theology and science coexist but each is assigned its own realm; third, science is assumed to explain all phenomena, and metaphysics is entirely rejected. The gradual growth of materialism in late seventeenth-century and eighteenth-century thought continued into the nineteenth and twentieth centuries, eventually creating a climate that has repudiated philosophical idealism.

Philosophical idealism is the belief that the form of an entity—a dog, a cart, or a king—is an independent, abstract reality, which individual dogs, carts, or kings reflect. Traditionally, an entity could be analyzed in two different ways: according to its form or according to its material composition. One could analyze the qualities of a dog that make it essentially a dog rather than another kind of entity: this is metaphysics. Or one could analyze the material components of the entity: this is physics, or "natural philosophy" in general. As Western society became increasingly concerned with economic development, it began to demand a coherent, unifying, universal science that could produce tangible, technological results. And it found metaphysics wanting. If "dog" is completely different from and essentially unrelated to "cart" or "king" or even "cat," no unified science could be constructed to treat them all. This does not mean that metaphysics cannot be a valid discipline pointing toward truth, but it does mean that it cannot be a predictive, quantifiable science producing the technical results that modern Western society demands.

On the other hand, since from the seventeenth to the early twentieth century matter was believed to be the underlying basis of reality and the common basis of all creatures, then matter could be the subject of a common science based upon general, common principles. The increasing prestige of natural science that resulted from its technical achievements gradually drew the attention of rational philosophers away from metaphysics and toward physics.

The first important philosopher of the new rationalism was Francis Bacon (1561–1626), whose book *On Atheism* (1612; second edition, 1625) was a dry, tolerant view of religion; it maintained that on the one hand no true atheism can exist because of the manifest existence of God, but on the other hand tolerance is necessary because the claims of no one religion can be demonstrated. Bacon's notion of the "idols of the marketplace" followed nominalist tradition in asserting that many general words, such as "Devil," were idols in that they did not correspond to anything external to the human mind.[4]

The most influential philosopher of the century was the moderate rationalist René Descartes (1596–1650). Descartes set forth his basic principles in his *Discourse on Method* (1637) and *Meditations on First Philosophy* (1641). We make no initial assumptions about the world at all, he said; we begin by looking for first principles, which by intuition we find innate within us. That God exists is obvious through the ontological argument: the idea of a perfect being is within us; such an idea could not emanate from our minds, which are obviously imperfect, but only from a perfect being itself, which is God. We proceed to explore the cosmos rationally, questioning at every step. We decide to accept our sense perceptions because they give us clear and distinct ideas and because God would not mislead us by giving us senses that do not convey true perceptions. Still, Descartes admonished, grave possibility of error enters whenever we accept any idea that is not clear and distinct.

Bacon had advanced the cause of the empirical method, but empiricism needed a philosophical framework to succeed, and Descartes provided that framework. He found its basis in Euclidean geometry: the universe is geometrically constructed as an infinite Euclidean space without boundaries. Assuming that the laws governing the behavior of bodies within this space are strictly mathematical, material, uniform, and unchanging, the mathematical structure of the universe provides a

---

4. F. Bacon, *Novum organum* (London, 1620), aphorisms 43, 59–60. Thomas Hobbes (1588–1679) argued even more forcefully than Bacon for materialism and religious skepticism in his *Leviathan* (London, 1651).

basis for certain scientific knowledge. As it turned out, Descartes was right in his assumptions though wrong in his mathematics, and when Newton produced his own *Principia*, the basis for a coherent scientific view of the world was established.

Descartes held to Christianity, but he absolutely separated the material universe from the spiritual world, leaving the act of creation as the only juncture between them. In the beginning of time, according to this view, God created the universe with its natural laws and then withdrew to allow it to function mechanically. In no other way does God influence the material world. We know the existence of the spiritual world by revelation, which God uses to supplement our natural understanding. On the basis of revelation we may accept the incarnation of Christ or the existence of angels or the Devil, but we must not accord them any influence in the world of nature. Descartes's cosmology, breaking any real connection between this world and God's, set the precedent for future Deism and atheism, which would gain strength once the view that space is infinite was supplemented by the view that time is infinite as well.

As religious tenets came increasingly under the eye of skeptical reason, Christians found themselves obliged, in response to critics, to confront openly the most difficult question for believers: the problem of evil. Descartes himself attempted to construct a rational theodicy to deal with the question. In his "Fourth Meditation," he began by asking whether the existence of God is consonant with certain observable phenomena such as sin, natural disasters, and human error. As a philosopher, he chose to dwell upon the problem of error. Why would God create beings capable of intellectual error? He divided the question into four sections: how is the possibility of error consistent with the existence of God; how is the actuality of evil consistent with his existence; what in human nature allows for the possibility of error; what in human nature allows for the actuality of error? His answer is a variant of what has come to be called the Free Will Defense: error is our fault, not God's, because we extend our will beyond the range where we have clear and distinct ideas. Yet Descartes sensed that God could have given us clear and distinct ideas to the extent that we *would* not make errors, even though we had the free will to do so. So why did God create us with limitations on our knowledge? Descartes's answer is a variant of what has been called the Esthetic Defense, essentially a demonstration of the metaphysical necessity of "evil" in the sense of imperfection. God could not create a perfect cosmos without creating something identical with himself; such a creation would only be an affirmation of God's own identity and not a real, differentiated cosmos; any real cosmos is not identical to God and thus is of necessity imperfect, containing metaphysical imperfections. Further, in creating something different from himself, it seems that God wishes to create a plenitude: that is, a cosmos full of things differing from God in different degrees. It follows that some creatures—humans, for example—will have limited intellect and will lack a perfect coextension of will and knowledge. Hence, error and, by analogy, other evils are necessary.[5]

Rationalists and latitudinarians such as Thomas Browne (1605–1682), John Locke (1632–1704), Baruch de Spinoza (1632–1677), Nicholas Malebranche (1638–1715), and John Toland (1670–1722) proposed that religion and morality are properly obtained not by revelation but by reason based on experience; the proper stance of religion, therefore, is open-mindedness and suspension of belief. Christianity is to be subjected to rational analysis, and anything not consonant with reason is to be rejected, certainly including the existence of the Devil.

Efforts to reconcile these rationalist views with Christianity were made by such deeply religious scientists as Blaise Pascal (1623–1662) and Isaac Newton (1642–1727), but Newton's system ended by undermining metaphysics even more thoroughly than Locke's had done, for he replaced logic as the basis of knowledge with empirical observation. As the empirical science that Newton did so much to establish grew in influence, little use was found for any statement that could not be empirically verified. In such a system the Devil was doomed. It is no wonder that Pierre Bayle (1647–1706) concluded after deep personal and intellectual struggle that the problem of evil was an insoluble, incomprehensible mystery, an *abîme*, an unplumbable depth.[6]

The most vigorous effort to construct a rational theodicy in this period appears in the closely related work of Leibniz and William King (1650–1729). Both King's *De origine mali* (1702) and Leibniz's *Theodicy* (1697–1705), written partly in response to Bayle, enjoyed wide influence; the very word "theodicy" was coined by Leibniz.[7] Leibniz re-

5. R. Descartes, *Meditationes de prima philosophiae*, ed. G. Lewis (Paris, 1970). See also B. Calvert, "Descartes and the Problem of Evil," *Canadian Journal of Philosophy*, 2 (1972), 117–126.

6. J. P. Jossua, *Pierre Bayle ou l'obsession du mal* (Paris, 1977). On the seventeenth century in general, see F. Billicsich, *Das Problem des Ubels in der Philosophie des Abendlandes*, 2d ed., 3 vols. (Vienna, 1952–1959), esp. vol. 2 on the rationalists.

7. William King's *De origine mali* (London, 1702) was translated into English by

versed the usual direction of reasoning about theodicy. Most thinkers began with the observed existence of evil in the world and argued on that basis that there must be limitations on the divine mercy or omnipotence. Leibniz began at the opposite end, with the existence of God, which he held to be self-evident. Leibniz asked why anything should exist. There are two logical possibilities: that nothing exists and that something exists. Why should anything at all exist? It is amazing that it does. The apparent tautology "what is, is" in fact makes the most essential of all metaphysical points: the absolute, noncontingent nature of what is. Being is absolute. Leibniz saw that once this point is really grasped, the ontological argument is compelling. Absolute being is absolute being; God is God.

An absolute being from which everything comes and upon which everything depends is omnipotent, Leibniz's argument continues. No principle exists outside of God that might limit him. Such an absolute being is also by definition perfect. And the absoluteness of his nature implies that he is unchanging. This means that the "rules" he lays down for his own being do not change; God in effect limits himself by his own rules. God creates a cosmos in which the principle of contradiction exists: in this cosmos a circle cannot at the same time be a noncircle; a circle cannot be a square, and by the rules God has set for himself, he cannot make a circle be a square. The notion that God "might have" been different and created differently introduces a false (indeed an impossible) contingency into the divine nature. God is absolutely what he is, so it is meaningless to say that he could be different or could have created a different world. He absolutely and necessarily creates the world that he creates. By "world," Leibniz means the entire cosmos; in the unlikely event that a plurality of universes exists, he subsumes them all under the term "world."

The cosmos is created by the flowing forth of the abundance of God's goodness, love, and created energy (*Theodicy*, p. 412). It is alive with God's life. Leibniz rejected pure materialism. If forms did not exist at all, then matter would be undifferentiated, and there would be no difference between the dog and the philosopher. He also discarded the

---

William Law in 1731. G. W. Leibniz, *Essais de theodicée sur la la bonté de Dieu, la liberté de l'homme et l'origine du mal*, appeared in Amsterdam in 1710. I cite *Theodicy*, trans. E. M. Huggard (New Haven, 1952). See also D. Copp, "Leibniz's Theory That Not All Possible Worlds Are Compossible," *Studia Leibnitiana*, 5 (1973), 26–42; L. Howe, "Leibniz on Evil," *Sophia*, 10 (1971), 8–17; J. Kremer, *Das Problem der Theodicee in der Philosophie und Literatur des 18 Jahrhunderts* (Berlin, 1909).

Cartesian notion of a mechanical universe wound up and left by a distant creator. Rather, he saw the entire cosmos as permeated by God and made up of a virtual infinity of monads that are not inert but really alive and possessing rudimentary mind and spirit. The monads form the cosmos according to a preexistent harmony fashioned by God. In such a universe, "whence does evil come? . . . We, who derive all being from God, where shall we find the source of evil?" (p. 135).

If God is both omnipotent and good, it would seem that evil cannot exist. But Leibniz refused to take the easy (and indefensible) road of declaring that evil is only apparent. He accepted the scholastic view that evil is *essentially* privation, that it has no essence of its own, but he and King both squarely faced the fact that the world (or at least the part of it that we experience) is full of real examples of real suffering. How can the existence of such suffering be reconciled with the existence of God? Leibniz and King stated the traditional view more clearly than ever before. Three kinds of evil exist: metaphysical evil, the imperfection of the cosmos as a whole; natural evil, suffering such as that caused by cancer; and moral evil, or sin (p. 136). They followed Descartes in arguing that these evils were not only compatible with God's goodness but were an absolutely necessary corollary of any created cosmos, any cosmos not identical with God. A cosmos identical with God would *be* God: it would have no existence of its own and thus no purpose; it would not be a real creation. Since only God can be pefect, the creation of any real cosmos entails the existence of imperfection.

In the infinite amplitude of his love, God wants to create the largest number of the best elements that can exist together in one cosmos. In an instantaneous calculation made in eternity, God computes the best possible world and creates it. This "decision" by God is uncontingent and eternal rather than temporally or ontologically sequential. It is impossible for every perfect good to be compatible with every other perfect good: the intense beauty of the mountain must be set off by the fertility of the plain; the good of free will must entail real choices for sin. No world that reconciles all perfections is logically possible.

Natural evils are the result of metaphysical evil, since no natural evil exists that is not necessary for the maximization of the compossible goods. If any evil that exists were removed, the cosmos as a whole would only be worse. It is hard for us to grasp how the removal of muscular dystrophy or tornadoes would make the cosmos worse, but our view of things is limited to an infinitesimal area of space and time. God wills natural evils, not for the sake of evil but for the greater good.

Leibniz follows Christian tradition in suggesting that some evils may exist to punish us, instruct us, or warn us, but he admits that the quantity and sharpness of evil is out of proportion to such purposes; we must simply recognize that we cannot at present understand what the function of seemingly disproportionate or gratuitous evil may be.

Moral evils God does not will at all, but he permits them as a necessary consequence of the greater good of free will. Here Leibniz and King parted company, for King argued that there was no cause at all of an act of free will, but Leibniz held that a freewill act was determined or at least prompted by the "previous representations of good or evil, by inclinations, or by reasons" (p. 406). King's argument, which followed Saint Anselm's, seems superior. For the argument arises that a world with free will need not contain so much sin as this one does. If one uses Leibniz's model, one is obliged to ask why God did not limit the scope of sin, but if one uses King's, the question does not arise. If there is no cause of a freewill act, and if the choice of good or evil is fully—not just technically—free, then a world in which beings with free will sin less is possible, but it does not follow that God could have created it. What he created was real freedom; free creatures make their own choices.

Questions of random sampling and statistics arise at this point, as Kant pointed out. Though God may not cause A or B to sin, he knows that a proportion of his free beings are statistically likely to sin, yet he creates the cosmos anyway. But Leibniz would reply again that this is the best possible world, given the existence of that great good, free will.

For this is the best of all possible worlds in the sense that it is the best possible mix of compatible goods. Leibniz was aware that we can imagine a better world than this one, but he argued that what we think we can imagine is impossible because of its inherent contradictions. The evils of the world are necessary components of a cosmos that could not exist without them and whose harmony we would see, if we had the ability, to be the closest possible approximation of perfection. This is the best world that is possible; indeed, given the omnipotence and benevolence of God, it is the only world that is possible.

A doctrine more congenial to the confident, progressive bourgeois society that was emerging after the intense, conflicted pessimism of the early seventeenth century can scarcely be imagined. Voltaire unfairly caricatured and pilloried the view in *Candide*, but it must be confessed that its genial light seems not to penetrate the heart of the darkness.

For all the speculations of the metaphysicians, the focus of both elite and popular attention in the seventeenth century was still on issues within the old world view. The venerable debate on free will was still continuing. On the Protestant side, Lutheran and Calvinist predestinarian ideas were challenged by Arminian (Jacobus Arminius, 1560–1609) arguments for free will; on the Catholic side, the predestinarian Jansenists (Cornelius Jansen, 1585–1638) were challenged by the freewill views of the Molinists (Luis de Molinos, 1535–1600) and the Jesuits. Both Protestant and Catholic predestinarians won a number of rounds in the debate, but by the eighteenth century freewill views had come to prevail practically everywhere in practice.

Other writers argued the fall of Adam and Eve. Some, following the "minimalist" position going back to Irenaeus, contended that the first parents had been in a state of childlike innocence before their sin, so that their fall was error as much as sin and became the occasion for the gradual soul-building of the human race. The opposing "maximalist" position, going back to Gregory of Nyssa and Athanasius, held that the first parents had been "godlike" before their sin, so that their fall was comparable in culpability and gravity to that of Satan. Augustine had adopted a middle position, which Milton tried to follow in portraying both the majesty and the innocence of Adam and Eve.[8]

The nature of angels was also a point of debate. By 1700, belief in angels had begun to be unfashionable among the intellectual elite, though early in the seventeenth century it had been affirmed as a matter of course and then later defended vigorously by theologians who saw in attacks on angelology the first muster of the war against God.[9] The decline of the angels by the end of the century is a sign of the decline of both the traditional view and of hermetic magic, which placed the angels in a natural, Neoplatonic scheme of the cosmos. The question of Satan's eventual salvation revived among a few Arminians as well as Anabaptists, though Protestants as a whole followed the almost universal judgment of Christian tradition that the apostasy of the angels was "irrecoverable, and their sin unpardonable; God sware unto them in his wrath, they should never more return unto his rest."[10]

8. J. M. Evans, *Paradise Lost and the Genesis Tradition* (Oxford, 1968), pp. 242–271.

9. See R. H. West, *Milton and the Angels* (Athens, Ga., 1955). John Salkeld's *Treatise of Angels* (1613) affirmed the traditional picture; George Sinclair's *Satan's Invisible World Discovered* (1685) cited eyewitness accounts of demons; G. Schott's *Magia universalis naturae et artis* (1657), pt. 3, gives the actual census of the number of the demons at about 2705×10^{57}. Thomas Heywood's *Hierarchie of the Blessed Angells* (1634) is a compendium of patristic and medieval doctrine.

10. Richard Montagu, *The Acts and Movements of the Church* (London, 1642), p. 7, quoted in C. A. Patrides, "The Salvation of Satan," *Journal of the History of Ideas*, 28 (1967), 472.

The tension between skepticism and credulity so common in the seventeenth century produced a new phenomenon, the "black mass," a strange combination of disbelief in Christianity and belief in the Christian Devil. The atmosphere for the black mass had been building through the centuries, both in witchcraft and in the numerous reported cases of demonic possession where the force of the demonic was very tightly bound to disturbances of the human unconscious, especially sexual aberrations. Catherine de Saint-Augustin (1632–1668), a nun in Quebec, was said to have been attacked by the Devil at the age of five, and for the rest of her life he assaulted her with every kind of temptation, including despair, lust, and gluttony.[11] In the possession of the nuns of Loudun and Louviers in France, the powers of Satan and of human sexuality were combined in an atmosphere of collective hysteria and hallucination cleverly exploited for political purposes. The possession of the nuns of the Ursuline convent of Loudun is well known. The hysteria centered on a priest named Urbain Grandier, a sexual libertine whose ironic wit had earned him many enemies, some of whom concocted a plot to ruin him by accusing him of debauching the nuns and causing them to be possessed by Satan. At least some of the nuns believed that they had been sexually molested by demons. At the convent of Louviers, a nun who had been seduced by her confessor before entering the convent was the focus of the posession. These phenomena differed from those of witchcraft in their attention to sex and in the involvement of priests—elements that became central in the new black mass, for nothing could be more blasphemous in a Catholic context than the sexual perversion of the sacraments presided over by a priest.[12]

In 1680 a number of priests were indicted for saying mass on the bodies of naked women at the center of a ring of black candles, of leading the congregation in intercourse with the women, of ritual copulation on the altar, of sacrificing animals, of murdering children and using their blood in the preparation of aphrodisiacs, of desecrating the Eucharist, of mixing children's blood and bodily fluids in the chalice, of invoking the Devil, and of making written pact with him. These black

11. G. Boucher, *Dieu et Satan dans la vie de Catherine de Saint-Augustin, 1632–1668* (Tournai, 1979).

12. W. D. Howarth, *Life and Letters in France: The Seventeenth Century* (London, 1965); A. Huxley, *The Devils of Loudun* (New York, 1952); G. Mongrédien, *Madame de Montespan et l'affaire des poisons* (Paris, 1953); H. T. F. Rhodes, *The Satanic Mass* (London, 1954); D. P. Walker, *Unclean Spirits: Possession and Exorcism in France and England in the Late Sixteenth and Early Seventeenth Centuries* (Philadelphia, 1981); G. Zacharias, *Satanskult und Schwarze Messe*, 2d ed. (Wiesbaden, 1970).

Mirror writing and signatures of the Devil and his cohorts from the alleged pact between Urbain Grandier and Satan, which was exhibited at Grandier's trial, 1634.

masses were supposed to have been said at the behest of courtiers or other influential people to procure political or sexual advancement. One of Louis XIV's mistresses, Madame de Montespan, was alleged to have used black magic to render the queen sterile and fix the king's sexual attentions on herself. As with the witch craze, however, once the madness began to touch people of such power and influence, it was doomed. After the execution for sorcery and murder of dozens of people—none of them from the noble and wealthy classes on which the scandal centered—the king terminated the investigation in 1682 and issued an edict eliminating prosecution for witchcraft and sorcery. The black mass— the product of the cynical, skeptical, yet credulous seventeenth century—vanished until it was revived in the late nineteenth century by literary poseurs.

The Protestant attitude toward such matters was quite different from the Catholic. Despite Luther's own use of them, the Protestant churches soon decided that exorcisms were superstitious, like consecrations, blessings, and holy water (a Somerset farmer reportedly said that "his mare will make as good holy water as any priest can"). The Puritan John Hall called exorcism "foul superstition and gross magic"; Anglicans abolished the office of exorcist in 1550. The argument was that the age of miracles had ended with the early church; what now prevailed was a rational nexus between divine providence, natural law, and individual faith. In such a world the Devil could not be repulsed by holy water, the sign of the cross, the Lord's Prayer, or exorcism; clergy could only pray over the victim, beseeching God's mercy. As Keith Thomas observed, this left the Protestants in a painful situation: their churches affirmed all the traditional doctrines of demonic obsession and possession but removed the traditional antidotes. Still the Protestants were at least spared most of the lurid features of Catholic exorcisms and their polemical uses.[13]

In the arts the process of shifting emphasis from transcendent evil to the demonic immanent in the human mind was slow and irregular, and the traditional Devil continued to play an important part in literature, especially in conservative Spain and its colonies.[14] Miguel de Cervantes

---

13. Thomas, pp. 51–55, 74–76, 265, 479–481.

14. See A. L. Cilveti, *El demonio en el teatro de Calderón* (Valencia, 1977); J. L. Flecniakoska, "Les rôles de Satan dans les 'Autos' de Lope de Vega," *Bulletin hispanique*, 66 (1964), 30–34; U. Müller, *Die Gestalt Lucifers in der Dichtung vom Barock bis zur Romantik* (Berlin, 1940); S. Sola, *El diablo y lo diabolico en las letras americanas (1580–1750)* (Bilbao, 1973). Boileau (Nicolas Boileau-Despréaux, 1636–1711) objected in his *Art poétique*

(1547–1616), Lope de Vega (1562–1635), and Calderón de la Barca (1600–1681) treated both vice and the Devil seriously but brought the Devil and humanity closer together by probing the psychology of evil.[15] In Protestant England, *The Pilgrim's Progress* of John Bunyan (1628–1688) also emphasized the internal demon of temptation and sin more than a transcendent lord of evil.[16]

Plays and poems dealing with the traditional story of Satan—including the war in heaven, the fall of the angels, and the temptation of Adam and Eve—continued to be popular all over Europe both before and after Milton's *Paradise Lost*.[17] The treatment of the subject by Joost van den

---

(1674) to the growing custom of including God, Devil, angels, demons, and saints in literature on the grounds that it made them merely mythical figures, as ancient literature had done to the pagan gods.

The visual arts paid much less attention to the Devil in this period than earlier, but Jean Fragonard (1732–1806) produced a humorous sketch of Satan terrified by the sight of a naked woman. Giuseppe Tartini (1692–1770) wrote a "Devil's Sonata," alleging that it was inspired by a dream in which the Devil came and played to him on the violin.

15. Lope de Vega, *Obras publicadas por la Real Academia Española* (Madrid, 1890–1913); Calderón, *Comedias, Dramas, Autos sacramentales* (Madrid, 1960–1967). The Devil appears in over twenty plays of Lope from 1585 to 1635, such as *Coloquio del bautismo de Cristo*, *El tirano castigado*, *El desengaño del mundo*, and *El villano despojado*. He takes various forms— sailor, merchant, procurer, shepherd, bandit, gypsy—and goes under names such as Astarot, Demonio, Dudoso, Asmodeo, Luzbel, Lucifer, Satan, Nembrot, Rengo, and "Principe del mondo o de los tinieblas." Calderón's *El mágico prodigioso* and other plays presented the Devil under the names of Demonio, Luzbel, Lucero, Baal, and Belfegor; Calderón also associated him with vices personified as demons: *culpa* (sin), *duba* (doubt), *apostasia* (apostasy), *herejia* (heresy), *idolatria*, *malicia*, and *odio* (hatred).

16. J. Bunyan, *The Pilgrim's Progress* (London, 1678). See R. M. Frye, *God, Man, and Satan: Patterns of Christian Thought and Life in Paradise Lost, Pilgrim's Progress, and the Great Theologians* (Princeton, 1960), esp. pp. 124–125. Bunyan's autobiography, *Grace Abounding* (1666), shows that he believed in the external existence of the Devil.

17. Phineas Fletcher, *The Locusts or Apollyonists* (1627); Serafino della Salandra, *Adamo caduto* (1647); Abraham Cowley, *Davideis* (1656); John Dryden, *The State of Innocence and the Fall of Man* (1674: a dramatization of Milton's *Paradise Lost*); Manz Noël, *Lucifer* (1717). After the first quarter of the eighteenth century, the genre rapidly declined. The debate as to the extent of the influence of such works on Milton is tangential to the history of the Devil. See A. B. Chambers, "More Sources for Milton," *Modern Philology*, 63 (1965), 61–66; W. Kirkconnell, *The Celestial Cycle: The Theme of Paradise Lost in World Literature with Translations of the Major Analogues* (Toronto, 1952); E. S. LeCompte, "Milton's Infernal Council and Mantuan," *Publications of the Modern Language Association*, 69 (1954), 979–983; J. W. Lever, "*Paradise Lost* and the Anglo-Saxon Tradition," *Review of English Studies*, 23 (1947), 97–106; I. Samuel, *Dante and Milton: The Commedia and Paradise Lost* (Ithaca, 1966). In a personal communication to the author, Professor C. T. Berkhout argues that Milton may have been influenced by the pictures in the Old English Junius manuscript but was unlikely to have felt the influence of the text, since he was scornful of Old English poetic diction and his eyesight was fading at the time when he would have had access to the manuscript. See Lucifer, p. 138.

Goya, Saint Francis of Borgia exorcizes a demon-oppressed dying man, while demons crowd around the bedside hoping to seize his soul. Oil on canvas, 1788. Courtesy of the Museo Catedralico y Diocesano de Valencia.

Vondel (1587–1679), one of the most eloquent and coherent, is contained in his two plays *Lucifer* (1654) and *Adam in Exile* (1664).[18]

The action of *Lucifer* begins among the angels in heaven soon after the creation of the world. Gabriel informs them that God had decided to become incarnate in humanity, thus granting to humans an honor denied the angels. Lucifer envies both this honor and the innocent sexual love between Adam and Eve.

Vondel's scenario raises logical problems. The incarnation is traditionally thought of as God's response to the fall of Adam and Eve, itself encouraged by the fallen Lucifer. There is no rational chronology in which the plan for the incarnation could precede the fall of Lucifer, for God's eternity and simultaneous knowledge of all events does not mean that he does not work with normal cause and effect within the time/space continuum. Besides, Vondel is telling a story that is set within time. Still, the failure of his scenario is not all his fault; it springs from the incoherence of the traditional Christian explanation of Satan's motives. Did Satan sin through pride in desiring to be like God; pride in trying to achieve his own salvation on his own terms and before the time was right; envy of God's position; envy of Christ's position in heaven; envy of humanity for being made in God's image; or envy of humanity for being dignified with the incarnation? The possibilities have never been sorted out satisfactorily, and the view that there is *no* cause of a true freewill action is the only logically coherent one.

Vondel goes on to show Lucifer—assisted by Apollyon, Belial, Beelzebub, and other untrustworthy angels—planning to raise rebellion in heaven. Like Faustus, Vondel's Lucifer repeatedly contemplates repentance and repeatedly rejects it on the double ground of pride and despair: he has made his choice and he will be what he is. Vondel's chronology is still peculiar, for Lucifer descends from heaven to cause the fall of Adam and Eve before he himself is cast down. This solves one problem in that it allows Satan to be bound in hell after his expulsion from heaven without needing to account for his escaping his bonds to visit Eden, but it introduces an awkward sequence of events and tends to equate the original sin of Lucifer with his temptation of humanity. This would mean that Lucifer had lived long in heaven before changing his mind and turning against God, a view that degrades the power and scope of inherent angelic knowledge.

---

18. Joost van den Vondel, *Adam in Ballingschap*, in *De Werken van Vondel*, vol. 10 (Amsterdam, 1937), pp. 94–170; Vondel, *Lucifer*, in *De Werken*, vol. 5 (Amsterdam, 1931), pp. 601–696.

Still in heaven, Vondel's Lucifer begins to consider that it may be better to rule in exile than to remain subordinate to the Lord. The good angels counsel submission, but Lucifer exclaims that God is unfair and unjust in setting the incarnate God/Man above the ontologically superior angels. The angel Uriel appears onstage to describe the great war in heaven to the audience and to recount how Lucifer, flung down from heaven, has been transformed into a hideous toad.

In his *Adam in Exile*, Vondel returns to a more traditional chronology in which Lucifer tempts the first parents after his fall from heaven. Since he has lost his open war with the Lord, he determines to attack in a more devious way by striking at him through his beloved creatures. Lucifer is under sentence of bondage in hell, where he is both captive and ruler, but God gives him license to tempt humanity. With the help of Asmodeus, Lucifer sends Belial in the form of a serpent to corrupt Eve, who in turn ruins Adam. Asmodeus reports the success of Belial to a delighted Lucifer, while Adam and Eve are expelled from Paradise.

It was John Milton who made the traditional story of the fall of angels and humanity into a scenario so coherent and compelling that it became the standard account for all succeeding generations. Milton was born in 1608 and seems to have been brought up a staunch Protestant; after 1637 the policies of Archbishop Laud drove him into increasing sympathy with the Puritans. But his religious views are not fully understood. His theology contained both Anglican and Calvinist elements, and in the 1650s he seems to have shifted toward Independency and Arminianism. By the late 1650s he had formulated a coherent, sometimes idiosyncratic theology of his own. The most relevant of his works are *Christian Doctrine* (*De doctrina christiana*, written in 1655–1660 though not published until 1825), *Paradise Lost* (1667, revised 1674), and *Paradise Regained* (1671).[19] He died in 1674.

Christian Doctrine, which Milton wrote at about the same time as he was composing *Paradise Lost*, was an effort to construct a logically coherent theology based entirely upon scripture. Like other Protestant writers attempting similar tasks, he was unaware of how much his interpretations and even his categories derived from tradition as well as the Bible. His views on the evil angels are essentially traditional. Too

19. Here abbreviated CD, PL, and PR. The best overall edition is F. A. Patterson et al., eds., *The Works of John Milton*, 18 vols. (New York, 1931–1938); the best edition of CD is *Christian Doctrine*, in *The Complete Prose Works* (New Haven, 1973), vol. 6. See also J. H. Hanford and J. G. Taaffe, *A Milton Handbook*, 5th ed. (New York, 1970).

much has been made of Milton's supposed heresies by critics who seem
not to understand the wide diversity of Christian tradition. It has been
said that Milton was not a trinitarian, which is an ignorant reading both
of the poetry and of *Christian Doctrine*. More plausible is the view that
Milton was an "Arian," but even this is anachronistic and too precise.
The most that can be said is that he tended toward subordinationism,
the view that the Son and the Holy Spirit, though truly God, are not
coeternal with the Father. Milton's belief that the cosmos was created
from the substance of God has a long traditional background, particularly among the mystics, and is consistent with the original ex nihilo
doctrine of the early church. His belief that angels may in some sense be
corporeal reflected the opinions of many scholastics, as did his view that
angels do not know everything from the moment of their creation.[20]

In Milton's scheme, God declared freedom for angels and humans
and, as a corollary of freedom, permits evil (CD 1.4). The Devil led the
angels in the revolt in heaven (1.9). After his expulsion from heaven, he
tempted Adam and Eve, who need not have yielded but freely chose to
sin (1.11). God became incarnate in Christ in order to destroy the
Devil's power (1.14). Here in outline is the wholly traditional diabology
of the *Christian Doctrine*. Milton made his mark on the subject not by a
departure from orthodoxy but by the poetic grandeur and detail that he
added to it.

The epic poems *Paradise Lost* and *Paradise Regained* cover almost the
entire span of Christian salvation history from the fall of the angels to
the redemption on the cross. Rather than following Milton's classical
device of beginning in the midst of the action, I take the two works
together and trace the argument chronologically. This does violence to
the poems, but my purpose is historical rather than literary.

Milton's own purpose was to offer a poetic theodicy:

> That to the highth of this great Argument
> I may assert Eternal Providence,
> And justify the ways of God to men. [PL 1.24–26]

Milton's theodicy combines the freewill argument with soulmaking.
God created the world good; moral goodness is impossible without free

---

20. LUCIFER, pp. 31–34, 172–173. See also West's *Milton and the Angels*, and R. H.
West, "Milton's Angelological Heresies," *Journal of the History of Ideas*, 14 (1953), 116–
123.

will; humans and angels are free to choose evil; some do so; God's providence, turning all to good, makes our fall the occasion for teaching us wisdom through trials and suffering; God ultimately redeems us through the incarnation and passion of Jesus Christ. In order to understand the origins of the drama we must return to the beginning and see how the fall of Satan prefigured and prepared that of Adam and Eve. The drama of Satan is not itself the point of the poems but the necessary background for the drama of humanity. Adam and Christ, not Satan, are at the theological (though not necessarily the dramatic) center of the poem. For Milton, as for the Christian tradition, evil is empty, mad, unreal, focused on unreality, and self-defeating.

Milton based the poems, as he did his *Christian Doctrine*, on the Bible, but in both he added a second level by using Christian tradition, and in the poems he added a third level—his own poetic and rhetorical embellishment. It is difficult to say how much of the poems Milton meant to be taken theologically. A poem may be very like a theological tract only if it is a very bad poem, and Milton was well aware that reality has many dimensions. Sometimes he expressed reality with a theological statement; sometimes with allegory, as in the figures of Sin and Death; sometimes with mythopoeic invention, as in the debate in Hell; sometimes with poetic convention, as in his description of the universe. He seldom made scientific or historical statements; his cosmos, like Dante's, is more deeply real than any one-dimensional statement could possibly be.

The question of whether Milton believed in his Devil must be understood in this multidimensional sense. He found the existence of the Devil clear in scripture; he also believed in Satan poetically. Shakespeare had brought the diabolical into the human psyche, and Milton returned the now humanized diabolical traits to the Devil. Milton's Satan shares with Shakespeare's villains an obsession with self and a willful ignorance of the reality of other creatures and of the cosmos as a whole. Satan's emotions are human and powerful because the poet drew that dark power from the depths of his own psyche. It is curious that this vividly powerful portrait of Satan should have appeared when belief in the Devil was rapidly declining among educated people, particularly in the worldly England of the Restoration, but the fact is that the image of the Devil retained its power in the human mind long after theological belief had faded.

The deep power of Milton's Satan raised a long-standing debate as to whether Satan was the real hero of *Paradise Lost*. The answer depends upon what one means by "hero." In a purely literary sense, the hero is the protagonist, the character who most moves the action along. Dryden and others in Milton's own time saw Satan as the hero in this sense. The action of the poem is the struggle between Satan on one side and Adam, Christ, and the Father on the other. That three characters—two of them divine—are needed on one side to balance one on the other indicates the dramatic power of the one. Further, since only one who changes can carry the action, the eternal and unchanging Father can scarcely be the hero, and even the Son is too remote and impervious. As protagonist, Adam has severe limitations: half the battle between God and Devil is already over before attention can focus on Adam, and he is too passive, too acted upon—by God, Eve, and Devil—to be the hero. (Some critics have argued that the dramatic hero is really Milton or even the Reader.)

But the literary sense of "hero" must be distinguished from the moral sense that is the real concern of this study. Was the character of Satan to be admired? Every reader is struck by his magnificence, a magnificence that had already appeared in the war in heaven as described by Milton's predecessors. For the war in Heaven to be credible and dramatic, it had to be a clash of uncertain outcome between mighty heroes, like the classical struggles of the *Iliad* and the *Aeneid*. But these epics did not have clearly defined villains as counterpoints to their heroes. Both Achilles and Hector are heroes; Aeneas' opponent Turnus is also a hero, and Milton deliberately transferred some of Turnus' attributes to his own Satan. Like Turnus, Satan could be both opponent and hero; indeed, he needed to be in order to make Christ's triumph in the war in Heaven noble and magnificent. Satan also shared some Stoic virtues with Aeneas, who in turn sometimes appeared in post-Vergilian literature as less than a hero or even as a traitor.[21]

Milton's predecessors had found no way out of the dilemma, but Milton was able to depict Satan as heroic and at the same time cast doubts upon his heroism by taking an ironic distance and showing in action, dialogue, and asides that Satan's apparent heroism is sham. It is

21. On the war, see S. Revard, *The War in Heaven* (Ithaca, 1980), esp. ch. 6. For Milton and Aeneas, see G. B. Christopher, *Milton and the Science of the Saints* (Princeton, 1982), pp. 62–66: "One may view Satan as a summary of the literary decay of Aeneas' reputation from Homer onward, so that he stands as the embodiment of what Calvin saw as the course of downward imagination." For Milton and Ulysses, see J. Steadman, *Milton's Epic Characters* (Chapel Hill, N.C., 1968), pp. 194–210. For the view that Milton intended his Satan as a criticism of epic heroes, see Steadman, pp. 211–212.

hard to retain a heroic picture of Satan when one is brought up against his incest with his daughter Sin, his ugliness (PL 2.115–116, 968–970; 3.681–685; 4.115–128, 835–840), his stench (9.445–446), his filth (10.630–634), and his grotesque parody of God (1.73, 110, 162–165, 247, 263; 3.375–382; 9.122–130; 10.444–454). Yet these are corrections to our first impulse to admire his rich, sensuous, lofty rhetoric and his determination to be true to himself, enduring every defeat and agony in his fierce adherence to his own identity in the face of a superior power determined to destroy him.

Milton certainly knew what he was doing when he made the character of Satan powerfully attractive. He intended the reader to be caught up in admiration, to feel the tug of attraction to the terrible, self-indulgent prince of darkness, to feel the pull of that darkness of self turned forever narrowly down into itself instead of opened up courageously to the broad world of light and beauty. He intended us to identify with the Devil and then, as the poem develops, to identify the gradual revelation of his viciousness and his impotence with the understanding of our own sin and weakness. Milton applied the characteristics of the epic hero to Satan so that the reader could see the emptiness of loveless heroism in a world governed in reality by love. Though the poetic personality of Milton's Satan is so strong that those unfamiliar with Christianity can mistake him for a noble figure (as the nineteenth-century Romantics did; see Chapter 5) *Paradise Lost* is best read in the spirit in which Milton intended it.[22] The poet seems almost to have warned against the distortion of his Satan when he addressed the Devil thus: "And thou, sly hypocrite, who now wouldst seem/patron of liberty" (PL 4.957).

The chronological beginning of *Paradise Lost* is midway in Book 5, where the archangel Raphael relates to Adam what "hath past in Heav'n" (5.554, 562). There are in effect two creations in Milton: the creation of the cosmos, the entire world seen and unseen, including angels and even, paradoxically, chaos; and the creation of the material universe. In the poem, Chaos is simply there from the beginning, without explanation, but in *Christian Doctrine* Milton explained that God created the cosmos by generating it from himself.

---

22. Modern writers favoring the view that Satan is the real moral hero include W. Empson, *Milton's God*, 2d ed. (Cambridge, 1981). Those defending Milton and Milton's own view include, above all, C. S. Lewis, *A Preface to Paradise Lost*, 2d ed. (London, 1960). See also D. R. Danielson, *Milton's Good God: A Study in Literary Theodicy* (Cambridge, 1982); R. Comstock, *The God of Paradise Lost* (Berkeley, 1986).

Some critics have viewed this as a heresy against the traditional idea that the cosmos was created ex nihilo, from nothing, but that criticism misunderstands the original ex nihilo position. The early fathers who argued for ex nihilo were expressing their opposition to the idea that chaos, matter, or any other principle is coeternal with God. There could be only one eternal principle. Later, many Christian theologians insisted that ex nihilo meant that God creates literally from nothing; that is, not from himself either but from some mysterious something called "nothing." This is a misunderstanding—indeed a contradiction—of the original ex nihilo view. A third position, favored by many of the mystics, was that the universe is an outpouring of God himself. It is not as if God sits there in the beginning with something called "nothing" outside of him from which he creates the cosmos. Nothing is nothing at all; there is nothing but God for the cosmos to come from. Pantheism, the notion that God is coextensive with the cosmos, is certainly a heresy in Christian terms, but panentheism, the idea that the cosmos is contained within God, is not.[23] In the beginning is God:

> Boundless the Deep, because I am who fill
> Infinitude, nor vacuous the space.
> Though I uncircumscrib'd myself retire,
> And put not forth my goodness, which is free
> To act or not. [PL 7.168–172]

This seems to mean that God could have chosen to make all of Chaos into coherent worlds but chooses instead to leave parts of it in an unformed state. Out of the rest he produces a real cosmos, real in the sense of its freedom to act apart from him, by voluntarily withdrawing the sphere of his omnipotence and thus allowing for a real distinction between the cosmos and God. The cosmos is God, but distinct from God-in-himself: it is the external expression of God.[24]

In the time after the initial creation and before the creation of the material universe, God calls the angels into being by the power of his Son, the Word (5.835–838). And then one "day" he calls all the hosts of heaven before his throne to announce:

> This day I have begot whom I declare
> My only Son, and on this holy Hill

23. CD 1.7; PL 3.708–709; 7.170–171. On ex nihilo theory, see LUCIFER, pp. 115, 118–119.

24. See LUCIFER, pp. 31–34.

Him have anointed, whom ye now behold
At my right hand; your Head I him appoint;
And by my Self have sworn to him shall bow
All knees in Heav'n, and shall confess him Lord. [PL 5.603–608]

Milton did not mean that the Son was literally begotten after the creation of the angels. He was using the term "beget," as many seventeenth-century writers did, to mean "exalt," as is clear by his other phrase for the "begetting": "that day / Honour'd by his great Father" (PL 5.662–663) and by other references to the Son's having created the angels (3.390–391; 5.835–838). The begetting of the Son by the Father is contrasted with the false boast of Satan to have been "self-begot" (5.860).

To the angelic hosts who gather around the throne of the Father, Milton attributes a sort of corporeal nature. He indicates through Raphael that he may be doing so only metaphorically (PL 5.569–571), because it surpasses human imagination to portray the life of pure spirits, but even the literal meaning is within the bounds of Christian tradition. Precedents exist not only in the Old Testament—as when Abraham entertained the three angels at table—but also among the scholastics. In any event, it is the spiritual nature of the angels that Milton emphasizes throughout.[25]

Among these hosts the greatest or one of the greatest was Lucifer. Milton preferred the name Satan, using Lucifer only three times in *Paradise Lost* and offering the poetic reason that the name was changed when the bright angel fell:

Satan, so call him now, his former name
Is heard no more in Heav'n. [PL 5.658–659]

The underlying reason is that Milton, attempting to build his theology on the Bible alone, found no justification in scripture for the name Lucifer.[26] The poet is deliberately unclear as to Satan's rank in heaven: he calls him an archangel, yet sets him in command of seraphim and cherubim, and names his lieutenant Beelzebub a cherub. Knowing that

25. On angels as spirits, see PL 1.423–425; angels eat: 5.406–452, 630–637; angels feel pain but cannot die except by annihilation: 6.327–347. See LUCIFER, pp. 41, 172–173.

26. The three mentions of the name Lucifer occur in PL 5.760; 7.131; 10.425. See SATAN, pp. 25–28, 130–131.

the Bible ascribes no angelic rank to Satan, Milton felt that the only point he needed to make was that Satan was of such dignity in Heaven that he naturally became the king of Hell. The poet was at pains to describe his godlike, princely nature and his terrifying stature:

> On th'other side Satan alarm'd
> Collecting all his might dilated stood,
> Like Teneriff or Atlas unremov'd:
> His stature reached the Sky, and on his Crest
> Sat horror Plum'd. [PL 4.985–989]

> [He] extended long and large
> Lay floating many a rood, in bulk as huge
> As whom the Fables name of monstrous size. [PL 1.195–197][27]

This great power is moved to envy, anger, and horror at the elevation of the Son above the angels:

> Fraught
> With envy against the Son of God, that day
> Honour'd by his great Father, and proclaim'd
> Messiah King anointed, could not bear
> Through pride that sight.
> . . .
> [Therefore] he resolv'd
> With all his Legions to dislodge, and leave
> Unworshipt, unobey'd the Throne supreme. [PL 5.661–670]

The rebellion of Satan therefore occurs before the creation of the material universe, including humanity.[28]

The selection of this chronology determined which of the possible reasons for Satan's fall could be adopted. On one level the Almighty is the cause of Satan's ruin: God chooses the cosmos as it is, including the fall of a great angel. The angel Abdiel tells Satan: "I see thy fall / Determin'd" (PL 5.878–879), and the absolute freedom and providence of God pervade the poem (1.211–220; 7.171–173). On the next level, however, God does not directly will things to be as they are, for he has

27. See also PL 1.129, 157, 209–222, 315–316, 324, 358, 589–593; 2.300; 4.828; 5.696–708. Compare Dante's Satan and the classical Titans.

28. CD 1.7: "It seems even probable, that the apostasy which caused the expulsion of so many thousands from heaven, took place before the foundations of the world were laid." This was traditionally the preferred account, though early hexaemeral writers placed the rebellion during the six days of creation.

given his creatures freedom. What God says of humanity's original sin also applies to Satan:

> So will fall
> Hee and his faithless Progeny: whose fault?
> Whose but his own? ingrate, he had of mee
> All he could have; I made him just and right,
> Sufficient to have stood, though free to fall. [PL 3.95–99][29]

The third level is the cause of Satan's fall, but there is none, since there can be *no cause* of a freewill act.[30] Still, on a fourth level one can speak of motives, if not causes.

During the course of the poem Satan's motives deteriorate from pride to envy to revenge.[31] Pride and envy are of course the traditional motives, and Satan's "obdurate pride" (PL 1.58) appears from the very beginning of the poem:

> He trusted to have equall'd the most High,
> If he oppos'd; and with ambitious aim
> Against the Throne and Monarchy of God
> Rais'd impious War in Heav'n. [PL 1.40–43]

The scholastics had rejected as absurd the idea that Satan could try to equal God and relied instead upon the usual Latin translation of Isaiah, *ero similis altissimo*, to vindicate their view that he was attempting only to be *like* God. Steadman has shown that Milton may have been using the Tremellius-Junius translation, *me aequabo exelso*, "I shall equal the most high," a much more arrogant boast. "Satan," Steadman observes, "desires to equal God in royal power, in strength, in freedom, in reason, in glory. The most common meaning, however, is parity in might."[32]

Satan himself confesses that "Pride and worse Ambition threw me down" (PL 4.40; cf. 2.10, 5.860) To pride he added envy of the Son. Envy of the Son is a traditional motive, but tradition was never consistent as to what it meant. It might mean envy of the Son's intrinsically

---

29. Milton asserts angelic and human free will in PL 9.344–356. He took the Arminian freewill position against the Calvinist position set forth by the Westminster Confession of 1647, which included total depravity, unconditional election, limited atonement, irresistible grace, and the perseverance of the saints.

30. LUCIFER, pp. 164–166.

31. See Lewis, *Preface to Paradise Lost*, and Evans, pp. 230–231.

32. Steadman, pp. 161–163. Cf. PL 5.922.

superior nature, or envy of his elevation to higher status in Heaven, or envy of his role of creator of the universe, or envy of his power to redeem fallen humanity. Milton made no clear statement. His chronology did not permit Satan to envy Christ's creation of or lordship over the universe, since the universe did not yet exist; still less could he envy the redemption, since humanity did not yet exist (the mention of the Messiah in PL 5.644 is an anachronism). Milton chose to focus on the dramatic moment of Christ's elevation by the Father and Satan's disdainful refusal to bend the knee, a moment dramatically similar to Satan's usurpation of God's throne in the mystery plays.[33]

Satan had a sense of "injur'd merit" (PL 1.98) at the Son's power, which seemed to him a "strange point and new" (5.855). To Milton, it was absurd that Satan should claim any merit, injured or otherwise, since no one has any merit that does not come as the gift of God. At God's request that the angels glorify the Son, Satan addresses his fellow angels with scorn: "Will ye submit your necks, and choose to bend / The supple knee?" (5.787–788; cf. 1.35–40; 4.50–70; 5.661–665, 772–802, 853–858). Once ruined, Satan adds revenge to envy (1.35–40; 2.336–373), and when humanity is created, he adds envy of humanity to envy of the Son (4.505–535). The degree of Satan's initial understanding of the situation is left unclear. Does Satan know that God is both good and omnipotent yet rebel anyway, or does he know that God is good and refuse to admit it to himself, or does he really think that God is an unjust tyrant?

In Milton's chronology, the first sin in the cosmos occurred at the moment that Satan willed to rebel. At that moment of decision, his daughter, Sin, sprang from his forehead, an image drawn from the birth of Minerva from the brow of Jove and in parody of Holy Wisdom, the personification of the Holy Spirit (PL 2.752–760). Satan's first act as a sinner is to persuade his fellow angels to rebel. He sees God as "Our Enemy" (1.188). He withdraws his followers from the hosts surrounding the throne of God and erects his own throne in the north of Heaven. Echoing seventeenth-century hatred of political innovation, Satan argues that the exaltation of the Son is an illegitimate novelty and a gratuitous insult to their dignity as angels. He declaims in favor of equality and democracy, an irony in the light of his eagerness later to wield the tyrant's scepter in Hell. In one of his specious rationalizations, he reminds them that they cannot remember the moment of creation,

33. LUCIFER, pp. 250, 251.

goes on to speculate that they might not have been created at all, and then leaps to the unwarranted conclusion that they actually were "self-begot, self-rais'd" (5.860).

> Our puissance is our own, our own right hand
> Shall teach us highest deeds, by proof to try
> Who is our equal. [PL 5.864–866]

One-third of the angels, including angels of every rank, join him in revolt.[34]

The immediate effect is war in Heaven,[35] a mad action on Satan's part, for it could have only one conclusion. To make a war against omnipotent divinity dramatically effective, it was necessary to portray some degree of valor and courage on the part of the rebellious angels, and Milton did this so enthusiastically as to introduce a scenario peculiar to him: he made the first stage of the war a stalemate between Satan's armies and those of Michael, so that God is obliged on the third day to send in the Son to cast the rebels down. Where Michael had been hard pressed, the Son easily triumphs and hurls the defeated rebels out of Heaven.[36] God could have chosen to destroy them utterly, but he refrains:

> Yet half his strength he put not forth, but check'd
> His Thunder in mid Volley, for he meant
> Not to destroy, but root them out of Heav'n. [PL 6.853–855]

Why does God not in fact annihilate them? Even Satan is surprised when God actually leaves them with the power to do more damage:

> Let him surer bar
> His Iron Gates, if he intends our stay
> In that dark durance. [PL 4.897–899]

34. Later, 9.141, Satan claims that "well nigh half" fell with him, but he is lying as usual. Cf. PL 5.668–907; 7.145; 9.141.

35. Revard, p. 135, points out that the early hexaemera tend not to support belief in a war in heaven, and both Luther and Calvin excluded it from their own interpretation of Revelation 12:19. But the war in heaven was well established in both the poetic and the theological interpretations of the Middle Ages.

36. PL 6.855–856. Cf. 6.262–353: Satan and Michael in combat; 6.478–652: the demons invent artillery; 6.680–801: the Father sends out the Son; 6.801–892: the Son's victory.

The answer is that God wishes to teach Satan that every effort to do evil is turned to good, to show him

> How all his malice serv'd but to bring forth
> Infinite goodness, grace, and mercy shown
> On man by him seduc't, but on himself
> Treble confusion, wrath and vengeance pour'd. [PL 1.217–220]

Whatever Satan does "shall rebound / Upon his own rebellious head" (3.85–86), and no matter how much he may learn from the action of God's providence, he can never be saved. Humanity can have a savior because the first parents were seduced by another being, but Satan will have none because he was the first to sin. Though this is illogical, since neither Eve nor Adam was compelled to sin, it is Christian tradition:

> The first sort by their own suggestion fell,
> Self-tempted, self-deprav'd: Man falls deceiv'd
> By the other first: Man therefore shall find grace,
> The other none. [PL 3.129–132]

Another result of the fall of Satan is the introduction of evil into the cosmos. Satan is the "author of evil" (6.262) as God is the Author of the universe. As a result of his sin, misery enters the world:

> How hast thou disturb'd
> Heav'n's blessed peace, and into Nature brought
> Misery, uncreated till the crime
> Of thy Rebellion? how hast thou instill'd
> Thy malice into thousands? [PL 6.266–270]

Having fallen from grace by choice, Satan and his evil angels are flung down from Heaven:

> Him th'Almighty Power
> Hurl'd headlong flaming from th'Ethereal Sky
> With hideous ruin and combustion down
> To bottomless perdition, there to dwell
> In Adamantine Chains and penal Fire. [PL 1.44–48]

With him fell all the angels that had taken his side:

Yawning hell closes over the fallen angels in a Gustave Doré illustration for *Paradise Lost*, 6.875. Engraving, 1882.

> Lucifer from Heav'n
> (So call him, brighter once amidst the Host
> Of Angels, than that Star the Stars among)
> Fell with his flaming Legions through the Deep
> Into his place. [PL 7.131–135]

They fell "thick as Autumnal Leaves . . . Cherub and Seraph rolling in the Flood" (1.302, 324). Nine days they fell through the air and nine days lay prostrate in the fiery lake (1.50–53; 6.871).[37]

> Nine days they fell; confounded Chaos roar'd,
> And felt tenfold confusion in thir fall
> Through his wild Anarchy, so huge a rout
> Incumber'd him with ruin: Hell at last
> Yawning receiv'd them whole, and on them clos'd,
> Hell thir fit habitation fraught with fire
> Unquenchable, the house of woe and pain. [PL 6.871–877]

In short, the angels plunge out of Heaven through Chaos into Hell. But where is this Hell?

Dante and tradition put Hell at the center of the Earth, because in the Ptolemaic cosmos the center of the Earth is that point farthest from God's heaven. And this farthest point is what Milton seems to intend:

> here thir Prison ordained
> In utter darkness, and thir portion set
> As far remov'd from God and light of Heav'n
> As from the Centre thrice to th'utmost Pole. [PL 1.71–74]

But in Milton's chronology the physical universe has not yet been created (CD 1.33). Later in the action Milton describes Satan's voyage from Hell across Chaos toward Heaven, from which the universe hangs pendant on a golden chain (PL 2.409–410, 1046–1055). If the universe hangs from Heaven, and both are separated by Chaos from Hell, where is Hell? The physical imagery that Milton uses to describe it is taken from the imagined interior of the Earth—the deep caverns, fiery lakes, and sulfurous smells go back to the Hebrew Gehenna—but his Hell is not in the Earth.

37. Nine is the traditional number of the heavenly spheres; Hesiod's Titans fell nine days; the intelligences that fell in gnostic and Neoplatonic thought fell through nine spheres; the angels fell for nine days in Langland's *Piers Plowman;* the traditional number of the angelic ranks is nine.

Where is it then? It is nowhere. This is the beauty of Milton's conception. The place where Satan sets up his throne and with his fallen comrades seeks to raise a new empire is precisely nowhere at all: a perfect metaphor for the absolute nonbeing of evil. Milton deliberately presents a self-contradictory, impossible picture of Hell. To begin with, the material world has not yet been created at the time of the angelic ruin, so how can Hell, despite its physical imagery, possibly be material? Everything is ambiguous: Hell is deep inside a material universe that does not yet exist; it is inside the created cosmos yet outside it; it is a place where the fallen angels dwell, yet it is within their hearts and is with them wherever they go: "which way I fly is Hell; myself am Hell" (4.75); it is a prison where they are chained yet from which they can issue forth; it encompasses time and motion yet is eternal; it is the other side of Chaos as the universe is the other side of Heaven; it is a place "where all life dies, death lives" (2.264). In short, it is nowhere and has no characteristics, the fit dwelling for those who have chosen nothingness over reality.

Now that the angels have fallen, God proceeds to the second creation, the creation of the material universe. He calls a new world into existence to redress the balance of the old, to make up for Satan's depredations in Heaven:

> But lest his heart exalt him in the harm
> Already done, to have dispeopl'd Heav'n,
> My damage fondly deem'd, I can repair
> That detriment, if such it be to lose
> Self-lost, and in a moment will create
> Another World, out of one man a Race
> Of men innumerable, there to dwell. [PL 7.150–156]

The race of humans will make up for the fallen angels, and when at last humanity is redeemed, humans will come and fill the empty places in Heaven (9.146–157).

In creating the material cosmos, the poet explains, God first produced Chaos from himself. Within Chaos was motion, and since time is the measure of motion, it is appropriate to speak of motion before the formation of the universe.

> As yet this world was not, and Chaos wild
> Reign'd where these Heav'ns now roll. . . .

Satan is chained for nine days on hell's burning pool. Doré, illustration for *Paradise Lost*, 1.209–220. Engraving, 1882.

> (For Time, though in Eternity, appli'd
> To motion.) [PL 5.577–581]

From this Chaos God forms the universe:

> I saw when at his Word the formless Mass,
> This world's material mould, came to a heap:
> Confusion heard his voice, and wild uproar
> Stood rul'd, stood vast infinitude confin'd. [PL 3.708–711]

In Milton as in Christian tradition, it is God the Son who does this work:

> And thou my Word, begotten Son, by thee
> This I perform, speak thou, and be it done;
> My overshadowing Spirit and might with thee
> I send along, ride forth, and bid the Deep
> Within appointed bounds be Heav'n and Earth. [PL 7.163–167]

Milton describes the process of creation in Book 7 (218–630) and the beauty of the created world in Book 8. The crowning glory of the universe is the human race, and that glory Satan will soon seek to mar.

But now, from the fiery lake, Satan surveys the darkness of Hell, a nowhere "filled" with fallen angels. He sees his lieutenant, Beelzebub, and then the whole shadowed host, whose chieftains Milton names (PL 1.381–521). Their natures remain angelic because their natures were created by God (1.315–316, 358–360; 2.430), but their wills have become evil, and their appearance gradually changes to match the distortion of their wills. One of the most striking devices in *Paradise Lost* is the reflection of the continuing deterioration of Satan's character in the increasing grotesqueness of his appearance. Most earlier writers described his deformation at the moment of his fall, and paintings show the bright angels turning into black, twisted shapes as they fall from heaven. But the warping of Milton's Satan continues on and on, forever.

> And in the lowest deep a lower deep
> Still threat'ning to devour me opens wide,
> To which the Hell I suffer seems a Heav'n. . . .
> While they adore me on the Throne of Hell,
> With Diadem and Sceptre high advanc'd
> The lower still I fall. [PL 4.76–91]

Though at first "his form had yet not lost / All her Original brightness, nor appear'd / Less then Arch Angel ruin'd" (1.591–593), it already bore the terrible marks of decline. Upon seeing his comrade Beelzebub for the first time in Hell, Satan exclaims, "O how fall'n! how chang'd" (1.84; cf. 1.313), sensing that the mark of ruin is also upon himself. And later, when the angels Zephon and Ithuriel remind him:

> Think not, revolted Spirit, thy shape the same,
> Or undiminisht brightness, to be known
> As when thou stood'st in Heav'n upright and pure;
> That Glory then, when thou no more wast good,
> Departed from thee, and thou resembl'st now
> Thy sin and place of doom obscure and foul. [PL 4.835–840]

Apparently unaware of how his continued treachery and lies only debase him further, he takes on a number of animal forms—the lion, the tiger, the cormorant, the vulture, the serpent—in order to deceive angels and men, and then complains that he is being degraded by doing so:

> O foul descent! that I who erst contended
> With Gods to sit the highest, am now constrain'd
> Into a Beast, and mixt with bestial slime,
> This essence to incarnate and imbrute,
> That to the highth of Deity aspir'd;
> But what will not Ambition and Revenge
> Descend to? who aspires must down as low
> As high he soar'd, obnoxious first or last
> To basest things. [PL 9.163–171]

As C. S. Lewis remarked, Satan is gradually reduced from bright angel to peeping, prying, lying thing that ends as a writhing snake.[38]

Rising from the fiery lake into which he has been pitched (and from which he is let loose for a time in order to learn the ways of Providence), Satan muses to his comrade Beelzebub on their present predicament and future plans. Condemning God as a tyrant and vaunting his own hatred and revenge, he calls for protracted warfare against the deity. All this is vain boast or blind madness, for Satan has always known—though he has pretended otherwise—that God is not evil and that his omnipotence precludes the success of any continued rebellion. But the Devil always prefers illusion to reality and distortion to truth, and because he longs to defeat God, he convinces himself that he can (PL

---

38. For the animals, see PL 3.431; 4.183, 192–196, 402–403, 431, 800; 5.658–659.

1.84–127). Beelzebub joins Satan in the delusion, pretending to his master that they had nearly succeeded in toppling the heavenly tyrant. But an undercurrent of worrisome reality crops up in Beelzebub's reply: he admits that they have been as completely ruined as angelic intelligences can be, and he supposes that God must be almighty, since no lesser power could have overcome their might (1.128–156). Indeed, all the demons participating in the infernal discussions have insight into reality that Satan lacks, and it is a measure of Satan's greater blindness as well as his greater evil that his plan loses the benefit of their insight.[39] Satan's response is the perfect expression of a completely corrupted will choosing evil for evil's sake:

> To do aught good never will be our task,
> But ever to do ill our sole delight,
> As being contrary to his high will
> Whom we resist. If then his Providence
> Out of our evil seek to bring forth good,
> Our labour must be to pervert that end,
> And out of good still to find means of evil. [PL 1.159–165]

This is a blunt plan for a counterprovidence: whatever God does good we will attempt to twist to evil; we hate good for the pure and simple reason that it is good.

Satan embraces his own evil:

>   Farewell happy Fields
> Where Joy for ever dwells: Hail horrors, hail
> Infernal world, and thou profoundest Hell
> Receive thy new Possessor; One who brings
> A mind not to be chang'd by Place or Time.
> The mind is its own place, and in itself
> Can make a Heav'n of Hell, a Hell of Heav'n. . . .
> Better to reign in Hell, than serve in Heav'n. [PL 1.249–263]

I affirm, he says, that my sole function and purpose is to embrace nothingness and to obliterate whatever is good so far as I am able. Again this is nothing but boast, for his anti-Providential schemes are illusion: in reality, divine Providence will turn every evil into good. Belial and the other demons rush about, planning to build an empire in Hell with Pandemonium as its capital, but the idea of making this stinking, smok-

---

39. Christopher, p. 80.

ing, filthy place—literally nowhere—into a comfortable kingdom is a paradigm of absurdity (1.271–621).

The Devil has his own schemes. God is planning a new world and a new race to take the place of the fallen angels. Very well: this provides us with our opportunity to strike the oppressor a blow; since we seem to have difficulty in defeating him in open war, we will effect our purposes by fraud and guile (PL 1.621–662). Satan's plot is, with the help of Beelzebub, to call a council of the chief demons where he will appear to consider their proposals, and then to have Beelzebub reintroduce his master's plan and sway the infernal host to accept it.

Satan opens the council:

> High on a Throne of Royal State, which far
> Outshone the wealth of Ormus and of Ind,
> Or where the gorgeous East with richest hand
> Show'rs on her Kings Barbaric Pearl and Gold,
> Satan exalted sat. [PL 2.1–5]

The throne upon which Satan apes the royal state of God in Heaven is, like all of Hell, a mad fantasm (cf. 5.755–771). Satan's opening address to his followers is equally mad, for he suggests that they have a chance to defeat the Almighty, that they may somehow turn their ruin to advantage and end up by acquiring greater glory than they had before their fall (2.11–42). Thus setting the unreal tone, the counterfeit prince opens a meaningless debate whose outcome he has already determined. Each demon makes his speech, not on the basis of a rational choice of plan but on the basis of his own ruling vice, which each disguises as a virtue.[40]

The savage Moloch rises first and counsels open war against "the Torturer," since they have nothing to lose. The only further punishment God could decree would be annihilation, and even that would be better than crouching here in chains. Out of pure spite and hatred of the enemy, Moloch—like some modern military leaders—plans a destructive war that he knows cannot be won (2.51–105).

Belial, the smooth-tongued orator, speaks next, using all the arts of rhetoric and charismatic charm to advance his own lazy, sensuous scheme. Moloch, he says, errs in deeming annihilation better than this, and in any event annihilation is not God's only alternative, for he could torment us with pains far more relentless and intense. Let us instead

40. Steadman, p. 253.

just settle down here in Hell and wait till God's wrath cools; perhaps things will get better. Belial's illusions are subtler and less obviously mad than Moloch's but still illusions, for Belial forgets whose fault their fall is. It is not up to God to cool his wrath, but up to the demons to repent, which Belial knows they will never do. Only they can better their own lot, and they will not do it (2.106–227).

Mammon's argument resembles Belial's, though representing avarice more than sensuality. Look here, he reasons, we cannot depose God and cannot regain Heaven; we will not repent, and if we did, we would only revolt again, for we could not bear to be up there with those namby-pambies singing "forc'd Hallelujahs." So let us build a city and an empire here, mining the rich earth to construct mighty towers and so profit from our fall (2.229–283). Mammon neglects to mention that the proud palaces they build in Hell will no more serve to save them than the proud towers they had erstwhile built in Heaven (1.670–751).

The assembled demons incline to the side of Belial and Mammon, but now Beelzebub rises to promote Satan's plan as if it were his own. Courtly, grave, recognized as second in command, he gets immediate respect. Calmly and politely, he exposes the illusions of the previous speakers, only to advance an equally mad course of action. We cannot rule or be happy here, he points out, because God is the real ruler even in Hell; whatever we may like to imagine, we are really prisoners in chains. God is in absolute control here, as everywhere in the cosmos. The conclusions that an unclouded mind would draw from that premise are obvious, but none of the demons has a clear intellect or a straight will. Their sin has twisted them for eternity: theoretically, they could repent; in fact, they will never do so. And so Beelzebub counsels not repentance but an indirect and stealthy attack upon the ruler they had not been able to dislodge by force. Beelzebub stirs the demons to contempt and hatred for humanity. Humans are happy while we are miserable, favored by God above the angels even though they are inferior, contemptible little creatures usurping our own place in the cosmos. If we cannot confront God directly, we will get at him by corrupting and ruining these little pets of his (2.310–378).

The demons enthusiastically embrace this plan to

> confound the race
> Of mankind in one root, and Earth with Hell
> To mingle and involve, done all to spite
> The great Creator.

But the plan is in vain from the outset: "thir spite still serves / His glory to augment" (2.382–386).

Now the demons must decide which of them will go to Eden and do the deed. Satan nobly volunteers, vaunting his courage and his initiative to his followers—a vainglory (contrasting with the Son's calm assumption of responsibility in Heaven) that is later debunked by the angel Gabriel, who points out that the real reason Satan went on the mission was to escape, if only for a while, the torments of Hell [PL 2.417–465; 3.235–236; 4.920–924). Sallying forth, Satan reaches the gate of Hell and there encounters his daughter, Sin. At first he fails to recognize her, for like her father, she has lost her comeliness: "I know thee not, nor ever saw till now / Sight more detestable," he exclaims. She reminds him that she had once pleased him so much that he had made incestuous love to her, begetting on her "the execrable shape" of his son (and grandson) Death—who in turn had raped his mother, producing a brood of monstrous offspring. The Devil, Sin, and Death are thus a monstrous parody of the Holy Trinity, the *circuminsessio* (mutual indwelling) of the three Persons of the Trinity disgustingly mirrored by this mutual incest (2.681–870). The parody is reflected in their dialogue, as when Sin addresses Satan in terms appropriate only to God:

> Thou art my Father, thou my Author, thou
> My being gav'st me; whom should I obey
> But thee, whom follow? thou wilt bring me soon
> To that new world of light and bliss. [PL 2.864–867]

The irony is that the new world where the perverted trio will soon make their home is the Earth. Here is already a hint of the freeway that Sin and Death will build to connect Hell and Earth (2.1024; 10.293–324).

The Devil now issues forth out of the gate of Hell into Chaos, a nonplace separating the nonplace Hell from the reality that is Heaven and the universe depending from it (2.871–1055). Leaving Chaos, he journeys toward the universe, while God watches his course across the void and already plans his response: the Son's willing sacrifice of himself for a humanity that Father and Son know will fall and will need redemption (2.1–145). Satan finally reaches the tenth or outermost sphere of the universe, the primum mobile; perching there, he looks down into the patient universe like a vulture spying out his prey. Descending to the sphere of the sun, he disguises himself as a cherub and there meets the angel Uriel; thence he comes down to Earth, alighting at last upon Mount Niphates near the Garden of Eden, the same mountain (Milton feigns) as that on which Satan would later tempt Christ (PL 3.416–742; 11.381; PR 3.252–265).

Sitting on Mount Niphates, Satan speaks his great soliloquy, which we might think honest soul-searching had we not been warned by our knowledge of Satan as well as by Milton's own caution (PL 4.1–10) that this is a being wholly committed to evil: the soliloquy is another imposture. And yet not entirely so. Satan's intellect, though coarsened and weakened, is still an angelic intelligence, and here it seems to glance sideways at reality before rejecting it yet again. Looking at the sun, Satan hates it for reminding him of what true light really is and of his pride and ambition in rising up against a ruler who had established him in bright eminence in Heaven and to whom he owed loyalty and love. He recognizes that the choice was his and that he is the author of his own misery (4.31–74). But quickly he passes from self-realization to self-hatred, from self-hatred to despair, and then back to hatred of God. The thought of repentance and submission enters his mind, only to be rejected immediately; he knows that he would only sin again. He knows which way his will is bent:

> For never can true reconcilement grow
> Where wounds of deadly hate have pierc'd so deep:
> Which would but lead me to a worse relapse,
> And heavier fall: so should I purchase dear
> Short intermission bought with double smart.
> This knows my punisher; therefore as far
> From granting hee, as I from begging peace:
> All hope excluded thus. [PL 4.98–105]

Uriel, observing Satan's soliloquy from afar, notices the contortions of his face as he ponders, and he realizes that this is no untroubled cherub but a grave threat to the innocent inhabitants of earth (4.75–130). The madness of Satan, implicit in his vain boasts from the beginning, appears explicit here to the observer and the reader.[41]

Satan travels on to Paradise, at whose beauties he looks down in the shape of a cormorant from a tree. Gazing at the loveliness of Eve and seeing Adam and Eve embracing in innocent union, he is again filled

---

41. Christopher, p. 83.

with envy and hatred (4.131–561). Meanwhile, Gabriel has set an angelic watch over Paradise to protect the first parents, and two of these guardian angels, Ithuriel and Zephon, come across Satan squatting like a toad at Eve's sleeping ear, whispering fantasms of sin and corruption into her dreams. Ithuriel touches him lightly with his spear, and at the touch he springs up in his own shape. They immediately recognize him as a demon but do not immediately realize that the fiend before them was once the high prince Lucifer. The Devil is angry at their failure to recognize him, but when Zephon rebukes him, telling him the truth about the change he has suffered, Satan is taken aback:

> Abasht the Devil stood,
> And felt how awful goodness is, and saw
> Virtue in the shape how lovely, saw, and pin'd
> His loss. [PL 4.846–849]

Still, his regret is not so much for the harm that he is doing and will do as for the loss of his own beauty and prestige.

The angels bring Satan before Gabriel, and the two great archangels—one fallen, one elect—begin a dialogue. Satan is contemptuous of Gabriel's loyalty and boasts again of his own courage and faithfulness to his comrades. Gabriel's reply is crushing in its clear and direct reasoning:

> O sacred name of faithfulness profan'd!
> Faithful to whom? to thy rebellious crew?
> Army of Fiends, fit body to fit head. . . .
> And thou, sly hypocrite, who now wouldst seem
> Patron of liberty, who more than thou
> Once fawn'd, and cring'd, and servilely ador'd
> Heav'n's awful Monarch? wherefore but in hope
> To dispossess him, and thyself to reign? [PL 4.951–961]

The focus of the poem has turned more and more upon Adam and Eve; Eve's dream, recounted in the fifth book, is the prologue to the central scene in the ninth book, in which the first couple commit their first sin. Though Satan has sat whispering as a toad in Eve's ear, in her dream she perceives him in the form of a beautiful angel who suggests the new joys that will be hers if she eats of the fruit:

> Taste this, and be henceforth among the Gods
> Thyself a Goddess, not to Earth confin'd,

Satan, brooding, contrasts his misery with the happiness of Adam and Eve.
Illustration by Doré for *Paradise Lost*, 9.97–98. Engraving, 1882.

> But sometimes in the Air, as wee, sometimes
> Ascend to Heav'n, by merit thine. [PL 5.77–80]

God had prepared the joys of Heaven for both Lucifer and Eve. The root of sin is that Lucifer had insisted on obtaining them not from God's grace but by his own force of will and supposed merit. Now he is suggesting to Eve the same falsehood, that she can achieve happiness by her own efforts. Adam warns Eve that this dream may proceed from an evil spirit rather than a good one; nevertheless, the dream prepares her for the actual temptation and fall in Book 9.[42]

That the fall of Adam and Eve is the central focus of the poem is clear from the very first words of the epic: "Of Man's First Disobedience." Satan, driven out of Paradise by Gabriel's command (PL 4.1015), now roams the Earth in search of an appropriate disguise in which to effect their ruin. He decides upon "the serpent subtlest beast of all the Field" (9.86), taking voluntarily the form into which he will later be turned against his will (1.34). For a moment he hesitates, contemplating the beauties of this Earth that he is about to defile. But it is not love and pity that make him pause; it is envy of Adam and Eve's enjoyment of the Earth and of God's creation of it. Unwilling to grasp the idea that God could have poured forth such beauty in pure and selfless love, his darkened mind can only conceive that God must have made this place as a second thought, to improve upon his own seat in Heaven. The only point Satan sees clearly is his own nature:

> The more I see
> Pleasures about me, so much more I feel
> Torment within me. . . .
> Nor hope to be myself less miserable
> By what I seek, but others to make such
> As I, though thereby worse to me redound:
> For only in destroying I find ease. [PL 9.119–129]

He does evil for its own sake even though it will make his own lot worse. Milton projected upon Satan the human tendency to launch self-righteous attacks upon others even at the risk of terrible consequences to the self. The Devil's ultimate joy will be "in one day to have marr'd /

---

42. See J. Steadman, "Eve's Dream and the Conventions of Witchcraft," *Journal of the History of Ideas*, 26 (1965), 567–574. It is possible that Milton had witchcraft in mind, but all the characteristics of the dream are part of general Christian diabology.

What he Almighty styl'd, six Nights and Days / Continu'd making"
(9.136–138). He pities himself, musing how unfair it is that he should
work so hard to accomplish these ends yet receive no thanks for his
efforts.

Finding the serpent—as yet an innocent beast—asleep, Satan creeps
into his mouth and possesses him (9.187–190). Unaware of the horror
awaiting them yet apprised by the angel of possible danger, Adam
suggests to Eve that they stay together, but she determines to walk in
the garden alone, a situation that Satan had hoped for and was quick to
exploit. On beholding her again, he hesitates for a moment; his senses
and intellect, which still retain a remnant of their original ability, perceive the power of her innocent beauty:

> Her graceful Innocence, her every Air
> Of gesture or least action overaw'd
> His Malice, and with rapine sweet bereav'd
> His fierceness of the fierce intent it brought:
> That space the Evil one abstracted stood
> From his own evil, and for the time remain'd
> Stupidly good, of enmity disarm'd,
> Of guile, of hate, of envy, of revenge. [PL 9.459–466]

Then his twisted will draws him back away from reality:

> But the hot Hell that always in him burns,
> Though in mid Heav'n, soon ended his delight. . . .
> Fierce hate he recollects, and all his thoughts
> Of mischief, gratulating, thus excites. [PL 9.467–472]

He addresses Eve, and Eve wonders aloud how a serpent can speak.
This is the perfect opening for Satan to explain that he had gained
wisdom by eating the fruit of the marvelous tree. Eve plays into his
hands by asking where the tree is to be found, and Satan is delighted to
show her. Oh well, says Eve, if this is the tree you mean, we might as
well not have bothered to come, for God has prohibited it to us. Satan
quickly exclaims at a tyrant that would forbid his creatures such access
to growth and fulfillment. The tree, he explains, will give them immortality, a happier life, and higher knowledge, including the knowledge of
good and evil. It will make them like gods, and God's only motive in
prohibiting it must be to keep them under his control (9.655–732).
Every word he speaks is not only a lie but the diametrical opposite of the

truth, for the tree will bring them death, a wretched life, and extra knowledge only of sin, and they will resemble demons more than gods. Eve is persuaded, both by her intellect, which responds to Satan's false reasoning, and by her senses, which urge her to desire the fruit. Her sin is no hasty, mitigated act; she thinks it through carefully before she plucks (9.733–780).

The act entails several dimensions in Milton's poem. First, it is a sin. Satan did not compel, and had not the power to compel, her to commit it. Her choice was her own, freely made after due consideration. Knowing full well that God had forbidden the fruit, she deliberately placed her will above God's. Thus the first sin of humans reflects the first sin of the angels. Humans, however, are less culpable: first, because they were tempted by an external agent; second, because their intellectual capacities are so much less. Satan before his fall possessed all the vast intellect of the angels; the first parents, on the other hand, were in God's image not through any comparability of intellect but in that their relationship with him was harmonious and undistorted. Satan's fall was a maximal plunge from the heights of Heaven to the depths of nowhere; Adam and Eve had much less distance to descend. The fall of humanity was a change from harmony to disharmony, from gentle innocence to hard alienation, but it was not a plunge from godlike heights to infernal ruin. Further, as Milton goes on to show, God brought good out of the disaster by making it a positive occasion for us to learn wisdom by suffering.[43]

With the fall of Eve the moment of drama is over: Adam's will soon follow. With horror he learns what Eve has done:

> O fairest of Creation, last and best
> Of all God's Works, Creature in whom excell'd
> Whatever can to sight or thought be form'd,
> Holy, divine, good, amiable, or sweet!
> How art thou lost, how on a sudden lost,
> Defac't, deflow'r'd, and now to Death devote? [PL 9.896–901]

But he knows that they are united forever man and wife, bone of bone and flesh of flesh, so his immediate and resolute choice is to remain by her. Yet his choice, like hers, is freely made against what he knows to be God's will. The consequences are sure and inevitable: Adam and Eve

---

43. On minimalism and maximalism, see Evans, pp. 242–271.

are driven out of Paradise to live a life of suffering and alienation from God, and the serpent is cursed. Satan understands what the curse means for him: eternal enmity between himself and the Deity; eventual ruin when Jesus Christ, the second Adam and son of the second Eve, will crush him underfoot (PL 10.172–181, 496–501, 1031–1036; PR 1.55). Sin and Death, Satan's misbegotten offspring, now build their freeway between Hell and Earth, polluting the world and, until the time of redemption, placing it under Satan's rule. The new world that God has called into being has become "that new world / Where Satan now prevails" (PL 10.256–257).

Satan has accomplished what he had planned, and he returns triumphantly from Earth to boast of his accomplishments to his followers. He appears on his richly bedecked throne shining in what little of his starlike glory remains, and all the fallen angels prostrate themselves in wonder and praise as he vaunts his deeds and proclaims his conquest of the earth. God is defeated, he tells them; Earth has been opened to sin and death, and I am its new ruler. Arise and take possession of the new world I have earned for you. All of a sudden his boasts are reduced to gross reality, for the angels ranked around the glittering throne room are taking on shapes more becoming to their true nature. Satan hears not the shouts of praise that he expects but the authentic voice of his attendant throng:

> So having said, a while he stood, expecting
> Thir universal shout and high applause
> To fill his ear, when contrary he hears
> On all sides, from innumerable tongues
> A dismal universal hiss, the sound
> Of public scorn; he wonder'd, but not long
> Had leisure, wond'ring at himself now more;
> His Visage drawn he felt to sharp and spare,
> His Arms clung to his Ribs, his Legs entwining
> Each other, till supplanted down he fell
> A monstrous Serpent on his Belly prone,
> Reluctant, but in vain, a greater power
> Now rul'd him, punisht in the shape he sinn'd,
> According to his doom; he would have spoke,
> But hiss for hiss return'd with forked tongue
> To forked tongue, for all were now transform'd
> Alike to Serpents all as accessories
> To his bold Riot: dreadful was the din

Satan returns to hell to boast of his defeat of Adam and Eve, only to find his followers transformed into loathsome serpents. Illustration by Gustave Doré for *Paradise Lost*, 10.519–521. Engraving, 1882.

Of hissing through the Hall, thick swarming now
With complicated monsters, head and tail. [PL 10.504–523]

Satan is reduced to the state of the beast he had used to seduce Eve. He had assumed that the curse God laid on him in Eden extended only to his eternal enmity with humankind; he had failed till now to see that he, like the serpent, was doomed to crawl upon his belly.

In *Paradise Regained*, Milton completes his diabology and Christology. *Paradise Lost* recounts the alienation between humans and God resulting from Satan's successful temptation of the first Adam. In the new poem, Milton describes the healing of that division by the resistance of the second Adam, Christ the Son of God, to a new temptation. Satan, who in the earlier poem loses all his majesty by his total humiliation, appears in the new one as merely cunning and devious. He has heard of a Son of God being born and does not know what this means. Is Jesus the Son of God only in the sense of being an inspired prophet? Or is he the incarnation of the divine Son himself?

Satan calls an infernal council to remind the fallen angels of God's curse upon the serpent and tell them that the child of Eve who was to crush them beneath his feet has now been born. God has proclaimed this child his "son," and we must find out what this means, says Satan, "for man he seems / In all his lineaments, though in his face / The glimpses of his Father's glory shine" (PR 1.91–93). Satan assures his followers that as he tempted Adam, he will set out again now in "hope of like success" (1.105). God in Heaven, observing the new plot, confides to Gabriel that he is permitting Satan to tempt Christ so that the Son may demonstrate his divine birth, proving to the Devil that the new Adam has the strength to restore the damage done by the first Adam and so break the power that the Evil One boasts over the earth (1.140–167).

When Christ goes out into the desert to pray, the Devil approaches him disguised as an old man in country clothing (PR 1.314). Still evading responsibility, Satan complains that he is an unfortunate victim whom misery, not sin, has brought low. The Son is not taken in: "Deservedly thou griev'st, compos'd of lies / From the beginning, and in lies wilt end" (1.407–408). No joy can make Satan happy, for he has chosen unhappiness, and he is most miserable when in the presence of joy; he is "never more in Hell than when in Heaven" (1.420).

Satan returns to Hell and warns his fellows that Christ is plotting to advance their ruin. God had granted them temporary powers on Earth because of the sin of Adam and Eve, but these are now about to be revoked (PR 2.121–146). Their response is a plan to tempt the "son" in the hope of ascertaining whether he is God and, if not, to ruin him as they had ruined Adam and thus avert the loss of their power.

The idea that the temptation of Christ was a test of his divinity is clear neither in scripture nor in tradition, but it was fairly common in medieval literature.[44] Milton's scenario posed both theological and literary problems. Satan must doubt the divinity of Christ, for if he were sure of it, one of two consequences would follow. Either he would not dare to tempt him at all, or else he would press his attack out of sheer hatred, knowing in advance of his certain defeat. The latter is tenable theologically but not dramatically, for it robs the action of the tension of uncertainty. A further dramatic weakness threatened: if Christ fully grasped his own divine nature, even if Satan did not, the tension would still be lost, for Father and Son would know the outcome from eternity, and the whole scenario would be an entrapment of the unwitting Devil. Milton rejected this approach; for him, the Son as a child does not know his divine origin and must be told it by his mother (PR 1.201–258). At the time that he goes out into the desert, Christ is aware that he is the Son of God in some sense, but like the Devil he is not sure what this means, and he debates within himself what he is supposed to do to fulfill his mission. The Father plans to use the temptation to enlighten both Satan and the Son. As God turns all evil into good, as he will later turn the crucifixion into salvation, God now turns Satan's test of Christ into the confirmation of Christ's divinity.

Meanwhile, in the demonic council the sensuous Belial suggests that they tempt Christ with women, but Satan chooses to use "manlier objects": honor, glory, and popular praise (2.153–171). He returns to the desert dressed in sophisticated clothing, and urbanely offers Christ food, riches, glory, and all the kingdoms of this world.[45] The temptations fail because Christ discerns that Satan can never offer anything but illusions. The Devil is not yet convinced and still wonders "in what degree or meaning thou art call'd / The Son of God, which bears no single sense" (4.516–517). I too am a son of God, he muses, or at least I was, and all men are sons of God (4.518–520):

---

44. LUCIFER, pp. 145–146, 153–154, 265–266.
45. Milton follows the order of the temptations in Luke, rather than that in Matthew, because Luke puts the temptation on the tower in the dramatically satisfying last place.

> Therefore to know what more thou art than man,
> Worth naming Son of God by voice from Heav'n,
> Another method I must now begin. [PR 4.538–540]

Setting Jesus upon the pinnacle of the Temple, Satan urges him to prove his divine power by hurling himself down and allowing the angels to catch him in his fall. Jesus replies: "Tempt not the Lord your God," both an affirmation of Christ's own faith in the Father and a warning to Satan not to tempt the Son. The crushing truth of that reply sends the Devil plunging back into the darkness (4.562). As Adam, by yielding to Satan's temptation, lost paradise for humanity, so Christ, by his resistance, regained it.

Satan cannot understand that Christ's motive in coming to Earth is love, for all that Satan understands is power. The heavenly choir warns him that he cannot hope much longer to "Rule in the clouds; like an Autumnal Star / Or lightning thou shalt fall from Heav'n, trod down / Under his feet." And "this repulse" is not yet "thy last and deadliest wound" (PR 4.618–622). In Christian tradition, Satan falls three times—or, more accurately, his fall is represented three times: first, in his fall from Heaven at the beginning of the world; second, in his defeat by Christ at the incarnation and especially at the passion; and third, in his final defeat and destruction at the end of the world. Milton showed the first in detail, hinted at the third, and described a crucial event in the second. Christ's passion was traditionally seen as beginning with the temptation in the desert and culminating in the crucifixion (although it could also be seen as beginning with the circumcision or even with the incarnation itself). Milton dwelt upon the temptation for the esthetic reason that it mirrors the temptation of Adam and that Christ's success in withstanding the temptation rectifies Adam's failure to withstand the first one; for the scriptural reason that it is the only direct confrontation between Christ and Satan reported in the Bible; and for the dramatic reason that it allows a dialogue between the two.

Milton's is the last convincing full-length portrait of the traditional lord of evil. In the eighteenth and nineteenth centuries, the concept would be worn down by rationalism and distorted by Romanticism.

4 *Satan Expiring*

The traditional world view supporting belief in the Devil had been undermined by Descartes, Spinoza, and Locke, while reaction against the witch craze made the Devil of all Christian doctrines the least attractive to the educated. The most vulnerable part of theology, the Devil thus helped weaken the old structure further, and the new philosophies and ideologies of the eighteenth century provided the tools with which to pull it down. Before 1700 the traditional Christian view was still accepted by many of the educated, but by 1800 most had abandoned it or modified it out of recognition.

The degree to which the eighteenth century actually "dechristianized" Western society is debatable, since the degree to which society had previously been Christian is also disputed. Among the minority of Europeans in 1700 who were literate, Christian education was often shallow; many, if not most, of the aristocratic and bourgeois leaders of society wore Christianity like a summer scarf over an outfit of hedonism or selfishness. Peasant religion was tied to the ritual life of rural communities; when in the course of the eighteenth and nineteenth centuries peasants and manual laborers left those communities for the growing cities, their religion, cut off from its parish roots and from nature, withered.

The secularization of Christianity had begun as early as the Reformation and Counter-Reformation, and the modernistic views of some Christian thinkers, notably the Jesuits, preceded and influenced the philosophes of the Enlightenment. The Jesuits divided the cosmos into a world of revelation and a world of nature. Nature, they said, is undistorted by original sin, an open book that God has written and in which any rational creature can discern God's plan. Though humanity's moral sense has been corrupted by the sin of Adam, its reason and even to a degree its will are unimpaired. Nature can therefore be understood and described by natural reason, which can discover and propound physical laws. Divine grace is necessary to salvation, but the individual is wholly free to accept or reject the offer of grace. Human nature is essentially good and, with God's grace, perfectible.

For the Jesuits, the world of grace and revelation was an extra dimension that God had superimposed upon the natural world. Once religion was seen in this way as an addition to nature, a superstructure built upon nature rather than the very core and being of the world, it could easily pass from seeming necessary to seeming merely desirable, and from desirable to merely nice or perhaps even absurd. Descartes, Locke, Leibniz, and Newton—like the Jesuits—all affirmed Christianity but created philosophical or cosmological systems that had no need of Christian explanations. Scientific explanations removed the *why* of the world and replaced it with the *how*. The ultimate reason for the regularities observed by science in physical nature was held to be unknown, and scientific "laws" were seen simply as descriptive statements of observed patterns. Thus the philosophes of the Enlightenment (the term indicates that they were not so much philosophers as propagandists for the new faith in reason, materialism, and empiricism) simply accepted the natural world of the Jesuits and rejected their supernatural world. As icing on the cake rather than the cake itself, religion could eventually be done away with.

Against this background the hostility of the Enlightenment to Christianity may be reassessed. The philosophes may be seen as following the Jesuits, only taking their arguments logically further. In this light the claims of the philosophes to be favoring "true Christianity"—defined as the ethical teachings of Jesus in a context of optimism, the perfectibility of humanity, the essential goodness of the world, social justice, and individual conscience—make sense. Such views indeed became the essence of liberal Protestantism and later of some liberal Catholicism. The philosophes may be seen as condemning not Christianity but the church, the organized religion that had, in their view, departed from the true message of Christ and become authoritarian, traditional, magical, conformist, ritualistic, pious, narrow, fearful of science and philosophy, and stuck in the dark illusions of sin, redemption, hell, and the Devil. This portrait was never more than a caricature; for example, the Catholic church did not oppose but rather fostered and patronized the advance of natural science, except where science challenged the fundamental epistemology of the church. Nonetheless, the caricature acquired rapid acceptance among intellectual leaders and set Christianity on the defensive. The French Revolution of 1789 and the other revolutions it inspired also posed a direct challenge to a Christianity that had come to rely on institutional and financial support deriving from a close relationship between throne and altar.

The widespread worldliness of the eighteenth-century church—both its moral laxity and its intellectual flabbiness—reduced its resistance to the challenges of Enlightenment and Revolution. Some Christians clung desperately to the old ways—in vain, for the old symbols were quickly losing their power and even their meaning. Other Christians equally vainly retreated, apologized, and adapted to materialism until Christianity was all but paralyzed by their concessions. Instead of upholding the independent epistemological basis of Christianity in experience, revelation, and tradition, they tried to ingratiate Christianity within the empirical framework—a tack that proved futile and ultimately self-destructive.

In the early part of the eighteenth century, Christianity was still strongly entrenched in society, but the process of compromise was already visible. In England, the adaptation known as latitudinarianism had already begun in the late seventeenth century. Archbishop John Tillotson (1630–1694) had argued that the beliefs of Christianity "are no other but what natural light prompts men to, excepting the two sacraments, and praying to God in the name and by the mediation of Christ."[1] Such ideas were advanced by John Locke's *Reasonableness of Christianity* (1695) and John Toland's *Christianity Not Mysterious* (1696). To the latitudinarians, faith was simple: the harmony of the cosmos proves the beneficence and omnipotence of the deity; theological elaborations such as original sin, redemption, resurrection, and of course the Devil are encumbrances to a Christianity that best travels light.

Deism, the logical extension of latitudinarianism, dominated intellectual circles both in England and on the continent by the middle of the century. Deists held that God exists, that he shows himself in nature, and that we worship him best by living constructive moral lives. Scrip-

1. Quoted in B. Willey, *The Eighteenth-Century Background* (London, 1940), p. 3. See also J. Delumeau, *Catholicism between Luther and Voltaire* (London, 1977); P. Gay, *The Enlightenment: An Interpretation*, 2 vols. (New York, 1966–1969); H. Günther, *Das Problem des Bösen in der Aufklärung* (Frankfurt, 1974); I. O. Wade, *The Structure and Form of the French Enlightenment*, 2 vols. (Princeton, 1977).

ture, tradition, miracles, revelation—all were to be discarded. Some Deists preferred to retain the name of Christian; others abandoned Christianity openly. The effect was the same: a nature religion with only a few ethical and emotional roots in Christian tradition. Voltaire once invited a visitor to view the sunrise at Ferney with him. When the sun appeared, the philosophe astonished his companion by prostrating himself and exclaiming, "I believe in you, Powerful God! I believe." Then, rising and dusting himself, he added: "As for monsieur the Son and madame his Mother, that is another thing."[2]

Conservatives tried to hold the line. One mode of defense was fideism, which, like medieval nominalism, accepted that Christianity could not demonstrate its truths rationally and declared that God's truths lay beyond the limits of human reason; our internal experience and faith teaches us that the cosmos is inscrutable, mysterious, and divine. This democratic mysticism, which Pascal had already espoused and which found support from George Berkeley and Joseph Butler, avoided the untenable claim that Christianity could rest on the same basis as science. This was a powerful position, and Voltaire recognized it as the most dangerous Christian riposte to Deism.[3] Fideism had a number of divergent effects. In its rejection of theological certainties, it led to a broad and undoctrinaire view that eventually merged with liberalism; on the other hand, it led to a return to reliance upon the rock of scripture.

This latter approach typified the Pietism and Methodism dominating many Protestant churches during the century. Pietism was by no means mere conservatism; like fideism, it rejected intricate doctrinal statements, was skeptical of tradition, and avoided the worldly cynicism that colored many of the established churches.[4] The forerunner of modern evangelical churches, the movement emphasized the simplicity of Chris-

2. Quoted in P. Gay, *The Enlightenment: An Interpretation*, 2 vols. (New York, 1966–1969), vol. 1, p. 122. Skeptical views of Christianity were also advanced by Thomas Woolston (1670–1733), Anthony Collins (1676–1729), and Joseph Priestley (1733–1804).

3. G. Berkeley, *Alciphron* (1732); J. Butler, *The Analogy of Religion* (1736). Voltaire attacked the view in his *Lettres philosophiques* (1734). For the revival of mysticism, see the work of William Law (1686–1761), and C. Musès, *Illumination on Jacob Boehme* (New York, 1951), which deals with Dionysius Andreas Freher's interpretation of Boehme.

4. In Germany the chief figures of Pietism were Philipp Jakob Spener (1635–1705), Nicholas von Zinzendorf (1700–1760), August Hermann Francke (1663–1727); in England, John Wesley (1703–1791) and John Whitefield (1714–1770); in America, Jonathan Edwards (1703–1758). On Wesley's views of the Devil, see R. W. Burtner and R. E. Chiles, eds., *A Compend of Wesley's Theology* (Nashville, 1954), pp. 96–97, 112–113.

tianity as opposed to the intricacies of theology, and the personal relationship between the individual and Christ as opposed to the historical Christian emphasis upon community. The Pietists feared that rational philosophy would lead to atheism and instead relied on feelings, emotions, and sentiments. What is needed for salvation, they said, is not assent to a creed but internal conversion, a radical personal change characterized by compunction for sin and abandonment of the sinful heart in a total yielding to God's grace and love. The movement was extremely democratic, for its adherents saw no need for ecclesiastical authority to interpret the truth. Each Christian, reading the Bible with faith in his or her heart, will have all the truth anyone needs; all believers are priests. Nor is there need for a hierarchy of learned theologians, for Christ's truth is simple and open to all.

Seeing less need for secular learning than for theology, the evangelical movement firmly repudiated the secular point of view. The revolutionary intellectual changes of the eighteenth and nineteenth centuries touched it little; unlike the "mainline" churches, it felt little need to accommodate. As a result, among all the movements of the eighteenth century, only Pietism strongly upheld the belief in Satan as attested by the Bible. And though they claimed to rely upon the Bible alone, the Pietists adopted traditional diabology almost completely, though with a new emphasis upon the personal. Since all Christians are priests, all are saints; the Devil makes war on each individual Christian, and each is responsible for fighting against him in faith, conversion, and attentiveness to the word. Preaching, not the sacraments, is the Christian's main weapon against the evil one. Alone in his closet, armed with the Word, the Christian does solitary battle with the enemy of man; and he carries the war to the enemy by going out into the streets and across the seas to uphold the banner of the gospel against sinners and heathen.

Among the established churches, at least among their educated elements, the work of accommodation proceeded. Intellectual and nominal Christians in the early part of the century tended to the cosmic optimism of King and Leibniz. Optimism resembled Stoicism more than Christianity; still, it was compatible with the liberal Christian view that denied original sin, salvation, and the Devil, and it adapted the old Christian arguments to its own approach to the problem of evil.

Optimism found its most eloquent spokesman in Alexander Pope (1688–1744), a Catholic English poet whose *Dunciad* (1728) and *Essay on Man* (1733–1734) had great influence throughout northern Europe. Leibniz's optimism had been a priori, beginning with God's omnipo-

tence and goodness and arguing from those premises that the cosmos
must be the best possible. Pope argued rather from design: the beauty,
order, and harmony of the cosmos constitute a demonstration of its
goodness. "One truth is clear," Pope proclaimed. "Whatever is, is
RIGHT."[5] Though our poor intellects cannot grasp how the apparent
flaws of the cosmos fit into its perfection, its overall harmony gives faith
that the cosmic order puts everything right. Our view is limited,

> But Heav'n's great view is One, and that the Whole:
> That counter-works each folly and caprice;
> That disappoints th'effect of ev'ry vice. . . .
> Look round our world; behold the chain of Love
> Combining all below and all above;
> [All tends to] the gen'ral Good. [*Essay*, 2.238–240; 3.7–8, 14]

Natural evils seem evil only because we cannot understand the mind of
God, and metaphysical evil is a necessity in any cosmos, since any
creation implies a hierarchy of being extending down from the greatest
Perfection to the least perfect being:

> All must full or not coherent be,
> And all that rises, rise in due degree;
> Then, in the scale of reas'ning life, 'tis plain
> There must be, somewhere, such a rank as Man. . . .
> Then say not Man's imperfect, Heav'n at fault;
> Say rather, Man's as perfect as he ought. . . .
> Vast chain of being, which from God began,
> Natures aetherial, human, angel, man. . . .
> Cease then, nor ORDER Imperfection name:
> Our proper bliss depends on what we blame.
>   [*Essay*, 1.45–48, 69–70, 237–238, 281–282]

From God down to the least thing extends the great chain of being,
eternally established by the Creator in the best of possible arrangements, from angel to man to beast to plant to stone, all static and fixed
in the eternal mind. Metaphysical and moral evils are necessary parts of
a divine scheme that transcends the limitations of our own poor minds.

Moral evil comes from human ignorance and folly, which produce a
ridiculous egoism that revolts against the perfect harmony:

5. Alexander Pope, *Essay on Man*, ed. Maynard Mack (London, 1950), 1.294; 4.145,
394.

> All this dread ORDER break—for whom? for thee?
> Vile worm!—oh Madness, Pride, Impiety! . . .
> Know then thyself, presume not God to scan;
> The proper study of Mankind is Man. [1.257–258; 12.1–2]

By education and moral correction the individual may learn to understand and accept his proper role in the world.

Optimism was a revolt against the traditional pessimism that postulated a humanity corrupted by original sin. For the optimists, an enlightened mind could discern the rational pattern of the cosmos and willingly assent to it. But optimism was attacked from opposite sides by philosophes and traditional Christians. Soame Jenyns' *Free Enquiry into the Nature and Origin of Evil* (1757), coming only two years after the great Lisbon earthquake of 1755, was the last gasp of complacency. The traditional Christian Samuel Johnson flayed optimism in his review of Jenyns in 1757 and in his novel *Rasselas* in 1759; the philosophe Voltaire excoriated it in his *Poem on the Lisbon Disaster* (1755) and his novel *Candide* (1759), in which he observed that optimism was the fad of maintaining that everything is good when in fact everything is wrong. The philosopher Denis Diderot took the pessimistic view that evils simply come from the impersonal forces of nature. Behind such intellectual attacks upon optimism lay the grim reality of growing urbanization and the beginning of industrialization.

The century thus moved toward greater skepticism and radicalism.[6] For the philosophes, Christianity had failed; they found it intellectually wrong and socially destructive. However diverse their views otherwise, they were virtually united in their opposition to Christianity; indeed, their anti-Christian program is the single clearest identifying feature of their movement. They invented the complimentary term "Enlightenment" (German; *Aufklärung;* French; *siècle des lumières*) for themselves and fixed it on the century as a whole. Peter Gay distinguished three generations of philosophes, each more alienated from Christianity than the previous one—the first led by Montesquieu and Voltaire, the second by Diderot and Rousseau, and the third by Kant, Holbach, and Jefferson. The philosophes first used the classics against traditional

6. Bishop George Berkeley (1685–1753) produced an original philosophy combining idealism, skepticism, and Christianity. Samuel Johnson (1709–1784) defended Christian orthodoxy by engaging the hostile intellectual trends of his day directly. On Berkeley, see J. P. Hershbell, "Berkeley and the Problem of Evil," *Journal of the History of Ideas*, 31 (1970), 543–554; on Johnson, R. B. Schwartz, *Samuel Johnson and the Problem of Evil* (Madison, 1975).

Christianity, especially Lucretius' *De rerum natura*, with its famous tag "Tantum religio potuit suadere malorum" (how much evil religion leads to). Then they discarded the classics in favor of scientific empiricism: religion could be of value only if restrained within the boundaries of natural reason.

The leader of the philosophes through most of the century was Voltaire (1694–1778).[7] An optimist until the 1730s, Voltaire gradually became a naturalistic Deist. The fact that we observe motion, design, and intelligence in nature, he said, makes the existence of God obvious, but about the nature of this God we can know absolutely nothing. True religion has no place for fanaticism, force, or threat; it is based upon natural morality and ignores dogma. "Adore a God, be just, and love your country": this for Voltaire was as far as religion should go. Christianity was false because it tried to make doctrinal statements about the unknowable; more, its fanaticism and superstition made it the cause of most of society's evils. By the 1760s, hatred of Christianity had moved to the forefront of Voltaire's mind, and he began to end his letters with the phrase *écrasez l'infame:* "crush the infamy" of the church. God is first cause and prime mover, but he has nothing to do with the daily working of the universe. Fearing nihilism, Voltaire saw that God was the necessary guarantor of the goodness of nature: if God did not exist, we would have to invent him. God has established Nature and Nature's laws, and if one frees one's mind from superstitious ignorance, one can discern the ethical laws of the cosmos and learn to live by them.

At one point Voltaire was tempted to say that since we know nothing about the existence of God, we know nothing about absolute good and evil, and the problem of evil does not exist. But he saw that this would lead to complacent optimism, mystical obscurantism, or moral relativism. Moreover, he was no cool or indifferent observer; he was outraged by the evils of the world. When the Lisbon earthquake of 1755 killed more than ten thousand people, his *Poème sur le désastre* demanded how a God and a Nature that produce such horrors could be good. Perhaps the world might eventually be improved, but if so, improvement would be achieved by human efforts. God and Nature are indifferent to human suffering, but the proper response is not to despair but

7. Voltaire, *Lettres philosophiques* (1734); *Traité de la métaphysique* (1734); *Poème sur le désastre de Lisbonne* (1756); *Candide* (1759); *Dictionnaire philosophique* (1764). See also P. Richter and I. Ricardo, *Voltaire* (Boston, 1980); J. S. Siegel, "Voltaire, *Zadig,* and the Problem of Evil," *Romanic Review,* 50 (1959), 25–34.

to cultivate one's garden; accepting that the world is evil, one should not worry about abstruse propositions but do one's best to improve it.

Evil was certainly not the product of the Devil, in Voltaire's view. He despised the Devil as a grotesque Christian superstition and considered *Paradise Lost* a "disgusting fantasy." He sought to undermine the doctrine by describing its historical derivation from ancient Near Eastern paganism and Iranian dualism, and by arguing that it was promoted by the church fathers to bolster the doctrine of original sin. He concluded ironically that "our religion has consecrated this teaching . . . and what the ancients considered an opinion has become, by revelation, a divine truth."[8]

The philosophes in general had relatively little to say about the dark lord, considering him too easy a target for their mockery. The victory over belief in Satan had already been decided by the victory over witchcraft, and since few educated Christians could be found to defend the Devil's objective existence, the philosophes appear to have considered it beneath their dignity to attack such a figure of straw.

The philosophes considered evil, on the other hand, an intensely real problem. In dismissing revelation, they removed the sanction of divine law from human behavior. For Voltaire, human nature was a product of nature—fixed, static, and discoverable by reason. But a problem immediately arises: if humans are a product of nature, then it follows that all of their behavior must be natural, and thus acceptable by natural standards. But that crime should be as acceptable as justice, or Christianity as valid as the Enlightenment, was intolerable to Voltaire; such a position provided no basis for his impassioned condemnation of tyranny and his advocacy of change. He realized that a universally accepted rational basis of law was necessary if the two extremes of anarchy and tyranny were to be avoided. He found his answer in the active, formative aspect of nature, *natura naturans*. This active Nature became a form of deity, for its rules were not merely descriptive but prescriptive. Nature permits some actions and condemns others. We can discern the eternal laws of Nature by reason, Voltaire asserted, and by reason teach ourselves to conform to them.

The later philosophes discarded this active Nature in favor of *natura naturata*, things simply as they are. Reason then no longer sought to discern the eternal commandments written in nature; there are none, claimed these thinkers. All we can do is observe things, and when we

---

8. *Essai sur les moeurs* (1756), Introduction, sec. 48.

observe them, we see not the static, universal Nature that Voltaire had
assumed but rather constant variety and change through time; there are
no universal standards and no prescriptive laws. Before the end of the
century, the lack of objective standards became the most troublesome
problem for the Enlightenment and led, in the Marquis de Sade, to the
realization of Voltaire's worst fears.

The foundations of belief in the Devil were particularly undermined
by the philosophical skepticism of David Hume (1711–1776).[9] Hume's
skepticism was radical though not quite complete. Human reason had
no power to obtain certainty about anything at all, he said—not even
matter, and certainly not God. We postulate the existence of a world of
nature outside ourselves in order to get along in life practically, but we
have no way of knowing whether it is really there or what it is. We
know it only through our impressions of it, which may be fallible. We
have no knowledge or science of absolute reality, of the world in itself.
Still, the impressions we receive follow certain patterns of regularity,
and from these we may construct "laws" of nature. These laws are not
necessarily descriptions of nature; rather they are descriptions of our
impressions of nature. They are descriptive, not prescriptive; they
organize what we have observed but cannot be binding upon nature
itself. Still, Hume believed it practical and necessary to assume the
regularity of these laws and therefore their predictability. If y has followed x a million times, we can assume that it will follow x the next
time. Hume's followers went further and made his system practically
prescriptive by insisting that observed regularities are immutable: y not
only will but must follow x the next time. They failed to realize that
there can be no empirical evidence for that statement, failed to see that
the assumption that observed regularities are immutable is an act of
faith.

Hume turned skepticism against religion with devastating effect. His
attack, which forms the philosophical basis of modern atheism, followed
five main lines. The first was epistemological: we can know absolutely
nothing about God or the transcendent, since the only valid knowledge

9. Hume, *A Treatise of Human Nature* (1739); *Philosophical Essays Concerning Human
Understanding* (1748; later issued as *An Enquiry Concerning Human Understanding*); *The
Natural History of Religion* (1757); *Dialogues concerning Natural Religion* (1779). See also T.
P. M. Solon and S. K. Wertz, "Hume's Argument from Evil," *Personalist*, 50 (1969),
383–392; J. Wolfe, "Hume on Evil," *Scottish Journal of Theology*, 34 (1981), 63–70; R. M.
Burns, *The Great Debate on Miracles from Joseph Glanvill to David Hume* (Lewisburg, Pa.,
1981).

is empirical knowledge (Hume specifically rejected all a priori arguments, including the ontological argument that God's existence is self-evident); consequently, any religious or metaphysical statement is meaningless. Strictly speaking, this is an agnostic position, for if we can know nothing about the transcendent, we cannot know that it does not exist. But Hume's empiricism and his Enlightenment distaste for religion led him to practical atheism. His second argument is psychological: the origin of all religion is the projection of human hopes and fears upon external objects. The third is historical: religion is a human invention that has developed in purely natural historical fashion from animism to polytheism to monolatry to monotheism. (Modern philosophers of religion agree that religion is a human invention but reject the evolutionary view as a simplistic distortion of historical facts.)

Hume's fourth and fifth lines of attack, dealing with the concept of miracle and the existence of evil, have been the most effective. In his "Essay on Miracles" (later included as the tenth chapter in the 1748 edition of the *Essays concerning Human Understanding*), Hume correctly reasoned that if he could disprove the possibility of miracle, he would thereby disprove the viability of a religion based upon such miracles as the incarnation and resurrection.

Hume urged that "a miracle is a violation of the laws of nature; and as firm and unalterable experience has established these laws, the proof against a miracle, from the very nature of the fact, is as entire as any argument from experience can possibly be imagined." However strong the evidence for a miracle, it cannot be as strong as the evidence against it, since the evidence against is derived from countless observations by countless witness. If *y* has been observed to follow *x* a million times, then one report that *y* did not follow *x* must be discounted. Even if all the historians of England reported that Elizabeth I had risen from her grave to govern England for three years after her demise, Hume would still disbelieve it, for that would be a violation of the thousands of millions of observations that people do not rise from the dead: "The knavery and folly of men are such common phenomena, that I should rather believe the most extraordinary events to arise from their concurrence, than admit of so signal a violation of the laws of nature."[10] Diderot later expanded on Hume's example. If one honest man reported that the king had won a battle at Passy, Diderot would be inclined to believe him, but if all Paris declared that a man had risen from the dead

10. Quotations are from ch. 10 of the *Essay (Enquiry)*.

at Passy, Diderot would not believe a word of it—not even, as Peter Gay added, if it were certified by a committee headed by Voltaire and D'Alembert.[11]

The difficulty with Hume's argument lies in the undemonstrated assumption that the "laws of nature" are without exception unchangeable, as well as in the more fundamental assumption that all knowledge is empirical. This leaves Hume in the odd position of being a dedicated empiricist denying the possibility of empirical observation of unique events on the basis of an unempirical act of faith in the regularity of "laws of nature."

In considering Hume's argument, an initial distinction should be made between a "miracle" and a "unique event." A unique event may be defined as an extremely unexpected and improbable conjunction of circumstances. A "miracle" assumes the intervention of God, the Devil, or any other "supernatural" figure in such a unique event. I set "supernatural" in quotation marks because the argument can be made that anything that occurs is by definition natural, so that if spirits act in the world they are part of the natural order. "Supermaterial" would be a better and more exact word. Hume argued against the possibility of miracles on two grounds. First, humans have no access to the minds of supernatural or supermaterial beings, if any such exist, and thus no way to ascribe any event to them. Second, and more fundamentally, he argued that a miracle is by definition a unique event, an event in violation of the laws of nature, which by the definition of natural laws cannot occur. One limitation of Hume's argument is that such a unique event may be only an apparent violation of the laws of nature. It is possible, on Hume's own assumptions, that we do not fully understand natural laws and must continue to modify them as new evidence arises. Thus the "unique" event might not really be unique; it might be a member of a class of rare events that needs to be incorporated into the natural laws that we have devised. It is also possible that the laws of nature change in space and time. It is possible too that the laws of nature are open to exception, that truly unique events do occur.

Hume is unquestionably correct in arguing that no proof of a truly unique event is possible, if proof requires the kind of regular observa-

11. Gay, vol. 1, pp. 147–148. The limitations of such a view appear in Thomas Jefferson's reaction to the discovery of meteorites by two professors from Connecticut: he said he would rather believe that two professors were liars than that stones could fall from the sky.

tions upon which we base our "laws of nature"; truly unique event cannot form part of an organizable body of data from which we can draw conclusions. But when he goes beyond saying that such events cannot be proved to saying that they positively cannot occur, his argument is circular and unpersuasive. It goes like this: no unique events have ever been observed; therefore the laws of nature are firmly and fully established; therefore they are unbreakable; therefore no unique events can possibly be observed. To the objection that unique events, such as the resurrection of Lazarus, have been reported, Hume replied that such reports occur only among barbarous and superstitious nations unaware of the laws of nature.[12]

Hume's assumption that natural laws cannot have exceptions is not valid. Conceive of two different models of our universe, A and B. We may live in either one or the other. In Universe A, metaphysical entities are active; in Universe B, they are not. Most people since Hume's day would assume that there is a presumption in favor of Universe B. In fact, neither model is more likely than the other.

In Universe B, science and history rule out the metaphysical as irrelevant to their fields of inquiry. And this is proper: the quantitative and empirical methods of science cannot be adapted to deal with metaphysical entities or their actions, and history is limited by the valid rule that the more unusual an alleged event, the more evidence is required to make it believable. For an absolutely unique event, then, such as the resurrection of Jesus, the amount of evidence must be infinite, and therefore any alleged unique event is ruled outside the boundaries of history. In Universe B, this is the way science and history proceed, and this is the way they proceed in the world we inhabit.

But if we look at Universe A, we find that history and science proceed in exactly the same way as in Universe B. The boundaries of history and science are drawn in exactly the same place, and the findings of history and science are exactly the same in Universe A, where the metaphysical does act, and in Universe B, where the metaphysical does not act. This is because history and science are constructed for the purpose of identifying natural phenomena and not for any other purpose. It follows that no evidence from science or history can have any weight at all in determining whether we live in A or B; there is no

---

12. If so, twentieth-century France must be included among superstitious and barbarous nations, as numerous well-attested miracles have been reported there; see François Leuret, *Les guérisons miraculeuses modernes* (Paris, 1950).

historical or scientific evidence for or against the metaphysical. Some people choose to assume that A is more likely than B, others that B is more likely than A. But their assumptions are made on grounds other than historical or scientific evidence. It is logically meaningless to say that historical or scientific evidence points to one universe or the other.

The statement is often made that the only truth is scientific truth. If this were true, then we would surely live in Universe B. The problem is that there is no basis upon which to make the statement other than an act of faith, and an act of faith assuming Universe A is equally valid.

If we are permitted to step beyond the boundaries of science and history and consider other kinds of evidence, is there any indication which universe is more likely? For example, what of the continued reports of alleged "miracles"? What of eyewitness accounts of events that seem to transcend the realm of knowledge defined by history and science? The difficulty of dealing with such alleged phenomena is enormous precisely because there is no accepted methodology for doing so. A given report may be false. A given report may be true but refer to a phenomenon that science may eventually be capable of explaining. A given report may be true and refer to something forever beyond science—but then how can we know what it is?

What then can we do in the face of reports of such phenomena? We can deny their possibility as an a priori act of faith: most people nowadays choose to do this, but they must understand that they do so simply on faith and out of personal preference, not on the basis of any evidence. We can accept the possibility of such phenomena but deny that there is any means of investigating them sensibly: this is reasonable if we choose to restrict ourselves to the borders that we have drawn around history and science; it is safe and gets us out of the frightening task of exploring uncharted space without understanding what kind of vehicle we need. But is it sufficient to deal with the world as it is actually experienced? Apparently not, since we actually experience things that do not fit within the boundaries of science. It may be possible in the future to discover methodologies for dealing with such possible phenomena; after all, many modes of scientific thought are now in use that a century ago would have been unimaginable. It is possible to conceive of a coherent world view embracing not only science and history but also phenomena beyond their boundaries; we need only assent to the mere possibility that we live in Universe A—and in fact, Universe A is at least as likely as Universe B. One cannot follow Hume in declaring that unique events in violation of "natural laws" absolutely cannot have occurred.

Hume found in the existence of evil the fifth promising line of attack on Christianity.[13] Christians cannot reconcile the existence of God with the existence of evil, he argued, without modifying their assumptions about one or the other. Either God is not omnipotent, or else God's goodness is totally different from human goodness, in which event it is meaningless to call him good. The existence of an omnipotent God can be affirmed only so long as we admit that his moral nature is absolutely incomprehensible to us. But such a God would no longer be the Christian God. Since it is a fact that we observe that the universe contains vast and intense evils, we cannot make any inference from this universe to the existence of God. Most radically and persuasively, Hume argued that it is logically illegitimate to argue from an imperfect effect (the cosmos) to a perfect cause (God) and then use the perfect cause to explain the existence of a cosmos observed to be imperfect. Thus nature does not, as both Christians and Deists argue, show forth the wonders of God; on the contrary, it leads to the conclusion that he does not exist.

This powerful argument devastated Deism more than Christianity, since Christians had always admitted that their beliefs rested upon faith as well as reason, but it removed from all theists the comfortable and ancient assumption that one could argue to the existence of God from observation of the cosmos. Henceforth, religion had to be argued on experiential grounds. If one experiences the existence of God, one can find ways of reconciling it with the existence of evil. But if one begins without that experience, the presence of evil points away from the existence of God. Hume concluded that no theodicy, Christian or otherwise, was verifiable. The irony is that Hume's devastation of religious theodicy cleared the way for a myriad of secular theodicies such as those of Hegel and Marx.

In all this the Devil seemed to Hume quite beneath his notice. If the existence of God and of miracles is removed, the subsidiary teachings of Christianity evaporate. In dismissing the likelihood of Christianity, Hume dismissed the likelihood of the Devil. His views provided a clear, rational basis for the Enlightenment attack on Christianity and for modern skepticism, in the twentieth century becoming so standard as to be accepted almost as common sense. They also—again ironically—cleared the way for William James, the will to believe, and the new theology of the late twentieth century.

13. For Hume's discussions of theodicy, see the *Dialogues*, pts. 10 and 11, and the *Enquiry*, pt. 8, sec. 2.

The analysis by Immanuel Kant (1724–1804) of the nature of concepts is the historical origin of the phenomenological approach to the Devil that I have taken in these books.[14] Like Hume, Kant realized that human knowledge was incapable of reaching absolutes, but unlike Hume, he believed that skepticism could be transcended. Kant maintained that we receive sense impressions from a world outside our minds, but that the data we receive are not necessarily inherent in objects "out there" but are rather in the sensations that jostle into our minds. Our minds organize these sensations into coherent concepts. These concepts, which we ourselves manufacture, are all that we can surely know. The thing-out-there, the thing-in-itself, cannot be grasped. All that we can grasp is the *phenomenon*, the concept that we create of the thing. We can be certain of our knowledge of phenomena. Though we do not create nature, we construct it by organizing it into meaningful patterns, and since we are the organizers, we can fully know what we have organized.

Kant believed that statements are meaningful only when they refer to objects of possible sense perception. Metaphysical statements about the transcendent—about God and the Devil, for example—are meaningless because they are purely analytical and tautological. The proof is that they always lead to contradictions: from initial transcendent premises, contrary and equally probable propositions can be deduced. This conclusion accounted for the wide divergence among theologians, and it created a devastating detonation in the foundations of Christian diabology, which over the centuries had produced many contradictory doctrines from its initial premises.

Kant's Pietistic Lutheran background drew him to the problem of evil. A philosophical optimist as a young man, he had abandoned optimism by the 1760s but also rejected rationalist skepticism and Enlightenment progressivism. Observation, he maintained, indicates that human nature is not basically good and that evil cannot be eradicated by education or other liberal schemes of improvement. Evil is universal and

14. Kant, *Kritik der reinen Vernunft*, "Critique of Pure Reason" (1781; 2d ed., 1787); *Grundlegung zur Metaphysik der Sitten*, "Foundations of a Meptaphysic of Mores" (1785); *Kritik der praktischen Vernunft*, "Critique of Practical Reason" (1788); *Über das Misslingen aller philosophischen Versuche in der Theodizee*, "The Failure of All Philosophical Efforts at Theodicy" (1791); *Die Religion innerhalb der Grenzen der blossen Vernunft*, "Religion within the Strict Boundaries of Reason" (1793). See also S. Anderson-Gold, "Kant's Rejection of Devilishness," *Idealistic Studies*, 14 (1984), 35–48; O. Reboul, *Kant et le problème du mal* (Montreal, 1971); P. Watte, *Structures philosophiques du péché originel: S. Augustin, S. Thomas, Kant* (Gembloux, 1974).

rooted in human nature. Kant's belief in radical evil scandalized his fellow philosophes.

Kant argued that the traditional Christian problem of evil is insoluble because it deals with noumena—absolute reality—unknowable to the human mind. Further, evil is by definition unexplainable and unjustifiable, for as soon as you justify or explain something, it can no longer be a real evil. He classified three types of evil: sin, pain, and injustice. Sin is the essence of evil; humans introduced it into the world, and it is an inherent part of human nature. Kant's view is a demythologized version of original sin. The essence of sin is the lie, which consists of the refusal to recognize the moral law and set it above our own egoistic desires. This is not a chronological event involving Adam and Eve and the distant past but a principle of human nature. The Devil is a transcendent a priori concept whose independent existence cannot be meaningfully argued. However, the Devil is an important symbol of radical evil in the world, which transcends individual human evils, going beyond anything that individual humans want or plan. Radical evil is truly demonic, but making a personal Devil rather than humanity the originator of sin does nothing to explain the origin of evil; it only removes the question one step further from experience.

Moral good and evil, said Kant, depend primarily on the motion of the individual conscience either toward or away from the universal good.[15] There is no zero position. Kant rejected the traditional Neoplatonic-Augustinian view that evil is the absence of good; he saw evil as a radical force within us. Good is a positive, and its opposite is not a zero but a negative.[16] It was the problem of evil that made Kant religious, though his religion was far from the Christian orthodoxy in which he was raised. Without evil, the cosmos could be seen as a perfectly functioning mechanism, but the existence of evil was a radical flaw, an absurdity, a scandal that could not be explained in purely naturalistic terms.

Kant's complex and abstract philosophy had a less wide effect than Hume's, which was used polemically by the atheist philosophes. The growth of atheism was a logical extension of the Enlightenment movement from rationalism to naturalism to materialism. If all knowledge is empirical knowledge based upon the observation of matter, then there is no room for God or Devil. Atheists such as Denis Diderot (1713–1784),

15. Kant distinguished between individual acts of will (*Willkür;* cf. Augustine's *arbitrium*) and the will as a whole (*Wille;* cf. Augustine's *voluntas*). See SATAN, pp. 205–207.

16. Actually, Kant contrasted virtue (+) with absence of virtue (o), and obligation (o) with culpability (−).

Claude Adrien Helvetius (1715–1771), and Paul-Henri Thierry, Baron d'Holbach (1723–1789) despised Deism as one step away from superstition.[17] The atheists held that the universe is material, infinite, and eternal, and that it was formed by chance and at random. It expresses both order and disorder, yet it follows mechanistic laws of nature. Human intelligence rises from purely mechanistic sources indifferent to human values. For such a cosmos, said Holbach, "a God such as the one theology paints, is totally impossible."[18] Yet the atheism of these philosophes may not have been complete, for they came close to making Nature itself a divinity, ascribing to the cosmos the infinite, eternal, absolute existence that medieval theologians had assigned to God. Nature, they believed, "is its own end—it has no other aim but to exist, to act, to preserve its own ensemble."[19] Matter is not a free agent, but must act in accordance with laws of nature.

The reason the atheists could not bring themselves to grasp the nettle of absolute atheism was that they feared moral anarchy as much as Voltaire had. Diderot argued that we can deduce moral principles from observations of human behavior. Having established empirically what human behavior is, we can derive rules of conduct by applying reason to what we have observed. We observe, for example, that our physical natures render us greedy and selfish; reason tells us that unrestrained selfishness ends up harming everyone, including ourselves; therefore, we use our reason to construct practical restraints upon ourselves in order to obtain a viable society. Such practical ideas underlay the Constitution of the United States of America, ratified in 1787. Diderot had none of the illusions of the optimists: if a comet were about to destroy the planet, he remarked, people would doubtless behave according to their lowest instincts. Civilization is built upon restraint.

For the atheists, good and evil were human constructs, practical aspects of human relationships, not absolutes. Matter produces mind, and mind creates the categories of good and evil. We have bodily, emotional, and intellectual needs and call evil whatever frustrates them. "Evil," then, is merely our own designation of a part of the workings of an indifferent nature. No "problem of evil" exists, since neither the

---

17. Diderot, *Pensées philosophiques* (1746); *De la suffisance de la religion naturelle* (1746–1750; published 1770); *Encyclopédie*, with Jean d'Alembert (1717–1783). Helvétius, *De l'esprit* (1758); *De l'homme* (1773). Holbach, *Christianisme dévoilé* (1767); *Système de la nature* (1770).

18. Holbach, quoted in I. O. Wade, *The Structure and Form of the French Enlightenment*, 2 vols. (Princeton, 1977), vol. 2, p. 315.

19. Willey, p. 162.

deity nor objective evil exists. These ideas, radically shocking in the time of Diderot and Holbach, had become orthodoxy by the late twentieth century. The atheists passed over the Devil with a few words of contempt. Holbach merely observed that "religion has found it necessary to enlist a crowd of hideous phantoms in its train."[20] Diderot's *Encyclopédie*, which had to be circumspect in order to pass the censors and make money, showed its disdain by limiting the article on the Devil to less than one column; by noting ironically that "the Ethiopians, who are black, paint the Devil white, in order to contradict the Europeans, who represent him as black: the one view is as well founded as the other"; and by describing the concept of demons as "an abyss of the human intelligence."[21] Diderot scoffed at the notion that an omnipotent deity could be constantly harrassed and obstructed by a spirit that he had created.[22] The playful, mocking attitude of the philosophes toward the Devil appears in the Hellfire Club, a group established toward the end of the century that met in the caves of Buckinghamshire with genial orgies and tongue-in-cheek diabolical rituals.[23]

The atheists' denial of objective meaning to good and evil left them with three alternatives. They could find a totally different basis for ethics, such as Diderot's consensus or some jurists' legal and constitutional traditions. They could admit that moral standards are purely arbitrary while insisting on the social necessity of upholding some set of standards. Or they could declare that we are free of all values, all morality.[24] From the last alternative Diderot and Holbach drew back in horror, but others did not shrink from following the argument to its end.

Donatien Alphonse François, Marquis de Sade (1740–1814), lent his name to sadism.[25] Whatever one thinks of Sade's practices, one must give him credit for taking the principles of atheistic relativism to their logical conclusions. Where Diderot and Holbach stopped on the brink of the chasm, Sade enthusiastically hurled himself in. To the intellectual atheism of the philosophes, he added a personal, vindictive hatred of God. If God exists, Sade exclaimed, he must be more vicious than

20. Holbach, *Système*, bk. 1, ch. 13 (p. 34 in Paris, 1821, edition).
21. *Encyclopédie*, s.v. "Diable" and "Démon."
22. Diderot, *La Promenade du sceptique* (Paris, 1747).
23. See J. B. Russell, *A History of Witchcraft* (London, 1980), pp. 131–132.
24. L. G. Crocker, *Nature and Culture* (Baltimore, 1963), p. 107.
25. Sade, *Dialogue entre un prêtre et un moribond* (1788); *Justine* (1791); *Juliette* (1797); *La philosophie dans le boudoir* (1795); *Les crimes de l'amour* (1800).

the worst of criminals. We can be grateful that he is a merely a phantom of the human imagination. The supernatural in any event only diverts us from our true calling: plumbing the depths of human vice. Sade ironically professed a belief in the Devil, using him for esthetic effect: "The Devil, more powerful than this villainous God, a being still in possession of his power, forever able to brave his author, incessantly succeeds, by his seduction, in debauching the herd that the Eternal reserved unto himself."[26] Madame de Saint-Arge, a character in Sade's novel *La philosophie dans le boudoir*, prays fervently to the dark lord: "Lucifer, sole and only God of my soul!"[27] But while Sade ironically made the Devil's program his own, he dismissed the ideas of God, the Devil, and beneficent Nature with equal contempt. Nature, far from being purposive, orderly, or kindly, is absolutely indifferent to the struggles of humanity. It smiles upon the success of the wicked at least as frequently as upon the struggles of the good—more, because the wicked are sensible enough to seize what they want. The supposed ruler of this world is a "Supreme Being of Wickedness. . . . The author of the universe is the most wicked, ferocious, frightening of all beings."[28]

In an intrinsically valueless world, Sade argued, the only sensible thing to do is follow one's own pleasures. Julien Offray de la Mettrie (1709–1751), another materialist though not an atheist, had already suggested this principle. One might not be happy pursuing sensuality alone, he conceded, but one could not be happy without it.[29] Sade advanced the theory without restraint. Whatever you feel like doing is good for you. If you enjoy torture, well and good. If others do not enjoy torture, they need not engage in it, but they have no business imposing their own tastes on you. Violations of so-called moral laws are both permissible and actually laudable, because they demonstrate the artificiality of such restraints and because the restraints impede the only demonstrable good: personal pleasure. Virtue and law are fantasies; mercy, love, and kindness are perversions that impede the natural pursuit of pleasure: "The greater the pleasure, the greater the value of the act."[30]

Since sexual pleasures are usually the most intense, they can be pursued without any restraint. Crime is even better than sex under

26. *La philosophie*, quoted in Crocker, p. 96.
27. *La philosophie*, vol. 2, p. 15.
28. *Juliette*, vol. 2, p. 349.
29. La Mettrie, *L'homme machine* (1747); *L'art de jouir* (1743).
30. Quoted in Crocker, pp. 404, 413.

some circumstances, because it can be more exciting, and a sex crime is best of all. The greatest pleasure comes from torture, especially of children, and if one humiliates and degrades the victim, the delight is further enhanced. Murder is an excellent stimulus, especially when preceded by torture and sexual abuse. Some will enjoy cannibalism, since feasting on the flesh of the victim may add to the intensity. The purest joy, exceeding even sensual pleasure, is to commit a crime purely for its own sake in a gratuitous act of what the ignorant call evil.

Sade may have belabored the point in the interests of argument, but he was right to do so. If there are no moral boundaries, there are no moral boundaries. Sade's fellow philosophes viewed him with particular disgust and horror because they recognized in him the logical implications of their own beliefs. If there is no God, no active principle of Nature, then Diderot's consensus and the jurists' tradition are of no particular value. Why should a child molester not be free to rape and torture his victims? Why should some mad fanatic not launch a nuclear war? Who is to call him mad or fanatic, since one person's madness is another's sanity? The objection that nuclear war would make more people unhappy than it makes happy has no force, for the idea of the greatest good for the greatest number has no more basis than any other moral principle. Sade himself dwelt wistfully on the pleasure one might feel in destroying the entire cosmos, "to halt the course of the stars, to throw down the globes that float in space."[31]

To dismiss Sade as an anomalous intrusion of Satanic values into the Enlightenment is to ignore the logical force of an argument based upon the premise of atheism. Most atheists and relativists shrink from his propositions in personal distaste, but they can offer no consistent objection to them. For example, to Freud's argument that civilization depends upon the restraint of our dark impulses, Sade could retort that civilization has no necessary value.

It can be argued that Sade's assumption that personal sensual pleasure is the fundamental value is both a precarious, unproven assumption and an inconsistent affirmation of at least one value in a valueless world. But if all values are equally precarious, then Sade's are no more unfounded than any others, and his argument that no one has any business imposing his own set of precarious assumptions upon others is valid. It might be objected that Sade's pleasures would disrupt other pleasures: if we did nothing but fornicate and torture, there would be no specialty restaurants or theaters, let alone physicians to tune our bodies to their

31. Quoted in Crocker, p. 428.

highest sensual pitch. But to this Sade could reply that of course one can find time for other pleasures and that if you prefer elegant dining to raping he would by no means deny you the choice. The core of Sade's doctrine is that he pays absolutely no attention at all to other people's choices, including those of his victims.

Sade forces us to face the dilemma. Either there is real evil, or not. Either there are grounds of ultimate concern, grounds of being by which to judge actions, or not. Either the cosmos has meaning, or not. If not, Sade's arguments are right. Sade is the legitimate outcome of true atheism, by which I mean the denial of any ground of ultimate being. The annihilation that hangs over the earth in the late twentieth century is, perhaps, the logical outcome of nihilism.

However destructive relativistic values were to the traditional religious view, an equally serious threat was mounted by science and history. Both modern science and modern history were established in the course of the eighteenth century, and their acceptance constituted the most dramatic revolution in human thought yet recorded.

Isaac Newton's *Principia mathematica* (1685–1687) replaced the old epistemology based upon logic with a new epistemology based upon observation. Christian diabology and theology in general had been based upon revelation, tradition, and logic. A devout Christian himself, Newton continued to affirm the old ways of establishing religious truth. But the implications of his empirical views expanded in ever widening circles for the three following centuries. Newton's empiricism, as adopted by the thinkers of the Enlightenment, laid the basis for scientism: the belief that all knowledge is scientific, empirical, quantitative. In such a view, religion and theology were either dismissed altogether or, at best, tucked away in a closet locked off from the sciences, which were deemed to constitute real knowledge.

Almost equally important in undermining diabology was the emergence of history, a second phenomenal revolution involving no less than the discovery of time.[32] Before the eighteenth century, the prevailing view was that the cosmos was relatively static: minor changes occur, but in their broad features the cosmos and the earth were created in the same shape and form they appear in today, complete with the species of life that exist in the world today, including humanity. Even though

---

32. On the new views of time, see especially M. T. Greene, *Geology in the Nineteenth Century: Changing Views of a Changing World* (Ithaca, 1982); A. Schweitzer, *The Quest of the Historical Jesus* (New York, 1948); S. Toulmin and J. Goodfield, *The Discovery of Time* (London, 1965).

Copernicus had placed the sun, rather than the earth, at the center of the universe, that had done little to dislodge humanity from its privileged place as the apple of God's eye. But now a series of discoveries were made that seemed to place humankind in an insignificant corner of space and time.

The chief obstacle to the atheist view of a world developed by random processes had been that not nearly enough time had elapsed for the random motion of particles to produce such a highly ordered and diverse cosmos. Atheists had no idea of the age of the earth, and the traditional Christian view—based upon chronology drawn from the Bible—that the earth was only six or seven thousand years old seemed plausible. But now, enormous reaches of astronomical, cosmological, and geological time began to open. These new vistas would change, forever, our view of the world.

In 1755, Immanuel Kant published his *General History of Nature and Theory of the Heavens*,[33] which claimed that the cosmos, including the earth, had gradually evolved over a period of millions of years, is still evolving, and will continue to do so indefnitely. Kant sought to expand space as well as time, suggesting that some nebulae are really island universes of stars remote from our own, although this idea was not generally accepted until the empirical demonstration of galaxies in the early twentieth century.

Between 1750 and 1850, a mutual interaction of geology, history, and astronomy gradually established an evolutionary view of the cosmos, the physical earth, and human society. Everything, it was observed, had a history, and everything in both the physical and the human world must be seen dynamically rather than statically. The Comte de Buffon (1707–1788) argued that the solar system and its planets had evolved gradually, and James Hutton (1726–1797) and Charles Lyell (1797–1875) vigorously advanced the view that vast amounts of time were needed to explain geological phenomena.[34]

A rearguard action was mounted in the form of catastrophism, which accepted that the earth had changed yet managed to preserve a short time-scale by arguing that changes had occurred through sudden, giant catastrophes. The biblical account of the flood was called in to reconcile religion and science. But catastrophism could not endure; the mounting

33. Kant, *Allgemeine Naturgeschichte und Theorie des Himmels* (Königsberg, 1755).
34. Buffon, *Histoire naturelle* (1749–1788); Hutton, *Theory of the Earth* (Edinburgh, 1788); Lyell, *Principles of Geology* (London, 1830–1833).

evidence of astronomy, geology, and finally (in the mid-nineteenth century) biology pointed to vast amounts of time, and the principle of uniformity—the idea that the physical laws operating today have always been operating at the same rate—gained increasing acceptance. The late twentieth century has modified many of these views. Evolution is no longer thought to have been so gradual and continuous as was once believed; modern physics sees no "center" at all to the universe, so that the idea that we are somehow tucked away in some insignificant outskirt of the cosmos is invalid, and the anthropic principle derived from quantum physics suggests that humanity (though in quite a different way from the medieval view) may yet in a sense be the center of the cosmos; new reflections on randomness and time suggest that even in billions of years the information of intelligent life by random processes is virtually impossible.[35]

Whatever the upshot of such contemporary discussions, eighteenth-century science and history shattered the traditional view. Educated Christians had assumed that the Bible was historically and scientifically reliable. But if the world were much older than the Bible indicated, that reliability was gone for part of the Old Testament; and if part, why not all; and if the Old Testament, why not the New as well? Such questions undermined scripture and tradition, the two most important bases of Christianity. They also undermined confidence in the historicity, and therefore the authority, of Jesus Christ himself, who now became the subject of intense historical investigation and criticism.

In the sixteenth and seventeenth centuries the frantic debates between Catholics and Protestants had already shredded confidence in tradition, for it was difficult to establish whose tradition was the authentic one. Protestant insistence that the truth of Christianity lay in its origins led to the use of the new historical tools to get back not only *to* the scriptures but eventually also *through* them to the "historical" Jesus behind the New Testament texts. This quest is gradually being abandoned in the late twentieth century, but, strangely, Protestant faith in the primitive past combined with historical criticism to undermine the authority of scripture, as faith was transferred from the words of scripture itself to those of influential biblical critics. Christianity was no longer defined in terms of what it had always been but in terms of what certain modern scholars (whose pronouncements often diverged widely)

35. See, for example, Paul Davies, *Space and Time in the Modern Universe* (Cambridge, 1977).

said that it should have been. Most of these scholars attempted to reinterpret scripture in accordance with the assumptions of eighteenth- and nineteenth-century scientific and historical materialism. This amounted to a curious compromise: educated people, refusing to rely on scripture and tradition but unready to discard them althogether, remade them to fit the preconceptions of their own day.

Biblical criticism focused most sharply on the person of Christ himself. It was argued that Jesus must be seen as a man of his own time, a peasant in an obscure corner of an ancient empire. His views were unadvanced, his ideas primitive. When he spoke of the Devil or demons, he merely reflected the ignorant superstitions of his day. That Jesus could have been divine or risen from the dead were outmoded notions. Ignorant himself, Jesus was surrounded by ignorant followers who muddled his message, so that the New Testament was riddled with error. Such was the confidence of the historical scholarship springing from the Enlightenment that it judged scriptural views valid only insofar as they conformed to the views of current historians.[36]

Some of this could have been avoided by more careful attention to the discoveries of Giambattista Vico (1668–1744). Vico demanded a skeptical, rational analysis of the changes in human behavior over the centuries, yet his skepticism provided the basis for a new and sophisticated idealism. Since we cannot know the nature of things "out there" but only our perceptions of them, it follows that our perceptions of human affairs are much more secure than our perceptions of external nature, because we make human affairs ourselves and thus know them from the inside. *Verum et factum convertuntur:* we know what we have made. This establishes the study of human concepts on a firm historical basis. Although we are incapable of discovering what the Devil is as a thing in itself, we are capable of establishing with complete certainty what the Devil is as a human concept, because we have created the concept. The only way to analyze such a concept is historically. We cannot investigate how closely it corresponds to the Devil-in-itself because we have no knowledge of things in themselves. We must define the Devil in historical terms. The Devil *is* the tradition of what he has been thought to be. Our historical knowledge of the Devil is infinitely more certain than any statement about anything "out there."[37] From Vico's perspective, the efforts of biblical critics and liberal Christians to reshape Christianity in

36. Among the most important historical critics of the Bible were Paulus (1761–1851) and Bruno Bauer (1809–1882). Their views and others' are discussed by Schweitzer.

37. Vico, *La scienza nuova* (1725–1730), ed. N. Abbagnano (Torino, 1966).

terms of "what we now know" was wrongheaded and pointless. We do not know what God's view of Christianity is, or what Christianity is "out there." We know only what Christianity has defined itself to be on the basis of scripture and tradition.

Ignoring this solution, liberal Christianity retreated hastily before the advance of science and biblical criticism, regrouping every so often to fight another losing battle before giving up new ground. By the end of the eighteenth century, advanced liberals had abandoned the core of Christian beliefs. Satan was a painful embarrassment to them, one of those outmoded ideas that Jesus had assumed because he was soaked in the ignorance or superstition of his times, or that the unreliable gospels had attributed to him. Many liberals also abandoned the idea of original sin (and therefore of redemption), and this left them peculiarly defenseless against the problem of evil. Relinquishing the traditional arguments, most tended to evade the question.

One liberal theologian who did confront the issue was Friedrich Daniel Ernst Schleiermacher (1768–1834), a pastor of the Reformed Church.[38] Revolting against a Pietist upbringing, Schleiermacher at first adopted Enlightenment religion, denying original sin, redemption, and the incarnation. Gradually he came to believe that the Enlightenment, in its distanced rationalism, had missed the main point of religion: the experience that we are always absolutely dependent upon something outside ourselves for our lives and our very being. Christianity could stand critically against the world and society only so long as it maintained its epistemological independence and did not become an appendage of current intellectual trends. Christianity must penetrate deeper than the bloodless rational religion of the Enlightenment, but it must also go beyond the narrow boundaries of traditional orthodoxy. Schleiermacher sought to overcome the limitations of the opposite views he had held in his youth and instead to build a new Christian system based upon the experience of absolute dependence.

Schleiermacher took evil to be an existential reality but replaced original sin with a progressive view similar in many ways to that adopted by John Hick in the late twentieth century.[39] Schleiermacher argued that humans are created weak and infirm, both as a race and as individuals. Inherent imperfections disorder our true nature, which is to seek union

38. Schleiermacher, *On Religion* (1799); *The Christian Faith* (1821–1822); *Brief Outline on the Study of Theology* (1830). Schleiermacher's discussion of the Devil appears in *The Christian Faith*, 1.1.1.2.

39. John Hick, *Evil and the God of Love*, 2d ed. (New York, 1979).

with God. Original sin is simply a metaphor for our inherent imperfection. Since God creates us imperfect, the "fault" is his, but he does it so that we may, by overcoming hardships and obstacles, gradually attain full maturity in our progress toward fulfillment in him. Our guide along the way is Jesus Christ, the perfect model and the mediator through which divine power enters the world to shape and direct it. The essence of the evil that we must overcome is egoism and the preference for worldly, finite goods over the true good, which is loving growth in God.

Schleiermacher addressed the idea of the Devil with a progressive eye toward eliminating it. However, many of his objections had already been considered by traditional diabology. (1) How could perfect creatures such as angels fall? (Christian theology had never proclaimed the angels perfect.) (2) If they fell because of envy, that would mean they were already envious and must already have fallen, a contradiction. (Theology had declared envy or pride the motives but not the causes of the fall, since a freewill act has no cause.) (3) The Devil's nature, including his intelligence, must have been so diminished by his fall that he could not be an effective enemy of God or man. (Theology had argued that Satan's will, not his nature, had been corrupted, and that he retained his natural intelligence, though darkened.) (4) Demons should be unable to cooperate against us, since evil beings hate one another. (But evil persons are often observed to cooperate with one another.) (5) Displacing the origin of evil from humanity to Satan does nothing to help explain it. (To this, theology had never had an adequate answer.)

Schleiermacher's most direct line of attack upon the Devil lay through the Bible: Christ referred to the Devil only offhand, he said, or in quoting proverbs, or in symbolic reference to evil humans, and the story of the temptation is a didactic tale without historical foundation. Christ and the apostles could not really have believed in such an unenlightened doctrine as the Devil, and if they did, we still need not believe it, since they were only drawing upon the superstitions common to their times. Schleiermacher, too, assumed that the views of his own age were standards by which those of other ages could be judged.

Schleiermacher also offered practical arguments against belief in the Devil. The concept of the Devil is a fusion of a number of diverse historical elements. (Voltaire had already offered this view, with more awareness than Schleiermacher that it applied to every element of Christian theology.) The idea of the Devil encourages people to shift responsibility away from themselves onto another being. (But traditional theology had always insisted that the Devil can never compel anyone's conscience and that responsibility for sin lies with the individual.) Belief in the Devil provokes despair if we come to believe that the Devil can foil God's plan for the world. (But tradition had always affirmed God's providence in transforming all evil efforts into good.)

Schleiermacher concludes that the Devil does not exist, though we may choose to use him as a convenient metaphor for evil. Underneath his conclusion lies a hidden syllogism: the idea of the Devil is unfashionable and embarrassing, yet Christianity is somehow true and the Bible somehow inspired; therefore, a complex system must be erected to explain away the fact that the New Testament teaches the existence and power of the Devil as a central point of eschatology.

The most visible intellectual change toward the end of the century was the transition from Enlightenment to Romantic thought. Jean-Jacques Rousseau (1712–1778) prefigured this transition.[40] An intensely emotional and inconsistent personality, he alienated the philosophes by professing Christianity, but his emotional, sentimental, esthetic religiosity—denying trinity, incarnation, redemption, and resurrection, yet claiming to feel the spirit of Christ within—alienated both Protestants and Catholics. In his distaste for what later came to be called "organized religion," he rejected the church and one of the fundamental aspects of Christianity, its communal nature, in favor of individual sentiment.

Rousseau confronted the problem of evil far less directly than Kant or Voltaire and less consistently than Sade. His view of evil was social rather than metaphysical; it was a human creation: "Man, look no farther for the author of evil: you are he."[41] Our nature is basically good; it is we ourselves who have corrupted it.[42] Rousseau did not object to culture in itself, which he regarded as both necessary and desirable, but he did observe that historically the cultures we have established have tended to enslave and corrupt us. We can be saved by our consciences, which are a divine instinct of goodness within us, a principle by which we can remove these evil, smothering influences and restore ourselves to

40. Rousseau, *La nouvelle Héloïse* (1761); *Emile* (1762), including bk. 4, "Profession de foi du vicaire savoyard"; *Du contrat social* (1762); *Confessions* (1782).

41. Rousseau, "Profession de foi." See also a letter of August 18, 1756, cited in L. G. Crocker, *An Age of Crisis: Man and World in Eighteenth Century French Thought* (Baltimore, 1959), p. 90: "I do not see how we can look for the source of moral evil elsewhere than in man, who is free, who has progressed, and thereby become corrupted."

42. "Tout est bien sortant des mains du Createur": *Emile*.

our natural goodness and to a natural social order characterized by liberty and equality. By education and social reform we can remove our errors, superstitions, vices, and repressive institutions and enter into a new era of light. These benevolent, progressive ideas influenced the American and French revolutions, which were on the whole hostile to traditional Christianity. But Rousseau's combination of revolution with vague religiosity also encouraged the Romantic revival of a God and the Romantic creation of Satan the noble revolutionary. By the end of the century, literature had begun to reflect these views.

Once the age of witchcraft was past, the Devil made relatively few appearances in literature until the later eighteenth century, and when he revived, it was in a new form. Theology and metaphysics were superseded by estheticism and symbolism. When Satan's metaphysical existence was dismissed, he became a symbol that could float free of its traditional meanings. He ceased to be a person and so could become a personality, a literary character playing a variety of parts.[43] (1) In some works, he continued to play his traditional role.[44] (2) Some used him as a symbol of human evil and corruption. (3) Some used him ironically or satirically to mock Christianity or to parody human folly. (4) Some used him as a positive symbol of rebellion against corrupt authority. Overall, the Devil continued to be a valuable metaphor for pure evil. Since human nature is mixed and few people are either wholly good or wholly evil, the Devil could be presented, as no human character could, as the hypostasis of the evil of the human spirit distilled to its essence.[45] There also began to appear hints of the sympathetic, Romantic Devil. Fol-

43. E. C. Mason, "Die Gestalt des Teufels in der deutschen Literatur seit 1748," in W. Kohlschmidt and H. Meyer, eds., *Tradition und Ursprünglichkeit* (Bern, 1966), pp. 113–125.

44. For example, Antoine-Louis Daugis's *Traité sur la magie* (1732); Dom Augustin Calmet's *Dissertation sur les apparitions des anges, des démons, et des esprits* (1746); Abbé Nicolas Lenglet-Dufresnoy's *Traité historique et dogmatique sur les apparitions, les visions, et les révélations particulières* (1751); Abbé Claude-Marie Guyon's *Bibliothèque ecclésiastique* (1771). These expressed varying degrees of credulity ranging from complete defense of the old tradition to mild skeptical criticism. See M. Milner, *Le diable dans la littérature française*, 2 vols. (Paris, 1960), vol. 1, pp. 52–61.

45. Among the most important new interpretations were Alain René Le Sage (1668–1747), *Le Diable boiteux* (1707), freely adapted for ironic purposes from *El diablo cojuelo* (1641) of Vélez de la Guevara (1579–1644). Le Sage's imitators included the Abbé Bruslé de Montpleinchamp's *Le diable bossu*, "The Hunchbacked Devil" (1708). See Milner, vol. 1, pp. 75–78. Daniel Defoe wrote an ironic *Political History of the Devil* (1726). On Defoe's use of the Devil in his novel *Moll Flanders* (1722), see R. Erickson, "Moll's Fate: 'Mother Midnight' and *Moll Flanders*," *Studies in Philology*, 76 (1979), 85–87.

lowers of Louis-Claude de Saint Martin (1743–1803), a pantheistic mystic, believed that the angels' first fall had been esthetic, a love of beauty so intense that they desired to grasp and possess it for themselves.[46]

A work that spans Enlightenment and Romanticism is the masterpiece of Faust literature, *Faust: Eine Tragödie*, by Johann Wolfgang von Goethe (1749–1832).[47] The place of *Faust* in the history of the Devil is ambiguous. On the one hand, Goethe's Devil, Mephistopheles, became one of the most influential literary creations of all time.[48] On the other, Mephisto is an immensely complex figure only one of whose components is the Christian Devil. Goethe himself took an ironically distant Enlightenment view of Christianity, drawing upon Christian symbolism but despising the church. His views shifted broadly throughout his life—his interests at one time or another embracing Pietism, mysticism, the kabbala, alchemy, folklore, Neoplatonism, liberalism, and many other vogues— and he made no effort to impose rigid consistency upon his masterwork. He began to work on *Faust* while still a very young man, about 1770, and he was still working on it near his death in 1832. It represents sixty years of the creative thought of an active and lively intellect, and it resists summarization and reduction to formulas.[49]

At the age of sixty-three, Goethe looked back and described the cosmology he had adopted as a young poet. God the Father produced the Son, and Father and Son produced the Holy Spirit. Together these three were complete and perfect, so that when they produced a fourth, Lucifer, he was necessarily imperfect. Lucifer created the angels. Impressed by his own creative powers, he concentrated more and more

46. Martinist works are discussed in Milner, vol. 1, pp. 111–120. Other influential literary works include Paul Weidmann's *Johann Faustus* (1775) and Freidrich Maximilian von Klinger's satirical *Fausts Leben, Thaten, und Höllenfahrt* (1791).

47. Goethe, *Faust: Eine Tragödie*, 2 vols. (Basel, 1949); C. Hamlin, ed., and W. Arndt, trans., *Faust: A Tragedy* (New York, 1976). I cite the German edition throughout. See also S. Atkins, *Goethe's Faust: A Literary Analysis* (Cambridge, Mass., 1958); A. P. Cottrell, *Goethe's View of Evil and the Search for a New Image of Man in Our Time* (Edinburgh, 1982).

48. The musical adaptations of Faust, for example, include Berlioz's *Damnation de Faust* (oratorio 1846; opera 1896); Liszt's *Faust-Symphonie* (1854–1857); Gounod's *Faust* (1859); Grieg's *Peer Gynt* (1890).

49. The *Urfaust*, composed during the period 1772 to 1775, was not published until 1887. *Faust: Ein Fragment*, written between 1788 and 1790, was published at Leipzig in 1790; Mephisto puts in his first appearance in Goethe here. *Faust: Eine Tragödie* consists of two parts, the first written between 1787 and 1806 and published in 1808, the second between 1825 and 1831 and published in 1832.

deeply upon himself, gradually losing touch with reality. Some of the angels remained aware of their true origin, but others followed Lucifer and retreated into selfishness. From Lucifer's self-absorption proceeded the material universe. It would have spiraled deeper and deeper into itself until it ceased to exist had not God in his mercy chosen to give it the positive power to open up to the light. From the tension between selfishness and openness, darkness and light, comes the tension in the world and in humanity between the downward-closing diabolical force and the upward-opening divine force. Goethe meant this as a symbolic structure more than as a literal theology, but it left lasting marks on the poem.[50]

Faust has no single meaning or even set of meanings. Goethe intended it to express the complexities and incongruencies of his own mind, of his culture, and of Western civilization as a whole. Thus a wide number of readings are possible. For the purpose of this book, I emphasize the place of Goethe's Mephistopheles in the tradition of the Devil.

Mephistopheles, like *Faust* itself, is as varied as the world. On even the most superficial level his nature is left unclear, for he sometimes appears to be Satan or Satan's equivalent and at other times only a minor demon (ll. 338–339, 1338–1340). In fact, Mephistopheles is much too complex, diverse, and ambiguous to be identified with the Christian Devil. Goethe gladly used and developed the myth, but he always vehemently denied the literal existence of the Christian Devil and even of Kant's principle of radical evil. Goethe kept the ambiguity pronounced, as part of Mephisto's function is to deny any dichotomy in nature, moral or otherwise. Mephisto appears both as the opponent of God and as the instrument of the divine will; as the creator of the material world and as God's subject; as the principle of matter against the principle of spirit; as evil against good; as chaos against order; as a stimulus to creativity; and in many other aspects. He is fundamentally a nature spirit representing the undifferentiated world as it presents itself to human experience. He is an invitation to the reader to face the multiplicity of reality.[51]

Such was the enormous influence of *Faust* that most of the literary Devils of the past two centuries have taken the suave, ironic, ambiguous shape of Mephistopheles. The shift from the Devil as theological person

50. "Dichtung und Wahrheit," in *Autobiographische Schriften*, cited by A. P. Cottrell, *Goethe's View of Evil* (Edinburgh, 1982), pp. 27–30.
51. See Jane K. Brown, *Goethe's Faust: The German Tragedy* (Ithaca, 1986).

to the Devil as literary personage was permanently fixed by Goethe. There have been exceptions, but writers wishing their theological Devils to be taken seriously as personifications of evil have had, since *Faust*, to overcome powerful resistance.

Mephistopheles is partly a Christian devil, partly an ironic commentator on society, partly a spokesman for secular, progressive humanism; mostly, says E. C. Mason, he is "simply a one-sided insistence on the seamy side of human life."[52] He has the ironic, aloof, critical, cold, judgmental qualities of the academics whom Goethe despised, characteristics that Faust shared but of which he was purged by his suffering. Mephisto's slick intelligence and superficial charm allow him to manipulate people, but on a deeper level he is a fool, for he fails to grasp that the essential reality of the cosmos is the power of love. He is foolish enough to make a bet against the all-knowing deity; he begins by playing the fool in heaven and ends by lusting after the angels. His combination of wisdom and stupidity is summed up when he admits that for thousands of years he has been resisting the irresistible power of God.[53]

Essentially blind to reality, Mephistopheles tries to negate and destroy it. He denies the value of existence and declares that the purpose of creation is to be destroyed. He hates beauty, freedom, and life itself; he causes the deaths of individuals and advocates ruinous social policies that destroy multitudes.[54] This nihilism is the essence of evil, and it comes indirectly from God (ll. 342–349). Like the traditional Devil, Mephisto is a liar and cheater, a master of illusion who repeatedly shifts his shape, appearing as a dog, a scholar, a knight, a fool, a magician, and a general. With sophistry, flattery, and gossip he sows doubt and distrust; he uses his magic to instill illusions, hallucinations, and dreams; as counselor of state he creates false wealth, and as a general he destroys armies by committing illusory troops to battle.[55] The spirit of chaos and disorder in the natural world, he also promotes disorder in society by disrupting justice.[56] He delights in cruelty and suffering.[57] He tempts

52. E. C. Mason, "The Paths and Powers of Mephistopheles," in *German Studies Presented to Walter Horace Bruford* (London, 1962), p. 93.

53. Ll. 1776–1784. For Mephisto's intelligence, see ll. 1362–1378, 6172, 10,075–10,076; foolishness, ll. 339, 1675; the riddle in ll. 4743–4750, 11,780–11,800.

54. Ll. 1338–1384, 1851–1867, 3711, 6255–6256, 6954–6962, 11,350–11,369, 11,544–11,550, 11,596–11,603.

55. Ll. 1506–1606, 1868–2050, 2300–2366, 2901–2912, 3050, 5985–6027, 8027, 10,547–10,781.

56. Ll. 1379–1384, 4611, 5465–5470, 6203–6208.

57. Ll. 3543, 3711, 11,350–11,369, 11,545–11,554, 11,636–11,707.

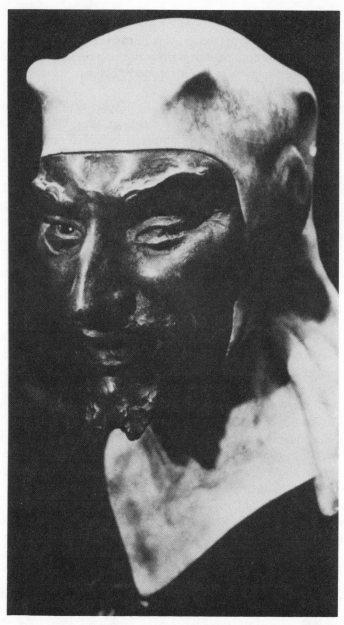

A bust by Morelli shows the devil as Mephistopheles, with his scholar's cap, forked beard, and sardonic face. Alabaster with ruby eyes. Florence, nineteenth century. Courtesy of Sylvie Mercier, photographe "La Licornière," Paris.

and threatens in his efforts to corrupt and is most pleased with the despair of the innocent.[58] Incapable of grasping what love means, he promotes coarseness and brutality in sexual relations.[59] He opposes social reforms and crushes a revolution against tyranny.[60] He regrets his unfallen past but refuses to repent, falling into the sin of despair.[61] Yet he speaks for Goethe in his ironic comments on philosophers, professors, fanatics, generals, clergymen, bureaucrats, politicians, and exploitative rulers.[62]

After a dedication and a prelude, the poem opens with the "Prologue in Heaven," where the Lord is surrounded by his heavenly courtiers, led by Raphael, Gabriel, Michael, and Mephistopheles. The setting immediately recalls the Book of Job, with Mephistopheles playing the part of Satan. The angels praise God for the beauty of the cosmos. But Mephistopheles shifts the focus from the cosmos as a whole to the condition of humanity. In spite (or because) of the alleged harmonies of the cosmos, humanity is wretched, brutish, unhappy, and unreliable. God reproaches him for this negativism, but Mephisto persists, pitying the human race: "I feel such compassion for their wretched lives that I hesitate to afflict them any more myself" (ll. 297–298). The Devil's presence in the heavenly court and his influence upon the Lord indicates that evil is part of God's design, inherent in humanity, the cosmos, and God himself. The Devil's role in the heavenly court is ironic, almost that of a heavenly jester or fool who cleverly indicates the failings of his Master. His disagreement with God over humanity hints at an Enlightenment rebellion against the tyrant, a Promethean sympathy for humans against the gods, and a proto-Romantic rebellion against abstract justice in the name of feeling and mercy. Yet the Devil also serves the Lord well. The Lord not only tolerates but ordains the evil that Mephistopheles plans, and he even confesses a little fondness for the Devil: "I have never hated you; of all the spirits who deny me, I blame the rogue the least. The activity of humans all too quickly slackens into laziness, so I give them a companion to push them and work on them and act as Devil" (ll. 337–343).

As the Lord had once called Satan's attention to Job as an example of a just and uncorruptible man, he now draws Mephistopheles' attention

58. Ll. 2321, 3543, 6792.
59. Ll. 2031–2036, 2513, 2603–2604, 4136–4143, 5775–5796, 6208, 6979–6983.
60. Ll. 4772–5064, 6063–6172, 10,242–10,344.
61. Ll. 1776–1784, 10,075–10,094, 11,809–11,816.
62. Ll. 4076–4095, 6587–6591, 7847–7950, 10,313–10,320, 10,783–11,042.

to Faust as representative both of individual genius and of humanity as a whole. The Lord observes that Faust is a faithful seeker after truth who will never turn away from his goal; he is proof that the creation of humanity was a good thing. Goethe distanced himself from the earlier Faust tradition in making the magician symbolize the plight of the human race as a whole. Faust is Job, Adam, Christ, Man. Where traditional Faust dramas had centered on the pact, Goethe's focuses on two wagers: one between Mephistopheles and God, and the other between Mephistopheles and man. Mephisto challenges the Lord: You say that Faust is steadfast? Then give me permission to tempt him. What can you lose? What do you bet that he will resist me? (ll. 312–314). Whether God actually takes the bet is unclear, but he does promise not to intervene on Faust's behalf (l. 323). Mephisto himself believes that the wager is on and that his license to tempt is unlimited, for he ignores God's stipulation that his power over Faust will end at the scholar's death (l. 315). The Lord knows that Mephistopheles will inevitably lose his bet, but Mephistopheles' playful need to see what he can do overwhelms his knowledge of his own certain defeat.

The "First Part" of the tragedy begins in Faust's study, where the great scholar is sunk in despair, because in spite of incessant intellectual effort he has been unable to penetrate the secrets of the universe (ll. 382–383).[63] He tries to gain entry into the world of spirits in order to obtain the occult knowledge that he requires; he will not understand for many lines that what he needs is not knowledge but love and concern for others. He hears the angels' chorus but lacks the faith to believe and fails to understand the importance of love (l. 765). In a book of magic he finds the symbol (*Zeichen*) of the Earth Spirit, the *Erdgeist*, which expresses the restlessness, striving, and desire that Faust feels within himself. Neither good nor evil, the *Erdgeist* is an elemental nature spirit beyond human values.[64] Faust pronounces the *Erdgeist*'s symbol, whereupon the spirit appears and asks who called it (l. 482). By blurring the question of whether Faust actually summons the spirit, Goethe puts further distance between himself and tradition; it needs to be unclear how much Faust is responsible and how much he is a victim of the Lord's arrangement with Satan.

The next scene takes Faust out of the study into streets populated

63. Wagner later echoes this desire to know everything: "Zwar weiss ich viel, doch möcht ich alles wissen" (l. 601).
64. "Zwei Seelen wohnen, ach, in meiner Brust" (l. 1112).

with taverners, students, wenches, and soldiers; here the scholar and his assistant Wagner drink and debate. Faust argues the beauty of nature and Wagner the glory of scholarship, both failing to enter into the real life going on around them. Faust complains that he feels two spirits within him, one drawing him to worldly pleasure and the other toward infinite wisdom (ll. 1112–1117). Both these ideals are flawed, for neither is rooted in love. As they talk, Faust points out a black dog sniffing nearby. Wagner takes it for an ordinary poodle, but Faust sees that it trails a streak of fire (ll. 1154–1155). Mephistopheles has appeared, and in one of the traditional Devil's favorite forms, a black dog. He comes unbidden by Faust's conscious will yet attracted by Faust's despair, which opens his mind to the Evil One.

Later, back in the study, the poodle appears again, takes a variety of disturbing shapes, and finally settles on the form of a wandering scholar.[65] Faust demands that the "scholar" declare his identity and guesses the truth: that he is a liar and a destroyer. Mephistopheles identifies himself as "a part of that power that ever seeks evil and ever does good"—does good because compelled by divine providence (ll. 1336–1337). He is also the spirit of negation and seeks to destroy all that has been created.[66] He openly proclaims that destruction and evil are his native element (ll. 1342–1345). Still, as the "Prologue" has suggested, evil is part of the cosmos because it is part of the stuff from which God has made the cosmos. Mephisto declares that he is a part of that dark chaos that gave birth to the light, and Faust understands him: "Thou art Chaos' wondrous son."[67]

In a continuing departure from tradition, Goethe has Faust suggest a pact to Mephisto, by which he hopes to gain access to Mephisto's occult powers (ll. 1413–1415). The Devil's own plan is to lull the scholar into mindless sensuality and thereby win his bet with God, and he sends spirits to Faust to induce sensual dreams and visions. When Faust awakens, he is not certain whether he has really seen the Devil or not (ll.

65. Both Dostoevsky and Mann imitated this scene, making the power to change shape characteristic of their own Devils.

66. "Ich bin der Geist, der stets verneint! / Und das mit Recht; denn alles was entsteht, / Ist wert, dass es zugrunde geht" (ll. 1338–1340).

67. "Ich bin ein Teil des Teils, der anfangs alles war, / Ein Teil der Finsternis, die sich das Licht gebar. . . . Des Chaos wunderlicher Sohn" (ll. 1349–1350, 1384). He is part of the darkness that gave birth to the light, because God brought the power of light into the darkness of matter. But Mephistopheles is lying by suppressing the truth, for the darkness of matter was secondary to the light and was produced only through the Devil's own fault.

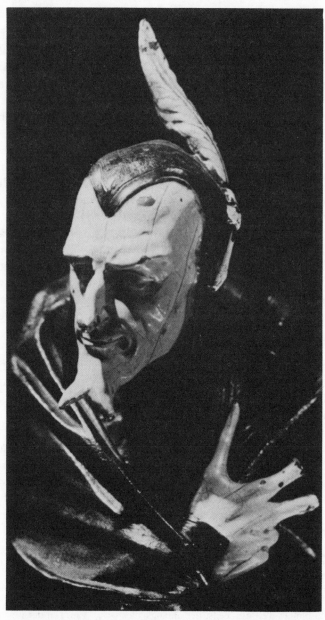

A nineteenth-century sculpture in bronze and ivory. The Devil as Mephistopheles, again with scholar's cap, forked beard, and sinister smirk. Courtesy of Sylvie Mercier, photographe "La Licornière," Paris.

1529–1530).[68] But Faust's curse on human existence (ll. 1587–1606) opens him further to the influence of the Devil, who has reappeared as a young nobleman. Mephistopheles offers to be Faust's servant in this world if Faust will be his in the next, forgetting the limitations that God has placed upon his power (ll. 1648–1659). The pact transposes into a second wager, which recapitulates the one made in heaven: Mephisto bets that he can make Faust abandon his quest, sink into luxurious sensuality, and bid the moment of pleasure linger; Faust bets that he will never cease to strive.[69] Mephisto urges him, and later his student, to abandon study and abstractions for "life's golden tree" (ll. 2038–2039). He treacherously omits the middle ground between pedantry and sensuality: the ground of generosity and love.

It is the failure to love that makes *Faust* a tragedy. Goethe's *Tragedy* is in deliberate contrast to Dante's *Comedy*. Dante's poem is a *commedia* because it focuses on the human situation, which, taken in itself apart from the cosmic context, is painfully flawed. Faust and Mephisto sign a pact, whose terms are deliberately left undefined (ll. 1734–1740). The pact is subsidiary to the bet, and both bet and pact are subsidiary to the human tragedy. Mephisto observes that if Faust had not made the pact, he would still be doomed, for God and Devil between them had set his fate (ll. 1866–1867). Mephisto will next attempt to corrupt Faust's intellect, emotion, and will, his ultimate purpose being to destroy him.[70]

The next scene, set in Auerbach's wine cellar in Leipzig, begins Faust's initiation into the sensual world. Believing that he has Faust in his power, Mephisto shows himself increasingly coarse and brutal as times goes on. In the scene in the Witch's Kitchen, this coarseness becomes pronounced, though he still maintains his ironic distance to the point of observing his own historical decline, noting that modern cultural fashion civilizes the Devil and removes his horns, tail, and claws. The cloven hoof remains, because it is easily disguised by shoes. (The lame Devil would become an important symbol in modern literature through Dostoevsky, Mann, and Flannery O'Connor.) Goethe suggested that the skeptical world is uncomfortable with symbols of evil and prefers the Devil comfortably disguised as a suave gentleman with only the hint of a hidden deformity (ll. 2499–2500). For the same reason, Mephisto no longer uses the name Satan, because every modern person considers

68. This uncertainty reappears in both Dostoevsky and Mann.
69. Tarry a while: "Verweile doch!" (l. 1699).
70. Cottrell, pp. 106–166.

the Devil a superstition—not that modern disbelief in Satan has made people any less vicious, he ironically concludes (ll. 2504–2509).

Mephistopheles lures Faust into deeper sensuality by playing upon his lust for the young girl Margarete (Gretchen). Mephisto cares little about Gretchen, for he sees that though he can ruin her life, he has no power over her soul (l. 2626). His purpose is to destroy Faust by helping him sink into lust and fornication and at the same time make him responsible for Gretchen's ruin, thus scoring a double blow against his soul. When Gretchen gives birth to her illegitimate child, she goes mad, drowns the infant, and is executed for her crime. Mephistopheles savors her destruction, for he has demonstrated the folly and corruption of all humanity and degraded love to sensuality and exploitation (l. 3543). But his success is hollow, for Faust's lust has become transformed into real love for Gretchen. Mephistopheles could not avoid doing the good that he despises: the sensuality he instilled in Faust has broken down the scholar's cold pedantry and opened his heart to tenderness and compassion. When Mephisto later takes Faust to a *Walpurgisnacht* where they see Gretchen wandering as a lost soul, Faust feels—against Mephisto's plan—the first pang of the remorse that will eventually save him.[71]

Mephistopheles is less evident in the tragedy's more abstract "Second Part"; when he does appear, it is as a shadowy magician and sorcerer— the emperor's "Fool"—urging disastrous social policies. But he is at work in a number of forms, undermining society and seeking to lead people to various false, mechanistic, or fantastic solutions to social problems. Only in the final scene does the focus return to the struggle for Faust's soul. The dying scholar has a vision of a better world created by human progress, while Mephisto sneers that Faust's life and that of humanity as a whole is all in vain (ll. 11,600–11,603). Mephisto claims Faust's soul, but the scholar has won his bets, for he has never ceased to strive and never settled down to a life of sensual ease. The Devil claims that he is entitled to the soul because of the contract, but the contract is void because Faust has learned to love. The Blessed Virgin welcomes Gretchen into heaven, as choirs of angels bear Faust's soul aloft, praising his eternal striving (ll. 11,936–11,937). Mephistopheles, his perceptions so absurdly dulled by evil that his response to the sight of the boyish angels is to fantasize about sodomizing them, has lost the bet, the soul, and the point of existence.

I have emphasized those aspects of Mephisto's character that best fit

71. A. Schöne, *Götterzeichen, Liebeszauber, Satanskult*, 2d ed. (Munich, 1982).

the Christian tradition. But in Goethe's *Faust*, things are never only what they seem. The Christian symbolism in the last scene, as throughout, is only esthetic. Faust is saved not from sin, in the Christian sense, but from the antiphonal errors of sensuality and arid intellectualism. His ascension into heaven is not the beatification of an individual but rather a program for the human race: we, like Faust, are called to abandon folly and seek a society based upon regard for others.

Mephistopheles is the most important literary Devil since Milton's, but a Devil resurrected in a non-Christian form in which he has lost his horns and tail, and covers his deformed foot with his shoe. The new Devil will take yet stranger forms in the Romantic period.

5   *The Romantic Devil*

The Revolutions of 1789–1848 shattered the ancient symbiosis of Christianity and the state that had begun a millennium and a half earlier with Constantine the Great. As the old political and legal systems were swept away in the wake of Napoleon's reorganization of Europe, the political powers of the monarchy and the aristocracy, on which the churches had often relied, were drastically reduced. Commercial and industrial elites gradually replaced the aristocracy as political and cultural leaders. The capitalist values of the new elite, with their emphasis on competition and profit, had little ground in common with Christianity.

Although the leaders of capitalist society still found it politically useful to embrace Christianity or at least to appear to do so, two underlying effects were increasingly felt: the religion of the leaders of society tended to become more nominal and superficial; and the intellectual leaders tended to become more openly skeptical of religious values. Further, with the industrialization that proceeded rapidly in much of western Europe during the nineteenth century, a large population shift occurred from the countryside, with its traditional religious customs, to the ugly cities with their anonymity and often cruel working conditions. The industrial proletariat, cut off from access to traditional values, tended to develop a sense of despair and meaninglessness that was eventually alleviated only by such new ideologies as Marxism. In such a society, belief in the transcendent waned, and Christian theology seemed to lose much of its relevance.

Attitudes toward these changes varied radically, and as the Revolution of 1789 came to symbolize the transformation of society, attitudes toward the Revolution often paralleled attitudes toward the Devil. Monarchists and traditional Catholics tended to view the Revolution as the work of the Devil and the restoration of the monarchy as the triumph of Christ the King over Satan. As political reactionaries made common cause with Catholics against the Revolution, republicans and revolutionaries attacked Christianity and rallied to the standard of its opponents—the greatest of whom was Satan. Christ is King, but kings are evil, and the greatest king is the greatest evil. Revolutionaries tended to perceive Satan as a symbol of rebellion against the unjust order and tyranny of the *ancien régime* and its institutions: church, government, and family. Not only radicals but also the bourgeois, who saw individualism and aggressive competition as virtues, were prepared for a shift in symbols. The traditional feudal Devil had been condemned as a rebel against his liege lord; the individualist Devil, struggling against hypocrisy, could be praised as a saint and martyr.

Such positive views of Satan were symbolic rather than literal. The depersonalization of Satan, his reduction to a symbol, and the unmooring of the symbol from Bible and tradition meant that the idea of the Devil could float free of its traditional meanings. The nineteenth-century Devil was good as well as evil, urbane as well as brutal, a proponent of love as well as a lord of strife. Since the history of the Devil in this period from the end of the eighteenth century to about 1860 is more symbolic than theological, the emphasis of this chapter is more literary than philosophical.[1]

The Devil and radical evil were not subjects that preoccupied the leading philosophers and theologians of the period. Materialism, pragmatism, and skepticism of religion dominated. Auguste Comte (1798–1857) formulated the theory of positivism, in which human society was assumed to have advanced through three stages: theological (the effort to understand by revelation), metaphysical (the effort to understand by logic), and positive (the effort to understand by empirical science). The positive stage, the modern period, was characterized by rejection of belief in anything that could not be demonstrated empirically and scientifically. Even though positivism rested upon empirically unverifiable acts of faith that overall human progress exists, that reality is ultimately

1. The Devil took on a variety of forms in art as well, often in satires combining skepticism of the traditional Devil with insight into human evil. The most notable is the long series of paintings by Goya (Francisco Goya y Lucientes, 1746–1828). See also the *Walpurgisnacht* of Ferdinand Delacroix (1798–1863), William Blake's numerous illustrations of the subject, and the famous engravings illustrating Dante and Milton by Gustave Doré (1832–1883).

material, and that the human mind can grasp this material reality, it was pressed with vigor; its influence became enormous.

Ludwig Andreas Feuerbach (1804–1872) used positivism to attack Christianity. Nothing exists except matter, said Feuerbach; anything else is mere speculation having no foundation. All the attributes we assign to God are actually human conceptions projected upon the deity. The same, naturally, is true of the Devil. Ethical philosophers such as Jeremy Bentham (1748–1832) and John Stuart Mill (1806–1872) constructed their systems without reference to a transcendent power of evil. Theologians avoided the question, and the most original theologian of the century, Søren Kierkegaard (1813–1855)—though he had much to say about alienation, anxiety, and despair—held that the concept of the Devil had become so trivial that it actually weakened our sense of the problem of evil.

The Catholic revival after 1815 did little to convince society at large of the Devil's existence. Still, the church continued to affirm its traditional teachings. Gregory XVI (1831–1846), fearing the identification of the church with fading royalism, tried briefly to free Catholic theology from scholasticism but soon restrained his liberalism; Pius IX (1846–1878) flirted briefly with liberalism but, shocked by the revolutions of 1848, returned to a rigidly traditionalist view. Joseph de Maistre (1753–1821) had already identified the Devil with revolution, disorder, disunity, moral degeneracy, and disrespect for proper authority, notably pope and king. Pius IX condemned liberalism in his *Syllabus errorum* (1864) and defended the return to scholasticism against those who, like John Henry Newman (1801–1890), favored a historical and developmental approach. The triumph of the scholastics was assured by the encyclical *Aeterni patris* of Leo XIII (1879), which declared Thomist theology eternally valid. In such an atmosphere, the objective reality of the Devil was widely assumed.[2] Until the 1960s, when Catholicism began to retreat from its own epistemological foundations in scripture and tradition, the existence of the Devil as a personal entity was included in the official line of the Catholic Church.

In Protestantism, growing disregard for church unity and for apos-

2. The First Vatican Council (1869–1870), in renewing the decree *Firmiter* of the Fourth Lateran Council (see LUCIFER, pp. 189–190), did not include the specific affirmation of the Devil's existence, though no contradiction of *Firmiter* on this point was implied. See First Vatican, *Constitutio dogmatica* no. 1: *De fide, caput primum, De Deo rerum omnium creatore*. For the First Vatican, see J. Mansi, *Sacrorum conciliorum nova et amplissima collectio*, vols. 49–53 (Graz, 1961).

Engraving from a nineteenth-century catechism, contrasting the death of the sinner (below) with the death of the just man (above). The sinner's guardian angel departs, while demons pull him down toward hell. Courtesy Photo Jean-Loup Charmet, Paris.

tolic succession had long undermined the authority of tradition; the increasing acceptance of higher biblical criticism undermined the authority of scripture as well. With the weakening of these twin pillars of Christian epistemology, first theologians, then preachers, and finally the laity questioned nearly every aspect of Christian belief: heaven, the soul, immortality, sin, redemption, and certainly hell and the Devil. By 1898 the English statesman and churchman William Ewart Gladstone could speak of hell as a shadowy thing relegated to the dusty corners of the Christian mind.[3] Unmoored from its epistemological anchor, liberal Protestantism drifted with secular trends and fashions, tending to reject the Devil (and eventually God) as old-fashioned and outdated. One growing trend of nineteenth-century theology was universalism, the belief that in the end everyone, including Satan, will be saved. Two groups may be distinguished: "soft" universalists holding to a weak, progressive optimism derived from the progressivism of liberal secularists, and "hard" universalists affirming the reality of evil but also the merciful plan of God to transform it into good.[4] In any form, universalism ran the risk of promoting relativism, undermining free will and moral choice, and denying radical evil.

Against liberal Protestantism a counterforce gradually asserted itself, exerted by those who continued loyal to the Reformation faith in scripture and who affirmed the incarnation, the resurrection, and other Christian doctrines on the authority of the Bible. Rejecting compromise with secularism and denying the validity of the higher criticism, these "conservatives," along with traditional Roman Catholics and Eastern Orthodox, tended also to affirm the reality of the Devil. However, the emphasis of conservative Protestants upon the Bible to the exclusion of tradition produced its own inconsistencies, for, like Luther, its exponents tended to ignore the fact that the Christian doctrine of Satan is more traditional than biblical. The kernel of the idea of Satan is certainly present in the New Testament, but the full doctrine developed only gradually. This poses no problem for one who perceives the essential historical and developmental nature of all Christian doctrine; however, for one who believes that the truth lies only in the earliest statements of Christian doctrine, the theology of the Devil is precarious—

3. Quoted in G. Rowell, *Hell and the Victorians: A Study of the Nineteenth-Century Theological Controversies concerning Eternal Punishment and the Future Life* (Oxford, 1974), p. 212.

4. Rowell, pp. 217–218.

along with other historically developed ideas such as the identification of Christ with the second person of the Trinity. Each in its own way, both "liberal" and "conservative" sides tended to cut themselves off from the historical development of Christianity which alone gives it form and definition. Cut off from a sound epistemological basis, Christianity as a whole continued to retreat in the face of the intellectually more consistent forces of positivism and materialism.

Even more than by positivism, the early nineteenth century was dominated by Romanticism, a fuzzy-bordered concept that developed in the second half of the eighteenth century. Less an intellectual movement than a literary and artistic reaction against the neoclassicism that had dominated the arts since the seventeenth century, Romanticism in various forms flavored Western thought through the 1860s and even down to 1914.

The elements of this vaguely defined movement included an emphasis upon the esthetic and the emotional as against the rational and the intellectual. Whether a thing was powerfully affecting was more important than whether it was true; the emotions were a surer guide to life than the intellect. This belief encouraged a psychological penetration that prepared for the birth of depth psychology later in the nineteenth century. Romanticism exalted the virtues of love, pity, and mercy against rational and scientific calculation, but the tendency to dismiss reason led to wishful thinking, individualism and selfishness, and a self-satisfied, elitist contempt for those considered less fine, noble, or sensitive. The focus upon the subjective and the interior life pitted the Romantics against both traditional Christianity and emerging science. The search for the emotionally and psychologically stimulating encouraged a taste for the miraculous, the supernatural, the weird, and the grotesque—witness the penchant for oriental tales such as the *Thousand and One Nights* early in the nineteenth century and for medievalism after 1815.

The late eighteenth-century concept of the "sublime" lay close to the heart of Romanticism. As expressed by its most articulate exponent, Edmund Burke (1729–1797), the sublime was to be contrasted with the merely beautiful.[5] The sublime in nature consisted of grandeur, obscurity, vastness, privation, and magnificence and was often accompanied

5. E. Burke, *A Philosophical Enquiry of the Origin of the Sublime and the Beautiful* (1757), ed. J. T. Boulton (New York, 1958). The term "sublime" ceased to be fashionable by 1800.

by the experience of terror in the beholder. In humanity it consisted of the individual quest for honor and glory against all odds. Terror, suffering, danger, and heroism were thought to tap the most profound and powerful human emotions and call forth the highest manifestations of the human spirit. God and the Devil were the ultimate symbols of the sublime, but Burke and the Romantics traced the sense of sublimity to inspirations in nature and humanity rather than to God.

Intensely concerned with the conflict of good and evil within the human breast, the Romantics used Christian symbols for esthetic and mythopoeic purposes, usually without much regard for their theological content, thus encouraging the unmooring of such symbols from their basic meanings. In a world view that eschewed logic in favor of emotion there were bound to be many contradictions. The Romantics' concern with good and evil led them to an intense ambivalence about the world. On the one hand they affirmed the optimistic faith that human progress would destroy tyranny and lead to a new world of freedom; on the other they saw humanity at the mercy of selfishness and viciousness. This ambivalence led some of the more thoughtful Romantics toward the coincidence of opposites: the eventual reunion of God and Satan, and the integration and transcendence of the opposing elements of the human psyche. The views of Carl G. Jung at the beginning of the next century were prepared for and anticipated by Romanticism.

The Romantics also expressed dissatisfaction with the bourgeois domination of ideas after the Revolution. Their esthetic bent encouraged them to adopt behavior, dress, manners, and views designed to *épater les bourgeois* and confound the philistines. Later in the century, when Romanticism transposed into decadence and dandyism, Oscar Wilde would flout convention with his green carnation, his velveteen suits, his poppy, his epigrams, and his scandalous sex life.

The Romantic distaste for the church was reciprocated, and clerical attacks on the Romantics only intensified their view that Christianity was evil and its opponents good. It followed that if the greatest enemy of traditional Christianity was Satan, then Satan must be good. This was a philosophically incoherent statement contradicting the core meaning of the Devil, and indeed the Romantics intended such a statement not as a theological proposition but rather as an imaginative challenge and a political program. In his rebellion against unjust and repressive authority, the Devil was a hero. The Romantic idea of the hero, derived from the concept of the sublime, stands in contradiction to the classical epic notion of the hero as one devoted to the welfare of his family and people. The Romantic hero is individual, alone against the world, self-assertive, ambitious, powerful, and liberator in rebellion against the society that blocks the way of progress toward liberty, beauty, and love; the Romantics read these qualities into Milton's Satan. Their admiration for Satan was not Satanism, however—not the worship of evil—for they made the Devil the symbol of what they regarded as good.

Four different aspects of the demonic in art exist. The first is a popular misreading of the artist's intention, as when an audience misunderstands the composer's use of musical dissonance as demonic. The second is a deliberate portrayal of the demonic—as in Moussorgsky's *Night on Bald Mountain* or Shostakovitch's *War and Peace* quartet—but with the intent of condemning the evil. The third is the actual exaltation of evil, as in the performance of certain rock music groups of the late twentieth century. The fourth, characteristic of the Romantics, is the deliberate shift of demonic symbols away from evil toward good. Since the Romantics' view of good was not radically different from the Christian view of good, and since the Romantics themselves were inconsistent in the degree to which they shifted the symbols, their symbolism was incoherent. Their tendency was to transpose the Christian God into a symbol of evil, the Christian idea of humanity into God (in the sense that humanity became the ultimate concern), and the Christian Satan into a hero.

Because of the difficulty inherent in shifting symbols so radically, some of the Romantics chose mythological figures other than Satan to represent the rebellious hero. The eighteenth century had transformed Brutus from traitor to revolutionary hero in its political symbolism; the Romantics in their moral and psychological symbolism would praise Prometheus and Cain (though not Judas). The merging of Prometheus and Satan was one of the crucial symbolic transformations. The traditional Prometheus and Satan had much in common: their rebellion against divine authority, their inevitable defeat and doom, and their sentence to be bound in eternal chains. But there was also a powerful difference: Prometheus did not challenge the gods from selfishness or hatred but from a desire to help humanity. The melding of the two heroes enabled the positive elements of Prometheus to be transferred to Satan, so that the Devil might also appear as a noble liberator of humanity.

The Romantic Satan was not always positive; he could also be evil, symbolizing isolation, unhappiness, hardness of heart, lack of love, insensitivity, ugliness, and sarcasm. The growth of medievalism helped to restore some of the medieval sense of the evil Devil, whom the Romantics saw as impeding the progress of the human spirit and as the representation of destructive forces within the soul. There was, then, no one Romantic Satan or even two, but virtually as many Satans as there were Romantics. Their use of Satan was seldom designed as serious intellectual comment on the principle of evil, and even when it was, it lacked any epistemological basis in logic, science, revelation, tradition, the Bible, or any other specific source. Whether one is a Christian, an idealist, a materialist, or a scientist, one finds such views incoherent and inconsistent.

The Romantic ideas of the Devil had little ultimate impact upon the concept of the Devil. Today one takes either the traditional view or the Enlightenment view, but rarely the Romantic view. Nonetheless, Romanticism did leave some traces: by dramatizing the real conflict of good and evil within the human spirit and by shaking Christian thought violently out of its complacency about the problem of evil, it laid the foundation for a twentieth-century revival of serious theological concern with the problem of evil.

One reflection of the Romantic treatment of evil was the Gothic novel or *roman noir*, popular first in Britain and then on the continent in the late eighteenth and early nineteenth centuries. By 1834, when the *roman noir* was already past its peak, Théophile Gautier wrote in *Le Figaro* that one could now scarcely read a novel, hear a play, or listen to a story without being beset by mystical, angelic, diabological, or kabbalistic concepts.[6] Like a twentieth-century horror film, the Gothic novel used—or degraded—the "sublime" to produce thrills. Its favorite theme was the decay underlying the veneer of the apparently good, rational, and familiar. It was rich in the wild aspects of nature and the world—crags, caves, and castles—as well as the grotesque and decadent in human nature. Physical and moral deformity, sadism, sexual frenzy, distant lands, and medieval times were typical elements. The macabre aspects of the supernatural, including witches, ghosts, phantoms, vampires, and demons, were especially favored. The Devil often made an appearance but less as a serious symbol of evil than as one among many evil monsters designed to entertain and thrill the reader.

One of the most demonic Gothic novels was Matthew Lewis' *The Monk* (1796), which had enormous influence on English, French, and

6. M. Milner, *Le Diable dans la littérature française*, 2 vols. (Paris, 1960), vol. 1, p. 520, citing *Le Figaro* of May 3, 1834.

German literature.[7] Written when Lewis was only nineteen, it contains ghosts, incest, poisons, visions, rape, drugs, and whatever else a sex-crazed adolescent mind of the time could conjure up. Ambrosio, a monk who outwardly appears ascetic, is actually boiling with sexual passions. Dominated by spiritual pride, this cleric of that notoriously degenerate and sensual body, the Catholic Church, is easily corrupted by Satan. Abetted by the Devil, he plunges into ever deeper and more grotesque vices, finally ravishing the virgin Antonia in a dark vault upon the brittle bones of long-deceased monks. For Antonia, "to linger out a life of misery in a narrow loathsome cell, known to exist by no human Being save her Ravisher, surrounded by mouldering Corses, breathing the pestilential air of corruption, never more to behold the light, or drink the pure gale of heaven, the idea was more terrible than She could support." She need not have fretted, for Ambrosio proceeds to murder her. English readers could enjoy the moral sense of being instructed about the evils of Catholicism while being entertained by Lewis's lurid prose. But Ambrosio's evil was limited to the narrow purviews of his author's adolescent lust; it fails to plumb the depths, as Sade had done and Lautréamont would do later. Further, such excesses were grist to the mills of satirists, who produced a number of parodies of the Gothic tale that served to trivialize the Devil further. Along with the specters and ghouls with which he was associated, Satan became more than ever a comic figure.

Perhaps the most original artist and writer of the period was William Blake (1757–1827), whose mythology and symbolism showed some Romantic characteristics but were so individual as to defy categories. Rejecting Christian orthodoxy and avoiding Christian worship, Blake nonetheless affirmed that "Man must and will have Some Religion: if he has not the Religion of Jesus, he will have the Religion of Satan."[8] Blake constructed his own religion; whether or not he believed in a spiritual reality beyond the human mind, he found the resources and symbols of his religion in his own imagination.

7. Other influential Gothic novels included Horace Walpole, *The Castle of Otranto* (1764); Ann Radcliffe, *The Mysteries of Udolpho* (1794); Walter Scott, *The Black Dwarf* (1816); Charles Robert Maturin, *Melmoth the Wanderer* (1820); Matthew G. Lewis, *The Isle of Devils* (1827). See also C. O. Parsons, *Witchcraft and Demonology in Scott's Fiction* (Edinburgh, 1964); and for other Romantic works dealing with the Devil, see the bibliographies in Milner and in H. Vatter, *The Devil in English Literature* (Bern, 1978).

8. W. Blake, *Jerusalem*, Pt. 52. A recent edition of Blake's works is G. Keynes, ed., *The Complete Writings of William Blake* (London, 1966).

William Blake's *Satan Watching Adam and Eve*, pen and watercolor, 1808, shows the envious Evil One already entwined with a serpent. Courtesy of Museum of Fine Arts, Boston.

Since his symbols lacked explicit consistency, it is difficult to define what he meant by the Devil. For Blake, as for the Romantics, both the Devil and God were morally ambivalent. Consequently, when Blake spoke of the Devil, he was only sometimes using the symbol in its conventional negative sense; and when he spoke of God, he was often using that symbol in an unconventional negative sense to mean something like what Christians meant by the term Devil. For Blake, what was good was the poetic imagination, artistic inspiration, creativity; and this could be called either God or Devil. The moment of poetic inspiration, he held, was always free from evil. Divinity for Blake was everywhere, a pulsing reality ever ready to express itself in music, art, or literature. Emotions, sensitivity, love, and commitment were all manifestations of the divine spirit, while "every obstruction to Art and to intuitive Genius is Satanic (evil)."[9] But this evil was manifest, Blake believed, in the traditional view of God, whom Blake called, among other unflattering epithets, Nobodaddy (no one's daddy); in this sense, God was an evil tyrant, like Shelley's Jupiter or Swinburne's "supreme evil, God."[10] A God who is the supreme evil is clearly the traditional Devil; by "God," therefore, Blake and the Romantics often meant "the Devil."

In other words, one must often look for the Romantics' idea of the Evil One under the name of "God." Their point in reversing the symbols was that the traditional Christian view had created a God who was really an evil tyrant. Blake believed that Jesus had understood the true religion of love, sensitivity, and spirituality but that Christians had forgotten that religion and created in its place a tyrannical system of reason and external morality. Blake viewed abstract reasoning as the heart of evil and despised Enlightenment rationalism at least as much as he did traditional Christianity. For him, the philosophes had been right in criticizing Christianity but entirely wrong in the direction they took. Reason was to be rejected in favor of feeling and love, just as feeling and love were to take the place of all external authority, whether of priests, kings, teachers, or parents. Like Rousseau, Blake believed that human nature was essentially good and needed only to be freed from false external restraints to allow loving creativity to spring forth. Yet Blake

9. Quoted in T. A. Birrell, "The Figure of Satan in Milton and Blake," in Bruno de Jésus-Marie, ed., *Satan* (New York, 1952), p. 391. See also R. D. Stock, *The Holy and the Daemonic from Sir Thomas Browne to William Blake* (Princeton, 1982).

10. A. C. Swinburne, "Choruses from Atalanta in Calydon."

also attacked the easy optimism of the Enlightenment. "Man," he said, "is born a Spectre or Satan, and is altogether Evil, and requires a New Selfhood continually."[11]

Blake's "Devil" therefore carried two opposite meanings. In his poem *Milton* (1804), Satan's self-righteousness makes him evil, yet his rebellion against the divine tryant makes him good. And for Blake, Milton's God is at least as evil as Milton's Satan.

Blake was naturally attracted by the idea of the coincidence of opposites, which appears most clearly in his *Marriage of Heaven and Hell* (1790), written in part to elucidate Emanuel Swedenborg's *Heaven and Hell*, which had influenced Blake earlier in his life. In the *Marriage*, Satan is the symbol of creativity. He is activity, energy struggling to be free. Milton, Blake believed, unconsciously realized that active "evil" is better than passive "good." "The reason Milton wrote in fetters when he wrote of Angels and God, and at liberty when of Devils and Hell, is because he was a true Poet and of the Devil's party without knowing it."[12] Jesus himself was really Satanic in that he acted from impulse, not from rules, and cheerfully "broke all the commandments."[13] The loving Jesus is contrasted with Jehovah, God the Father, Milton's judgmental God, who is really evil.

No goods or evils were absolute for Blake. "All Deities reside in the Human breast," and no element of the psyche is wholly good or evil.[14] True evil arises from the lack of integration of psychic elements; true good from the balance, union, and integration of the opposites. For the original title page of the *Marriage*, Blake drew an angel and a demon embracing. Reason and energy, love and hatred, the passive and the active, apparent good and apparent evil, must all merge in a transcendent, integrated whole of which creativity will be the leading spirit. The true God is poetic creativity, that spirit, poet, maker, who makes not only art but in a real sense the entire world, for the whole cosmos is a creation of the poetic spirit. Whether Blake ultimately believed that the external cosmos is a poem of a Great Creator or that humans create their own cosmos is unclear. Disdaining reason as a guide to ultimate truth, Blake made no effort at philosophical or cosmological consisten-

---

11. *Jerusalem*, pt. 52.
12. W. Blake, *The Marriage of Heaven and Hell*, "The Voice of the Devil."
13. *Marriage of Heaven and Hell*, conclusion.
14. *Marriage of Heaven and Hell*, "Proverbs of Hell."

William Blake's *Christ Tempted by Satan to Turn the Stones into Bread* depicts the Devil as a wise old man, in a deliberate statement of moral ambiguity: Christ and Satan appear almost as doublets locked in a dance. Watercolor with india ink and gray wash, 1816–1818. Courtesy Fitzwilliam Museum, Cambridge.

cy. The true God expressed itself in human creativity: that was all he needed to know.

The First Book of Urizen (1794) again shows the interchangeability of the terms "God" and "Devil." Urizen is the old creator God, the Ancient of Days, the blind tyrant; he represents Jehovah, the Old Testament God of laws, the principle of reason. His act of creation is evil because it sets rules and limits (Greek *horizein:* to limit) in the cosmos, which otherwise would be free to express its creativity. Against Urizen stands Orc, representing revolution and the force of liberation from blind tyranny, yet the violence and hostility of Orc make him Satanic in the evil as well as in the good sense. All of Blake's mythical supernatural beings, the Zoas, have Satanic qualities of one kind or another—nature itself is an ambivalence of good and evil—but in all this confused struggle there is a groping toward brotherhood and love. Blake was Christian enough to see this ideal best expressed in Jesus, and he considered it a cruel irony that the followers of Jesus had remade him into a version of his tyrant Father: "Thinking as I do that the Creator of this World is a very Cruel Being, and being a worshiper of Christ, I cannot help saying: 'The Son, O how unlike the Father!'"[15]

No one familiar with Blake can fail to sense his deep empathetic understanding of evil, most poignantly stated in "The Sick Rose":

> O Rose, thou art sick!
> The invisible worm
> That flies in the night,
> In the howling storm,
> Hath found out thy bed
> Of crimson joy:
> And his dark secret love
> Does thy life destroy.[16]

Blake and the Romantics opened the doors of perception into the depths

---

15. Quoted in K. Raine, *William Blake* (London, 1970), p. 86. See also K. Raine, *Blake and Tradition*, 2 vols. (Princeton, 1968), vol. 2, pp. 214–238, for the figure of Satan in Blake. Blake was as creative in the pictorial arts as in poetry. Among his artistic works dealing with Satan are *The Marriage of Heaven and Hell* (1790); *The Good and Evil Angels* (1795); *Satan Watching Adam and Eve* (1808); *Satan Tempting Christ to Turn the Stone into Bread* (1816–1818); *Christian and Apollyon* (from Bunyan; 1824); *Michael Binding Satan* (c. 1805); *Satan Killing the Children of Job* (1825); *Satan Smiting Job with Sore Boils* (c. 1826–1827); *Satan, Sin, and Death* (c. 1808).

16. *Complete Writings*, p. 213.

of the psyche to a degree unprecedented except by the mystics, and in this sense they advanced the understanding of the true nature of evil. It is in such understanding, rather than in their idiosyncratic and incoherent use of symbols, that their contribution to the concept of the Devil is to be sought.

Blake was followed in England by the poets of high Romanticism, such as George Gordon, Lord Byron (1788–1824). Byron revolted as a youth against his Calvinist upbringing and remained throughout his life an opponent of traditional Christian views of evil. Of original sin and redemption he asked: "What have we / Done that we must be victims for a deed / Before our birth, or need have victims to / Atone for this mysterious, nameless sin?" Still, like Blake, Byron was sharply aware of the problem of evil; indeed, it was the degree of evil in the world that convinced him that the Creator could not be good. His Cain demands, "And yet my sire [Adam] says he's [God's] omnipotent. / Then why is evil, he being good?" Later, Lucifer asks Cain, "What does thy God love?" And Cain can only reply, "All things, my father says, but I confess / I see it not in their allotment here." When Lucifer claims to be eternal himself, Cain quickly counters by asking whether he can do humanity any good and, if so, why he has not done it already. Lucifer's riposte is just as quick: Why hasn't Jehovah?[17]

In such a world, Byron was torn between the Romantic optimism that human liberty would eventually triumph and a pessimism derived from his observation of reality. Lucifer speaks from cruel knowledge of the fate awaiting us, the descendants of Cain: "The sixty-thousandth generation shall be / In its dull damp degeneracy, to Thee and thy son" (*Cain*, 2.276–278; cf. 2.424–432). Human dignity lies in eternal striving toward freedom, even though we must not expect to succeed. Metaphorically speaking, we once lived in an age of innocence from which we have fallen owing to our self-consciousness. This self-consciousness has bound us to a set of tyrannical laws, rules, and rational postulates that imprison and starve the life of the soul. Through knowledge of love and liberty we can rebel against the tyranny of government, church, philosophy, science, and morality, all of which repress our divine creativity. The act of artistic creation is the best rebellion against this stifling conformity, a thrust toward freedom and intensity of experience. For Byron, the natural harmony of seals and sparrows was not

17. Byron, *Cain*, in *The Poetical Works of Lord Byron* (London, 1960), 3.88–91; 1.144–147; 2.490, 515–517.

enough for humans, who require a balance of harmony and intensity. The poet, rebelling against the forces of convention and tyranny, is linked with the great figures of rebellion in the Christian and classical traditions: Satan, Cain, and Prometheus.

Byron's Devil appears in a number of forms.[18] The poetic drama *Cain: A Mystery* (1821) best expresses Byron's views of evil and rebellion. The poet reconstructs the character of Cain, adding to the original figure in Genesis the Promethean elements of benevolence toward humanity and the Satanic (Miltonic) elements of the sublime. The character Lucifer is himself ambivalent, good in his support of Cain's rebellion against tyranny, yet evil in his ironic distance from human suffering. His essential flaw is that he lacks the love needed for redemption.

Early in the poem Lucifer instructs Cain that God rules the world with rigid, unjust laws. Cain's wife/sister Adah expresses the traditional line that God is both good and omnipotent (1.387–388), but for Byron, Jehovah is ambivalent, both evil and good (1.137–163). Jehovah is a pathetic symbol of human striving, creating world after world in an effort to alleviate his loneliness and isolation, and one after another finding them defective and destroying them. Cain is enraged at such apparent wantonness, but it is Jehovah's nature. Like humanity in general and the poet in particular, Jehovah is both maker and destroyer (1.147–163, 264, 529–530). Lucifer is ready to announce the double truth that Jehovah is both good and evil and that the cosmos he has created is both beautiful and cruel. In this he speaks for Byron: any understanding of the world that sees only the beauty or only the cruelty is false. In the light of Jehovah's ambivalence, it is unclear whether he puts the tree of the knowledge of good and evil in the garden to help or hinder us, and whether Adam and Eve were justified in taking its fruit for themselves. The conflict between the demands of Jehovah and those of Lucifer represent a conflict within the human soul, not between good and evil but between various ambivalences that should be transcended and integrated but may perhaps never be.

Lucifer sneeringly asks Cain who the real Devil is: Lucifer, who wanted Adam and Eve to have knowledge and prompted the serpent to tell them the truth about the tree, or Jehovah, who drove them out of

18. In *The Deformed Transformed* (1824), an unfinished drama modeled on *Faust*, the Devil is "a stranger" later named "Caesar"; in *The Vision of Judgment* (1822), Satan appears as a haughty dignitary; in the dramatic poem *Manfred* (1817), the hero Satanically (in the good sense) defies the evil lord Arimanes (Ahriman), who is Satanic in the evil, tyrannical sense.

the garden into exile and death (1.204–207, 220–230). But though Jehovah is lawbound, insensitive, and sometimes cruel, the rebellious Lucifer is at least as evil as his counterpart—really more so, because Jehovah, for all his faults, feels the pull of creative love, which Lucifer cannot grasp (2.515–531). Though he promotes intellectual freedom and progress, Lucifer is deliberately blind, self-absorbed, and selfish. He argues for creativity but ultimately creates nothing. While inveighing against God's cold rationality, he himself uses reason and dialectic cynically in order to make his argument. He lies to Cain, suppressing the truth that he shares in the world's cruelty. Cain, already dissatisfied and bitter, listens to him readily when he appears, whereas to Adah, Lucifer is scarcely visible.[19] Worst of all, Lucifer rejects the only road to a good cosmos, the integration of himself with Jehovah, preferring instead to blame everything on God and demanding that humans replace their servitude to God with servitude to himself. His vindictiveness and hatred of God's cosmos is limitless:

> All, all will I dispute. And world by world
> And star by star and universe by universe
> Shall tremble in the balance, till the great
> Conflict shall cease, if ever it shall cease,
> Which it ne'er shall, till he or I be quenched. . . .
> He as a conqueror will call the conquered
> Evil, but what will be the good he gives?
> Were I the victor, his works would be decreed
> The only evil ones. [2.641–651]

Lucifer has the Miltonic/Satanic virtues of grandeur and sublimity and the Romantic heroic virtue of rebellion and persistence against odds. He speaks for Byron when he praises

> Souls who dare us their immortality,
> Souls who dare look the omnipotent tyrant in
> His everlasting face and tell him that
> His evil is not good! [1.137–140]

Lucifer's lack of love, however, means that the strife in the cosmos will continue until the cosmos is destroyed. Ultimately, Lucifer's evil lies in his desire to live forever independently of God (1.116). His claim

---

19. God is always invisible: *Cain* 1.500–505.

to be everlasting (1.121) is true only in the sense that he is everlastingly alienated by his failure to embrace the love that would be death to selfishness.

Both Jehovah and Lucifer are within Cain and know his thoughts (1.100–104). Cain, representing humanity in general, resolves the conflict between the two forces in the wrong way. Instead of integrating them, he follows Lucifer's suggestions and attacks the Jehovah side of himself. Prompted by Lucifer, he kills his brother Abel under the delusion that he is striking a blow against the tyranny of Jehovah. His desire for vengeance blots out love; his search for abstract justice blinds him to the flesh-and-blood reality of his brother. His act reinforces humanity's failure to open itself to the love that would knit us together. Byron believed that however unlikely the chances of success, we must keep struggling to reverse that failure and to integrate good and evil. Both God and Devil partake of the Satanic, but neither is truly evil. The truly Satanic is the unresolved tension between them. True evil lies in the opposition of the two psychic principles, true good in their reconciliation.

Percy Bysshe Shelley (1792–1822) was interested from his youth in the demonic and the occult for their esthetic effects of terror and sublimity. Shelley was expelled from Oxford in 1811 for publishing a pamphlet called "The Necessity of Atheism," and throughout his life he continued to reject traditional Christianity and all "organized religion." He gradually adopted a personal religion of the spirit of love in nature and in humanity but refused to call his spirit God because of the cruelty associated with the Christian deity. Jesus himself, he argued, had taught the gospel of love in rebellion against organized religion. Shelley's religion was evolutionary, almost vitalistic, influenced by Erasmus Darwin and similar to the idealistic progressivism of Hegel: the spirit of love is moving humanity and the cosmos toward a better, freer, more loving future. Shelley was deeply aware that evil is continually blocking this benign progress, but he rejected the Christian Devil on the basis that all we can know is the product of the human mind. Shelley perceived Satan as the symbol of the obstructive and regressive tendencies within humanity.

On the Devil and Devils (1820–1821) reveals Shelley's intense preoccupation with the problem of evil. Manicheism, he believed, was no more true than Christianity, but it fit the psychic facts better. The Manichean view that there are two spirits of balanced power and opposite dispositions represented an insight into the divided state of the human soul. The Christian view of a Devil subject to the divine will, especially the diluted Satan of Christian liberalism, seemed to Shelley to evade psychic reality. Yet Shelley was as ambivalent about the figure of Satan as Blake or Byron. On the one hand he insisted that a truly Satanic figure was needed to express the reality of human evil; on the other he took Satan as the symbol of the progressive spirit rebelling against the established forces of repression. Like Blake, he admired Milton's Satan as the greatest literary example of the spirit of sublime rebellion, the archetypal Romantic hero pledging his very essence to the struggle against tyranny.

Nothing can exceed the energy and magnificence of the character of Satan as expressed in "Paradise Lost." It is a mistake to suppose that he could ever have been intended for the popular personification of evil. . . . Milton's Devil as a moral being is as far superior to his God as One who perseveres in some purpose which he has conceived to be excellent in spite of adversity and torture, is to One who in the cold security of his undoubted triumph inflicts the most horrible revenge upon his enemy. . . . Milton . . . alleged no superiority of moral virture to his God over his Devil. And this bold neglect of a direct moral purpose is the most decisive proof of the supremacy of Milton's genius.[20]

Chagrined as Milton would have been at this interpretation of his epic, it epitomized the Romantics' reading of it, and in this sense Milton's Satan became the greatest of the Romantic Devils, the archetype of the Romantic hero.

For Shelley, evil was better represented by the demonic in humanity than by Satan, whose moral character he saw as good or at least ambivalent. In *The Cenci* (1819), a play in the Gothic vein, Francesco Cenci is a totally evil character who callously seduces his daughter and rejoices at the death of his sons. Francesco represents the extension of the process, visible in Shakespeare's Iago, of transferring evil from an external power to the human soul. What need have we of a Devil, Shelley seems to ask, when we have humanity? The Devil is a figure that we invent in order to project our own vices upon something external. It is we who are the source and center of evil, not he.

In *Prometheus Unbound* (1820) Shelley used Prometheus (as Byron used Cain) as the symbol of rebellion. In the preface Shelley claimed similarities between his work and *Paradise Lost*: he meant Prometheus to resemble Milton's Satan in courage, majesty, and opposition to omnipo-

20. Shelley, *Defence of Poetry* (Indianapolis, 1965), p. 60.

tent tyranny; however, like Byron, he saw the drawbacks in making Satan the hero of a poem. Even the Romantic Satan was too ambivalent, for Shelley needed his hero to be the incarnation of love, whereas Satan was ambitious, envious, aggressive, and vengeful as well as a rebel. Prometheus was a better symbol; his rebellion, defeat, and bondage were the result not of his faults but of his love for humanity. Prometheus symbolizes Christ, who sacrifices himself for the good of his people; humanity, which struggles toward freedom under the guidance of the spirit of love; and the poet, whose love and creative word are weapons against the darkness. Thus the symbolic cluster around Prometheus comprises Christ, humanity, the poet, Shelley, and Satan (in his good aspects). Prometheus' antagonist is Jupiter, a wholly evil tyrant; the symbolic cluster around Jupiter includes Jehovah and Satan (in his evil aspects).

Prometheus is a Titan, a member of the race that classical mythology represents as impious rebels against the Olympian gods. But Shelley's Prometheus loves humanity and is distressed to see it kept in bondage and ignorance by the Olympians. The poem begins with a reproach to Olympian Jupiter, whose haughty arrogance sets him forever apart from the reality that is love. Prometheus' gift of knowledge to humanity is rewarded by Jupiter with a terrible punishment: the noble Titan is chained to a rock for eternity, while a bird of prey, "heaven's winged hound," plucks at his liver—which is eternally regenerated in order to prolong his torment. Prometheus' self-sacrifice parallels that of Christ, but his predicament is also that of humanity, for we too are bound by the tyrant's chains. Still, we place these chains upon ourselves, for we know the truth and refuse to act by it. Jupiter is only a projection of the tyranny that lies within: our own willful ignorance, selfishness, and vengefulness. Prometheus will not be freed until his understanding of himself and reality allows him to cease cursing his fate, the cosmos, and the gods. He must cease hating Jupiter and learn to pity him for his choice of coldness and isolation.

Shelley's optimism exceeded Byron's: to Shelley, the world of freedom and love seemed really obtainable. Evil proceeds from the human mind, from our own choice of selfishness and hatred. To eliminate the evil in the world, we have only to decide to do so. Since we have created Jupiter in our own minds, we can also dismantle him and create a better god. This new god would emerge not from hatred and rebellion, even rebellion against tyranny, but from love for everyone, including ourselves and the Jupiter we have created. Jupiter's chief evil is his refusal to abandon his own arrogant isolation, which makes him inferior to

Prometheus, who can learn to love. If we can integrate and transcend the opposition of Prometheus and Jupiter within ourselves, we shall be ready to proceed on the road that winds upward in peace through the green country of understanding, freedom, and love.

Shelley's wife Mary (1797–1851) had a darker view. Mary Shelley's *Frankenstein, or the Modern Prometheus* (1818) has enjoyed an enduring popularity as entertainment, though the author's philosophical message has generally been ignored. Mary Shelley drew upon the Gothic love of monsters and horrors to entertain, and *Frankenstein* was a bridge between the Gothic and the modern horror tale. It is also one of the original sources for science fiction, for she made some important changes in the Gothic plot: the creator of the monster, Dr. Frankenstein, is no longer a sorcerer or a magician but a scientist; the monster is no medieval demon or specter but a material being of flesh and blood manufactured in a laboratory. *Frankenstein* replaces the old supernatural horror with modern positivist horror.

The author hardly meant this break to be a clean one; indeed, Frankenstein and other human characters in the novel repeatedly call the monster "daemon," "fiend," "devil." But here Mary Shelley's intent was ironic, for the evil lies not so much in the monster as in the humans who create him. The monster becomes evil only because he has been taught evil by humanity. In this lies another shift of symbols, for here humanity symbolizes the creator whose own pride and selfishness spill out to spoil creation; yet the monster (who has no name) also represents the innocent, open aspect of humanity corrupted by its experience of evil. The individual human, Mary Shelley implied, is born innocent and debased; he is destroyed by the viciousness of the world around him. The monster cries out, "I was benevolent and good; misery made me a fiend. Make me happy, and I shall again be virtuous."[21] The monster teaches himself to read from *Paradise Lost* and other books; he compares himself with Adam, who was created good but became miserable, and to Satan, who was wretched in his isolation. Yet even Satan, he exclaims, had his "fellow-devils" (p. 136). As the people whom the monster encounters shun, fear, and despise him, his character is steadily more deformed until he becomes the murdering fiend that people assume him to be.[22]

The monster's last hope of reform lies in Frankenstein's promise to

<hr>

21. Mary Shelley, *Frankenstein* (London, 1818), p. 101.

22. A factual antidote to this pessimism is the life of the historical Elephant Man, who was treated with equal horror and contempt yet maintained a generous heart.

construct a female companion for him, but in the midst of the new experiment the scientist is shaken by revulsion and destroys both the half-formed woman and the equipment. Now the monster pursues his creator with unremitting vengeance, while the latter in turn seeks out his creature to destroy him. Like Byron's God, Frankenstein has made a world that he regrets and wishes to destroy. As each seeks the other, it becomes clear that Frankenstein and his monster are one and the same; they represent two warring aspects of human character. If only we could transcend the conflict within us, Mary agreed with her husband, we could enter a world of peace—but Mary seems closer to Byron in her pessimistic conclusion. After a weird, extended chase through the limitless Arctic night, the two finally meet. But Frankenstein dies of the exhaustion of his long pursuit, and the monster, feeling both frustrated revenge and frustrated love for his creator, vanishes forever into the icy darkness. No reconciliation or integration occurs: both aspects of Frankenstein, both aspects of humanity, perish.

The Gothic, medieval, and marvelous had broad appeal in Germany and France, as well as in England. Nevertheless, François-René de Chateaubriand (1768–1848), virtually the founder of French Romanticism, was an opponent of revolutionary change and therefore saw Milton's Satan differently from Byron or Shelley. His long essay on *Paradise Lost* in *Le génie du christianisme* (1802) expressed admiration for the grandeur of Milton's Satan as the finest product of the Christian imagination but concluded that Satan's rebellion against legitimate authority made him less hero than villain.

By reintroducing the Devil as a serious symbol at the very outset of French Romanticism, Chateaubriand set a tone that was followed throughout the century by other leading authors. In the prose epic *Les Natchez* (1826), Satan appears as a hazy, ill-defined spirit of evil who exhorts the pagan American Indians against Christianity. The Satan of *Les Natchez* wavers on the border between personality and symbol, for the most chilling, evil figure is not Satan but René, the model for a long line of villains in French literature. In *Le génie du christianisme*, Chateaubriand praised the poetic symbolism, ritual, ceremony, symbolism, and morality of Christianity while showing little interest in its traditional theology. His immensely influential prose epic *Les martyrs* (1809) is set during the persecution of the early Christians by the emperor Diocletian, to which the royalist Chateaubriand parallels the persecutions under the Revolution and the Terror. Imitating Milton in a scene where Satan addresses a council of his demonic followers in hell, Chateaubriand painted the Devil as promising fair treatment of humanity while secretly plotting its ruin. As Satan encouraged the Roman persecution of the Christians and did his evil work through Diocletian, so he prompted the Terror and worked his will through Robespierre. To drive his point home, Chateaubriand even had Satan quote the "Marseillaise."[23]

Unlike Chateaubriand, most French writers who followed him in reviving interest in the Devil treated Satan with ironical skepticism or else used him—along with demons, ghosts, and specters—to produce *frissons* of Gothic horror. Many serious writers felt that the Devil had become too trivialized to use effectively in treating evil and preferred to portray evil in such human characters as Chateaubriand's René. Stendhal (1783–1842), famous for his gibe that "God's only excuse is that he does not exist," painted the demonic human figure of Julien Sorel in *Le rouge et le noir* (1830), and Honoré de Balzac (1799–1850) addressed real evil not in his Gothic novels but in his *Comédie humaine*, in which he laid open the cruelty, stupidity, and vice natural to humanity without the intervention of the Devil.[24]

A few writers followed Chateaubriand in taking Christian symbols more seriously. As a child, Alfred de Vigny (1797–1863) had been fascinated by Raphael's painting of Michael slaying the dragon, and Satan remained a powerful symbol throughout his life. Byron's *Cain* reinforced the young poet's interest in the Devil, but his use of Christian mythology was entirely esthetic, for he regarded the Christian

23. Chateaubriand, *Les martyrs*, ed. V. Giraud (Paris, n.d.), p. 141: "Le jour de gloire est arrivé."

24. One writer who made much of demonology was Collin de Plancy (1794–1881) in books such as *Le diable peint par lui-même* (1819), *Démonomanie* (1820), and *Dictionnaire infernale* (1818); see *Dictionnaire infernale: Edition princeps intégrale* (Verviers, 1973). Charles Nodier (1780–1844) used the Devil with ghouls and ghosts to enhance his tales of Gothic horror; Nodier and other French writers of the *roman noir* were following the lead of Jacques Cazotte (1719–1772), whose *Le diable amoureux* (1772), a demonic horror story, influenced both French and German writers. Irony and the excitement of horror surround the figure of Satan in the works of E. T. A. Hoffmann (1776–1822), Jean Paul Richter (1763–1825), and Christian Friedrich Hebbel (1813–1863); see Hoffmann, *Die Elixiere des Teufels*, 2 vols. (Berlin, 1815–1816), and Richter, *Auswahl aus den Teufels Papieren* (n.p., 1789). Jules Michelet (1798–1874) transferred these literary attitudes to pseudohistory in his book on the witch craze, *La sorcière* (1862). Eugène Sue (1804–1875) and Balzac preferred to satirize the evil that exists within humanity. In addition to his "human comedy," Balzac also produced a *Comédie du diable* (1830), in which he uses a banquet of demons to satirize human folly. See also J. P. Houston, *The Demonic Imagination: Style and Theme in French Romantic Poetry* (Baton Rouge, La., 1969).

notion of a good, omnipotent deity as absurd. Since human life is wretched and miserable, the Christian Deity must be either perverted or powerless, and Vigny preferred to think that he did not exist at all. Vigny's works are a cry against the complacency of Christian optimism, a demand that we face the problem of evil with eyes open and without illusion. *Le jugement dernier* and *Satan*, two unfinished poems written between 1819 and 1823, preceded his masterpiece, *Eloa, ou la soeur des anges*.[25] Eloa is a female angel born from the tear that Jesus shed at the death of Lazarus (John 11:35). Her heart is full of compassion for her fellow creatures, and because she finds everyone happy in heaven, she sets out to wander the cosmos in search of someone who needs her help. She hears of an outcast angel who is alone and sad, in need of love and companionship. Unaware that this is Satan and that Satan has committed real evils, she sheds a tear of pity for him as Jesus had wept for Lazarus. Satan, of course, chooses to conceal the truth about himself; he convinces her instead that he is misunderstood:

> He whom they call wicked is really a Consoler
> Who weeps for the slave and frees him from his master,
> Who saves him with his love and with his own suffering.
> Since he is enshrouded in the same common misery,
> He can give the wretched a little sympathy and sometimes blessed
>   forgetfulness. [*Eloa*, 2.212–216]

Vigny's Satan, a pale, voluptuous youth, is the archetype of the languishing beauty that the Romantics idealized. He is torn by Eloa's presence. He knows that he has sinned from pride and arrogance, and he is racked by remorse and grief that he is cut off from the beauty of heaven. Yet he cannot overcome his hatred of God. He uses his beauty, his feigned innocence, and his assumed compassion to impress Eloa, shedding tears as false as those of Jesus and Eloa had been sincere. His response to Eloa's love is as idiotic as Mephistopheles' response to the young angels in *Faust*: he determines to seduce her. Eloa resists, worried about his hostility to God: "How can you love me, if you do not love God?" (3.116). At last she yields, but just at the moment when he shows for an instant a sincere wish to repent, she is distracted and fails to understand him. The moment missed, he returns to his hatred. Under such conditions, Eloa's love cannot relieve his misery, and he drags her

25. Vigny, *Eloa*, published in his *Poèmes antiques et modernes* (Paris, 1826).

Antoine Wiertz, *Angel of Evil*,
right panel of the triptych *Christ
at the Tomb*. Here the ancient tradition that the Devil can appear
as an angel of light blends with
the Romantic conception of the
beauty of Satan. Oil on canvas,
1839. Courtesy Royal Museums
of Fine Arts of Belgium, Brussels
(Collection Wiertzmuseum).

with him down to hell. Only in the last line of the poem does she begin to grasp the truth: "Who are you then?" she cries; the response is, "Satan" (3.268).

The poem expresses a deep pessimism about the ability of love to overcome the bitter barriers of hatred and despair. In this, Vigny's vision was like Byron's. Although he planned a sequel, *Satan sauvé*, in which the dark lord would at last be redeemed,[26] the optimistic poem was never finished, and we are left with a vision that is bleak. Nonetheless, in spite of his religious skepticism, Vigny achieved a more empathetic and psychologically convincing portrait of Satan than had anyone else since Milton himself. It remained for Victor Hugo to deepen the character of the sad, isolated Devil and to render it even more poetically sympathetic.

The Satan of Victor Hugo (1802–1885) is, with that of Byron, among the most effective of the Romantic Devils. Beginning as a rationalist, Hugo as a young man experienced an esthetic conversion to Catholicism but soon abandoned it. Hugo's ideas were never fixed; throughout his life he pursued a wide variety of views—mysticism, gnosticism, occultism, pantheism, materialism, dualism. In true Romantic fashion, Hugo made his judgments less on intellectual than on esthetic and emotional grounds. He insisted upon a God of pity and mercy, hating the traditional doctrines of original sin, salvation through crucifixion, and hell. Humanity was intrinsically good, he believed, and God intrinsically benevolent. He saw the Christian idea of God as false but Jesus himself as a noble, loving teacher of a beautiful ethic, a model for the pursuit of real truth, which is love.

The alleged tension between Jesus and Christianity that characterized so many Enlightenment and Romantic thinkers, and found intellectual roots in the biblical criticism attempting to discover the "historical" Jesus behind the "Christ" of tradition, raises fundamental questions. It has recently been argued that the philosophes and Romantics were revolting not against Christianity but against a false Christianity that perverted the true teaching of Jesus, and that therefore they were "true" Christians as against traditional Christians. This view, which has found many adherents among those who reject "organized religion" in favor of an ethical, esthetic, or sentimental attachment to Jesus, contains a number of incoherencies and inconsistencies. The "historical Jesus" has not been found and almost certainly cannot be found; we have no way

26. Portions were posthumously preserved in Vigny's *Journal d'un poète* (Paris, 1867).

of knowing, historically, what Jesus "really" said or did. What history can do, and with great security and accuracy, is show the development of Christianity and of the view of Christ within Christianity; that is, what we can know historically of Christ is the traditional view of Christ as it developed through the ages. The only way of defining Christianity objectively is to define it as what it is historically. Other definitions all rest upon unproven assumptions. The statement, therefore, that "Christianity is really something other than what it has historically been" is not a meaningful statement, because it rests upon unverifiable and unvalidatable faith assumptions. Hugo and the Romantics *felt* that they had got to the real Jesus behind Christianity. That is possible, but it is not capable of verification.

That Hugo had no rational defense of his view was less important to him than the evidence of his feelings; nonetheless, he could use reason when he liked. He was intensely aware of the problem of evil, and his own kindness and generosity led him to repudiate a God who was able to prevent evil yet chose not to do so. He also rejected the traditional Devil, adapting to his purpose the traditional Platonist/Christian argument of privation: evil is a negation, and no negation can truly exist; only the positive exists. If evil were God, nothing would exist; but we observe that something is. The principle of being must therefore be good.[27]

Though he denied the existence of an absolute evil, Hugo was acutely concerned with the effects of evil in the world. Humanity, basically good, was moving gradually toward perfect love and liberty, he believed, but its progress was blocked by cruelty and by a selfishness attracted to the glamor of evil. Yet we did not create the world, nor did we create the shadow within us, so we are to be pitied for our misfortune rather than blamed for our sin.

With Hugo's ever-changing interests, his use of the Devil was diverse and inconsistent. Since he shared the Gothic love for the medieval and the macabre, his Devil was a fantastic figure, fiend, or monster used to excite terror or thrills; he was a prop in dramas about the Middle Ages such as *Notre-Dame de Paris* (1831), used along with grotesques, witches, and hunchbacks to convey a sense of weird medieval darkness. Medieval settings allowed Hugo to indulge himself in fantastic scenes on the excuse of offering an ironic comment on the supposed medieval mind.

27. *Postscriptum de ma vie* (Paris, 1901), August 25, 1844. On Hugo, see C. Villiers, *L'univers métaphysique de Victor Hugo* (Paris, 1970).

They also permitted him to satirize the Catholic church by satirizing the alleged medieval expression of its views. That Hugo's Middle Ages bore little resemblance to historical reality blunted neither their popularity nor their effectiveness.

Satan was also the symbol of the Revolution. In Hugo's early days, under Chateaubriand's influence, this meant that Satan was a symbol of evil; later, when Hugo came to see the Revolution as advancing human progress, the Satan of the Revolution came to symbolize good. Satan could represent oppressive societies and governments, or he could mean the opposite: rebellion against oppression in the name of freedom. He could be used as one side of an ambivalent duality Satan/God, good/evil, which represented the alienation of humanity from its own inherent goodness. Hugo felt deeply that alienation, defeat, sadness, and regret are as inherent in evil as cruelty and selfishness, and he painted a dimension of evil that hitherto had been neglected: the poignant sadness and isolation of the sinner. Satan was a metaphor of the longing of creation and humanity to be reintegrated into that loving spirit of life from which they had exiled themselves by their own foolishness and selfishness.

Hugo had an optimistic faith that reintegration would occur. A passionate universalist, he believed that the spirit of light is infinite in its mercy and would eventually restore all its lost creatures to the union of love. Until that happy moment, evil would remain a stark reality. "Satan is gluttony; he is a pig that devours thought; he is drunkenness, the dark depths of the drained cup; he is pride lacking knees on which to kneel; egoism, rejoicing in the blood in which his hands are soaked; he is the belly, the hideous cave wherein rage all the monsters that dwell in us."[28]

In his preface to *Cromwell* (1827), a historical drama in verse, Hugo declared the grotesque—in which he included the Devil—a necessary element in modern literature; his *Odes et ballades* (1826) portrayed the demonic in folkloric and medieval style. In his *Pitié suprême* (1879), he demanded the abolition of hell and the merciful pardon of all creatures. In "Les mages" (in *Contemplations*, 1856), he saw evil as the opposite of good: "Humans call it barbarism and crime, the sky calls it night, and God calls it Satan" (ll. 578–580). He could also see the Devil as Mephistopheles—mocking, ironic, supercilious, and world-weary in the mode favored by the French:

28. *Postscriptum*, 1852–1854.

The fellow had troubled eyes,
And on his furrowed forehead
The distortion of two horns
Were quite visible.
His forked foot was bursting his stockings.
Enjoying his leave from hell, he breathed the fresh air;
Though his teeth were not false
His glances were not true.
He came to earth poised for prey.
In his hands with their iron talons
He clutched a hunting permit
Signed by God and countersigned by Lucifer.
He was that worthy Devil Beelzebub.
I recognized him right away:
His undisguisable grimace
Gave him the air of a wicked deity.[29]

The deepest portrait of Satan since Milton is in Hugo's unfinished trilogy of long narrative poems: *La légende des siècles* (in which God and Eblis, the Devil, make a wager on their respective creative powers), *Dieu*, and *La fin de Satan*.[30] The plan of the whole was to portray the destruction of evil by Liberty, opening humanity to light, freedom, and love. In *Dieu*, published posthumously (1891) in extended fragments, Hugo speaks of the Devil as the shadow of God, having no real or even possible existence. "God," he said, "has no Devil hidden in the folds of his robe." In *La fin de Satan*, begun in 1854 but also published posthumously (1886), the Devil is a vivid and convincing personality; he has truly sinned, truly distorted himself and the world through his blindness and selfishness, yet the pain and suffering of his own alienation render him sympathetic. He represents the lack of equilibrium, peace, and balance in the cosmos and the alienation of humanity from its proper repose in love and liberty. Like Satan, we are so wrapped up in our interior world that we cannot see the reality around us; we isolate ourselves from it, though it speaks to us in every tree, bird, and human voice. Miserable as we are, the spirit of love nonetheless draws us toward it, and in the end all will be saved. How could it be otherwise?

29. "Les bonnes intentions de Rosa" in "L'éternel petit roman," from Hugo's *Chansons des rues et des bois* (Paris, 1865).

30. V. Hugo, *Poésie*, 3 vols., ed. B. Leuilliot (Paris, 1972). *La fin de Satan* appears in vol. 3, pp. 216–301. Since Hugo never finished the poem, its text and organization are unsettled; thus the following references are to general sections rather than specific line numbers.

The spirit of the world is infinitely loving and merciful, desiring all to
return to him; against that love who could prevail forever? Further, evil
is nothing in itself; it can exist temporarily as privation, but the end of
time will refine out such imperfections; the opposites will be reconciled,
and the cosmos will be reintegrated in liberty and love.

The poem begins with the fall of Satan. As he falls, his angelic nature
is transformed: "Suddenly he sees himself growing bat wings; he sees
himself becoming a monster; as the angel in him died, the rebel felt a
pang of regret." His prideful envy of God turns into the more bitter
envy of regret: "God shall have the blue heavens, but I a dark and
empty sky." A fearful voice retorts, "Accursed one, around you the
stars shall all fade away." He falls, year after year, for millennia, and as
he falls, the stars gradually disappear, leaving the sky darker, emptier,
more silent, until only three faint points of light remain—then only
one. On this last, dimming star he concentrates all the efforts of his
depleted being.

> Toward the star trembling pale on the horizon
> He pressed, leaping from one dark foothold to another. . . .
> He ran, he flew, he cried out: Golden star!
> Brother! Wait for me! I am coming! Do not die yet!
> Do not leave me alone. . . .
> The star was now only a spark. . . .
> The spark
> Was now only a red point in the depths of the dark gulf. . . .
> Hoping to make the star glow more brightly,
> He set himself to blowing on it as one would on coals.
> And anguish flared his fierce nostrils.
> He flew toward it for ten thousand years. Ten thousand years,
> Stretching out his pale neck and his mad fingers,
> He flew without finding a single place of rest.
> From time to time the star seemed to darken and die,
> And the horror of the tomb made the dark angel tremble.
> As he approached the star,
> Satan, like a swimmer making a supreme effort,
> Stretched his bald and taloned wings forward; a wan specter;
> Gasping, broken, exhausted, smoking with sweat,
> He collapsed at the edge of the steep bank of darkness. . . .
> The star was almost gone. The dark angel was so weary
> That no voice, no breath was left to him.
> And the star was dying beneath his anguished stare . . .
> And the star went out.[31]

31. Section "Nox facta est."

The struggle between Satan and God occupies three sections: "The Sword" (*Le glaive*), dealing with the Old Testament period: "The Gibbet" (*Le gibet*), representing the New Testament; and "The Prison" (*La prison*), representing the modern world. In the Old Testament, Satan struggles to negate or at least minimize God's influence upon humanity. God succeeds in purifying humanity only temporarily and only by destroying the entire world in the flood—a strange manifestation (Hugo observed) of divine love. A feather falls from the wing of the ruined angel, and that feather takes the form of a beautiful angel (like Vigny's Eloa), whose name is Liberty. Thus Satan's evil rebellion contains within it the angelic sign of future return to liberty and love.

In modern times, God allows Liberty to descend to the pit and visit Satan. God also gives her permission to go to the earth and free humanity, but she must have the permission of Satan as well. At first, still brooding selfishly on his own wrongs, he refuses to grant it, but moved by her pleas at last, he grudgingly pronounces the necessary word: Go! Liberty encourages humanity to rebel against evil and to destroy the prison—symbolized by the Bastille—that keeps us from our freedom. The Revolution, then, fulfills the mission of the angel of Liberty under the permission of both God and Devil. The work of reconciliation begins.

Satan feels the pain of knowing that the entire cosmos rejects him:

> Throughout the universe I hear the words: Go away!
> Even the pig sneers to the dungheap: "I despise Satan."
> I feel the night thinking that I dishonor her. . . .
> Once, that pure white light, the dawn,
> Was I. I! I was the splendid-browed archangel. . . .
> But I was envious. There was
> My crime. The word was spoken; the divine lips
> Pronounced me evil! And God spat me out into the pit.
> Ah, I love him! That is the horror, that is the flame!
> What will become of me, abyss? I love God!
> Hell is his eternal absence,
> Hell is to love, to cry, "Alas, where is my light,
> Where is my life and my illumination?
> [When first I fell, I boasted:]
> This God, world's heart, this bright Father
> Whom angel, star, man and beast bear within,
> This center round which his flock of creature nestles,
> This being, source of life, alone true, alone necessary,
> I can do without him, I the punished giant. . . .
> Yet I love him! . . .

I know the truth! God is no spirit, but a heart.
God, loving center of the world, connects with his divine fibers
The filaments and roots of all living things.
[God loves every creature]
But Satan, forever rejected, sad, condemned.
God leaves me out; he stops with me; I am his boundary.
God would be infinite if I did not exist. . . .
A hundred hundred times I repeat my vow,
I love! God tortures me, yet my only blasphemy,
My only frenzy, my only cry, is that I love!
I love enough to make the sky tremble! But in vain!

Now God responds in what Hugo planned as the denouement of the poem. Satan cries out: "Love hates me!" But God replies:

No, I do not hate you! . . .
O Satan, you need only say, I shall live!
Come; your prison will be pulled down and hell abolished!
Come, the angel Liberty is your daughter and mine:
This sublime parentage unites us.
The archangel is reborn and the demon dies;
I efface the baleful darkness, and none of it is left.
Satan is dead; be born again, heavenly Lucifer!
Come, rise up from the shadows with dawn on your brow.[32]

This poignant portrait of the Devil expresses a poetic moral view: our selfishness and stupidity alienate us from the reality of the cosmos, which is love, but love is unlimited, patient, merciful. It waits until we understand that selfishness, anger, and pride are nothing in themselves, nothing but a blind refusal to see, nothing but negation of reality. Once we open our eyes a chink, love's illumination floods in, and with horror and shame we see that we have been standing, alone, staring down into our own darkness. But the first glimmer of love in our dim eyes brings an immediate response. When we are ready, love will fill our darkness to bursting, until there is nothing left but light.

The Romantic reversal of symbols sometimes went to extremes.[33]

32. These passages are from sections "Hors de la terre" III and IV, concluding: "L'archange ressuscite et le démon finit; / Et j'efface la nuit sinistre, et rien n'en reste. / Satan est mort; renais ô Lucifer céleste! / Viens, monte hors de l'ombre avec l'aurore au front."

33. Gérard de Nerval (the pen name of Gérard Labrunie, 1808–1855) used a phrase in his revision of *Le diable amoureux* that Baudelaire would later make his own: "Mon cher Belzébuth, je t'adore." On Nerval, see R. E. Jones, *Gérard de Nerval* (New York, 1974).

The abbé Alphonse Louis Constant (1810–1875), who began by believing in the Romantic goal of integrating God and Satan, was led by George Sand to believe that Satan lay unjustly condemned under the curse of an arbitrary God. Plunging into the occult, Constant changed his name to Eliphas Lévi and wrote a number of books portraying Satan as a positive spiritual force. The French Satan was often political, and Lévi's was no exception, though his development was the opposite of Hugo's: in the 1840s, Lévi's Satan was the symbol of revolution and liberty, but after Lévi came to admire Napoleon III, Satan became the hieratic support of law and order.[34] The occult, positive interpretation of Satan laid the foundation for the Satanism of the end of the century, an occasionally serious if tiny movement attracting the naive and foolish as well as literary poseurs.

Apart from the solemnity of Hugo and the pompous Satanism of Lévi, irony, parody, and whimsy were the dominant treatments of the Devil throughout the nineteenth century. The greatest master of irony was Théophile Gautier (1811–1872), who wrote a comic version of *Faust* called *Albertus* (1832) and a satire on Hugo and Vigny, *Une larme du diable*, "A Tear of the Devil" (1839). In Gautier's work the prince of darkness appears as a witty dandy, elegant and soigné, masking his malevolence behind his refined appearance.[35]

Gautier's short story "Onuphrius" (1832) shows his ironic Devil most clearly. Onuphrius, a young dandy poet and painter obsessed by medievalism and the marvelous, begins to see the hand of the Devil in everything; finally the Devil really does appear, smearing his paints and poems, ruining his strategy at checkers, and spoiling his love affair. At a literary soirée where Onuphrius is to read his verse, the Devil sits behind him, catches all his words in a little net, and transforms them into pompous and ridiculous phrases. Gautier's description of the Devil is so perfect a picture of the ironic Mephistopheles that it has become a stock figure in art, opera, literature, and cartoons: a young, handsome

---

34. Milner, vol. 2, pp. 246–256.

35. *Albertus ou l'âme et le péché* (Paris, 1832), in *Poésies complètes de Théophile Gautier* (Paris, 1970), vol. 1, pp. 127–188. Strophe 114: "Ce n'était pas un diable / Empoisonnant le soufre et d'aspect effroyable, / Un diable rococo.—C'était un élégant / Portant l'impériale et la fine moustache, / Faisant sonner sa botte et siffler sa cravache." *Une larme du diable* appears in Gautier's *Oeuvres complètes*, vol. 8: *Théâtre, mystère, comédies et ballets* (Geneva, 1978), pp. 1–52. Also note his "Deux acteurs pour un rôle," in Gautier, *Contes fantastiques* (Paris, 1974), pp. 165–178, in which an actor playing the Devil is replaced on stage by the Devil himself.

man with regular, sardonic features; a red imperial and mustache; green eyes; thin, pale, ironic lips; and a knowing look. The perfect dandy, he wears a black coat, red waistcoat, white gloves, and golden spectacles; on one long, delicate finger he sports a large ruby.[36] He instills not fear or hatred but ironic laughter. He is, in effect, cynical, valueless modern man looking at himself in a mirror.

In portraying Satan as a dandy, Gautier and his imitators, themselves dandies, ironically linked themselves to the Devil, and it is a deliberate coincidence that the favorite victims of Gautier's Evil One were poets and painters, artists like the author himself. The dandy was esthetic and elegant, disdaining convention, dressing and speaking so as to draw attention to himself and to shock the philistines, using exotic and bizarre words and images, spurning morality in favor of the pursuit of the delicate, arrogantly sensitive, self-absorbed, affecting the air of living on a higher plane of being, witty and charming rather than truthful or sincere. Many levels of irony exist in a story such as "Onuphrius." The poet mocks the traditional Devil, whose existence he assumes is absurd. He also ironically argues that belief in the Devil is as reasonable as belief in God: "The existence of the Devil is proved by the most respectable authors, exactly as is that of God; it is even an article of faith."[37]

On another level, Gautier satirizes himself and his fellow artists in the gullible, emotional, naive Onuphrius, so easily frightened and made such a fool of by the insolent dandy demon. And the dandy demon is also an ironic portrait of the other side of the contemporary artist. All these clever ironies lie beneath an overt satire of the contemporary taste for the magical and the miraculous. The story is a glittering mockery of everything it touches: God, Devil, cosmos, humanity, art, and the artist himself.

By midcentury, a number of attitudes were fixed in the artistic imagination: the moral ambiguity of both Devil and God; their possible integration; psychological empathy for Satan as representing the human mind lost in ignorance and selfishness yet yearning for the good; the use of Satan as an ironically distant voice with which to satirize the human condition. With the newer poets, Romanticism began to shade off in two directions: naturalism, which spurned the supernatural and the internal in favor of realistic descriptions of everyday life; and Dec-

36. "Onuphrius," in *Contes fantastiques*, pp. 23–62; the description appears on pp. 53–56.

37. Onuphrius, p. 34.

LE MIROIR DU DIABLE

The cover of an 1856 toy box demonstrates the trivialization of the Devil.

adence, which combined some elements of dandyism with exploration of the depths of human corruption, especially sexual depravity.

As early as 1828, long before the emergence of the Decadents, a group devoted to the occult and macabre began to meet at Victor Hugo's house to read works featuring skeletons, daggers, fiends, grave-yards, corpses, ghosts, incantations, pacts, and demons. Beginning in February of 1846 another circle of young poets, dedicated to shocking the philistines, collaborated in a session celebrating the seven cardinal sins and dedicated their work to Satan in words that might better have been left unspoken, even for dramatic effect:

> To thee, Satan, fair fallen angel,
> To whom fell the perilous honor
> To struggle against an unjust rule,
> I offer myself wholly and forever,
> My mind, my senses, my heart, my love,
> And my dark verses in their corrupted beauty.[38]

Satan, a theatrical prop for the dandies, was a serious symbol for the anarchist Pierre Joseph Proudhon (1809–1865). "Come, Satan," he prayed, "you who have been defamed by priests and kings, that I may kiss you and hold you against my breast."[39] Such ideas, which became fashionable with Baudelaire and his associates, have led some modern critics to speak of the Satanism of the nineteenth century. A few real Satanists certainly existed, but the term needs to be more carefully delineated.

The poseurs who feigned Satanism for esthetic effect cannot be considered real Satanists; nor can those such as Proudhon, who used a Satan in whom they did not personally believe as a symbol of political or social rebellion. The tendency of some nineteenth-century Christians to term Satanists those who denied the existence of both God and Satan

38. Quoted in Milner, vol. 2, p. 243. "A toi, Satan, bel archange déchu, / A qui le périlleux honneur échut / De guerroyer contre un pouvoir injuste, / Je m'offre tout entier et sans retour, / Mon esprit, mes sens, mon coeur, mon amour, / Et mes sombres vers dans leur beauté fruste."

39. Quoted in Milner, vol. 2, p. 260, from Proudhon's *De la justice dans la révolution et dans l'église* (1858). In Italy, Giacomo Leopardi (1798–1837) wrote a Satanic revolutionary hymn, "Ad Arimane," in 1833; see his *Opere* (Milan, 1937), vol. 2, pp. 391–396. Giosuè Carducci (1835–1907) composed a liturgy to Satan, "Inno a Satana," in *Inni civili* (1869), *Edizione nazionale delle opere di Giosuè Carducci*, 16 vols. (Bologna, 1935–1957), vol. 2, pp. 377–385. See also Carducci, *Satana e polemiche satanistiche* (Bologna, 1879).

is even less logical. The few eccentrics who took the view that only Satan exists and not God, or that both exist but that Satan is good and God evil, are not real Satanists, either, for they were merely reversing terms emptily. If one calls Satan the good, loving, merciful creator of the cosmos, one is simply applying an unconventional name to God.

The term Satanist is properly applied only to the tiny number who believe that Satan is a personal principle to true evil, selfishness, and suffering, and who worship him as such. It is not helpful to apply the term to Baudelaire and his colleagues, for true Satanism was extremely limited and had little cultural influence.

Charles Baudelaire (1821–1867), an important figure in the transition from Romanticism to naturalism and decadence, renounced the church as a young man. Skeptical by nature, he extended his doubts to scientism as well as religion; he regarded the facile material progressivism of his day as pathetically absurd, and atheism seemed to him incapable of dealing with alienation and evil, the deepest realities of human existence. Like Hugo and the Romantics, Baudelaire was an esthete; he had no systematic theology or philosophy, though he enjoyed speculation more than most of the Romantics and was intensely concerned with moral issues. In later life he considered himself a Catholic, and though he was never close to orthodoxy, his work was permeated with Catholicism and his preoccupation with sin as intense as that of a Jansenist.

Baudelaire's concern with evil in no way made him its advocate. He detested hypocrisy, stinginess, and cruelty; he felt it as a grievance that God had not filled up the world with beauty, love, and justice. He honestly acknowledged that evil is attractive as well as destructive: "In each person two tendencies exist at every moment, one toward God and the other toward Satan. Spirituality, the call to God, is a desire to mount higher; animality, the call to Satan, takes joy in falling lower."[40] Evil destroys by drawing us down into blind selfishness, isolation, and alienation, but this darkness has its attractions, which everyone feels and only hypocrites deny. Baudelaire was pitiless in his determination to remove the blindfold of hypocrisy from his own eyes and from those of others. Observing that George Sand denied the existence of the Devil, he caustically observed that it was to her personal interest that the Devil and hell should not exist.[41] Baudelaire well understood the

---

40. Baudelaire, *Journaux intimes*, ed. J. Crepet and G. Blin (Paris, 1949), no. 11. See also G. Bataille, *Literature and Evil* (London, 1973).

41. *Journaux intimes*, no. 17.

power of sensual pleasures, particularly over the young, but Satan's most powerful weapon was *ennui* (the esthetic equivalent of theological *acedia* and of materialist boredom), a sense of lassitude in the face of the utter futility of life.

Baudelaire felt the pull of the positive Satan, who appears in his verse as the Romantic champion of liberty as well as the incarnation of hypocrisy, and the poet perceived in the rebel angel the most perfect type of masculine beauty. But more often, Baudelaire took Satan as the symbol of human evil and perhaps even as a personal entity. In a letter to Flaubert, he wrote, "I have always been obsessed by the impossibility of accounting for certain sudden human actions or thoughts without the hypothesis of an evil external force."[42] Like all Christian writers with intense introspective powers, Baudelaire was well aware of the sudden and unannounced irruption into the mind of intensely destructive images, desires, and feelings, which can be explained only by reference to a power beyond the conscious mind—whether it comes from outside, as in traditional Christianity, or from the unconscious, as in depth psychology. Baudelaire was skeptical of the skeptics. "My dear brothers," he wrote, "never forget, when you hear the progress of the Enlightenment praised, that the Devil's cleverest ploy is to persuade you that he doesn't exist."[43]

Baudelaire's masterpiece was his collection *Les Fleurs du Mal* ("The Flowers of Evil"), to which should be added his prose poems entitled *Le Spleen de Paris*.[44] In both collections, the struggle between good and evil, sensuality and spirituality, *spleen* and *idéal*, was central. Though the censors and some of Baudelaire's own followers seem to have mistakenly read his intent as destructive, his message seems clear from the very outset of the *Fleurs*, which commences with a famous address "To the Reader":

> Stupidity, error, sin and stinginess
> Garrison our minds and enslave our bodies. . . .

42. Letter of June 26, 1860, in Baudelaire, *Correspondance*, 6 vols., ed. J. Crépet (Paris, 1947–1953), vol. 3, p. 125.

43. "Le joueur généreux," in *Le Spleen de Paris*, ed. Y. Florenne (Paris, 1972): "Mes chers frères, n'oubliez jamais, quand vous entendrez vanter le progrès des lumières, que la plus belle ruse du diable est de vous persuader qu'il n'existe pas."

44. The first edition of the *Fleurs* appeared in 1857; a second in 1861; a third posthumously in 1868. Owing to deletions by the censor and to additions, the three differ significantly. See the critical edition by J. Crépet and G. Blin (Paris, 1942), and *Les fleurs du mal: Texte de la deuxième édition*, ed. J. Crépet and G. Blin (Paris, 1968). *Le Spleen* first appeared in 1860.

On evil's pillow, Hermes Trismegistus
Slowly rocks our enthralled minds,
And the rich metal of our wills
Is vaporized by this learned alchemist. . . .
It is the Devil who pulls the strings that move us:
We find charm in the most disgusting things;
Each day we take another step down into hell,
Deadened to horror, through stinking shadows. . . .
Reader, you recognize this delicate monster,
Hypocrite reader, my likeness, my brother![45]

Such words may be taken as a rejection of evil, as a pessimisic statement of its inherence in humanity, or as ironic acceptance of evil on the part of the poet and artist, who alone in society has the vision and honesty to recognize it within himself.

Baudelaire seems to have meant all three. His work contains examples of the reversal in which the Christian God becomes evil and Satan the center of a symbol cluster that includes art, the poet, humanity, beauty, sentiment, revulsion against injustice, and even Jesus, who defends such values against the tyrannical Father.[46] Toward the cruel Jehovah one can feel only revulsion, combined with sympathy for his great foe. "There is no fiber in my trembling body," the poet exclaimed, "that does not cry, 'Dear Beelzebub, I adore you!' "[47] The lines come from "The Possessed," a poem whose persona is either mad or inspired, possessed by a demon whose moral value is ambivalent. "Hymn to Beauty" (*Hymne à la beauté*) is also ambivalent: beauty may come from God or from Satan; to the poet it does not matter which, for beauty itself is the supreme esthetic ideal. That this beauty serves both kindness and crime is no surprise in a universe that is itself wholly ambivalent.

The poet's "Litanies to Satan" (*Les litanies de Satan*) have often been cited as a sign of his Satanism, a view that neglects the fact that they arise from a literary tradition and that they are to be read, like all of Baudelaire's poems, with an awareness of irony and on several levels. The Satan whom Baudelaire praises is on one level the traditional Chris-

---

45. "Tu le connais, lecteur, ce monstre délicat, / —Hypocrite lecteur—mon semblable—mon frère!"

46. *Fleurs*, "Le reniement de Saint Pierre": "What does God make of this flood of curses that daily rises toward his angels? Like a tyrant gorged with flesh and wine, he drifts off to sleep on the sound of horrible blasphemies. . . . Ah, Jesus, do you remember Gethsemane, where in your simplicity you knelt and prayed?"

47. *Fleurs*, "Le possédé"; "O mon cher Belzébuth, je t'adore" is the line from Nerval.

tian Satan; on another, Jesus; on another, the ambivalence of the human
heart; and on yet another, the artist and the terrible double-edged sword
of creativity:

> Prince of the exile, you have been wronged,
> Defeated, you rise up ever stronger. . . .
> You who, even to lepers and accursed outcasts
> Teach through love a longing for Paradise. . . .
> You who know in what corners of envious nations
> God hoards his precious gems. . . .
> You who teach us to console the frail and suffering
> By mixing saltpeter and sulfur. . . .
> Glory and praise to you, lord Satan, in the highest,
> Where once you reigned, and in the depths
> Of hell, where you lie defeated and dreaming.
> Let my soul one day, in the shadow of the tree of knowledge,
> Rest next to you.

Baudelaire, who would die reconciled to the church, dedicated the
Fleurs to that great mocker Théophile Gautier. He did not know quite
how to take the demon that troubled him, but he realized that it would
never leave him alone:

> The Devil is active at my side;
> He swims around me like the impalpable air;
> I swallow him and feel him burning my lungs,
> Filling them with an eternal, guilty desire.
> Sometimes, knowing my great love of art,
> He takes the shape of a seductive woman,
> And under the false pretenses of cafard
> Accustoms my lips to the taste of forbidden potions.
> He leads me far from the face of God,
> Panting and broken with weariness, into the midst
> Of the deep and deserted plains of ennui
> And thrusts into my confused sight
> Dirty clothing, open wounds,
> And the bloody costume of Destruction.[48]

48. *Fleurs*, "La déstruction." Some of Baudelaire's contemporaries shared his serious
concern with the Devil: for example, Jules Amédée Barbey d'Aurevilly (1808–1869), a
Catholic dandy who held that Satan was an essential element in Christian theology. See
Barbey's *Les Diaboliques* (Paris, 1874). Others were Leconte de Lisle (1818–1894), who
wrote a poem entitled "Tristesse du diable," and Gustave Flaubert, author of *La Tenta-
tion de Saint Antoine* (Paris, 1968), esp. pp. 241–243.

Paul Verlaine (1844–1896) read Baudelaire's *Fleurs* at the age of fourteen and became his most devoted disciple and a leader of the Decadent movement. Verlaine coined the name "accursed poets" (*poètes maudits*) for the group who imitated Baudelaire's Satanic symbolism without his serious concern for the problem of evil.[49]

Arthur Rimbaud (1854–1891) died a Catholic after having spent his early career attacking authority, including church, education, and parents. For Rimbaud, who burned out young and abandoned the artistic life, the Devil was the symbol of the dull authority that suppresses and crushes artistic freedom, the only true good. His collection of prose poems *Une saison en enfer* ("A Season in Hell") was dedicated to the Devil with the words, "Dear Satan . . . you who love the absence of descriptive and didactic faculties in the poet, I dash off for you these few hideous leaves from the notebook of a damned soul."[50] Full of pretension, self-absorption, and despair, the poet sees himself as the battleground between the forces of God and Satan, sin and innocence, good and evil, past and present. The poet is at one and the same time intensely involved in the struggle and, like the Devil, coolly detached from it. Unlike Hugo, Rimbaud calls less for integration and transcendence of the conflicting sides of the personality than for simply accepting them and regressing with them to a preconscious state of the soul where good and evil are undifferentiated.

The most truly Satanic of the Decadents was Isidore Ducasse (1846–1870), who wrote under the name Lautréamont. He argued that we must renounce all evasions and face evil in its most intense and shocking forms; he then made the transition from facing evil to reveling in it. A follower of Sade, Lautréamont argued that creative cruelty was a mark of genius and of honesty; he took Baudelaire's contemptuous attack upon hypocrisy as an excuse to explore the most loathsome recesses of his own soul. Maldoror, the persona of his dark masterpiece *Les chants de Maldoror*, is a combination of Sade, Satan, and Ducasse himself; he contemplates or commits an endless series of perverted outrages.[51]

It is unclear whether Lautréamont was mad; he clearly did not practice, or seriously advocate practicing, everything that came to his mind.

49. See P. Verlaine, *Poèmes saturniens* (Paris, 1866); *Jadis et naguère* (Paris, 1884), which contains "Crimen amoris," a poem on the salvation of Satan; and *Les poètes maudits* (Paris, 1884).

50. Rimbaud, *Une saison en enfer*, in *Oeuvres de Jean-Arthur Rimbaud* (Paris, 1904), pp. 215–259.

51. Lautréamont, *Les chants de Maldoror* (Paris, 1868).

Yet the ironic dandy posing as a Satanist and mocking his own secret vices found himself excited by his fantasies, and the distance between ironic evil and true evil foreshortened and attenuated. Maldoror sees a child sitting on a park bench and immediately imagines a hog gnawing away her genitals and burrowing through her body. He dreams of torturing young boys and drinking their blood and tears. When he kisses a baby, he fantasizes about slashing its cheeks with a razor. Vampirism, necrophilia, blasphemy, bestiality, incest, bondage, pederasty, multilation, murder, and cannibalism obsess him.

In *Maldoror* the poet intended to paint a true picture of the human soul free from all hypocrisy: "Maldoror was born evil. He admitted the truth and said that he was cruel" (1.3). But Lautréamont, reacting against the bland Enlightenment-Romantic assumption that human nature was essentially good, plunged to the other untenable extreme. Just as the belief that humans are good raises the question where evil comes from, Lautréamont's dark universe leaves the presence of good unexplained. To a degree he meant Maldoror as an evil joke, a pose pointing the way to surrealism and dadaism. It is true that Maldoror's excesses are so bizarre as to be ridiculous as well as horrible, yet the author seems to have opened himself up to dark forces beyond his conscious control. Maldoror begins by boasting that he causes his "genius" to "paint the delights of cruelty" (1.4) and ends by killing an angel who has been sent to save him, thus symbolizing his rejection of redemption (5.8).

In America the tendency was even stronger than in Europe to detach serious studies of evil from works dealing with the Devil and to relegate the latter to tales of whimsy or horror. Neither Nathaniel Hawthorne (1804–1864) nor Herman Melville (1819–1891), both of whom made the study of human evil their central concern, had much use for the Devil even as symbol. Hawthorne's only serious use of Satan is in his story "Young Goodman Brown." The Devil appears when Brown yields to despair. "My faith is gone," Brown exclaims. "There is no good on earth; and sin is but a name. Come, devil; for to thee is this world given." Satan appears, takes him to a witches' sabbat in his fantasy, and persuades him of the Calvinistic (and, as Hawthorne sees it, Satanic) view that human nature is essentially corrupt. For Hawthorne, Brown is doomed because he despairs of humanity and fails to trust in God's goodness.[52] Melville's Moby Dick is one of the most polysymbolic

52. "Young Goodman Brown" appears, with other tales dealing with evil, in

figures in literature, but one of the symbols is demonic. Moby Dick is determined to destroy humanity body and soul; when at the end he bears down upon the *Pequod* to annihilate it, he does so with "retribution, swift vengeance, eternal malice."[53] In Melville's *The Confidence Man* (1857), the Devil appears as a cosmic trickster on a Mississippi steamer, the *Fidèle*, which begins its voyage on All Fools' Day. It is a ship of fools blinded by dreams of naive greed, ready to betray one another for profit, and all ultimately tricked by the Confidence Man, the eternal Cheater, the shapeshifter who appears in a variety of personalities and forms. It is the story of simple Christlike love overwhelmed and effaced by Satanic confusion and cynicism, symbolized by the motto that one of the characters tacks up in his shop: "No Trust." Melville's pessimism would be taken further by Mark Twain, as Hawthorne's deep probing of secret evil would be taken further by Dostoevsky, but Twain and Dostoevsky represent a dark view more attuned to the modern than to the Romantic era.

The horror story, an American adaptation from the Gothic novel or *roman noir*, had its first great expression in Edgar Allan Poe (1809–1849).[54] Like the Gothic writers, Poe wrote to entertain and to thrill, not to investigate evil seriously, though he was well aware of its power. It is indicative of the Devil's decline that when Poe wrote of real evil, as in "The Pit and the Pendulum," "The Cask of Amontillado," and "The Facts in the Case of Monsieur Valdemar," the Devil plays little part; he is a presence only in Poe's comic tales. In "The Devil in the Belfry," for example, the Devil causes the bells of a Dutch church to toll thirteen. In "Never Bet the Devil Your Head," a reprobate named Toby incautiously enters into a wager with Satan, and "a little lame old gentleman of venerable aspect" supernaturally causes an accident in which Toby loses his head; the doctors fail to replace it properly, and eventually Toby notices its loss and dies. This sort of whimsical tale, loosely derived from folklore, is typical of American Devil stories. The favorite

---

Hawthorne's *Mosses from an Old Manse* (1846). On Hawthorne, Poe, and Melville, see H. Levin, *The Power of Blackness* (New York, 1958).

53. H. Melville, *Moby-Dick; or, The Whale* (Berkeley, 1981; originally published 1851), esp. chs. 41, 51, 135. H. R. Trimpi, "Melville's Use of Demonology and Witchcraft in *Moby-Dick*," *Journal of the History of Ideas*, 30 (1969), 543–562, provides full demonstration of the diabolical theme.

54. See *The Complete Works of Edgar Allan Poe* (Boston, 1856). "The Devil in the Belfry" is in vol. 3, pp. 252–264; "Never Bet the Devil Your Head," vol. 4, pp. 342–356. The most influential of Poe's followers was Howard Phillips Lovecraft (1890–1937). See also Washington Irving's "The Devil and Tom Walker" (1824).

theme among American (and other Anglophone) writers has been the bargain with the Devil, which affords opportunity for everything from broad humor through satire to wit. It also permits virtuosity in devising new ways for the protagonist to outwit the Devil or to be outwitted by him.[55]

The development of music in the nineteenth century produced a change that some writers have associated with the demonic. The idealist view is that some music is more inherently harmonious with the cosmos than other music—that is, it reflects divine or cosmic order more closely. In this view, Bach or Mozart, for example, wrote "truer" or "better" music than Chopin or Stravinsky. Harmonious composers might introduce discords in order to make a musical point, sometimes explicitly to portray evil itself, but disharmonious music is less good, less true, less real—perhaps even demonic. The discordant reflects the chaotic, the disruption of the cosmos and of God's orderly plan.

Beginning with Beethoven, however (or even Mozart in his late quartets), composers deliberately introduced disharmony, mainly to give both the music and their emotions freer rein. Many composers of the Romantic period wanted their music to integrate all human experience—emotional as well as rational, evil as well as good—and used disharmony for this purpose. A few, such as Paganini, and François Boieldieu in his "Valse Infernale," ironically claimed to have been inspired by the Devil. Modern composers such as Stravinsky have employed disharmony to discredit and supplant the idealist view. But whether one can call some kinds of music better or more real than others depends upon whether one believes that music can reflect the cosmos and whether one ultimately believes that the universe is cosmos or chaos.[56]

55. Examples include I. Azimov, "The Brazen Locked Room," *Magazine of Fantasy and Science Fiction* (November 1956); M. Beerbohm, "Enoch Soames," in M. Beerbohm, *Seven Men* (New York, 1920); S. V. Benét, "The Devil and Daniel Webster," in *Selected Works of Stephen Vincent Benét* (New York, 1937); T. Cogswell, "Impact with the Devil," *Magazine of Fantasy and Science Fiction* (November 1956); M. A. DeFord, "Time Trammel," *Magazine of Fantasy and Science Fiction* (November 1956); H. Ellison, "The Beast That Shouted Love at the Heart of the World," in I. Azimov, ed., *The Hugo Winners* (New York, 1971); U. K. LeGuin, "The Ones Who Walk Away from Omelas," in Le Guin, *The Wind's Twelve Quarters* (New York, 1975); J. Masefield, "The Devil and the Old Man," in Masefield, *A Mainsail Haul* (London, 1941). A good collection is B. Davenport, ed., *Deals with the Devil* (New York, 1958).

56. For the Devil in music, see S. Leppe, "The Devil's Music: A Literary Study of Evil and Music," Ph.D. diss., University of California, Riverside, 1978; R. Hammer-

The literary imagination dominated the concept of the Devil in the nineteenth century, but by midcentury literary and artistic interest in the Devil had began to diminish. He had been milked dry of much of his horror and even of his comedy. The growth of realism and naturalism, with their shift away from the metaphysical, and the gradual but continual rise of positivism returned the literary focus on evil to the human personality. Still, the inconsistencies and vagaries of the Romantic uses of the symbol had tended to dissipate and blur its meaning, and with secularism and materialism slowly replacing Christianity as the dominant world view of Western society, belief in a personal Satan dwindled rapidly even among professed Christians. At the same time, the decline of Romanticism and of the literary Devil eventually led to the return of the symbol to the theologians. When the figure of Satan eventually regained some of its power in the twentieth century, it was in the traditional rather than in the Romantic mode. Meanwhile, powerful statements about evil would be made by Nietzsche, Twain, and above all Dostoevsky, who understood evil better than anyone in his century and whose dark vision became a model for the modern age.

---

stein, *Diabolus in musica: Studien zur Ikonographie der Musik im Mittelalter* (Bern, 1974). The Devil appeared frequently in nineteenth-century and early twentieth-century music, especially in opera: Daniel Auber, *Fra Diavolo* (1830); Michael Balfe, *Satanella* (1858); Arthur Benjamin, *The Devil Take Her* (1932); Hector Berlioz, *La damnation de Faust* (1846); Arrigo Boito, *Mefistofele* (1868); Ferruccio Busoni, *Doktor Faust* (1920); Anton Dvořák, *The Devil and Kate* (1899); Charles Gounod, *Faust* (1859); Douglas Moore, *The Devil and Daniel Webster* (1938); Vincenzio Tommasini, *Le diable s'amuse* (ballet, 1950).

6 *The Devil's Shadow*

The transformation of society by industrialization and urbanization continued at an increased rate in the later nineteenth century; agnosticism spread beyond philosophical and literary elites to the educated public at large. To this growing secularization of society, four great thinkers—Darwin, Marx, Nietzsche, and Freud—lent the weight of their authority. Recent historical opinion views the "warfare" between science and religion as both unnecessary and largely illusory, but whatever the underlying realities, the perception of an opposition between the two took on a reality of its own.[1]

Charles Darwin (1809–1882) was the most influential of the biologists who, following the lead of geologists and historians, were adopting a gradual, evolutionary view of the cosmos, a view shortly to be reinforced by astronomy and physics. Evolutionary biology dismissed the idea that the species had been fixed from the beginning and the idea that humanity was unrelated to other species but created by a special act of God. The hypothesis that the human race had evolved from less complex animal forms was set forth in Darwin's *Origin of Species* (1859) and *Descent of Man* (1871). Humanity had already been apparently removed from the center of space, and the evolutionary view also seemed to remove it from the center of time. The idea grew that humans are

---

1. On the new view of the relationship between science and religion, see D. C. Lindberg and R. L. Numbers, eds., *God and Nature: A History of the Encounter between Christianity and Science* (Berkeley, 1986), and R. L. Numbers, "Sciences of Satanic Origin: Adventist Attitudes toward Evolutionary Biology," *Spectrum*, 9 (1979), 17–28. On the origins of evolutionary thought, see S. Toulmin and J. Goodfield, *The Discovery of Time* (New York, 1965).

insignificant creatures crawling on the surface of a minor planet on the outskirts of one of billions of galaxies in a universe billions of years old. The concept of a cosmic struggle in which humanity had any importance faded. There seemed little room in the new world view for either God or Devil.

The intellectual confrontation between evolution and creation could have been conducted on an intelligent and dispassionate plane, and some thinkers did perceive that there was no necessary conflict between them: God's creative plan for the cosmos could be based upon an evolutionary process, and Genesis could be read as a poetic statement that God created the cosmos and humanity for his special purposes, a view consistent with divine inspiration and beyond the power of science to refute. For the most part, however, extreme creationists formed a bizarre unity with reductionist scientists in asserting that the author of Genesis, millennia before the invention of either science or history, intended to make statements of historical or scientific truth. The creationists insisted that since the Bible is scientifically true, evolution must be false; the evolutionists insisted that since evolution is true, the Bible must be false. The educated public thus confronted an unnecessary dichotomy between science and religion. Those choosing the side of science were increasingly inclined to reject traditional religion as a whole, while those choosing the side of the Bible retreated into bunkers to build up barricades against Darwinism. The whole controversy, founded on a failure to understand that different kinds of truth may be stated in different forms, continues to the present.

A more explicit and fundamental challenge to traditional religion was mounted by Karl Marx (1818–1883) and Friedrich Engels (1820–1895), followed by a variety of Marxist thinkers and activists. Marxism, which arose out of the German intellectual milieu of the mid-nineteenth century, is based upon positivism and materialism and explicitly rejects the existence of the transcendent. Marxism, like any other system, is based upon unproven a priori assumptions, some of which involve severe internal contradictions. Marxism is best understood as a kind of religion based on faith: Marxists claim that knowledge must derive from empirical observation, yet the materialist assumptions of Marxism cannot be empirically demonstrated. Marxists claim that all analyses of society are subjective because distorted by class views, save only their own analyses, which are objective and undistorted. That any one historical view should be free from the limitations that history places upon all historical views is unlikely enough from the beginning; and it is contradicted by the historical evidence itself, for Marxism rises out of nineteenth-century intellectual and social roots whose limitations are easily identifiable.

Marxism did not simply imply atheism, as Darwinism did: it affirmed it categorically. Matter, Engels argued, is absolute. It is its own cause. It is infinite, and therefore in its infinite dialectic it inevitably at some point in space and time produces intelligent beings. No transcendent mind or purpose is in any way indicated. Good and evil are merely human constructs. Still, they are not relative: since Marxism takes an absolutely objective view of human society and its needs, it provides an objective view of human morality and therefore of good and evil. The early Marx attributed evil to the inherent alienation of human consciousness from the material universe that produced it; later, he declared that alienation and its attendant evils resulted from the exploitation of human beings by one another, an exploitation arising from class differences. The chief sources of alienation are private property and the division of labor. Bourgeois capitalism, for example, creates evil by exploiting peasants and workers; bourgeois imperialism creates evil by exploiting the populations of other countries. When communism triumphs, Marx declared, class differences and the exploitation they engender will disappear, and evil will cease.

Against the formidable assaults of Darwinism and Marxism (as well as Nietzschean nihilism and Freudianism, discussed below), Christians tended to rush into blind obscurantism on the one hand or capitulation on the other. Retreating in disarray, they sacrificed belief in one doctrine after another, like Siberians tossing their babies off the sled to the wolves, in a frantic effort to placate materialism. The Devil was one of the first beliefs to go. The obscurantist side of Christianity, including both Catholic Thomism and Protestant Biblical inerrancy, was oddly reinforced by decadent Romanticism and occultism in producing a revival of demonology toward the end of the nineteenth century. Interest often focused on possession, and even as Jean Martin Charcot (1825–1893) and Freud were producing psychological explanations of alleged possession, conservative Christians were defending exorcism. Christians thereby painted themselves into a corner and blurred necessary distinctions.

Catholic thought, especially after the 1848 revolutions, when it swerved to the right, was determinedly traditional in its diabology, relying upon the councils of Braga, Fourth Lateran, and Trent and upon the writings of Thomas Aquinas.[2] The *Rituale Romanum* continued to include the rite of exorcism and specified standard tests of the validity of alleged cases of possession. Great care must be taken to avoid being duped by fraud, it pointed out, but if the allegedly possessed person can understand a real language completely unknown to him, or demonstrates certain knowledge of distant or future events, or manifests physical strength far beyond his natural capacities (tests that were not unreasonable when originally formulated but that seem naive in the light of modern psychology), then demons might be thought to be involved. On August 4, 1879, Leo XIII issued the bull *Aeterni Patris* affirming the timeless validity of Thomistic theology, which firmly included the existence of the Devil in its world view. The Catholic Church thus remained, until the 1960s, in accord with the Eastern Orthodox Church and with conservative Protestants in defending the reality of the Devil's personal existence.

Mainstream, liberal Protestant theology, on the other hand, tended to deny or at least ignore the Devil. Friedrich Schelling took the position that the doctrine of Satan was traditional rather than biblical and could thus be discarded. Like many liberals, Schelling suggested vaguely that the Devil could nevertheless be retained not as a person but merely as a symbol of evil.[3] Others were more specific in defining Satan as a metaphor for human sin, a view that gradually became standard in liberal Protestantism.[4] Albert Réville argued—as did many twentieth-century liberals—that diabology and demonology were part of the cultural milieu of New Testament times that Jesus and the apostles absorbed and accepted; the Devil and demons were mere relics of primitive polytheism that Jesus and Paul downplayed, concentrating instead upon human responsibility.[5]

It is evident to the dispassionate observer, however, that if one dismisses the Devil (who appears in the New Testament more frequently than the Holy Spirit) as a superstition of the time, then one is entitled to

2. LUCIFER, pp. 95–190, 193–206.
3. F. Schelling, *Philosophie der Offenbarung*, 2 vols. (Stuttgart, 1858).
4. See H. Martensen, *Christian Dogmatics* (Edinburgh, 1866). J. S. Banks, *Manual of Christian Doctrine*, 4th ed. (London, 1893), and W. Beyschlag, *New Testament Theology* (Edinburgh, 1895), took Satan as a metaphor; W. N. Clarke's widely used *Outline of Christian Theology* (Cambridge, 1894) ignored him altogether.
5. A. Réville, *Histoire du diable, ses origines, sa grandeur, et sa décadence* (Strasbourg, 1870).

dismiss the resurrection, the incarnation, and indeed the whole idea of revelation—in which case the dispassionate observer may be forgiven for supposing that the entire New Testament is so riddled with superstitious misconceptions as to be altogether dismissed. On the whole it is more credible to suppose that the writers of the Gospels and the Epistles actually meant what they said about the existence and power of the Devil.

Writers such as William James (1842–1910), who were not embarrassed by their religious beliefs, did not feel obliged to protect Christianity by excising its integral parts. James, who understood that "the world is all the richer for having a devil in it, so long as we keep our foot upon his neck," described some examples of direct intuitive experience of the Devil and courageously faced the radical nature of evil: "It may be that there are forms of evil so extreme as to enter into no good system whatsoever. . . . The evil facts are as genuine parts of nature as the good ones."[6]

While Christians were disagreeing on the Devil, the decadent Romantics made Satan something of an esthetic fad at the end of the century.[7] Some accusations of Satanism verged on the hysterical. Catholic and other conservative Christians attacked the Freemasons as Satanists, while Rosicrucians and other occultists attacked one another with equal fervor.[8] The surge of interest in the occult seems to have represented the stunted expression of an inherent religious feeling whose normal channels had been obstructed by positivism and skepticism.

The more Faustian varieties of occultism enjoyed a certain intellectual following for which the groundwork had been laid by Eliphas Lévi (1810–1875). In the year of Lévi's death, Madame Helena Blavatsky (1831–1891) founded the Theosophical Society; the Hermetic Order of the Golden Dawn, which counted W. B. Yeats, Algernon Swinburne, Oscar Wilde, and other litterateurs among its members, as well as the unspeakable Aleister Crowley (1875–1947), was founded in 1887; in the order, Yeats took the occult name "Demon est Deus Inversus" (the Devil is God inside out).[9]

6. W. James, *The Varieties of Religious Experience* (New York, 1902), pp. 50, 161.

7. For *fin-de-siècle* Satanism, see G. Zacharias, *The Satanic Cult* (London, 1980).

8. The Rosicrucians were founded in 1610 and enjoyed increasing strength in English-speaking countries in the 1870s and 1880s. On accusations of diabolism against the Freemasons, see, for example, J. Doinel, *Lucifer démasqué* (Paris, 1895), or D. Margiotta, *Le palladisme: Culte de Satan-Lucifer dans les triangles maçonniques* (Voiron, 1895).

9. H. S. Levine, *Yeats's Daimonic Revival* (Ann Arbor, 1983), p. 9; see also S. de

Blavatsky's *Secret Doctrine* presented the most coherent of these occult systems. In Blavatsky's views—combining the ancient gnostics, modern occultism, Eastern religions, and her own original ideas—the Devil is the shadow side of Jehovah, the darkness without which the Light could not shine so clearly. Lucifer is a necessary part of creation, a part of the divine pleroma, the Logos, and so is assimilated to Christ. He is the Lightbearer, Hermes, the divine messenger. Jehovah is a cold, distant deity who created the world only through the intervention of the angels. There are three groups of angels: the Self-created, the Self-existent, and the Fire-angels. When Jehovah ordered the world created, the first two groups followed his commands strictly and achieved pale copies of themselves, but the Fire-angels rebelled and made humankind with knowledge and therefore true freedom. It is the Devil whom we have to thank for our intellects, our wills, and our knowledge, for it was he who opened the blind eyes of the automata that Jehovah intended. "Satan, the serpent of Genesis, [is] the real creator and benefactor, the Father of Spiritual Mankind."[10]

The most infamous diabolism of the period was exposed by the novelist J.-K. Huysmans (1848–1907), a friend of Verlaine and the *poètes maudits*. When Romanticism split into naturalism and Decadence, Huysmans tried to bridge the gap; he wrote naturalistically but was also a leader of the Decadents. Decadence was characterized by estheticism, sensuality, and fascination with such psychosexual aberrations as incest, sadomasochism, bestiality, and prostitution; the Decadents invoked the Marquis de Sade and Lautréamont as their heroes. Writers such as Huysmans combined naturalism with Decadence, describing the life of the cities realistically but characterizing it as false, desolate, and meaningless. Under the influence of Nietzsche, the esthetes and sensualists claimed to create their own meaning through their emotions, sensitivities, desires, and perversions. Decadence had even less a sense of community than Romanticism and arrogantly exalted the esthetic elite above the great unwashed mass of the vulgar and unenlightened. Decadence was a revolt against both the established order and the growing

---

Guaita, *Le serpent de la Génèse* (Paris, 1891), and *Essais de sciences maudites*, 3 vols. (Paris, 1915–1920). Stanislas de Guaita (1860–1897) and the continental Rosicrucians who followed him tried to reconcile science and religion in a new occult system in which the Devil was a substratum of matter, the "plastic and imaginative soul of the world" (*Le serpent*, pp. 103–104).

10. H. Blavatsky, *The Secret Doctrine*, 2 vols. (London, 1888), vol. 1, pp. 443–456; vol. 2, pp. 241–257, 532–564 (quotation from p. 254).

"Une fête aux enfers" (a party in hell). The poster announces a café-concert c. 1880, and indicates the reduction of the Devil to a joke.

concept of democracy. One of the quintessential novels of Decadence was Huysmans' *A rebours* (1884), but it is *Là-bas* (1891) that earns him a place in the history of Satan.[11]

Huysmans began working on *Là-bas* in 1887; his initial plan was to write a novel based on the historical figure of Gilles de Rais, a fifteenth-century child molester and mass murderer whom the Decadents found fascinating. Interest in Gilles led Huysmans to medieval withcraft and demonology, then to the black masses of the reign of Louis XIV, and finally to curiosity about contemporary Satanism. He went to Bruges to visit the nototious canon Louis van Haecke, who was said to practice secret obscene rites. Huysmans then began an affair with Berthe Courrière, a friend of the even more notorious defrocked priest Joseph-Antoine Boullan.

Boullan (1824–1893), an ordained priest with a doctorate from Rome, became the lover of a nun, Adèle Chevalier, who claimed to be able to effect miraculous cures; the pair traveled about dispensing medications compounded of feces and consecrated hosts. When Adèle gave birth to their bastard child, they sacrificed it as a mass on December 8, 1860. The crime remained undiscovered until much later, but from 1861 to 1864 Boullan was sent to prison for selling fake medicines. In 1869, imprisoned again by the Holy Office in Rome, he composed his journal, the *Cahier rose*, which came to light later and confirmed all that was rumored about his Satanic crimes. Returning to Paris later that year, Boullan resumed his former practices, but his true nature was not yet known, and he was widely employed as an exorcist, in which capacity he taught nuns and other victims how to receive "incubi" in secret sexual practices. Enough of the truth finally came out that he was defrocked by the archbishop of Paris in 1875. He then set himself up as a magician and made his living by fake healings, clairvoyance, and erotic rituals.

At this point Huysmans entered the scene. Berthe Courrière put him in touch with Boullan, and Boullan sent his priestess and housekeeper Julie Thibaut to visit Huysmans to find out whether the writer could be trusted. Reassured, Boullan sent Huysmans copious materials on magic, incubi, and the black mass, attributing the gross practices of the black mass not to himself but to Stanislas de Guaita and the Rosicrucians. Guaita and other occultists indignantly tried to convince Huys-

---

11. J.-K. Huysmans, *Là-bas* (Paris, 1891). See also G. R. Ridge, *Joris-Karl Huysmans* (New York, 1968).

mans that Boullan was lying, but they were unsuccessful. When writing *Là-bas*, Huysmans refused to model his villanious priest, Canon Docre, after Boullan; he used Canon van Haecke of Bruges as the model instead.

The novel is a fictional account of Huysmans' own experiences in writing it: the protagonist is an author named Durtal who begins by investigating Gilles de Rais, becomes interested in modern Satanism, and meets Dr. Johannes (Boullan) and the repulsive Canon Docre (Haecke). In the course of his research, Durtal attends black masses in Paris and describes one presided over by Canon Docre. Docre and his congregation meet secretly in a darkened room decorated in black and lighted only by flickering candles. Docre, who wears the cross tattooed on the soles of his feet so as to tread on the Lord with every step, feeds consecrated hosts to mice and mixes feces and urine with the sacrament. While heavy incense smoulders, drugs are handed around, the Devil is invoked, and a hymn to Satan is intoned. A long litany of blasphemies and insults to Christ is read out, with choirboys saying the responses. The drugged congregation howls and rolls on the floor. The priest sexually abuses the host in front of the congregation, and women come forward to eat of it while the men violate the choirboys. *Là-Bas* became both popular and notorious in the Europe of the 1890s, but Huysmans, repulsed by what he had become involved in, soon converted to Catholicism and left the Decadent movement.

Unlike Decadence and occultism, mainstream philosophical and ethical thought in the period touched radical evil seldom and the Devil almost never. The leading ethical writers shifted from metaphysical and teleological concerns to cultural relativism, contextual ethics, and materialist utilitarianism.[12]

The work of Friedrich Nietzsche (1844–1900) was the most radical and ultimately the most influential.[13] Nietzsche's unremitting and in-

12. See, for example, the works of J. S. Mill (1806–1873), F. Brentano (1838–1917), W. G. Sumner (1840–1910), W. Windelband (1848–1914), J. Royce (1855–1916), H. Bergson (1859–1941), E. Troeltsch (1865–1923), H. A. Prichard (1871–1947), G. E. Moore (1873–1958), and M. Scheler (1874–1923).

13. Nietzsche's major works include *Die Geburt der Tragödie* (Leipzig, 1871); *Die fröhliche Wissenschaft* (Leipzig, 1882); *Jenseits von Gut und Böse* (Leipzig, 1885); *Zur Genealogie der Moral* (Leipzig, 1887); *Also Sprach Zarathustra*, 4 vols. (Chemniz, 1883–1891); *Der Wille zur Macht* (Leipzig, 1901); *Ecce homo*, published posthumously (Leipzig, 1908). The chief edition is the *Grossoktav-Ausgabe*, 2d ed., 19 vols. (Leipzig, 1901–1913); a new critical edition, *Kritische Ausgabe* (Berlin), is underway, with 30 volumes planned. See also P. Lenz-Medoc, "The Death of God," in Bruno de Jésus-Marie, ed., *Satan* (New York, 1952), pp. 469–496.

Cover of a book of Jehan Sylvius, published in Paris in 1929. The naked woman on the altar, the horned Devil, and the Satanic pentagram illustrate the title *Black Masses* and the late nineteenth-century penchant for such thrills, as seen in the works of J.-K. Huysmans.

tensely courageous determination to face reality as it was without wishful thinking led him to repudiate the idealism of Hegel; his refusal to compromise led to a mental illness that incapacitated him from 1889 to the end of his life. He insisted that God, idealism, metaphysics, Platonism, transcendence, absolute standards of morality, and being and meaning themselves are dying or dead illusions. All speculative philosophy is merely the hollow echo of the philosopher's own hopes and fears. Theology is nonsense, Romanticism self-indulgence. Above all, Nietzsche hated facile optimism, wishful thinking, and self-delusion of any kind. The only behavior worthy of humanity, he maintained, is completely honest confrontation with reality. Nietzsche was a nihilist, demanding that we recognize that we can obtain no absolute knowledge of any kind. Denying positivism, he maintained that we cannot know absolute reality but only human formulations of reality. He deliberately demolished all traditional epistemologies, showing that even Descartes and Kant had assumed too much. The only thing we can know is what we directly experience, he asserted, and the only thing we directly experience is thought. We cannot even know whether there is a thinker; all we know is *es denkt:* "thought is being thought."

Because the meaning of the world, if there is any, is forever hidden from us, we must create meaning ourselves. We do this with the "will to power," by which Nietzsche did not mean aggrandizement but simply the assertion of our autonomy. Since no external or transcendent value exists to validate our will, the will creates values and meaning for itself. The "superman" (*Übermensch*) asserts charge of himself and validates himself. Although Nietzsche's thought was later perverted by the Nazis and others, he did not himself intend the "superman" to impose his own views upon anyone else: the true superman is aware that he has created his own values for himself and does not confuse them with external reality or absolute principles.

A valid construction of reality, said Nietzsche, must not rest upon fantasy: it must be empirically rooted in true human experience, which is primarily suffering and despair. Most world views are constructed to avoid this tragic view, but the result is cultures built upon illusion and easily destroyed. (Nietzsche would have viewed the nuclear death march of today as the natural extension of such illusions.) Only total honesty, integrity, and courage in facing reality will save us from destruction; we overcome evil and despair only by recognizing them, facing them, and bringing them under the control of the will. Since the cosmos has no transcendent meaning, the meaning of life lies in the joyful creation of meaning for the cosmos. Nietzsche angrily thrust aside "weak pessimism" as well as optimism and would have despised the tendency of the late twentieth century to wallow self-indulgently in meaninglessness and despair; rather, one must use nihilism to overcome nihilism, will to overcome meaninglessness, and joy to overcome despair:

> Now we celebrate, certain of universal victory,
> The festival of festivals:
> Our friend Zarathustra comes, the guest of guests!
> Now the world laughs, the cruel curtain parts,
> And the wedding feast of Light and Darkness is set.[14]

Nietzsche viewed Christianity as the dominant illusion, the dominant evasion, of Western society, but he was hostile to all religions and to the very idea of a God or any transcendent principle, even a principle of nature. In *The Joyful Wisdom* (1882) he recounted the tale of the madman who rushes into the marketplace declaring that God is dead; when no one believes him, he realizes that he "came too early." Hegel and Heine had already spoken of the death of God, but Nietzsche's parable popularized the idea among the educated classes. God was not yet gone, Nietzsche saw, but he was on his deathbed and would soon disappear—an idea revived in different forms in the later twentieth century by Martin Buber's "eclipse of God" and by the "death-of-God" theologians. For Nietzsche, the idea of God arose from two sources: the misinterpretation of natural events, and the psychological projection of our own hopes and fears.

Nietzsche had personal respect for Jesus, who, he said, taught us how to live in courageous authenticity, but he considered Christianity an evil perversion of Jesus' intentions. An empirical examination of morality, Nietzsche argued, shows that there is a master morality and a slave or herd morality; Christianity is the worst of slave moralities, based upon weakness, fear, pity, duty, and submission. The historical success of Christianity lies in its pollution of the masters with the slaves' idea that lack of power is a virtue. The followers of the "pale Galilean" thus rob us of the will to power that is our only hope of salvation. The traditional Christian Devil is a vulgar concept for which we have no need.[15] Still,

14. *Jenseits*, Nachgesang 279.
15. *Jenseits*, trans. W. Kaufmann, *Beyond Good and Evil* (New York, 1966), p. 48.

he was influenced enough by Romanticism to speculate about a positive role for the Devil. If God represents authority, repression, imposed order, and cold logic, then the Devil represents the creative force of love, feeling, and joy, and as such he is the "most ancient friend of wisdom" who "keeps us as far away from God as he can."[16] Nietzsche identified the Devil with Dionysius, who was for him the rich, ambivalent, but generally positive symbol of creativity, chaos, fertility, destruction, sexual license, and courage. Under the influence of Nietzsche and Romanticism, Dionysius and Pan became popular symbols in the art and literature of the end of the century.[17]

The blows to Christian belief dealt by Darwin, Marx, and Nietzsche were matched by that dealt by Freud. The four pillars of Christian belief are scripture, tradition, reason, and experience. The first three had already been called into question by philosophy, history, and biblical criticism. Now the fourth—personal experience—was questioned by psychoanalysis, which compared religious experience with neurotic experience. Until the late nineteenth century, psychology had been a branch of philosophy. With the growth of scientific medicine, psychology achieved its independence and moved in the direction of becoming a science, though its basic methods and epistemology are still unsettled.

Modern psychology for the most part rejects religion as an illusion and seeks the roots of good and evil not so much in the "conscious" as in the "unconscious." Indeed, modern psychology tends to avoid the term "evil"; "evil" is perceived as a metaphysical term, and "violence" a sociological one. Psychologists usually prefer to speak of "aggression," for which several large categories of explanation are offered. Depth psychology explains aggression in terms of neurotic repression; social psychology explains it in terms of group behavior; ethnographers refer it to the survival of animal competition for food and sex; and behaviorists think of it in terms of learning and conditioning. For most psychologists, God and Devil are only projections of the psyche, expressions of elements of the unconscious.

Sigmund Freud (1856–1939), the founder of psychoanalysis, attempted a scientific exploration of the unconscious.[18] The influence of

16. *Jenseits*, epigram 4.129.
17. See, for example, Arthur Machen's story "The Great God Pan," in Machen, *The House of Souls* (London, 1922), pp. 167–243. The motif appeared even in children's stories, such as Kenneth Grahame's *The Wind in the Willows* (London, 1908). For a history of Pan in literature, see P. Merivale, *Pan the Goat-God* (Cambridge, Mass., 1969).
18. Freud's most relevant works are *Totem und Tabu* (Leipzig, 1913); *Eine Teufelsneurose*

Freudianism has waned in the late twentieth century, so that philosophers no longer feel obliged to adjust their views to fit it; still, Freudian views have dominated Western thought for so long that many have become part of accepted "common sense." One of those ideas is that religion is a mere psychological phenomenon whose origins and nature can be not only explained but explained away—thus the hostility between biology and religion is supplemented by hostility between psychology and religion (psychologists who differed, such as William James, have been widely dismissed as old-fashioned).

Insisting that religious systems were illusions founded upon faith assumptions, Freud lacked Nietzsche's understanding that the same could be said for his own or any other system. He denied that religious experience might correspond to any reality whatever, and his hostility increased with age. *Totem and Taboo* (1913) criticized religion as neurotic; in *The Future of an Illusion* (1927) Freud claimed scientific proof that religion is a mere neurotic response to "the crushing power of nature," an illusion with which we seek to temper the terror of death. "Religion," he wrote, "consists of certain dogmas, assertions about facts and conditions of external (or internal) reality, which tell one something that one has not oneself discovered and which claim that one should give them credence."[19] Freud did not seem to notice that this statement applies equally to science, that the great mass of believers in science accept assertions they have not discovered for themselves and do not understand, simply on the authority of professional scientists.

Freud argued that religion is a variety of neurosis on the grounds that both provoke "pangs of conscience following an omission of neurotic or religious rites"; that both isolate such rites from ordinary life and set them apart as sacred with the feeling that "one must not be disturbed" while practicing them; that both are characterized by the conscientiousness with which details are carried out, by feelings of guilt, by repression of instincts, and by compulsive acts of penance. Freud granted that religion was different from other neuroses in that religious rites are stereotyped and neurotic ones varied; religion is usually public

im seibzehnten Jahrhundert (Leipzig, 1924); *Die Zukunft einer Illusion* (Leipzig, 1927); *Der Mann Moses und die monotheistische Religion* (Amsterdam, 1939). See Freud's *Gesammelte Werke*, 18 vols. (Frankfurt, 1952–1968), and *The Complete Psychological Works of Sigmund Freud*, 24 vols. (London, 1952–1974). See also L. de Urtubey, *Freud et le diable* (Paris, 1983); H. L. Philp, *Freud and Religious Belief* (Westport, Conn., 1956).

19. Freud, *The Future of an Illusion*, trans. W. D. Robson-Scott (Garden City, N.Y., 1957), p. 43.

and neurosis private; religious symbols are widely understood and individual ones wholly idiosyncratic. But he failed to see that he was describing the obsessional aspects of religious practice and that most people are far from obsessive in practicing their religion; he missed the distinction between rational conscientiousness and compulsiveness; and he failed to distinguish adequately between neurotic guilt, rational guilt (conscious recognition that one has done wrong in an individual instance), and existential guilt (the intuition that the cosmos and our own souls are intrinsically out of joint, that something needs to be put right). He was also inconsistent in recognizing the value of repression in producing art, music, law, and other aspects of civilization while rejecting its value in producing religion. In other words, Freud did not simply condemn neurotic religion; he condemned religion itself as neurotic.[20]

Although Freud did not believe in metaphysical evil, he early became fascinated with the Devil as a symbol of the dark, repressed depths of the unconscious. When a librarian called his attention to a manuscript containing the story of a seventeenth-century Austrian who had made a pact with the Devil and had been rescued by the Mother of God, Freud wrote a book (*Eine Teufelsneurose*) on the case. In this and his other works, he developed a diabology whose central point was that "the Devil is clearly nothing other than the personification of repressed, unconscious drives."[21] Since the Devil traditionally took on many forms and shapes, Freud was able to identify him with an equally diverse number of neuroses—most generally, with the counterwill created by unconscious repression. For example, a woman wishes to nurse her baby but develops an illness that prevents her from doing so; the woman has unconsciously repressed her disgust with the process; the repression creates a *Widerwille*, a counterwill that expresses itself in her incapacity. Thus the unconscious works against our conscious will just as the Devil was traditionally supposed to do. Because Freud believed that sexuality is the most frequently and powerfully repressed force, he thought the Devil particularly represented the power of repressed sexual drives, which often cause people to act against their conscious will. Noting the frequent traditional connection of the Devil with anal imagery (in Luther, for example), Freud considered him especially the symbol of repressed anal eroticism.

20. Philp, pp. 21–37.
21. Freud, "Character und Analerotik," *Sammlung kleiner Schriften zur Neurosenlehre*, 2d ser. (1909), p. 136.

Most important, the Devil was a *Vaterersatz*, a substitute for the seductive father, a concept that Freud emphasized in the earlier part of his career. Repression of the father's sexual abuse of a child, seductive behavior on his part, or the child's own fantasies of paternal seduction create a powerful force in the child's unconscious that is readily personified as the Devil. Freud took as evidence the stories of witches copulating with the Devil at sabbats, bolstered by witch accounts of the Devil's large, serpentlike penis. A seductive mother or nursemaid could also produce powerful repressions in the child, who might express them later in terms of sorceresses, witches, phallic mothers, or *vaginae dentatae*. As Freud later moved away from his emphasis upon the seductive father, he came to regard the Devil more as a symbol for any hatred of a parent; in this view the Devil represents the child's repressed desire for the parent's death. Still later, he saw the Devil as a symbol of repressed fear of death or death itself. In short, the Devil always represented whatever element of the unconscious Freud saw as most in opposition to the conscious will.

Freud's followers introduced variations. Ernest Jones developed a full psychoanalytic theory of the Devil, beginning with the idea that religious beliefs are fantasies arising from the repression of impulses condemned by religion.[22] The force of the repressed libido expresses itself in images of incubi, witches, demons, and the Devil. In a sense, Jones suggested, Christians are right in seeing the Devil as their chief opponent, for he represents the libidinous energies that the Christian religion has tried to eradicate. Like Freud, Jones made the Devil the symbol of repressed instincts, especially those relating to relationships between father and child. The Devil can symbolize either the father whom the child hates and wishes to destroy or the child who defies or revolts against the father. The Devil, witches, fearsome goddesses, and other evil figures are always linked to problems of authority and repression. They are fierce and irrational deities with whom one does not debate or exchange views; they must be either obeyed or defied.

One of the most important discoveries of depth psychology, for the study of diabology, is the power of negative projection. When we are unaware of the process of repression within ourselves, we project the negative elements that we refuse to recognize within ourselves onto others, especially onto individuals and groups that we identify as enemies or potential enemies. Since I surely cannot be cruel or greedy, the

22. E. Jones, *Nightmares, Witches, and Devils* (New York, 1911).

source of the cruel and greedy feelings that I sense within me must be X, whom I dislike. This now justifies my hostility to X. The more powerful my own repressed cruelty, the more cruel I imagine X to be. If the feelings are powerful enough, I may self-righteously judge that such a cruel person as X is a menace to society and ought to be re-moved—by force, if necessary. I may end by venting my own hidden cruelty upon X, justifying it on the basis of his alleged cruelty, which I have myself projected upon him.

Freud's disciple Melanie Klein perceived the relationship between negative projection and a process she called "splitting." Splitting arises from the desire to preserve the absolute goodness of a beloved object by denying that there is any imperfection in it; any evil or imperfection must be transferred from the beloved object to something else. This behavior, Klein observed, is normal among young children, who split people and objects into good and bad categories, idealizing the good and projecting evil upon the other. The child is especially concerned with keeping a perfect image of the beloved parent. The child will often make radical shifts in his or her perceptions as a result of splitting: if once any evil is admitted to exist in the idealized object, the child may quickly move it from the good category and perceive it as entirely evil. As the normal person develops, he or she gradually accepts ambivalence and progressively restricts the spheres of absolute goodness and absolute evil. Every individual and group, however, seems to retain some degree of need to split and to make absolute positive and negative projections, though the tendency is in inverse proportion to emotional maturity. Klein perceived the tendency to divide the cosmos between a good and evil metaphysical force as a fixation of the immature tendency to split rather than to recognize ambivalence.[23]

Among Freud's associates, the most independent and original in his approach to religion was Carl G. Jung (1875–1961).[24] Jung took religion

---

23. M. Klein, *Contributions to Psycho-Analysis* (London, 1965), pp. 221–224, 288, 346, 358, 366; P. Heimann, "A Contribution to the Re-evaluation of the Oedipus Complex— The Early Stages," in M. Klein, ed., *New Directions in Psycho-Analysis* (New York, 1957), pp. 23–25.

24. On Jung and Jungianism, see *Evil*, ed. the Curatorium of the C. G. Jung Institute (Evanston, 1967); H. L. Philp, *Jung and the Problem of Evil* (London, 1958); J. A. Sanford, *Evil: The Shadow Side of Reality* (New York, 1981); R. A. Segal, "A Jungian View of Evil," *Zygon*, 20 (1985), 83–89; M.-L. Von Franz, *The Shadow and Evil in Fairy Tales* (New York, 1974). Among Jung's most helpful works are his *Modern Man in Search of a Soul* (New York, 1933); *Answer to Job* (New York, 1954); *Psychology and Religion* (New Haven, 1960); "Septem sermones ad mortuos," in *Memories, Dreams, Reflections* (New York, 1961), pp.

far more seriously and more positively than the Freudians; seeing it as a necessary part of the psyche and human civilization, he judged its expressions to be psychologically valid rather than neurotic. As to whether God and the Devil have metaphysical reality, he did not always speak consistently. Essentially, he considered them myths—but for Jung, myths are not idle inventions; they are powerful and omnipresent psychological realities.

The center of Jung's system, which he called analytical psychology, is the process of individuation or integration, which restructures the individual so as to integrate positively the power of the unconscious with that of the conscious. Psychological wholeness and health depend upon becoming aware of the elements of the unconscious, facing them squarely, and integrating them into one's consciousness in the light of reason. Jung distinguished sharply between suppression, a healthy process by which we consciously reject something, and repression, an unhealthy process in which we unconsciously deny feelings and refuse to deal with them. Repressions create a force in the unconscious that may burst out in inappropriate and destructive behavior. Jung differed radically from the Freudians in insisting that the powerful contents of the unconscious are not exclusively the product of repressions; some elements of the unconscious, he said, are part of a collective unconscious transcending the individual and embracing all of humanity. The physical structure of the brain, the product of genetic evolution, is similar in all *homo sapiens* and thus produces similarities in basic constructs of unconscious thought that Jung called archetypes; these in turn tend to produce structurally similar myths or images. In order to achieve a psychological whole, therefore, each of us must come to terms with both the personal and the collective aspects of our individual unconscious.

In such a view, the Devil is much more powerful than in Freudianism, for he is not only the expression of individual repressions but

---

378–390; and essays found in his *Collected Works*, 20 vols. (New York, 1957–1979), including "The Shadow," vol. 9:2, pp. 3–7; "The Fight with the Shadow," vol. 10, pp. 218–226; "Good and Evil in Analytical Psychology," vol. 10, pp. 456–458; "Psychology and Religion: The Definition of Demonism," vol. 18, p. 648. Other humanistic psychological works on evil include E. Becker, *Escape from Evil* (New York, 1975); E. Becker, *The Structure of Evil* (New York, 1968); L. Doob, *Panorama of Evil: Insights for the Behavioral Sciences* (Westport, Conn., 1978); E. Fromm, *The Anatomy of Human Destructiveness* (New York, 1973); R. May, *Power and Innocence* (New York, 1972). On some modern scientific psychological approaches to aggression, see R. G. Geen and E. I. Donnerstein, eds., *Aggression*, 2 vols. (New York, 1983).

also a reflection of the autonomous, timeless, and universal collective unconscious. Like Freud, Jung took possession seriously as a psychological rather than a spiritual manifestation, a neurotic or psychotic state that occurs when shadow elements replace the ego in controlling the personality. Jung associated particular archetypes with the Devil: the Wise Old Man who has learned wisdom through suffering; the Trickster, or Hermes, the divine messenger telling us about the irrational unconscious; the anima or animus, representing the repressed female side of a man or the repressed male side of a woman; the serpent or ouroboros, representing the one and the all, the beginning and the end, the conjunction of opposites; and what he called the Shadow.

Jung rejected modern religion's tendency toward activism and extraversion, pointing out that the introvert observes and experiences internal, psychic events as sharply and directly as the extravert experiences external events; thus the introvert is more likely to have a powerful experience of God or Devil. Modern society's readiness to dismiss the Devil is a sign of its shallowness, its unwillingness to face the reality of evil. It is particularly absurd for the church to shirk reality in this way, Jung argued, for in doing so, it becomes a positive-thinking society incapable of a full understanding of either the human personality or the cosmos, unable to deal with human cruelty or with the terrifying hand of God in natural disasters. Good and evil are not subjective or relative but rooted in a collective reality greater than the individual.

For Jung, evil is as real as good; it is a necessary part of the cosmos and indeed of God.[25] Jung's model for the cosmos and for the psyche was the "coincidence of opposites," a concept derived from the medieval mystics and from Nicholas of Cusa in particular.[26] God is totally beyond any of our categories, Jung believed. Only the totality of God is absolute, not any of the categories that we project upon him. When we say that God is good or God is powerful, we are using human categories that cannot restrict God and are as far from God's reality as the earth is

25. Jung denied the traditional idea of evil as privation, but he did not understand it. Privation theory does not deny the real power of evil in the cosmos or in the human personality but rather denies it ultimate metaphysical being: i.e., denies that it proceeds from God's Being itself. It likens evil to cold, which is an absence of heat but which can kill by draining heat away. Jung himself used this imagery in calling evil "the eternally sucking gorge of the void," bleeding life, joy, color, and love out of the world. See "Septem sermones contra mortuos," pp. 382–383, 386, 389.

26. For Nicholas, see Lucifer, pp. 275–283. Some critics have mistaken Jung for a dualist because of his emphasis on evil; quite the contrary, he was a strict monist, positing good and evil as two aspects of a whole.

below the heavens. Good and evil are human categories; they reflect certain realities in the cosmos; but no human category, and therefore neither good nor evil, can limit God. God must be perceived as a coincidence of all opposites: he is great and small, old and young, just and merciful, and so on, just as Nicholas of Cusa had said. But Jung took a step that Nicholas did not dare take: God is also both good and evil. That is to say that God embraces and unites in himself all that humans categorize as good or evil. Jung argued that the Christians had been right to symbolize the multiplicity of the godhead by calling it a Trinity rather than a Unity, but that they had not gone far enough, for the Christian Trinity seems to exclude both the principle of evil and the feminine principle. Jung's solution was always fuzzy and inconsistent: he suggested a Quaternity but his fourth person was sometimes the feminine principle and sometimes the Devil. He was cautious enough to balk at a Quinity, knowing from his reading of the gnostics that one could go on adding persons to the godhead forever.

The good Lord and the Devil, Jung argued, are but two sides to the fullness of reality, which he called the pleroma: "The shadow belongs to the light as the evil belongs to the good, and *vice versa*." Without darkness to define it, light could not appear good.[27] Evil and the Devil are real; they are part of creation, part of God's stuff. By rebelling against the good Lord, Lucifer carried out the fullness of God's plan, for his challenge to God produces a deeper and higher wisdom. The Devil is an enormously powerful energy in the cosmos which, if ignored and denied, will burst forth with a destructiveness proportional to the degree of its repression; if admitted and absorbed, its energy can be turned toward the greater good. Repression leads to mental illness on the individual level and to ruin on the collective level; acceptance and incorporation lead to individuation, health, and creativity. Jung cautioned that the demonic energy is never neutral; if it is not channeled toward the constructive, it will burst with equal power into the destructive. The modern refusal to accept the reality of the Devil is a cause as well as a symptom of impending destruction.

Jung accepted the Devil as a mythical symbol rather than as a metaphysical entity in the Christian sense. His term "the Shadow" is not entirely congruent with the Christian Devil. The Shadow is a force of the unconscious, a primitive psychological element lacking moral con-

27. Jung, *Modern Man in Search of a Soul*, pp. 41, 215; "Septem sermones contra mortuos," p. 382.

trol. It is primarily part of the personal unconscious, consisting of repressed material. Since what is repressed varies with the individual, the individual Shadow does not necessarily correspond with the social, collective, or metaphysical view of evil; for example, the Shadow of a criminal personality might consist of a number of elements that society considers good. Jung also suggested the existence of a collective Shadow, the Shadow of a group, society, or nation, which manifests itself in mass phenomena such as racism or violent revolution, or in cruel leaders such as Hitler or Stalin. Beyond both individual and collective Shadows, an archetypal Shadow may also exist, though Jung was not clear on this point. At times he suggested that the demonic Shadow, consisting of repressed material that might become destructive if not integrated, could be distinguished from the Satanic Shadow, which was intrinsically evil and sought to suck everything down into the eternal vacuum and void. The archetypal Shadow, representing evil as perceived collectively by all of humanity, would be close to absolute evil, close to the traditional Devil. The more the Shadow—whether individual or collective—is repressed and isolated, the more violent and destructive it becomes, often expressing itself in negative projections. In modern war the most destructive forces of the collective and perhaps archetypal Shadows are released. The enemy is dehumanized, turned into a group of demons, monsters, or subhumans.

We can defeat evil, Jung argued, only by recognizing it, naming it, and raising it to the level of the conscious. When brought out into the light, the dark power loses its poison; it can be placed under the command of reason and turned in the direction of constructiveness, individuation, and wholeness.

Most professional psychologists have dismissed the concept of evil as a metaphysical abstraction, preferring to work with other abstractions such as the social concept of violence or the more strictly psychological concept of aggression. Recently, however, some psychologists have begun to think that a concept akin to the old concept of evil is necessary in order to describe the phenomena they encounter. In their long psychiatric practice with criminals, S. Yochelson and S. Samenow observed that certain personalities are so completely founded upon lies and self-deception that traditional sociological and psychological remedies have no effect. A substantial number of criminals are people who freely choose a life of crime, and the criminal's behavior is "caused" by the way he thinks—not by his family, peers, or neighborhood. The criminal is a "victimizer, a molder of his environment, rather than a mere product of that mold."[28] Rex Beaber, professor of medicine at the University of California, Los Angeles, was led by his long practice with violent criminals to ask whether there is "an extra force, a dark force, that works through humans and perpetrates terror."[29] Such views avoid the danger of relying upon palliative measures, whether liberal or behaviorist. The sense of radical evil also permits the examination of questions of value that scientific psychology is by definition unequipped to undertake.

As psychology struggled to define evil, the literary Devil continued to appear in the Romantic guise of Satan the hero or Satan the noble penitent, but as Romanticism declined into Decadence toward the end of the nineteenth century, the Devil reflected the then fashionable traits of irony and cynicism. In many writers, the Devil is a tiresomely repeated reflection of the poet himself: artistic, rebellious, cruel, sensual, and devouring.[30]

The strongest symbol of literary diabolism in this period was Mephistopheles, who reveals the folly and futility of human life. One of the bleakest representatives of this genre is Mark Twain's *Mysterious Stranger*. This work, which Twain (1835–1910) began in 1897, has appeared in three different versions.[31] Twain's original idea was to write the story of an unfallen angel who bore the name of the chief of the fallen angels, a "young Satan" who would be numinous and powerful and who would

28. S. Yochelson and S. Samenow, *The Criminal Personality*, 2 vols. (New York, 1977), vol. 1, p. 104; see also S. Samenow, *Inside the Criminal Mind* (New York, 1984).

29. R. Beaber, "The Pathology of Evil," *Los Angeles Times*, January 6, 1985. See also M. S. Peck, *People of the Lie* (New York, 1983), and Dorothy Rowe's argument in *The Construction of Life and Death* (New York, 1982) that people are responsible for building their own world view.

30. Christopher Pearse Cranch (1813–1892), *Satan: A Libretto* (Boston, 1874), presented Satan as a symbol of the wild aspects of life and nature. For Wilfrid Blunt (1840–1922), in *Satan Absolved: A Victorian Mystery* (London, 1899), God forgives Satan and makes him his new incarnation; Satan, sad and weary, takes up the infinite task of saving this wretched world. For Marie Corelli (1855–1924), *The Sorrows of Satan* (London, 1895), humans and demons are fellow sufferers in a cruel universe constructed by a remote deity. George Santayana (1863–1952), *Lucifer, or The Heavenly Truce*, 2d ed. (Cambridge, Mass., 1927), distinguished between Lucifer, the noble Romantic rebel who asserts his autonomy against an autocratic God, and Mephistopheles, who is full of malice and hatred. See also G. Meredith, "Lucifer in Starlight," *Oxford Book of English Verse* (Oxford, 1921), p. 942; and *The Picture of Dorian Gray* and *Salome* by Oscar Wilde (1854–1900).

31. The early version, *The Mysterious Stranger*, was edited in 1916 after Twain's death by A. B. Paine and F. A. Duncka; it is sometimes called "the Eseldorf version." A second is entitled *The Chronicle of Young Satan*. The third, sometimes called "the Printshop version," is *No. 44, The Mysterious Stranger* (Berkeley, 1982).

sardonically reject conventional religion and ethics; he would represent a positive rebellion of clarity, reason, and humanity against the evil of convention and obscurantism. The "young Satan" would first appear to readers as evil, but Twain's irony would reveal that he was really good. The categories were confused and shifting, and Twain struggled with the book for years without ever quite bringing it off, yet the story remains unforgettably disturbing.

In the earliest version, a stranger suddenly appears in a medieval Austrian village. He offers his name as Philip Traum ("Dream"), but the reader soon learns that he is really "Young Satan," the nephew of the Dark Lord. Young Satan's magical tricks make fools of the villagers; he ridicules conventions, unmasks frauds and hypocrites, and teaches the young boys a catechism that mocks Christianity. He appears to be an irresponsible though charming trickster, but on occasion an appalling cruelty flashes out to the surface: to amuse the boys, for example, he creates a village of tiny people—and then crushes them under his thumb. Here Twain allowed Satan's real character to rise to the surface in order to make a terrifying statement on the nature of God, for Satan's cruelty to the tiny village represents God's cruelty to the village of real people. Is Satan God? Is the world evil, or merely idiotically amoral? Twain could not decide, could not find an effective balance between originality and tradition. In the last version, the stranger is no longer "Satan" but a mysterious "Number 44," whose moral ambivalence was easier to portray.

Still, Number 44 leaves his young Austrian friend at the end of the story with a black and powerful statement of emptiness. Critics have taken the passage in a number of ways, but its fundamental nihilism and solipsism are clear, and its words of pure pessimistic negation may constitute the core of the Devil's message to the dawning twentieth century.

Nothing exists; all is a dream. God—man—the world—the sun, the moon, the wilderness of stars; a dream, all a dream, they have no existence. *Nothing exists save empty space—and you!* . . . And you are not *you*—you have no body, no blood, no bones, you are but a *thought*. I myself have no existence, I am but a dream—your dream. . . . Strange! that you should not have suspected, years ago, centuries, ages, aeons ago! for you have existed, companionless through all the eternities. Strange, indeed, that you should not have suspected that your universe and its contents were only dreams, visions, fictions! Strange, because they are so frankly and hysterically insane—like all dreams: a God who could make good children as easily as bad, yet preferred to make bad ones; who could have made every one of them happy, yet never made a single happy one; who made them prize their bitter life, yet stingily cut it short . . . who mouths justice, and invented hell—mouths mercy, and invented hell—mouths Golden Rules, and forgiveness multiplied by seventy times seven, and invented hell; who mouths morals to other people and has none himself; who frowns upon crimes, yet commits them all . . . and finally, with altogether divine obtuseness, invites this poor abused slave to worship him! . . . It is true, that which I have revealed to you: there is no God, no universe, no human race, no earthly life, no heaven, no hell. It is all a Dream, a grotesque and foolish dream.

These words, which the traditional Satan might easily have uttered himself, are Twain's last literary statement. They form a bridge between Romantic Satanism and Nietzschean nihilism, a bridge from which the road to the despairing meaninglessness of the late twentieth century runs straight and broad. The narrator's response, and the last words of the book, are: "He vanished, and left me appalled, for I knew, and realized, that all he had said was true."[32]

Other writers used Mephistopheles to ironic or cynical ends, though with less than Twain's devastating directness.[33] Mephisto was also the subject of light satire, as in the story "Enoch Soames," by Max Beerbohm (1872–1956). An unpopular and disappointed writer, Soames sells the Devil his soul in exchange for foreknowledge of whether he will be famous a hundred years later. The Devil spirits him off to the British Museum Reading Room (neither Mephisto nor Beerbohm foresaw that it would become the "British Library Reading Room" and be moved to a new building) on June 3, 1997, where poor Soames, consulting the catalogues, learns to his horror that his work has remained totally obscure.

Once the Devil had become a figure of satire or amusement rather than terror, his truly frightening aspects were transferred to monsters derived from folklore or created by science fiction. *Dracula*, by Bram Stoker (1847–1912), followed Mary Shelley and Poe in this direction, and eventually Satan became simply one of a huge cast of evil creatures in a chaotic chamber of horrors. Late twentieth-century films such as Steven Spielberg's *Poltergeist* (1982) illustrate this chaos, incoherently muddling horrors from theology, folklore, science fiction, and the occult.

32. *No. 44*, pp. 186–187.
33. Similar cynical views were put forward by Mario Rapisardi (1841–1912), Anatole France (1844–1924), Guy de Maupassant (1850–1893), H. L. Mencken (1880–1956), and G. B. Shaw (1856–1950).

An original effort at a human diabology is *Un uomo finito* ("A Finished Man") by Giovanni Papini (1881–1956). Papini grew up an atheist but converted to Catholicism after the First World War; when he published *Un uomo finito* in 1912, he was already taking the problem of evil seriously. The book is both a fictional autobiography of Papini's early life and a fictional account of the Devil's own career: the author made his own career the symbol of Satan, and Satan the symbol of the demonic in the human mind. The unnamed protagonist is both Papini and Lucifer.

The book begins with the protagonist's childhood. He is isolated from other children and adults by his sense of alienation, his feeling of being almost of another race. His alienation and pride feed on one another, and he grows up introspective, aloof, solitary, and contemptuous of other people, especially those of his own age. Hated and rejected by them, he yearns for heroic stature and heroic action that will prove him their superior. Isolated and unhappy, he builds a fantasy life and soon discovers that knowledge is his best weapon against a hostile world. He desires to learn everything and begins ruthlessly to master knowledge, not out of love and openheartedness but out of pride and self-defense. He contemplates with pleasure the self-destruction of the human race that will leave the earth "revolving pointlessly in the heavens."[34]

As a young man, Papini's protagonist revolts against God and humanity with "all the force of his Satanic spirit" (p. 78). He recruits as disciples brilliant intellectual comrades dominated by hatred, competition, and rebellion. To these he preaches his religion, which is at first a vague pantheism and then a dogged solipsism: nothing exists but his own mind; the cosmos is a mere projection of his mind (p. 104). He founds a journal, *Leonardo*, aimed at the destruction of Christianity and the spread of his relativistic ideas. Like Faust, he turns his knowledge to the love of power, a sign of the irrationality of his supposed rationalism and of the growing hatred that is filling the gap in his soul left by the lack of love (p. 166).

He plans a great literary work—"a cosmic poem, a universal drama, an infinite scene"—that would lift him further above his contempo-

34. G. Papini, *Un uomo finito* (Florence, 1912), p. 73: "Suicidio in masso, suicidio cosciente, concordemente deliberato, tale da lasciar sola e deserta la terra a rotolare inutilmente nei cieli." The phrase encapsulates the equation between human destructiveness and the Devil's hope of destroying God's plan for the world.

raries than Dante and Goethe were above theirs (p. 224). When his journal, his poem, and his career all fail, he at last recognizes that he cannot become God and plunges into an orgy of self-pity and self-justification: fate has given him the wrong family, the wrong education, the wrong friends. He writes a work to justify himself, which, with masterful irony, turns out to be *Un uomo finito* itself. He boasts of the heroic scale of his failure.

The center of the protagonist's sinfulness, as Papini was coming to understand even as he wrote, is his failure to recognize that he is evil.[35] Lacking love and forgiveness of himself as well as of others, he wallows in the feeling that he is only mud and muck (p. 339), and this radical sense of worthlessness and meaninglessness impels him to sacrifice his own happiness and that of others to his quest for a heroic life. He chants a hymn to his alienation: "I was born a revolutionary. . . . Whoever rules the world, I shall oppose him. The essential expression of my spirit is protest; the spontaneous posture of my body is assault with bayonet; my natural mode of speech is invective and insult. On my lips every song of love becomes an anthem of revolt" (p. 383). With lucid irony, Papini saw in his own act of writing *Un uomo finito* the final boast, the final act of self-deception. In point of fact, the final joke is on us, for Papini's protagonist is not only Satan and Papini but also the intellectual reader.

In 1953, long after his conversion, Papini returned to the subject and wrote a sketch for what he called a future *summa diabologica*. He dismissed the modern tendency to take the Devil as a mere symbol of human sin rather than a personal, transcendent power of evil. Nonetheless, he argued, the transcendent Devil is increasingly immanent and realized in human nature, so that any successful modern diabology must be built upon observation of human evil. For Papini, the Devil has three separate but integrated functions: he is a rebel against God and the order of the cosmos; he is a tempter and enemy of humanity; but he is also a collaborator with God, who would not tolerate him if he did not fill some ultimate function in the cosmos. The Devil is not an atheist; he has seen God and knows that he is under the divine power. God uses the Devil and evil to do what is necessary to accomplish salvation. Without the Devil—without the tension between good and evil—poetry, art, philsophy, and statesmanship would be impossible. If there

---

35. "Diabolical people don't believe in the Devil," Papini observed in "Cristo e santi"; see *I classici contemporanei italiani*, vol. 5 (Verona, 1962), p. 111.

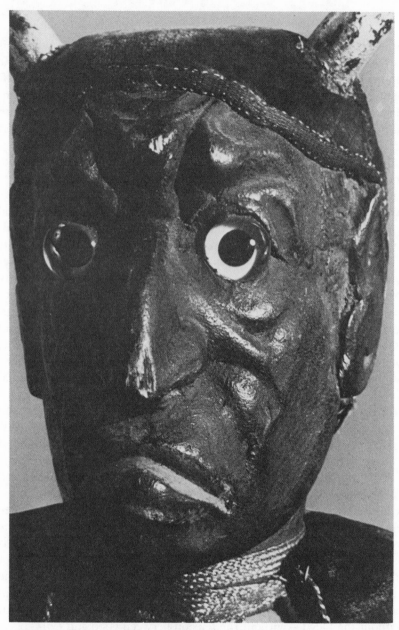

Marionette from the theater of the Jardin des Tuileries in the period 1880–1908. This poor Devil's face reflects irony and malice turned to defeat. Cliché des musées nationaux. Courtesy of Musée National des Arts et Traditions Populaires.

were no spiritual combat, there would be no spiritual growth, no room for moral freedom. Josiah Royce once summed up this point of view: "The best world for a moral agent is one that needs him to make it better."[36]

The life and works of Feodor Mikhailovich Dostoevsky (1821–1881) represent the most intense struggle with evil of the entire period.[37] As a youth, Dostoevsky was attracted to nihilism, anarchism, atheism, and revolution. A friend of the radical Vissarion Belinsky, he became eloquently antireligious. He was imprisoned for his political views and sentenced to death. In a reprieve that was itself an act of cruelty, he was stood up against a wall to be shot, only to have the sentence commuted to exile at the last moment. This event and the four years in a Siberian convict prison that followed deepened the darkness of his outlook. He abandoned radicalism in favor of Christianity, first adopting a vague populist religion, then flirting with Catholicism, and eventually reentering the Orthodox Church.

Rejecting Western politics and religion, he found in Russian spirituality the compassion, the intense sense of sin and suffering, that offered hope of salvation. His ideal was *sobornost*, the ancient Russian ideal of a communion of believers centered on the love of Christ and on mutual responsibility and charity. Dostoevsky worked fiercely to purge his life and his ideas of the slightest touch of facile optimism. The community of love can be realized, he believed, only by eschewing all illusion and squarely facing the human condition. No view of the world was worthy that did not give full attention to sin and suffering. Dostoevsky's thought became increasingly more spiritual and more Christian as he grew older, and in his late novel, *The Brothers Karamazov*, his full vision of spiritual and communal love opened up in the characters of Father Zossima and Alyosha Karamazov.

For Dostoevsky, the Devil was a transcendent power but one best

36. J. Royce, *The World and the Individual* (New York, 1959), vol. 2, p. 340.

37. I am unable to read Russian, but Dostoevsky's importance forces me to make an exception to the rule that I do not discuss writers I cannot read in the original. I use the Constance Garnett translations of *Crime and Punishment* (1866), *The Idiot* (1868), *The Possessed* (1872; alternatively known as *The Devils*), and *The Brothers Karamazov* (1880). On Dostoevsky, see V. Cerny, *Dostoevsky and His Devils* (Ann Arbor, 1975); I. Dolenc, *Dostoevsky and Christ* (Toronto, 1978); P. Evdokimov, *Dostoievsky et le problème du mal* (Paris, 1978); J. Fletcher, "Literature and the Problem of Evil," *Theology*, 79 (1976), 274–280, 337–343; J. Frank, *Dostoevsky*, 3 vols., in progress (Princeton, 1976–).

observed in human behavior. The Devil's home is not hell but the human soul. He is a shadow whose form and substance are filled out by the cruelty of sinners and the suffering of the weak and the poor. Dostoevsky grasped the reality of evil and of the Devil intensely and intuitively. He insisted that in order to overcome and master evil, we must name it for what it is and respond to it with love, for evil is not the last word in the cosmos; the last word is the God who is love.

Each normal human being experiences an internal struggle between good and evil. Dostoevsky frequently portrayed this struggle in "doublets": two characters each displaying one side of a whole personality, the evil side of which must be integrated and transformed by love if it is not to be destroyed. The human demonic incarnates the Devil, who is an intellectual seeking knowledge without love; a liar presenting a false view of the world and human relationships; a doubter and a cynic; an individualist reveling in his own isolation, despising the people and lacking any sense of community. The hell he inhabits is alienation from love, from community, and from God. In *Crime and Punishment*, Raskolnikov, having murdered the old usurer and her sister, is haunted by a doublet composed of the angelic Sonia and the demonic Svidrigaylov. In *The Idiot*, Myshkin is set against Rogozhin—through Rogozhin is not evil enough to be fully demonic, and Myshkin, while he is a kind of fool for Christ, is too ineffective and isolated to be a saint.

The Possessed (or *The Devils*) is Dostoevsky's first thorough exploration of the demonic. When he began the novel, he planned to center it upon the false world view of Verkhovensky and the other political revolutionaries, but he gradually shifted his focus to Stavrogin, the spiritual rebel. Shatov speaks for Russia, Christ, and *sobornost;* the engineer Kirilov represents pure intellectualism cut off from feeling and community, a pride of intellect and illusion of self-sufficiency characteristic of the intellectual devil. Pyotr Stepanovich Verkhovensky, the political rebel, is also a sensualist whose plan is to destroy society and to build a new world devoted to vice. His atheism rejects the reality of the cosmos as well as that of God; wrapped up in his fantasies of sensuality and power, his own mind is his cosmos, and he is blind to reality.

The central figure of *The Devils* is Nikolai Vsevolodovich Stavrogin, whose name conveys both pride and suffering: Nikolai, conqueror of nations; Vsevolodovich, master of all; Stavrogin, from the Greek *stauros,* the Cross. Stavrogin is torn between evil and guilt, but at every crucial moment when a choice is to be made, he chooses evil. He has conformed his will to Satan and given himself over to the Devil. Stavrogin is capable of great charm; he talks well, is convivial, and appears bluff and friendly; yet he excels in self-deception as well as the deception of others. Underneath his facade lurks an unquenchable hunger for power, self-sufficiency, and independence from his fellow humans. Composed, cold, and careful, Stavrogin lacks all tenderness, compassion, empathy, and enthusiasm. His ultimate suicide expresses the meaningless selfishness of his entire life.

Stavrogin's spiritual state is expressed most sharply in the episode involving Matryosha, which the censors deleted for decades, depriving the book of much of its meaning. Matryosha is the twelve-year-old daughter of Stavrogin's landlady. Stavrogin works patiently at seducing the child and finally succeeds. Dostoevsky, who seems to have controlled his own pedophilic tendencies with painful determination, regarded the seduction of a child as the most shameful possible crime. Worse, Stavrogin accomplishes the seduction totally without love or joy, feeling only a monstrous combination of lust and despair. Aware of his own corruption, he chooses not to resist it and succumbs to a fatalistic indifference as to whether he is discovered and punished. The child, obsessed with shame and guilt, hangs herself; Stavrogin's eventual fate is to follow her example. His immediate response to the girl's suicide, however, is to enter into a grotesque marriage with Maria Timofeyevna Lebytkin, an idiot cripple. His motives here are even more lifelessly diabolical than in the seduction of the child: he marries Maria to punish himself for Matryosha, to mock Maria, to make light of marriage, to flout every value—even the value of personal success—and to pursue a directionless curiosity to see "what would come of it." Underlying all his behavior is the conviction that life is an empty, meaningless absurdity.

Later, Stavrogin determines to confess to the holy priest Tihon. He presents himself with that combination of diffidence and frankness that constitutes charm but can be a clever facade for a dark, complex, and chaotic personality. Tihon asks Stavrogin whether he has really seen the Devil, and Stavrogin replies in an ironic tone: "Of course I see him. I see him just as plainly as I see you. . . . And sometimes I do not know who is real, he or I."[38] The presence of a saint such as Tihon always compels the Devil to utter the truth, and though Stavrogin tries to protect himself with mockery, he finds himself revealing his true self to the priest. Tihon, sensing the chaos in this man, retains his distance.

38. F. Dostoevsky, *The Possessed*, trans. C. Garnett (New York, 1936), p. 697.

Stavrogin jeers that of all people a priest ought not to doubt the Devil's presence in Stavrogin's soul, but Tihon cautions, "It's more likely a disease." Certainly the Devil exists, the priest admits, and certainly he can possess people, but it is prudent to be cautious about affirming his presence. Again the Devil is forced to bear witness to the truth: Stavrogin bursts out in reply, "I do believe in the Devil, I believe canonically, in a personal Devil, not in an allegory, and I don't need confirmation from anybody" (p. 697). Stavrogin intends to mock what he takes as Tihon's simplicity, but of course the simple truth is that he needs no confirmation because he experiences the Devil in his soul directly.

Stavrogin continues to suppose that he is playing with Tihon. "Is it possible to believe in the Devil without believing in God?" he inquires with a smile, and Tihon's reply is itself ironic: "That is quite possible. It's done right and left" (p. 698). The confession proceeds on the knife edge between salvation and damnation. Stavrogin is free, even this late, to open his heart and accept reality, and at one point that possibility becomes poignantly acute. "I love you," he suddenly cries out to Tihon, and to the Christ who speaks in Tihon. The saving grace rises in his heart, but his life has been so long lost in lies that he loses the moment; he is so used to self-deception that he does not realize when at last he sees the truth.

But God is patient; Stavrogin boasts that he feels no repentance for his crime, yet a minute later—caught unaware by pity—he declares that he would gladly die to make it not have happened (p. 711). He has even had a full confession of his guilt printed up and plans to distribute it. Some modern critics, influenced perhaps by the examples set by twentieth-century criminals and writers, have intepreted this as a shameless boast of sin, a boast that in the context of his confession would be the utmost blasphemy. But that is not his state of mind at this moment. Neither lust nor pride dominate him, only despair. The planned publication is a deliberate act of self-degradation, a recognition of total and irredeemable corruption. Stavrogin knows that even though God has compelled him to reveal the truth in spite of himself, his confession has not been made with honesty or love. "I know for a certainty that I am doomed," he says, and his absentminded breaking of a small crucifix between his fingers as he speaks symbolizes his rejection of salvation (p. 717). He returns to his mocking tone, telling Tihon that his whole purpose in coming was "to forgive myself. That's my chief object" (p. 727).

Perhaps even the confession was not Stavrogin's last chance. The meaning of his suicide note is eternally ambiguous: "No one is to blame. I did it myself." Are the words a final act of mocking pride, a boast that he was autonomous to the end, independent, isolated, refusing to be obliged to the community even for his own death? Or are they a last burst of true self-recognition? If so, they are immediately negated by the suicide itself, which in the Orthodox Church is an unforgivable sin. Stavrogin is one of the most perfect expressions in literature of a person who has given himself fully and truly to the Devil, a person who quickly snuffs out every flash of redeeming grace that springs in his soul, a person who condemns himself to the lightlessness of joyless sin and despair. He is an incarnation of the essential sadness of sin.

The Devil is very close in *The Devils;* in *The Brothers Karamazov* he confronts us face to face. The family Karamazov may be regarded as a set of character traits that together constitute a whole personality. The father, Feodor Pavlovich, is an irresponsible sensualist whose personality is reflected in the eldest of the three legitimate sons, Dmitri. The second son, Ivan, is an intellectual motivated by a prideful and cynical desire for knowledge. The youngest son, Alyosha, is of all Dostoevksy's characters closest to the author's own ideal—a spiritual, thoughtful, friendly, and cheerful young man who, unlike his brothers, inherits his mother's sweetness rather than his father's corruption. Alyosha is drawn to God through love of community; he knows that if one loves fully, one's love spreads out into the community. Unlike the ineffective Myshkin (in *The Idiot*), Alyosha is practical enough to translate his spirituality into effective action. In the end it is Alyosha's life that is the only effective answer to his family's corruption. The illegitimate son, Smerdyakov, is motivated by hatred and envy, owing to his inferior origin and position. The most important character outside the family is Father Zossima, Alyosha's confessor: Zossima is Alyosha at a mature age, a man of deep spirituality and love whose life is lived according to the principle of *sobornost* that people can be truly free only when they learn to act freely in loving cooperation with the community. The selfless love of *sobornost* conforms a person to Christ; individualism, with its attendant selfishness and envy, conforms a person to Satan.

Smerdyakov falls under the influence of Ivan's atheistic, individualistic ideas, which provide him an intellectual rationalization for his own hatred and envy. Ivan argues that the principle of God is that of a necessary being to whom all is permitted, and since God does not exist, it is the human individual to whom all is permitted. God does not exist, and "there's no devil either," Ivan tells his father—but Ivan forgets that if an individual may take God's place, he may also take the Devil's.[39] Ivan is too selfishly clever to follow his own moral relativism to its logical ends, but the stupid Smerdyakov translates Ivan's theories into action and murders their father. Circumstantial evidence indicates that the eldest brother Dmitri is responsible for the crime, and he is arrested, tried, and convicted.

The plot of the novel is less important than its philosophical sections, and Dostoevsky himself declared that the heart of the book is the "Pro and Contra" section, Book 5, in which Ivan and Alyosha discuss the existence of God. Ivan's argument in favor of atheism has never been surpassed in its intensity. The heart of his argument is the existence of evil. Human beings are infinitely worse than beasts because they are artificially cruel, and the idea that God would tolerate, much less create, such creatures is evidence that he cannot exist. Ivan's examples of evil, all taken from the daily newspapers of 1876, are unforgettable: the nobleman who orders his hounds to tear the peasant boy to pieces in front of his mother; the man who whips his struggling horse "on its gentle eyes"; the parents who lock their tiny daughter all night in the freezing privy while she knocks on the walls pleading for mercy; the Turk who entertains a baby with a shiny pistol before blowing its brains out (pp. 283–287). Ivan knows that such horrors occur daily and can be multiplied without end. "I took the case of children," Ivan explains, "to make my case clearer. Of the other tears with which the earth is soaked from its crust to its center, I will say nothing" (p. 287). "If the Devil doesn't exist," Ivan declares, "but man has created him, he has created him in his own image and likeness" (p. 283).

To the theory that all these horrors somehow fit into a divine harmony beyond our poor powers to conceive, Ivan replies with contempt: "If all must suffer for the eternal harmony," he inquires, "what have children to do with it, tell me, please." And he concludes, "I can't accept that harmony. . . . I renounce the higher harmony altogether. It's not worth the tears of that one tortured child. . . . Imagine that you are creating a fabric of human destiny with the object of making them happy in the end, giving them peace and rest at last, but that it was essential and inevitable to torture to death only one tiny creature . . . would you consent to be the architect on those conditions?" (pp. 290–291). Ivan allows himself none of the evasions that most of us use to

39. F. Dostoevsky, *The Brothers Karamazov*, trans. C. Garnett (New York, 1912), p. 160.

avoid the problem. He is struggling with the deepness of evil and sees no way through it. He awaits Alyosha's rebuttal, half hoping to be convinced.

Alyosha has little to say. He has argued "that suffering will be healed and made up for . . . that in the world's finale, at the moment of eternal harmony, something so precious will come to pass that it will suffice . . . for the atonement of all the crimes of humanity" (p. 279). But he isn't confident: "My brothers are destroying themselves . . . my father too. It's the 'primitive force of the Karamazovs.' . . . Does the spirit of God move above that force? Even that I don't know. . . . Perhaps I don't even believe in God" (p. 262). When Ivan poses the crucial question, "Would you consent to be the architect on those conditions?" Alyosha quietly replies, "No, I wouldn't consent" (p. 292). Yet Alyosha's final word is that God's forgiveness for us far surpasses our forgiveness for God. The only possible answer to Ivan is Alyosha's life, Father Zossima's life, Christ's life. Aloysha stands as silent before Ivan as Christ stood before Pilate. There is no argument that can overcome Ivan's objections; there is only love.

Ivan presses Alyosha further with the shocking parable of the Grand Inquisitor (pp. 292–314). Ivan sets his tale in sixteenth-century Seville, where Christ comes a second time to earth. Christ raises a little girl from the dead and performs other miracles. The people recognize and love him, but the Grand Inquisitor, a cardinal who is the chief ecclesiastical authority in Seville, orders his arrest. When Jesus appears before him, he says that Jesus has no right to come back and add to his revelation; he had left the church in charge, and the church now has everything under control. It is best to leave things as they are, the inquisitor explains, for people do not really want love and freedom. They prefer authority, and by coming again, Christ is interfering with the authority he has granted to the church. The Grand Inquisitor is an atheist—or more: he refers to the Devil as "the wise and mighty spirit in the wilderness" and informs Christ that "we are not working with Thee—but with *him*. . . . It's long—eight centuries—since we have been on *his* side" (p. 299).

Dostoevsky singled out the Catholic Church because of his dislike of Western ideas and because of the schism (eight centuries old) between the Catholic and Orthodox churches. Still, Dostoevsky's intent is to condemn the whole Christian church and indeed all human institutions. The Grand Inquisitor is the symbol of everyman, for we each prefer our comforts and our prejudices to the shattering truth thrust upon us by Christ. The inquisitor's reaction is ours. He condemns Jesus, sentences him to death, and in the end commutes the sentence to banishment with the awful words: "Go and come no more. . . . Come not at all, never, never!" (p. 311). To the inquisitor, as to Pilate—and as Alyosha to Ivan—Jesus has no response. None would be effective: those who choose to blind themselves are blind, and those who refuse to accept healing remain blind. In his argument with Alyosha, Ivan had condemned God; in his parable, he condemns humanity as well. Even if a merciful God of love exists, Ivan suggests, he has no effect upon creatures such as we.

As Alyosha's life answers Ivan's argument, Father Zossima's life answers Ivan's parable, for soon after the Grand Inquisitor passage, Dostoevsky introduces the biography of the priest who lives for the community. "Brothers," Zossima says, "have no fear of men's sin. Love a man even for his sin, for that is the semblance of Divine love and is the highest love on earth. Love all God's creation, the whole and every grain of sand in it. Love every leaf, every ray of God's light. Love the animals, love the plants, love everything. If you love everything, you will perceive the divine mystery in things. Once you perceive it, you will begin to comprehend it better every day. And you will come at last to love the whole world in an all-embracing love. . . . My brother asked the birds to forgive him; that sounds senseless, but it is right; for all is like an ocean, all is flowing and blending; a touch in one place sets up movement at the other end of the earth" (pp. 382–383). Understand evil, Zossima entreats, but understand too that joy and love triumph over evil. Hell is "the suffering of being unable to love" (p. 387). As for atheism such as Ivan's, it is the product of the Faustian attitudes of Western society, the cold pursuit of knowledge without love. To be fully human, we must recognize that we are the children of God.

Ivan's denial of the existence of the Devil is a denial of the demonic in himself, but both burst back upon him in the form of a vision or nightmare. Ivan first sees the Devil as a handsome and charming gentleman who is a bit down on his luck, but, true to his nature as a trickster and shapeshifter, Satan keeps changing his appearance before Ivan's eyes. His expression is "accommodating and ready to assume any amiable expression as occasion might arise" (p. 771). People say I am a fallen angel, he admits disarmingly, but really I am just an old gentleman, and "I live as I can, trying to make myself agreeable" (p. 776). Shapeshifter that he is, the old gentleman is the Devil, and more. He is mankind in general. "Satan sum et nihil humani a me alienum puto," he says: "I am Satan and consider that nothing human is alien to me" (p. 777). The original tag from Horace, of course, is "Homo sum: I am a *human* and consider nothing human alien to me." Satan's version states his identity as both Devil and man as well as underlining the demonic in human nature. More particularly, the Devil is Ivan himself. Ivan is aware of this, though he also senses that the demonic has less power over him than it claims: "You are the incarnation of myself," he exclaims to the apparition, "but of only one side of me" (p. 775).

Satan's reply to this comment has misled many critics. He obligingly agrees with Ivan: "I am only your nightmare, nothing more" (p. 777). According to his own admission, Satan is only a part of Ivan's unconscious rising to the surface in a deluded vision. But this same Devil has already shown himself a master of tricks and lies, and his eager assent to the idea that he is an illusion should immediately warn the reader that Dostoevsky intends us to suspect that he is more. Later, when Ivan catches the Devil telling him an anecdote that Ivan had made up himself and offers this as proof of the vision's unreality, the Devil urbanely replies, "I told you that anecdote you'd forgotten, on purpose, so as to destroy your faith in me completely" (p. 784). It is the Devil's cleverest ploy—for Dostoevsky as for Baudelaire—to convince us that he does not exist. Satan's efforts to make Ivan believe that he does not exist succeed in catching not only Ivan but readers and critics who assume that Dostoevsky intended the Devil to be no more than a projection of Ivan's unconscious. When Ivan angrily flings his wine glass at the Devil, Satan ironically approves—"He remembers Luther's inkstand"— and obligingly disappears (p. 790). His disappearance is followed immediately by the entrance of Alyosha bearing yet another proof of the Devil's real action in the world—the news that Smerdyakov has hanged himself.

The struggle of unbelief against belief in Ivan's dialogue with Alyosha and in Ivan's dialogue with Satan is a struggle in the mind of the supercharacter whom all the Karamazovs represent and who, ultimately, is Dostoevsky himself. Dostoevsky's faith, and his belief in the Devil, were built upon a mature and deep experience of evil and of the grace that overcomes evil, of intellectual doubt and the love that overcomes doubt. The last word of the Karamazov brothers is Alyosha's affirmation of the resurrection to a loving community of friends, along with his attention (like that of Jesus) to the simple pleasures of this world:

"Certainly we shall all rise again, certainly we shall see each other and shall tell each other with joy and gladness all that has happened!" Alyosha answered, half laughing, half enthusiastic. "Well, now we will finish talking and go to the funeral dinner. Don't be put out at our eating pancakes—it's a very old custom and there's something nice in that!" laughed Alyosha. "Well, let us go! And now we go hand in hand." [p. 940]

Dostoevsky's was the most deeply Christian vision of the world of his time, a vision steeped in in intense understanding of evil yet nurtured by the conviction that the greatness of evil is outweighed by one greater than evil, that the reality of emptiness is filled by the greater reality of grace. This is the essence of the Christian view; pessimism about human nature combined with hope in saving grace.

This vision became faint in the world after the wars. Materialism increasingly took the place of Christianity as the underlying world view of Western society, and the elevation of matter to the status of ultimate reality implied the ultimate reality of its characteristics—lifelessness, lack of intelligence, and intrinsic meaninglessness. "The personal, the sensible, and the conscious came to be seen as a second-class reality that must face up to the impersonal 'real world' and submit to the 'reality principle': the blind forces of economic change, the dialectics of class struggle, the survival of the fittest."[40] The monstrous events accompanying the world wars seemed confirmation that the world was meaningless as well as wretched. Suffering had always existed, but now suffering had no meaning. In such a world, the idea of the Devil continued to wane, while the activity of radical evil continued to grow.

40. F. Turner, "Escape from Modernism," *Harper's Magazine*, November 1984, p. 50.

7 The Devil in a Warring World

Since 1914 the suffering of humanity has reached a new intensity with the world wars, the Holocaust, the Cambodian genocide, famine, and the threat of nuclear extinction. As of 1986, nuclear weapons equivalent to more than fourteen thousand million tons of TNT are in existence. As few as two hundred million tons—a tiny proportion of the arsenal—dropped on cities, nuclear power plants, and oil refineries could bring about a "nuclear winter" that would exterminate every living vertebrate on earth. Appallingly, many people are sunk in such dull stupor that they do nothing to resist such madness. The Devil has been defined as the spirit that seeks to negate and destroy God's cosmos to the extent of his power. May not the force urging us to deploy nuclear weapons be the same force that has always striven to negate being itself? In this uttermost crisis of our planet, we cannot dismiss the possibility.[1]

Under the shadow of such monstrous collective evils as Auschwitz and Hiroshima, the Romantic obsession with individual emotions fades to insignificance. The huge collective forces of modern societies with their bureaucratization of responsibility have produced what Hannah Arendt called the banality of evil. Forms are filled out so that Jews may be herded efficiently into gas ovens; maps with anonymous coordinates are issued so that bomber crews may burn schools and hospitals without

1. For the principle of evil in modern society see H. Arendt, *Eichmann in Jerusalem*, 2d ed. (New York, 1976); Arendt, *On Violence* (New York, 1970); J. Ellul, *Violence* (New York, 1969); L. Kolakowski, *Religion, If There Is No God* (New York, 1982); C. Nugent, *Masks of Satan* (London, 1983).

a twinge of conscience. In such a world the Devil surely finds it more effective to sit behind a desk than to roam the world like a lion.

In the middle and late twentieth century, Christian tradition continued to decline; for the first time since the conversion of the Roman Empire, the majority of people in the homelands of Western civilization were growing up in almost complete ignorance of the most basic teachings of religion. This vacuum has to some extent been filled by Marxism (itself a variety of religion) and liberal progressivism, both of which profess a faith that humanity will advance—though progressives generally leave the goal of that supposed progress undefined. This Faustian trust in humanity's ability to solve its own problems, along with a baseless faith in the goodness of human nature, has reduced intuitions of good and evil to psychological phenomena unrooted in any transcendent reality and explained in physical, mechanistic terms. The result is a vague but pervasive moral relativism.[2] Popular relativism assumes that we know nothing absolutely except the proposition that we know nothing absolutely. No values are transcendent; all are wholly relative according to individual or societal preference. Truth also depends upon preference: endless intellectual fads grip Western intellectual circles one after another, because the criterion for the validity of an idea has become its novelty rather than its approximation to truth.

As the twentieth century approaches its end, society is dominated by two views whose incompatibility is seldom recognized: on the one hand, relativism, nihilism, and cultural despair; on the other hand, faith in human progress. The incoherence of these two ideas is absolute, because it is impossible to make progress without a goal. If your goal is Boston, then every step you take in the direction of Boston constitutes some small progress; but if you have no destination, then even a jet flight of ten thousand miles is no progress at all. If no transcendent values exist, then all goals are relative, arbitrary, and changing, and the idea of overall progress is nonsense. It is a lie that we can have both realtivism and progress. Perhaps we cling to the lie because of the terror of having no hope at all.

2. Confusion is so great that Einstein's theories of relativity are widely assumed to be applicable to moral relativism. It is also assumed that the randomness found in subatomic behavior disproves transcendent order; in fact, however, both mathematically and physically, randomness at the microlevel produces regularities at the mesolevel and macrolevel, so that the behavior of molecules and galaxies remains generally regular and predictable. The clearest explanation of modern physics for the layperson is H. Pagels, *The Cosmic Code* (New York, 1982).

In a fearful world where hope rests upon such illusions, neither God nor the Devil has a place. Attacks upon the existence of transcendent evil have led inevitably to assaults upon the existence of transcendent good, and belief in both the Devil and God has declined drastically since the eighteenth century. Though the decline of belief in evil has not been accompanied by any decline of the action of evil in the world, by the 1980s belief in the Devil had disappeared except among conservative Catholics, charismatics, conservative Protestants, Eastern Orthodox, Muslims—and a few occultists.

The revival of the occult that began in the 1960s, part of the anti-establishment and countercultural movement sometimes known as "New Age" thinking, included an element of diabology. The popularity of such films as *Rosemary's Baby* (1968) and *The Exorcist* (1973) encouraged an interest that had its origins in the repression of the sense of radical evil, in fear of the bomb and societal violence, in cultural despair, and in the need to fill the void left by the absence of traditional religion by something resembling religion. The sociology and history of the occult revival need a definitive study, but the sociologist Hans Sebald has suggested that in a society where traditional religion, scientistic materialism, and New Age radicalism are at a standoff in the midst of pervasive relativism, such forms of radical rejection of all values are not surprising. Belief in the Devil increased substantially from 1965 to 1975, and although the fad is subsiding, many elements of Satanism survive in popular culture.[3]

In retrospect, the Satanism of the 1960s to 1980s will be seen as an odd form of chic. A distinction should be made among "Satanic" groups. Some are merely frivolous, like the so-called Temple of Set with its breathless sexual hedonism in occult trappings. Others, whose prototype was the Manson family, practice real cruelty. A third variety that pretends holiness is exemplified by the Jim Jones cult that in the name of Christianity led hundreds to grotesque suicide in the Guyana jungle.[4]

Anton Szandor LaVey founded his Church of Satan in 1966; in 1975 a schism produced the Temple of Set. Their *Satanic Bible* is a melange of hedonistic maxims and misinformed occultism. Like most occult

3. H. Sebald, "New-Age Romanticism: The Quest for an Alternative Lifestyle as a Force of Social Change," *Humboldt Journal of Social Relations*, 11:2 (1984), 106–127. See also C. Z. Nunn, "The Rising Credibility of the Devil in America," *Listening*, 9 (1974), 84–100.

4. See James Reston, *Our Father Who Art in Hell* (New York, 1981).

In the twentieth century the Devil became only one of a number of symbols of evil and fear. Abraham Rattner, *Place of Darkness*, 1946. Oil on canvas. Courtesy, Indiana University Art Museum, Hope Fund.

The Devil in a Warring World 255

groups, LaVey's claims ancient origins; it pretends to arise from the cult of the God Set (Seth) in ancient Egypt.[5] For modern Sethians, the Devil is no fallen angel but a hidden force in nature beyond the power of science or religion to explain. The notion that Satan is evil (they claim) has come from his detractors over the ages, whereas he really is identical with the hedonistic nature spirit Set.

Aside from the fact that Set was not a hedonistic nature spirit and that there is no etymological connection between Set and Satan, the claim is meaningless: it asserts that everything humans know about the concept of Satan is in opposition to the absolute, objective reality of Satan. It ignores the fact that we have no way of knowing the absolute reality of Satan, whatever it might be. The only thing that we *can* know about Satan is the human concept of Satan. The idea that the Devil is good, not evil, has further dimensions of irrationality, because the human concept of Satan was developed in Mazdaism, Judaism, Christianity, and Islam precisely for the purpose of personifying radical evil. Satan is by definition evil. The claim that the evidence in favor of the good Devil has been destroyed, leaving only the evidence of his "detractors," is equally silly. For one thing, it constitutes an admission that the theory is based upon no existing evidence at all. For another, even the possibility of such "evidence" does not exist, because it would contradict the very definition of the subject. It is as if I were to argue that the term "Parliament" really refers to the KGB.

In short, the claims are not so much wrong as inherently meaningless. A proposition may be right or wrong only if it is internally coherent and can be subjected to testing. A proposition that contradicts itself is not simply wrong; it is absolutely without meaning. I have taken trouble with these absurdities not because the Temple of Set is itself important but because similar unawareness of the simple rules governing propositional knowledge has been increasing in literature since the Romantic period.

Similar objections can be made to the teachings of the "Process Church of the Final Judgment," which, like all sects, was rent by numerous heresies and schisms but whose underlying idea was that three or four deities—Jehovah, Christ, Lucifer, Satan—were in the process of unifying.[6] Although the cult of Charles Manson lacked any

5. On the Egyptian god Seth, see DEVIL, pp. 77–82.
6. See W. S. Bainbridge, *Satan's Power* (Berkeley, 1979). The "Process Church" had absolutely no connection with the academic school of process theology derived from the thought of A. N. Whitehead and C. Hartshorne.

pretense of theology or diabology, Manson seems to have been influenced by the "Process Church." Manson claimed to be both Christ and Satan, and argued that Jesus had really been a sensualist whose true ideas had been suppressed by "priestly creeps." Manson's follower Tex Watson announced, when he came to murder Sharon Tate, "I am the devil; I'm here to do the devil's work."[7] The Manson cult resembled the Jones cult in that it was devoted to radical evil without being explicitly Satanist.

Overt Satanism faded rapidly after the 1970s, but elements of cultural Satanism continued into the 1980s in "heavy metal" rock music with its occasional invocation of the Devil's name and considerable respect for the Satanic values of cruelty, drugs, ugliness, depression, self-indulgence, violence, noise and confusion, and joylessness. Groups and artists such as AC/DC, Black Sabbath, Dio, Motley Crue, Judas Priest, Iron Maiden, and Ozzy Ozborne made extensive use of demonic imagery. Ozzy Ozborne featured such titles as "Speak of the Devil," "Sabbath, Bloody Sabbath," "War Pigs," and "Iron Man/Children of the Grave." The jacket of Dio's first solo album portrayed a bestial Devil wielding a chain. Some numbers are "backmasked" to express diabolical messages, but backmasking is an unnecessary game, since the overt lyrics are often diabolical enough. Motley Crue used the Satanic pentagram as its symbol; the group's song "Red Hot" includes the following lines:

> Fight for the black shark—see what evil brings
> Can't you see we're out for blood
> Love from a shot gun
> License to kill
> Can't you see we're out for blood—
> The kids scream in fright through the night
> Loving every bite with delight.[8]

The Crue's "Shout at the Devil" contains these words:

> He's the wolf screaming lonely in the night
> He's the bloodstain on the stage
> He's the tear in your eye

7. V. Bugliosi, *Helter-Skelter* (New York, 1974), pp. 175–177.
8. "Red Hot" (Nikki Sixx, Mick Mars, Vince Neil) © 1983 Warner-Tamerlane Publishing Corp. & Motley Crue Music Company. All rights reserved. Used by permission.

> Been tempted by his lie
> He's the knife in your back
> He's rage—
> Oh, He's the razor to the knife . . .
> Shout shout shout shout at the Devil.[9]

Such groups usually disclaimed connection with real Satanism. Rooted in adolescent resentment of authority, they used the terms and symbols of the occult to express cultural rebellion rather than personal belief. They also found that demonism afforded commercial shock value. "We've got some of the loudest, grossest, sickest songs you've ever heard in your life," Nikki Sixx of Motley Crue is reported to have said. "We're out to make any song we've done before sound like a nursery rhyme."[10]

Many people could and did listen to such music without being converted to evil lives, but constant semiserious propaganda for evil has had decomposing effects on silly and weak minds. One result has been a rash of appallingly degenerate crimes, including the violation of children and the mutilation of animals. Only a society determined to deny the existence of radical evil at any cost could continue to tolerate such phenomena.

The Devil no doubt has some interest in cultural despair, Satan chic, and demonic rock groups, but he must be much more enthusiastic about nuclear armament, gulags, and exploitative imperialism, and it is to such problems as these that the serious philosophy and theology of the latter twentieth century has properly been directed. Yet, paradoxically, cynical despair and sharpened determination to confront evil have grown at the same time.[11]

---

9. "Shout at the Devil" (Nikki Sixx) © 1983 Warner-Tamerlane Publishing Corp. & Motley Crue Music Company. All rights administered by Warner-Tamerlane Publishing Corp. All rights reserved. Used by permission.

10. *Hit Parader*, January 1985, p. 13.

11. Some of the more important philosophical works of the later twentieth century dealing with evil include E. Harris, *The Problem of Evil* (Milwaukee, 1977); A. Hofstadter, *Reflections on Evil* (Lawrence, Kan., 1973); N. R. Moehle, *The Dimensions of Evil and Transcendence: A Sociological Perspective* (Washington, D.C., 1978); C. Musès, *Destiny and Control in Human Systems* (Dordrecht, 1985); N. Sanford and C. Comstock, *Sanctions for Evil* (San Francisco, 1971); P. Siwek, *The Philosophy of Evil* (New York, 1951). Among the most helpful theological works are A. Farrer, *Love Almighty and Ills Unlimited* (New York, 1961); M. Kelsey, *Discernment: A Study in Ecstasy and Evil* (New York, 1978); J. Maritain, *God and the Permission of Evil* (Milwaukee, 1966); M. Nelson and M. Eigen, eds., *Evil: Self and Culture* (New York, 1984); A. Olson, *Disguises of the Demonic* (New York, 1975); F.

The tension between the acute sense of evil and the cynical dullness of cultural despair dominated postwar existentialism. Albert Camus (1912–1960) courageously faced the question of evil in a world without transcendent values in such works as *L'étranger* (*The Stranger*, 1942), *La peste*, (*The Plague*, 1947), *L'homme révolté* (*Humanity in Revolt*, 1951), and *La chute* (*The Fall*, 1956).[12] *La peste* describes the effects of a terrible episode of bubonic plague on the life of a French Algerian city and the efforts of its inhabitants to make sense of it. The honest and faithful priest Paneloux tries and fails to explain the plague as part of God's mysterious plan for the world; the secularist Dr. Rieux knows that one must simply continue to do one's best in a world where such horrors have no meaning except in the resistance that we offer to them. Camus's work was both deep and compassionate, and it accurately described the state of mind prevailing in post-Christian Western society, but the hope of constructing meaning without transcendent values is ultimately futile. In a truly meaningless world, the courage and honesty of a Rieux is intrinsically no better than selfishness or even cruelty.

The emptiness of existentialism became clear in the work of Jean-Paul Sartre (1905–1980). Sartre's play *Le diable et le bon Dieu* (1951) pits God and the Devil against one another with the conclusion that neither is real and that it is up to humanity to supply its own meaning to a meaningless world. The bankruptcy of such a view was obvious in Sartre's embrace of bureaucratic Soviet communism. His play *Huis clos* (*No Exit*, 1947), best exhibits the underlying despair of existentialism. The characters sit silent and isolated in the darkness, endlessly masticating their grievances, self-blinded and self-immured in a dungeon of their own making.[13]

Western theology—Jewish, Catholic, and Protestant—has been subjected to radical transformation by Auschwitz and Hiroshima. The horrors of the twentieth century have shattered the optimistic progressivism that characterized theology before 1914 and have forced its attention upon radical evil. Leszek Kolakowski has insisted that we

---

Sontag, *The God of Evil* (New York, 1970). Strong treatments of the problem of evil are S. Davis, ed., *Encountering Evil* (Atlanta, 1981); J. S. Feinberg, *Theologies and Evil* (Washington, D.C., 1979); D. Griffin, *God, Power, and Evil: A Process Theodicy* (Philadelphia, 1976); J. Hick, *Evil and the God of Love*, 2d ed. (New York, 1977); N. Pike, ed., *God and Evil* (Englewood Cliffs, N.J., 1964); A. Plantinga, *God, Freedom, and Evil* (New York, 1974); G. Wall, *Is God Really Good?* (Washington, D.C., 1983).

12. See B. Mijuskovic, "Camus and the Problem of Evil," *Sophia*, 15:1 (1976), 11–19.
13. On Sartre, see J. Amato, *Ethics, Living or Dead* (Marshall, Minn., 1982), pp. 100–107.

experience evil directly and intuitively: when we observe an act of cruelty, we do not engage in a complicated process in which we subject factual, neutral data to value analysis by the criteria of an abstract ethical system; we react with certain knowledge that the act is evil. The work of Jerome Kagan and other psychologists indicates that children possess such direct intuition by the age of three and retain it unless society drives it out. The transpersonal evil of an Auschwitz or a Hiroshima, which surpasses individual evils qualitatively as well as quantitatively, can also be intuitively grasped. Yet the complex, twisted arguments of modern relativism can rob a person of that intuitive grasp of moral reality, and many theologies still follow the skeptical spirit of the times and evade the intuition by ignoring or denying radical evil. Kolakowski has observed that the question of Satan is not trivial, for it involves the question of God's responsibility for evil.[14]

In liberal Protestantism the tendency to wed theology and biblical criticism in an effort to "demythologize" Christianity has continued to dominate in spite of the neoorthodox revival of Karl Barth and his followers, and the insights of Carl Jung and Mircea Eliade on the value of myth. Conservative Protestantism tends to reject the "higher criticism" and continues to base its views upon scripture. Conservative Protestants claim, like their Reformation forebears, to rely solely upon the Bible, which they consider to be inerrant. In reality, they often unwittingly follow traditional arguments. Nowhere is this clearer than in their teaching on the Devil, which is, like that of the Reformers themselves, based upon patristic and scholastic exegesis and tradition.

Relatively unified before the 1960s, Catholicism has since then tended, like Protestantism, to split into traditional and liberal camps: the one emphasizing the guidance of the Holy Spirit in the development of tradition and recognizing the dangers of undermining the authority of apostolic succession; the other reacting against the long dominance of Thomism by a radical move away from tradition and an openness to the process of demythologizing. The traditionalists, aware of the virtually unanimous opinion of the church throughout the ages on the existence of Satan, continue to affirm it; the liberals discard the doctrine as old-fashioned and contrary to the discoveries of biblical criticism.

The heated discussion of the question since the 1960s reflects a division of opinion as to the essential nature of the church. The traditional,

14. Kolakowski, pp. 112–113, 179–181; J. Kagan, *The Nature of the Child* (New York, 1984).

Thomist view could still be found in midcentury, and the Second Vatican Council (1962–1965) itself referred to the Devil in a variety of contexts. The Roman Missal of 1970 retained reference to Satan in the liturgy of the mass, and the baptismal liturgies for both adults and children continued to include rejection of the Evil One. Still, even before the 1960s, change had begun, as Gabriel Marcel, Karl Rahner, and others prepared the way for a break with scholasticism. When the Second Vatican released the pressures for change, transformation was rapid. In their zeal for reform, those opposing scholasticism often confused scholasticism—especially the Jesuit expression of it—with Catholic doctrine as a whole and flung the baby out with the bathwater, forgetting that the existence of the Catholic Church depends upon the validity of a tradition guaranteed by the Holy Spirit.

The *Catholic Encyclopedia* of 1967 shows a marked shift from the edition of 1907 in the direction of treating the Devil as a symbol of psychological forces rather than as an external reality, and a poll of theologians taken in 1974 indicated that Catholic theologians were rapidly gaining on Protestants in their skepticism: more than one-third of the Catholics agreed with some three-quarters of the Protestants that the New Testament speaks of the Devil only as a reflection of the dominant world view of the first century, and that the Devil was a symbol rather than a real personality. The leaders in this shift in Catholic opinion were Herbert Haag in Germany, Christian Duquoc in France, and H. A. Kelly in the English-speaking world, who found many enthusiastic followers in denying the Devil's existence and many more who took an agnostic position on the subject. In 1976, the death of young Anneliese Michel of Klingenberg during an exorcism approved by the bishop reinforced support for the skeptics' viewpoint.[15]

The attack on the existence of the Devil has been based on a wide variety of grounds, ranging from doctrine to social practice. In theology, the strongest argument is that the Devil does nothing ultimately to explain the *mysterium iniquitatis*, the problem of evil. Shifting the original blame from humans to angels does not explain the introduction of evil into the world. In this view the Devil is an unnecessary hypothesis, and it would be better to return the question of good against evil to the context of the human mind from which it arose. The cosmic struggle between transcendent good and evil is a projection of the human experience of particular goods and evils, and all the evil in the world can

15. M. Adler, ed., *Tod und Teufel in Klingenberg* (Aschaffenburg, 1977).

be explained in terms of human sin. Further, it is meaningless to call the Devil a person or personality, since the only kind of "person" that we know is a human being, and the Devil obviously cannot be a person in the human sense. Thus the Devil is no more than a projection of human categories upon an unknowable transcendence.

The skeptics have bolstered their theological position with biblical and historical arguments. They submit that the concept of the Devil has roots in pagan mythology and in religious traditions, such as Mazdaism, that are extraneous to biblical revelation. The postexilic Hebrews injected him into their tradition in an effort to shift the responsibility for evil from the Lord onto another being, and there is no clear picture of the Devil in the Old Testament. Nor do the New Testament references to him show a consistent pattern. They seem to have been meant symbolically, and each one can effectively be replaced by the terms "sin" or "evil." Against indications in the New Testament that Jesus took the Devil seriously, the skeptics have responded variously: Jesus did not himself refer seriously to the Devil, for the evangelists merely put such words into his mouth; Jesus and the apostles referred to the Devil only because they had to communicate to people in terms of the first-century world view; Jesus and the apostles did actually believe in the Devil, but their belief was part of the first-century world view, along with the belief that the sun revolves around the earth; the ideas of Jesus can be divided between those having universal significance and those, such as the reality of the Devil, that are ephemeral and relevant only as historical curiosities.

Despite the unanimous Christian tradition affirming the existence of the Devil from earliest times, the argument that belief in Satan is not part of the core of faith finds a firm basis in the undisputed fact that no creed or council ever required it. Less firm and more nimble is the argument that conciliar statements on the Devil's existence can be rejected as part of an outdated world view. Of the ecumenical councils, only the Fourth Lateran and Trent give the Devil significant attention, and the Fourth Lateran did not explicitly define the existence of the Devil as a matter of faith. It did mention his nature and activity prominently in the first and main theological canon, but because the two sentences dealing with the Devil are subordinate to the main point of the canon—the universal sovereignty of God—the skeptics argue that it was not an important matter to the council.[16]

16. See LUCIFER, pp. 189–190.

It is possible to read the council's attitudes quite differently, however. First, the section in which the Devil appears is the most important section of the most important statement issued by the council. Second, the sentences constitute a significant part of that statement, both quantitatively and logically. Next, the language of the council clearly implies that the existence of the Devil is not a question for debate but an already settled matter that is not in need of definition. Finally, since the council was aiming the statement against the Cathar dualists with their exaggeration of the Devil's powers, it presented a perfect opportunity to question Satan's existence had there been any inclination to do so.

In the end, the skeptics are forced to fall back to the position that the council had a primitive, mistaken world view. They argue the need to correct "bad tradition," and it is of course true that no tradition based upon a falsehood can be valid. But the question of what constitutes "bad tradition" is extremely delicate; such an argument could undermine the entire basis of apostolic succession upon which the Catholic Church claims to rest.

The skeptics have also argued that belief in the Devil is socially destructive, encouraging negative projection and demonization of outsiders, and weakening human responsibility for evil by attempting to shift it onto another being.

Conservatives mounted a vigorous counterattack against the skeptics in the 1970s. A homily of Pope Paul VI on June 29, 1972 (reported in the *Osservatore romano* on June 30, 1972), was followed by a formal allocution by the pope on November 15, 1972. The pope ordered a formal study of the issue by the Sacred Congregation of the Faith, which produced a long, anonymous article in the *Osservatore romano* on June 26, 1975, presenting the pope's position. Supported by a number of theologians, especially Cardinal Joseph Ratzinger, the pope defended diabology on biblical and traditional grounds.[17] Biblical critics re-

---

17. Citing Matt. 6:13, 12:43; Mark 1:12–13, 5:8–9, 8:28–34; Luke 11:18–26, 22:31, 22:53; John 12:31, 14:30, 16:11; Acts 10:38; Rom. 7:23–24, 16:20; Gal. 5:17; Eph. 2:1–2, 4:27, 6:11–16; Col. 1:13; 2 Thess. 2:3–11; Rev. 12–13. On the argument that the Lord's Prayer refers specifically to the Devil, see J. Carmugnac, *Recherches sur le "Notre Père"* (Paris, 1969), pp. 305–319. On the modern Catholic debate on the Devil, see especially C. Duquoc, "Symbole ou réalité?" *Lumière et vie*, 78 (1966), 99–105; A. Greeley, *The Devil, You Say* (New York, 1974); H. Haag, *Abschied vom Teufel* (Einsiedeln, 1969); H. Haag, "Ein fragwürdiges römisches Studiendokument zum Thema Teufel," *Theologische Quartalschrift*, 156 (1976), 28–34; H. Haag, *Teufelsglaube* (Tübingen, 1974); W. Kasper and K. Lehmann, *Teufel-Dämonen-Besessenheit* (Mainz, 1978); H. A. Kelly, *The Devil, Demonology, and Witchcraft*, 2d ed. (Garden City, N.Y., 1974); H. A. Kelly, *Le diable et ses démons* (Paris, 1977; from the 1974 English edition with additions); Paul VI, "Confront-

sponded that the scriptural arguments offered by the pope were naive and that they evaded the fundamental issue of whether the New Testament even intended to offer a coherent diabology.

The arguments against the skeptics range, like those of the skeptics themselves, from biblical criticism to questions of immediate practicality. Biblical criticism itself hardly presents a unified voice: critics and exegetes differ, sometimes sharply, on the meaning and importance of passages. Further, biblical criticism, like all scholarship, often intrudes contemporary assumptions into our understanding of the past, thus blurring efforts to get at a literal understanding of scripture. The best sense of "literal" is the original intent of the author, and to get at that original intent means stripping away not only the encrustations of tradition but the encrustations of modern historical and scientific assumptions. The best literal reading of the New Testament seems to show Jesus struggling not only against individual sins but also against a power of evil that transcends the merely human. "Every facet of Jesus' life was dominated by his belief in the reality of demonic forces. Whether or not it makes sense or is embarrassing for contemporary thought is entirely beside the point."[18]

The suggestion that Jesus' belief in the Devil was only part of a primitive world view poses serious dangers. Each culture and each age seems determined to believe its own world view the absolute truth, but if history shows anything, it shows that world views shift and that all are equally precarious. There is no reason to assume that either the first- or the twentieth-century view is the true one, and no more reason to suppose that either is as a whole superior to the other than that French society is superior to Chinese. The fallacy of chronocentrism is dangerous for all scholars, but for scholars of a Christian persuasion it is particularly odd to maintain that Jesus and the apostles were primitive people who were not as enlightened as we. Since belief in the Devil permeates the New Testament, it follows that if belief in the Devil is rejected, any other belief expressed by the New Testament—including belief in the incarnation and the resurrection—is subject to the same treatment, and some theologians have not shirked this implication.

The historian—Christian or not—observes that Christianity is based upon the Bible and tradition and that it can be meaningfully defined only in reference to scripture and tradition. A doctrine that departs

ing the Devil's Power," *The Pope Speaks,* 17 (1973), 315–319 (trans. of the pope's address "Liberarci del male" in *Osservatore romano,* 15 November 1972).

18. J. Kallas, *Jesus and the Power of Satan* (Philadelphia, 1968), p. 202.

sharply from scripture and tradition cannot in any meaningful sense be called Christian. Again, it is like arguing that what people have been calling Parliament for six hundred years is really something else. Since both scripture and the earliest and most unanimous Christian tradition affirm the existence of the Devil, the skeptics' denial reduces Christianity to a vague cloud of residual emotional attachments to a Jesus whose real nature we cannot know. Such demythologizing leads to a "Christianity" that no Christian before the eighteenth century, including the apostles, would even have recognized.

Whether the Devil exists depends upon one's definition of the Devil and the conceptual framework within which one is operating. That the Devil does not and cannot exist "scientifically" or "historically"—that is, his existence cannot be demonstrated by scientific or historical methods—does not mean that he cannot be said to have existence in some other framework. The term "existence" has no necessary meaning prior to human categories. The confusion is evident in the skeptics' argument that the Devil cannot be a person. Certainly the Devil is not a person in the same way that a human being is a person, but in fact we do have a conception of "person" beyond a human being: we would, for example, call an extraterrestrial being a "person" if it possessed such attributes as consciousness, intelligence, and will, no matter how different from ours. Although the use of the term "person" for human "person," "person" of the Trinity, extraterrestrial "person," or angelic "person" is clearly analogical, an underlying, univocal ground is common to all in consciousness, intelligence, and will.

Another skeptical argument, that demonic possession as described in the New Testament is better explained in terms of modern medicine and psychiatry, is irrelevant to the Devil. It improperly conflates demons and Devil—physical distress and moral evil—into one category. Medicine may understand physical symptoms better than demonology does, although there is no logical reason why a given physical complaint may not have both physical and spiritual causes. But the Devil represents moral evil, and science and medicine by definition cannot treat questions or morality. The concept of radical evil embodied in the Devil cannot be outmoded or superseded by any developments in science.

Against the skeptics' view that belief in Satan is socially undesirable, it is clear that demonization of enemies goes on equally effectively in Soviet communism and other ideologies that deny the existence of the Devil. Nor does belief in the Devil seem historically to have impaired moral responsibility as much as the modern belief that behavior is determined by environment. Skepticism about the Devil often leads to skepticism about radical evil, producing a false optimism and a reliance upon palliatives.

On the whole, the skeptics' view is based less upon biblical criticism or history than upon the current world view. But the dispassionate historian knows that all world views are precarious; progress in one place is matched by decline in another; our science is better than Paul's, but our theology may be a good deal worse.

Some theological efforts to face radical evil in the twentieth century have struck off in new directions. One of the most original was that of Karl Barth (1886–1968), founder of Protestant neoorthodoxy. Barth differentiated three elements of reality: God, God's creation, and *das Nichtige* or "nothingness." Nothingness is that which God does not create. Being neither God nor God's creation, "nothingness" lacks all true being. Yet it is not totally without existence, for it springs into life on its own in an area from which God withdraws his creative power. God constructs the cosmos in such a way that he limits his creative power in an area in which "nothingness" can arise on its own. There are two kinds of evil: evil resulting from the finiteness of human nature, and *das Nichtige*, which actively resists and denies God and is totally destructive and unredeemable. Barth's nothingness, unlike Jung's, was in no way a part of God, so that there is no evil side of God and no coincidence of opposites uniting good and evil (31.2; 50.2).[19] The Devil is part of nothingness, the lie underlying all lies (31.2; 51.3). The Devil and evil exist within creation but are not part of God's work: they are nothingness, chaos, opposition to real being (3.2; 33.1; 50.3; 51.3). Although the Devil has no real being, he has enormous power to distort and destroy, like a vacuum. His aim is the destruction of the cosmos, and the evidence of his power is his influence over humanity (33.1). God allows the Devil wide scope to pursue this plan of annihilation, but God also summons up against him God's *opus proprium*, the power of creation directed against nothingness (50.3–4).

Although given a new perspective, Barth's views are very similar to traditional privation theory, and they face similar difficulties. Nothingness must either derive from God (which Barth denies) or else be a principle other than God, a power limiting God (which would lead to dualism). Barth enhances the danger of dualism by denying the tradi-

19. References are to K. Barth, *Kirchliche Dogmatik*, 13 vols. (Zollikon, 1939–1967); the translation is *Church Dogmatics*, 13 vols. (Edinburgh, 1955–1976).

tion that the Devil was originally an angel created by God—since Barth's Devil is pure nothingness, he has no created nature—but Barth avoided dualism by insisting that nothingness is contingent upon God's creation, for its opposition to reality entails the prior existence of reality. It is also entirely dependent upon God's permission to operate.

Barth always emphasized the human struggle between good and evil more than the cosmic struggle between God and Devil. Still, the absoluteness of evil with its innate hunger to harm for the sake of harming can be best grasped in the figure of a superhuman power.

The Jesuit paleontologist Pierre Teilhard de Chardin (1881–1955) invented an optimistic, progressive theology drawing both upon traditional mysticism and scientific evolution. For Teilhard, creation is a process stretching from the alpha point at the beginning of time to the omega point at the end of time. This process is God's plan for the world. The cosmos develops under God's direction and as a manifestation of the divine principle, beginning with the creation of the inanimate, proceeding through increasingly complex molecular structures to the creation of life, then to intelligent individuals, and—in the future—to a new kind of mind as individual intelligences knit themselves into a noetic whole. This divine process cannot be stopped, but it can be inhibited and thwarted where the living, organic process is "deadened" or "crystallized." The Devil is the symbol of resistance to the divine process.[20]

The contemporary theologian Jim Garrison (1921–) uses Hiroshima as a symbol of the qualitative difference in twentieth-century evil. No world view is valid that fails to integrate Hiroshima into its experience, he contends. To confront Hiroshima is to confront the transcendent mystery of God's darkness. "I have learned," says Garrison, "that to seek God is like holding a light in the darkness. As the light increases, the circumference of the darkness also expands."[21] God ultimately uses evil for the good, but this does not make evil an illusion. Evil—cold, cruel, and intrinsically destructive—is not merely a human category but a transcendent reality. God creates real evil.[22] How this can be true we cannot know, since God transcends every human category. However, we can know our experience of God, and that experience, both personally and biblically, is ambivalent. "God as experienced [is] as savage and terrible as God is merciful and forgiving" (p. 26). We need to

20. P. Teilhard de Chardin, *Le phénomène humain* (Paris, 1955).
21. J. Garrison, *The Darkness of God: Theology after Hiroshima* (London, 1982), p. 8.
22. Citing Job 16:12–17; Jer. 45:4–5.

overcome our "monopolar" prejudice that God is only good and move to a "bipolar" view that sees God as integrating genuine good and genuine evil in an ultimately benevolent synthesis (pp. 170, 173–174).

How God's ultimate benevolence integrates evil we cannot understand, Garrison continues, but we know that he is benevolent through personal experience, biblical revelation, and logic. A God who did not create an ultimate justice would be imperfect and therefore not God. For a Christian, the mystery centers in the crucifixion, in which God both inflicts and suffers agony himself. The passion of Christ is God's demonstration to the world that he himself shares its suffering. Hiroshima is a new crucifixion, a new revelation of our own darkness and God's. Nuclear war is the threat that the earth may die as Christ died. "Since Hiroshima, we must speak of God and humanity co-creating the apocalypse" (p. 207). The Devil is the shadow side of God. "It is impossible to experience God as *summum bonum* before experiencing him as antinomy. . . . All opposites are of God: light and dark, good and evil, crucifixion and resurrection" (pp. 173–174). There is the danger of concluding that the shadow side of God is also worthy of worship, but the shadow has no positive value except when integrated, and part of the process of integration is the struggle against evil. The Devil is the symbol of the unintegrated evil that we must oppose with all our might.

The theologically reflective novel *To an Unknown God* by the Rumanian exile Petru Dumitriu (1924–) argues that it is impossible to know whether the Devil exists as an independent personality but that he is a needful symbol of radical evil.[23] Evil infinitely surpasses human evil; it is as vast as the cosmos, as immense as God. God is an antinomy, one face being beauty, joy, and love; the other a "terrible visage of God, toleration of evil, fear, anguish, disquiet, hunger and thirst, physical pain, excruciating agony." Yet although natural evil is terrible enough, "in all creation there is nothing as cruel as human malice." Of all beings that we know, only humans take knowing pleasure in cruelty. "Wanting to do harm implies a secret communion, an identification of the human being with his victim, an empathy between the two: he puts himself in his victim's place and relishes a suffering he understands" (p. 58).[24]

The modern denial of the Devil's existence, Dumitriu suggests, is an escape from responsibility. It "is not just a simple refusal to personify

23. P. Dumitriu, *Au dieu inconnu* (Paris, 1979); I was unable to obtain the original and used the translation by J. Kirkup (New York, 1982).

24. Empirical confirmation seems to exist in the phenomenon of mass murder such as that reported in "The Random Killers," *Newsweek*, November 26, 1984, pp. 100–106.

Evil . . . it is a refusal of the very notion of guilty intent, of culpability, of sin" (p. 59). Modern society's search for genetic or environmental causes of evil behavior is an evasion. We have true moral freedom, and every evil act is culpable. The dignity of humanity depends on the existence of genuine evil, for without it we are mere programmed machines (p. 61). The Devil's favorite axiom is the deterministic excuse for evil. His second is that we project our own evil upon scapegoats and deny our own responsibility. Another is that one can be so guilty as to block out the hope of grace and change. Another is that evil is far too complex to solve, so that we approach nuclear war with complicated schemes of disarmament rather than with the simple decision to turn away from destructiveness to love.

Modern literature, like philosophy and theology, had to choose whether to face or to evade the horrors of the twentieth century. The intensely cynical period after the First World War produced works such as *Satan, the Waster* by Vernon Lee (the pseudonym of Violet Paget, 1856–1935), in which Satan is the symbol of the nationalism, patriotism, and futile heroism that waste human lives in war. Films such as *Apocalypse Now* (1979), *Mephisto* (1982), and *Sophie's Choice* (1982) made the same point for later wars; the most convincing demonic figure in cinema may be the concentration camp officer who forces Sophie to make her unspeakable choice.[25]

Twentieth-century writers tended to move rapidly from moral outrage at evil through disgust and despair to utter cynicism. In 1926 André Gide exclaimed, "Have you noticed that in this world God always keeps silent? It's only the Devil who speaks. . . . His noise drowns out the voice of God. . . . The Devil and God are one and the same; they work together. . . . God plays with us like a cat tormenting a mouse. . . . And then he wants us to be grateful to him as well. . . . Cruelty! That's the primordial attribute of God."[26] Cynical indifference to real values had become a dominant attitude by 1982, with Jeremy Leven's novel about Satan going to a psychoanalyst.[27] It's unfair that he was expelled from heaven, he explains, because "I'm Jewish, like God." He learns that God resents him because of his literary ambitions. The Devil is slick, obscene, and valueless, like the novel itself. The Devil,

---

25. The film derives from William Styron's novel *Sophie's Choice* (New York, 1979).
26. A. Gide, *Les faux-monnayeurs* (Paris, 1925), pp. 498–499.
27. J. Leven, *Satan: His Psychotherapy and Cure by the Unfortunate Dr. Kassler, J.S.P.S.* (New York, 1982).

An Allied poster from World War I shows Kaiser Wilhelm II demonized. 1915.

like the cosmos, can be reduced to a meaningless formula: "Devil $= y^4 + my^2 - x^4 + nx = 0$."

The most ambitious cynical treatment of Mephistopheles was the unfinished *Mon Faust* (1941) of Paul Valéry (1871–1945). Valéry's Mephisto is ironic, cynical, and aloof from real human suffering. He first appears as a tall, lean clergyman dressed in elegant but not quite contemporary style. His speech is also little off: he speaks Italian with a Russian accent. His goat ears betray the truth, but on the whole his person is pleasing, for, as he explains, he is more successful with people when he does not appear as a monster. To his chagrin, he soon learns that the modern world is unimpressed with him in any form. Faust dismisses him: "I'm afraid that I can't conceal from you that you seem a bit out of style. . . . You don't hold the great place in the world that you used to. . . . The whole system of which you were an essential part has fallen into ruin and dissolution."[28]

By the middle of the twentieth century it had become difficult to portray the traditional Devil effectively without either disguising him mythologically or else presenting him in the lurid format of the horror tale. In the 1960s and 1970s a number of successful horror novels and films contributed to a brief revival of interest in Satan. Of these Ira Levin's *Rosemary's Baby* (1967) and William P. Blatty's *The Exorcist* (1971), were the most successful, and, coincidentally, the most theologically plausible. Although *The Exorcist* luridly exaggerated traditional concepts, it retained a degree of faithfulness to them. The films of the late 1970s and early 1980s, however, perfectly illustrate the underlying collapse of the tradition, with their bouillabaisse of unrelated horror clichés.

Serious treatments of the personification of evil have often been presented in the form of fantasy or science fiction in order to overcome the prevailing skepticism of the time. In *Inferno* (1976), Larry Niven and Jerry Pournelle constructed a compelling and theologically accurate science fiction version of Dante's vision. Twentieth-century mythology tends to transfer demonic or angelic qualities from "supernatural" entities to supposedly "scientific" extraterrestrials. The films *2001* (1968) and *2010* (1985) present angels in the form of disembodied extrater-

28. P. Valéry, *Mon Faust: Ebauches* (Paris, 1946), pp. 52–54. See also Aldous Huxley (1894–1963), *The Devils of Loudun* (London, 1952); Dorothy Sayers (1893–1957), *The Devil to Pay* (London, 1939); Roland Duncan, *Death of Satan* (New York, 1954); Albert Lepage, *Faust et Don Juan* (Paris, 1960).

restrials, and the 1978 remake of *The Invasion of the Body Snatchers* featured extraterrestrials whose hissing, darting tongues, cruelty, and ability to shift into human form reproduced the traditional characteristics of demons. J. R. R. Tolkien (1892–1973) cast the struggle between transcendent good and evil in the fantasy world of Middle Earth. *The Lord of the Rings* is, like *Beowulf*, implicitly Christian though explicitly set in another world. Tolkien's Sauron, the dark lord of Mordor, is associated with the Devil through the serpent or dragon (Greek *sauros*), and the evil wizard Saruman's name resonates both with *sauros* and with the evil deity of Mazdaism, Ahriman.[29]

The mythical statement in modern literature truest to the tradition appears in the work of C. S. Lewis (1898–1963).[30] Lewis' most original contribution was the suggestion that demons are motivated by both fear and hunger. Cut off from the source of real nourishment, they roam the world seeking human souls to devour in a terrified effort to fill the famished void; when thwarted, they will turn and devour one another. But no amount of eating can mitigate their infinite emptiness, for they will not eat of the bread of life, which alone can satisfy. *The Screwtape Letters* (1942), in which this idea is set forth, purports to be a series of communiqués from a senior demon, Screwtape, to his nephew Wormwood; they offer practical advice on the corruption of humanity, specifically of the one human assigned to Wormwood. Here the Devil shows his interest in the opportunities afforded evil by everyday human weaknesses. Irritation with another person's expression or tone of voice, envy of someone else's success, social posing, contempt for others' opinions, pride of knowledge—all such human frailties offer the Devil points of leverage in his efforts to detach us from God. Lewis saw that most of us confront the Devil in these petty guises far more often than we espy him high on a throne of royal state.

In Lewis' *Perelandra* (1943) and its companion "deep space" novels, Mars, Earth, and Venus are populated by intelligent beings, and each

29. J.R.R. Tolkien, *The Lord of the Rings* (London, 1954). See also William Golding, *The Lord of the Flies* (London, 1954); Nikos Kazantzakis, *The Last Temptation of Christ* (New York, 1960).

30. The first novel of Lewis' space trilogy, *Out of the Silent Planet*, appeared in 1938; the second, *Perelandra*, in 1943; and the third, *That Hideous Strength*, in 1945. *The Screwtape Letters* was published in 1942, and the Narnia series of children's books between 1950 and 1956. Lewis also treated evil in *The Great Divorce* (1945), and dealt with natural evil in *The Problem of Pain* (1940) and the deeply personal *A Grief Observed* (1961). *Mere Christianity* (1952) is a lucid theological essay containing treatments of both natural and moral evil.

planet is ruled by an "oyarsa" (angel). Mars is inhabited by older civilizations that have successfully withstood temptation and live in harmony with Maleldil, the creator. In consequence of original sin, Earth is under the power of a "bent oyarsa," an evil archon, and Maleldil has quarantined it from the other planets.[31] Perelandra—Venus—is a paradise into which temptation has not yet intruded. Its inhabitants are beautiful plants and animals and one intelligent couple, the Lord and Lady, the Adam and Eve of this fresh new world. The black archon sends a scientist named Weston from Earth to introduce sin onto Perelandra by corrupting the Lord and Lady. Maleldil responds by sending Ransom, an Oxford don, to counter him. Weston and Ransom must compete to persuade the Lord and Lady of Perelandra to their views, for the first Perelandrans, like Adam and Eve, have complete freedom of will; the Devil cannot, and God will not, compel them.

Weston's name indicates that he represents not only the setting star, the Devil, but also Faustian Western humanity with its efforts to bend the world to its own desires. In the previous novel, Weston had attempted to exploit the inhabitants of Mars for the "good" of humanity; his ethic is humanism of the aggressive, imperialistic kind that ignores the rights of other species and defines progress in terms of the increasing human domination of whatever part of the universe we can lay our hands on. In the time between the action of the first novel and *Perelandra*, Weston's blind devotion to Faustian knowledge and power has opened his soul to the dark angel, and by the time he arrives on Venus, he has permitted his own personality to be submerged. He feels "guided" and "chosen" but lacks the discernment to realize who it is who is guiding him. Ransom suspects the Devil's presence in the scientist's willingness to lie, cheat, and falsify scientific evidence to advance the cause that he imagines to be that of triumphant humanity but is really that of the bent archon, who acts in him and through him (pp. 95–96).

Maleldil has made Perelandra a sea planet where beautiful floating islands are filled with flowers and peaceful animals. The Lord and Lady, first parents of the intelligent population to come, are given the freedom of the planet, the only restriction being that they never pass the night on the dry, fixed land. Their trust must be in Maleldil, who guides the floating islands for their good, rather than in the illusion that

31. C. S. Lewis, *Perelandra* (London, 1943), p. 23: "the black archon." Archon is a New Testament name for Satan, the "prince" of this world.

they can hold and hoard God's gifts on the unchanging land. The evil archon's purpose is to persuade the Lady to trust her own will and convince her husband to do the same. Through Weston he uses every cunning rhetorical trick, including ostensibly reasonable arguments that conceal the empty gulf beneath (pp. 116–118). When not whispering lies to the Lady, he engages Ransom, whom he senses to be connected with that other "ransom" who undid his work on Earth, in endless clever debates. God and the Devil, he says, are representatives of the same Force whose patent will is the domination of the universe by technological humanity. It is according to this will, Weston shams, that he has come to prepare Perelandra for development by the inhabitants of Earth.

Weston's ingenuity in the debates is astonishing, and though Ransom uses every defense to the limit of his abilities, he gradually realizes that reason cannot defeat a being who cares nothing for the truth and whose essence is pure unreason. Whenever Weston suspends his busy intent for a moment, he lapses into the idiot emptiness of evil. Among the creatures of the floating islands is a species of small, froglike animals. To his horror, Ransom discovers that Weston has been wandering mindlessly about slitting the frogs open with his fingernails and leaving them to die in agony. This cruelty for cruelty's sake compels Ransom to confront evil not in its fancy dress of philosophical argument but in its naked simplicity as an "intolerable obscenity which afflicted him with shame. It would have been better, or so he thought at that moment, for the whole universe never to have existed than for this one thing to have happened" (pp. 108–109). The suffering of the little animals is intolerable, and the cruelty that deliberately causes their suffering is even more intolerable.

The vacant idiocy behind Weston's intellectual facade reveals itself more and more. His smile "seemed to summon Ransom, with horrible naiveté of welcome, into the world of its own pleasures, as if all men were at one in those pleasures, as if they were the most natural thing in the world and no dispute could ever have occurred about them" (p. 110). Weston's evil is far beyond vice; vice is the search for sensual pleasures, which have at least some root in reality, but Weston's search is for pure abstraction—an abstraction which he has alleged to be the welfare of humanity but which is, in fact, simple annihilation.

The culmination of Weston's rhetorical temptation of the Lady is a perfect perversion of intellect. He describes the divine generosity of Christ's sacrifice on Earth, observes that that redemption would not have occurred without original sin, and concludes that it is Maleldil's hidden purpose that sin be done on Perelandra so that another incarnation may occur. Ransom summons his last intellectual strength to rebut him: God brings good out of evil and the greatest good out of the greatest evil, but it is never God's will that evil be done. Weston, seeing his most subtle argument undone, suddenly and without warning throws back his head and howls like a dog. The scene is modeled on the transformation of Devil into hissing serpent in *Paradise Lost*, and its effect is the same revelation of the mindless fury beneath evil's clever facade.

At last Ransom realizes that verbal struggle with the Devil can only be endless. The Oxford don Lewis wrote *Perelandra* during the war against Hitler, and the Oxford don Ransom sees that God calls him to fight crudely and physically against the physical body that the Devil is using. Sick with fear and repulsion, he hesitates. But Maleldil, with the words "My name also is Ransom," reminds him that Jesus did not argue the Devil down; he died on the cross.

The hideous battle begins, hand to hand and nail to nail. In a lull, the Devil makes a last, insidious attack on Ransom's reason. Conceding that evil truly exists, he rushes to a hideous conclusion: what Ransom fails to grasp, he insists, is that evil is the *only* reality; happiness and kindness are a thin veneer over a reality of torture, terror, and despair: "That is the real universe, always will be. That is what it all *means*" (p. 167). For a moment Ransom is overwhelmed, but then he sees that it cannot be true, for we experience a cosmos that is full not only of suffering but also of compassion, tenderness, and generosity. Revived, he resumes his horrible physical struggle, most of which occurs in hellish darkness in the interior of the only mountain on the planet. There Ransom breaks the Devil's physical and moral power and ascends the mountain as Dante did the mount of purgatory.

Lewis intended to show that the war between good and evil is no abstraction but a series of individual choices, each of which is cosmic in its implication: each choice for good, however small, wins strategic ground against the enemy. Lewis knew that this real world of ultimate values is out of the range of vision of materialist society. But for him, it was the material world that is "aslant," out of focus (pp. 141–142, 198). God and the Devil are reality; the illusion is our conviction that they do not exist.

The world of Georges Bernanos (1888–1948) was also rooted in

Adolf Hitler surrounded by admirers in a café. The glamour and attraction of powerfully charismatic evil figures illuminates the psychology of the Devil.

Christian orthodoxy, but of a more somber and pessimistic cast.[32] An idealistic royalist who left his friends and the reactionary *Action française* when they cooperated with the fascists and Vichy, Bernanos had formed part of the interwar Catholic Renaissance in France, along with Paul Claudel, François Mauriac, and Antoine Péguy. The growth of materialism, economic greed, war, and weapons technology seemed to them to indicate that power was becoming increasingly concentrated in the hands of an evil enemy. Bernanos was always more spiritual than rational in his theology, and he believed that the remedy was less in intellectual debate than in radical spiritual change. A true view of the world, he perceived, must take full measure both of its evil and of the power of grace to save it. Without the love engendered by grace, all human ideologies and efforts can only work us further down into Satan's power.

For Bernanos as for Lewis, the struggle between good and evil in the individual soul is the microcosm of the cosmic opposition between God and Devil, and human sin is part of the greater shadow that we call evil. Evil is not a mere human category but a real thing whose ultimate characteristics are nothingness and immobility. It is essentially incomprehensible because it has no essence; its heart is the void. This nothingness is a cosmic coldness whose tendrils reach out, penetrating our minds and beckoning us to join it in hell. The secret source of the evil of humanity, it squats in the deepest part of the conscience, exuding hatred of God and love of death. Deadly sin lies in associating ourselves with this nothingness, with a "conscious complicity in Satan's ruses, a lucid acceptance of his power to corrupt and a willingness to come to terms with him."[33] The desire for nothingness is planted deep in us, and under its influence we can turn our gaze so far away from the light that we can see only the darkness and choose it for its own sake.[34] The symptoms of this choice are pride, which separates us from love; lying,

32. The best edition of Bernanos' novels is G. Bernanos, *Oeuvres romanesques* (Paris, 1961), whose page numbering I follow throughout. The relevant titles in chronological order are: *Sous le soleil de Satan* (Paris, 1926); *L'imposture* (Paris, 1927); *La joie* (Paris, 1929); *Un crime* (Paris, 1935); *Journal d'un curé de campagne* (Paris, 1936); *Nouvelle histoire de Mouchette* (Paris, 1937); *Monsieur Ouine* (Paris, 1943). On Bernanos and evil, W. Burkhard, *La génèse de l'idée du mal dans l'oeuvre romanesque de Georges Bernanos* (Zurich, 1967); M. Kemp, *Manifestations of Satan in Two Novels of Georges Bernanos* (Hemel Hempstead, 1976); J. P. Santen, *L'essence du mal dans l'oeuvre de Bernanos* (Leiden, 1975).

33. J. E. Cooke, *Georges Bernanos* (Amersham, 1981), p. 33.

34. Bernanos, *Sous le soleil de Satan*, pp. 221, 237.

which separates us from truth; and despair, which separates us from mercy.

The power of evil holds sway over most of Bernanos' characters, especially liberal and worldly Christians, bureaucrats, anticlericals, stingy bourgeois, cynical peasants, and loveless intellectuals. Mediocrities who sense that things are wrong but acquiesce because it is easier than resisting evil, ideologues who put their convictions in place of compassion, and intellectuals who seek knowledge with soulless curiosity are the most guilty. At times in the late 1940s, Bernanos came close to falling into despair himself. "To hell with this world," he exclaimed, "crouched over its nuclear arsenal, yellow with hatred, and its heart absolutely empty of love."[35]

The heroes of Bernanos' novels are those who resist the power of Satan in themselves and in others. Their loving, honest simplicity makes them unpopular, alienated, and exploited, because society is so poisoned that it cannot stomach the bread of life. The bitterness of this vision led some critics to accuse Bernanos of gnostic dualism, but nothing in his work violates traditional theology. Satan is "the rebel angel who said no only once, but once and for all, in an irrevocable act in which he engaged his entire substance."[36] If the evil characters are joined to Satan, the suffering of the good characters joins them to Christ. The power of evil in the world is always and everywhere overcome by the power of grace.

Satan is the personality at the heart of evil just as Christ is the personality at the heart of good. Bernanos did not doubt the existence of either, and as a child he claimed direct intuitive experience of Satan. Without belief in Satan, he argued, one cannot fully believe in God. The world is riddled with evil, and deliberate blindness to that fact obscures the truth about the world and therefore the truth about God. The scale of evil in the world far transcends what humanity could cause itself, and all efforts to improve the world without understanding this transcendence are doomed to failure. The tendency of twentieth-century writers such as Anatole France to treat the Devil ironically and comically, Bernanos observed, is a clear sign of evasion of reality, and their popularity indicates that Satan has us in his power.

Bernanos' Satan has a double character: on the one hand he is harsh,

---

35. Quoted in Cooke, p. 42.
36. G. Bernanos, *Le crépuscule des vieux* (Paris, 1956), p. 19.

powerful, and threatening; on the other, empty and banal. The Devil makes himself appear threatening but can never overpower us or compel us to sin, as his vaunted power is under God's control. His purpose, which is mere idiot destruction and annihilation, is totally meaningless. His laugh is joyless and mocking, the supercilious laugh of the cynic who knows all the angles and understands nothing. The Devil wants us to believe that life is meaningless, to sin without even taking joy in sinning, to live a life of joylessness and gray depression while indifferent to the suffering of others. "I am," Satan boasts, "the door that is forever closed, the road that leads nowhere."[37]

Satan, Bernanos observes, has little trouble entering our minds, for we eagerly open our intellects and wills to him. Satan works with great facility on the intellect, for he is the greatest of logicians.[38] He uses philosophy and rhetoric to persuade us that we are mere random collections of particles, that we have no dignity, that we have no freedom of choice, that we can live effectively from day to day without facing ultimate choices. He perverts ideals: the desire for freedom into anarchy and armed rebellion, duty into mindless obedience, harmony into imposed order and tyranny, love into lust, equality into conformity, humility into mediocrity, charity into curiosity.[39] His mode of persuasion is always imposture, always the lie, always the effort to make things seem what they are not. Bernanos was intensely aware of the struggle within himself as well as within humanity as a whole. On earth, each of us is a battleground, he said: "Between Satan and himself God builds us as his last rampart. For it is through us that century after century the same Hatred seeks to reach him; it is in this poor human flesh that the unspeakable murder is consummated."[40]

Bernanos began his first novel, *Sous le soleil de Satan* (*Under Satan's Sun*), in the dark days of World War I and published it in 1926. The metaphor is the dark light and intolerable coldness of Satan's sun, the false sun or anti-sun, the empty hole in the sky that is the sign of the Devil's power over us in the world. The main section of the novel concerns Abbé Donissan, the vicar of the village of Campagne and later curé of Lumbres. Donissan is modeled on St. Jean Vianney, the holy curé of Ars. Like Bernanos' other heroes, he is completely and intensely

---

37. Bernanos, *Journal d'un curé de campagne*, p. 1046.
38. Bernanos, *L'imposture*, pp. 380–382.
39. Cited in Cooke, p. 32.
40. Bernanos, *Soleil*, p. 256.

devoted to God. As a result, he has no close friends; isolated and vulnerable, he is subject to fits of despair. His soul is open to deep intuitions of good and evil. At one point, lost on a country road, he encounters a jovial little man who offers to help him (pp. 167–184). Friendly, sympathetic, and full of insight, the man gains Donissan's confidence; he guides him, gives him his cloak, and even rocks him to sleep. The good fellow drops hints as to his real identity: he lives nowhere; he is "married to misery"; he has a sharp, whinnying laugh. But because Donissan is lonely and needs a friend, the priest allows himself to be duped. "I will be your true friend," the man assures him. "I will love you tenderly."

Gradually, Donissan senses who his new friend really is, and at last the little man identifies himself: "I am Lucifer, the lightbearer, but the essence of my light is an intolerable coldness" (p. 175). The Devil senses in his intended victim a surprising coldness and rigor of his own, a hard, unbendable resistance to evil. Frustrated, he intensifies his efforts: "Stop mumbling your prayers," he sneers, "your exorcisms aren't worth a pin" (p. 177). When Donissan looks into his companion's eyes, he is almost overcome with fear, and sweat runs down between his shoulderblades. The Devil picks up a stone from the road, holds it up, and jeeringly offers the words of Eucharistic consecration (p. 178). When Donissan observes that the Devil is forever crushed under the weight of his own misery to the point of nothingness, Satan, momentarily overcome by the truth, hurls himself down into the mud, racked by terrible spasms—a revelation of his character comparable to the scenes in Milton and C. S. Lewis where his bestiality is revealed in sudden animal behavior. Satan recovers his poise for a hideous temptation: he shifts his shape into a perfect double of the priest, a double whose eyes are a mirror in which Donissan reads written large all his own fears and doubts (p. 180). Donissan has the anguished sense that there is no difference between him and his double and that resistance is therefore impossible.

Nevertheless, the priest pulls himself together and bids the Devil go; then, on the verge of victory, he is undermined by hidden flaws: curiosity and vanity. Impressed by his own ability to resist and curious as to how far he can push Satan, he takes the offensive, demanding that the Devil surrender all his influence over the people of his parish. Satan immediately senses the return of opportunity and offers the priest an irresistible bait. Today, he tells him, God has granted you a special grace (p. 182). Donissan demands to know what it is. "You'll see,"

Satan replies. The priest, overcome by both curiosity and pride, cries "I'll get your secret. I'll wrest it from you if I have to follow you where you live to do it. I don't fear you" (p. 181).

The Devil replies with a mocking laugh, and Donissan realizes that he has lost sight of the fact that God's grace rather than his own merit has enabled him to resist. He trembles in shame, recognizing that any victory over such an adversary is fragile and precarious and that he must prepare to resist another assault. Satan leaves him with the confident threat that he will return and that when he does, Donissan will embrace him and cherish him under the illusion that he is God.

Back in Campagne, Donissan encounters a young girl on the road and astonishes them both by relating to her the story of her secret guilt. The gift that God has given him is the gift of seeing into souls. It is a genuine grace that will last all his life, and whenever he is asked how he does it, he responds that a great pity wells up within him for those who seek his help, and somehow from that pity comes the power.

Years later, when Donissan has become curé of Lumbres, the Devil makes good his threat to return. The priest is summoned to the bedside of a child dying of meningitis. The call comes when he is in one of his moods of deep depression, and when he reaches the child only to find him dead, a cold despair grips him so furiously that his heart seems to fail. All his sins and weaknesses surge over him: his despair that the horrors of the world are too great for God to overcome, his anger at God for the child's death and for his own failure to help, his doubt in God's redeeming love, his idle curiosity to see what God can really do, and his hidden pride at his spiritual gifts. Swept away, he asks that God raise the child from the dead. The request is made not out of love but out of pride and anger, and it fails, for God yields only to love: "Dieu ne se donne qu'à l'amour" (p. 268). So when the child's eyes slowly open for an instant, it is not the child who looks up at him, but the one he had met years before on the dark road to Campagne. The priest starts back with horror, the eyes close, and the child mercifully returns to death. The effects of Donissan's sin, however, do not vanish so quickly, for the child's mother, whose hopes that her child might live had been raised for a moment, now suffers redoubled anguish. Bernanos' testimony, through the priest of Lumbres, is that the greatest saints are subject to the greatest temptations, but that grace, incomprehensibly and sometimes violently, breaks through.[41]

41. *Soleil*, p. 308: "Toute belle vie, Seigneur, témoigne pour vous; mais le témoignage du saint est comme arraché par le feu."

Bernanos shows the interior nature of Satan in his *Journal d'un curé de campagne* (*Diary of a Country Priest*). Satan has persuaded the foolish twentieth century to believe that his complex sophistication is more real than the simplicity of God. The one thing that could save us from destruction, loving God and neighbor, is considered naive and simplistic, no match for complicated economies, negotiations, and armaments. "Sometimes I think," Bernanos comments, "that Satan, who seeks to lay hold of the mind of God, not only hates it without understanding but understands it all in reverse. Without realizing it, he struggles against the current of life instead of flowing with it, and he exhausts himself in absurd, horrifying efforts to redesign all of creation in the exact opposite of reality" (p. 1087). His favorite reversal of reality is to transform love into hatred. "Hell," the holy young curé tells one of his selfish, empty parishioners, "is to cease to love" (p. 1157). The earth is muffled in the dark coldness of Satan's loveless light, and without the love that breaks through the pall, Bernanos' vision would be as pessimistic as some of his critics have maintained. But love's light pricks at the warm center of this dark world. The last words of the country priest are: "Tout est grâce": all is grace (p. 1259).[42]

Thomas Mann's novel *Doktor Faustus* (1947), the greatest reworking of the Faust motif since Goethe, is at the same time rooted in tradition and deliberately unorthodox.[43] Mann (1875–1955) grew up a Protestant, married a Jew, lived in Catholic Munich, and was caught up in secular politics and thought. Later, he was forced by his repugnance for Nazism to search for a deeper world view and found a guide in that direction in the writings of Dostoevsky. Never an orthodox Christian, he became something of a Christian humanist.

Mann began work on *Doktor Faustus* in 1943 and completed it two years after the war, in 1947. The central character, Adrian Leverkühn, is Faust; he also represents Luther, Nietzsche, Wagner, and Germany, especially Germany since 1918. Depressed by the decay of European civililization and its complete collapse in Germany, Mann reversed Goethe's optimism, returning to the pessimism of the original Faust book, in which Faust was damned; in damning Faust, Mann condemned the Faustian drive of twentieth-century Western society. The ruin of Adrian Leverkühn, like that of Germany in 1945, is complete.

---

42. Demonic figures in other Bernanos novels include Ouine in *Monsieur Ouine* and the priest Cénabre in *L'imposture* and *La joie*.

43. I cite T. Mann, *Doktor Faustus*, in the Fischer edition (Frankfurt, 1967). See also D. Assman, *Thomas Manns Roman "Doktor Faustus" und seine Beziehungen zur Faust-Tradition* (Helsinki, 1975).

Still, Mann's pessimism, like Bernanos', left room for hope, for Adrian's love for his little nephew Nepomuk is a sign that the curse of love-lessness is not complete and that he—and Germany—may yet be redeemed.

Mann places a skeptical narrator between himself and the reader, Serenus Zeitblom, whose name—"Timebloom"—marks him as a man of his age. Zeitblom's views, an odd blend of Catholicism and materialism, religion and skepticism, are sometimes but not always congruent with Mann's own. Mann used Zeitblom to keep his own views deliberately remote, unobtrusive, and even ambiguous, for the novel can be interpreted in both Christian and secular terms.

Zeitblom's friend Adrian, a brilliant young musician, begins his career by studying theology and philosophy. Repulsed by the aridity and inhumanity of these subjects, he dabbles in magic and makes a bargain with the Devil, giving up joy and love in return for brilliant success as a composer. He gains all that he wishes in terms of creativity and acclaim, but at the end of the traditional twenty-four years he must render up his soul. The terrible moment comes at a concert to which Leverkühn has invited his musical friends to hear a preview of his last and greatest composition, appropriately named *Dr Fausti Weheklag*, "Dr. Faustus' Lament." Seated at the piano, Leverkühn breaks down and tells his guests that he has made a pact with Satan, that he has rejected a life of moderation, affection, and love because he could not stand to be cut off from communion with deeper powers. He declares that he is damned and falls senseless to the floor. The audience thinks him mad, and he is taken off to the asylum. His mind has, in fact, been ravaged by syphilis, but the audience does not realize that his confession is in a sense true. In the madhouse, he attempts suicide in the vain hope of saving his soul with the sacrifice of his body. He never regains his mind or his freedom, and he dies in 1940 on the date of Germany's great triumph over France.

Demonic forces of darkness, madness, and negation permeate the novel. From youth onward, Adrian repeatedly encounters the Devil in human form: as Capercailze or Auerhahn (drawn from the Faustbook), who teaches Adrian the secrets of the sea and the inhuman immensity of space (chs. 27, 43); as the art historian Helmut Institoris, whose name recalls the sinister medieval witch-hunter Heinrich Institoris (p. 381); as the stammering music teacher Herr Kretschmar, who praises creative chaos (chs. 8, 9); as Martin Schildknapp, the charming translator, ladies' man, and fraud (ch. 20); as Dr. Zimbalist, the red-haired physician (ch.

19); as Saul Fitelberg, who wants to take Adrian through the air on his cloak and show him the glories of artistic fame (ch. 37); as Dr. Erasmi with his red face and pointed beard (ch. 19); as Clarissa Rodde, who keeps a sulfur-yellow tomcat named Isaac and who has a penchant for the macabre (pp. 262, 379); as Hetaera Esmeralda, the name of the butterfly that Adrian's father keeps in his collection of dead things, and of the whore who infects Adrian with the syphilis that first intensifies his creativity and then drives him mad (chs. 19, 22); as the pimp who leads him to Esmeralda and who resembles the Satanic Dr. Schleppfuss (ch. 16).

Most demonic are the theology professors who represent the perverse futility of the modern intellectual. Professor Kumpf, a Luther figure who converses heatedly with the Devil and hurls biscuits at him in the corner, is "on close though naturally strained terms with the Evil One" (p. 130). Dr. Eberhard Schleppfuss lectures on the Devil, theodicy, and evil. His name, "Dragfoot," indicates his crippled intellectuality, the deformity of his spirit, and of course the Devil himself, who is often lame or deformed and who in Goethe keeps his cloven foot hidden from view. Schleppfuss is obsessed with the problem of evil, for which he offers a variety of theological explanations: God allows evil for the sake of free will; God's goodness consists in his ability to bring good out of evil; the highest good rests in the transcendence and integration of good and evil. Schleppfuss uses modern knowledge such as psychology to make demonology more understandable and intelligible to the modern world. Zeitblom—and apparently Mann himself—considers such obsession with evil a concession to evil and suggests that the abstract ideology of Christianity, like the abstract ideology of Nazism, is a demonic retreat from human reality and affection (pp. 133–149).

Mann found this demonic tendency to abstraction deeply embedded in the German spirit, with its inwardness, mysticism, unworldliness, and inclination to the metaphysical. True Christianity, Mann held, is centered on the Great Commandment to love at all costs, whereas German theology had made Christianity an abstract science and so turned it into a monster. He saw the Satanic character of ideology in our readiness to set it above the welfare of individuals.

Satan himself appears to Adrian at Palestrina in Italy. The place is where the great polyphonic composer Giovanni da Palestrina was born; the time is 1912, just before the great war; together they symbolize the doomed beauty of European culture. The Devil appears just at that time and place to shatter the harmony in Europe and in Adrian's heart (pp.

294–333). The interview between Leverkühn and the Devil is modeled explicitly on that between Satan and Ivan Karamazov. Mephisto changes his shape and his conversation to fit Adrian's moods. He first takes the form of a short, frail man with reddish hair and eyelashes, a pale face, a crooked nose, and bloodshot eyes. His clothes are not quite right: he wears a cap, a striped shirt under a checkered jacket with sleeves that are too short, yellow shoes, and suggestively tight trousers. In the course of the conversation, however, he shifts from confidence man to intellectual, carrier of physical disease, theologian, medical specialist, procurer, criminal, successful man of the world, lecturer—whatever fits the mood of Adrian's mind, because he speaks entirely out of Adrian's own memories and knows only what Adrian knows.

After long, pedantic discussions of theology and music, Mephisto explains that he is going to special trouble for Adrian because of his great talent and offers him the twenty-four years of success in return for Adrian's acceptance of the curse that he is not to love (pp. 331–332). This dark pact rises from Adrian's own being. He is already enslaved by ambition, indifferent to friends and family, and infected with syphilis, and his acceptance of the Devil's bargain only confirms the direction that his will has already taken.

Mann deliberately makes it difficult for us to discern his view of the Devil through all the refractive planes that exist between the author and the reader. Mann speaks only through Zeitblom, who relates what Adrian has told him, and Adrian reports what the Devil says. When the Devil boasts that he is the only one who understands religion and that liberal theologians understand nothing, he seems to be telling the truth as Mann sees it, but most of the time he is true only to his own nature, which is the lie. The reader must also beware of accepting Zeitblom's skeptical view that the Devil has no reality beyond Adrian's mind, for Zeitblom makes other statements about the Devil that are dubious. He blunders, for example, in assuring Adrian that there is nothing diabolical about Kretschmar, the musician.[44] Many modern critics, themselves blooms of their own time, have too readily accepted Zeitblom's position. They observe that Adrian's syphilis is responsible for the hallucination, which is true, but they neglect the multiple levels of reality in the novel. Adrian's moral weakness has opened the door to a

---

44. P. 251: "Nein, mit dem Teufel hast du nichts zu schaffen." Cf. his other odd error on p. 249: "Wer an den Teufel glaubt, der gehört ihm schon" (whoever believes in the Devil already belongs to him).

darkness that transcends his personal consciousness. When the interview is over, the skeptics point out, Adrian finds that the coat and blanket he had used to protect himself from the diabolical cold are still in the closet, just as Ivan Karamazov found the wine glass he had thrown at the Devil unbroken. But in traditional diabology the Devil always works through illusions and often leaves no physical trace of his presence. Like the traditional Devil, Adrian's visitor sees through each of Adrian's psychological evasions and warns him that they will not help him. Besides, Zeitblom himself is uncertain; he says he would be mad to believe that Adrian has had a real visitor, yet he shudders at the thought that the entire, cynical, bitter dialogue came from his friend's own mind alone.

Mann's own position was ambiguous. "From the very beginning," he observed, "the Devil makes his presence felt in the novel, but appears personally to arrange the pact in the middle. Zeitblom tries hard not to believe in his reality. So do I."[45] The Devil himself says, "You see me, so I am here for you. Is it worth asking whether I am real? Isn't what is real what really works; isn't reality experience and feeling?" (p. 385). At Leverkühn's funeral, Zeitblom sees a veiled, mysterious figure who vanishes as the last clods of earth fall on the coffin (p. 676). Is Zeitblom finally seeing the Devil, or is this a hallucination of his own? Mann does not intend a definite answer, for he felt the power of the demonic intensely and was aware that we have no way of knowing whether it is an external or internal reality. Whatever the source of Mann's Devil, he is no figure of whimsy but a power fiercely intent upon the destruction of the individual and of the world.

That the Devil's curse, powerful though it is, can be resisted is demonstrated by Adrian's intense suffering when his little nephew is dying of meningitis; the child's agony draws from Adrian a terrible curse against the Devil, the cosmos, God, and himself—against the whole order of existence that allows an innocent, loving child to die writhing in pain (pp. 627–636). But the curse is humanizing, for his love for this single human being contradicts the terms of his demonic pact. Nepo's suffering gives Adrian the anguish of love that he needs for his salvation, and for the first time he begins to have "something Christlike about his face" (p. 640). His pain allows him for a moment to pierce illusion to the inner warmth of the world. Later, the last note of the doomed oratorio *Dr Fausti Weheklag*—the last musical note that the

45. Quoted in G. Bergsten, *Thomas Mann's Doctor Faustus* (Chicago, 1969), p. 203.

composer leaves to the world—is a sustained high G on the cello, a tone of mourning that is transformed as it is uttered into a light in the darkness.

The work of Flannery O'Connor (1925–1964) was devoted to penetrating reality by piercing illusions.[46] She described her subject as "the action of grace in territory held largely by the devil."[47] That territory is the human soul, particularly in our modern, secular society. With the Devil's help we have extruded a thick rind around our souls that can be pierced only by the action of grace. The thicker the rind, the more violent must be the thrust necessary to break through. Deeply American and southern, O'Connor drew upon Hawthorne, Melville, Poe, and other American explorers of darkness; deeply Catholic, she drew upon Bernanos and the European Catholic revival.

O'Connor believed that we are entangled in a complex world that we ourselves have constructed, a dim and dark world made comically absurd by our own foolishness and sin. God illuminates the darkness with shafts of light and grace, but we often refuse to recognize them, preferring our own opaque illusions to the clarity of reality. Every word and action of daily life has moral implications affecting the entire cosmos; to make this convincing, O'Connor set her stories squarely in the everyday comedy of human behavior and the stark immediacy of the southern landscape. She knew that readers must see the actuality of the everyday world sharply and clearly before they could be convinced of the action of evil and grace. Her stories are rich in symbols, but they are public symbols derived from Christianity and accessible to everyone. Sin and grace operate in real people; O'Connor knew that unless materialized in good, rich earth, they become pallid abstractions. Although she often wields her love of humanity like a sharp weapon, the purpose of her satire is charitable. Like a prophet, she expresses in words that burn her

46. I cite the works of Flannery O'Connor in the following editions: *The Complete Stories* (New York, 1979); *The Habit of Being* (New York, 1979); *Mystery and Manners* (New York, 1969); *The Violent Bear It Away* (New York, 1960); *Wise Blood* (New York, 1952). I deeply appreciate the extraordinary kindness, generosity, and wisdom shown me by Flannery O'Connor's close friend and editor Sally Fitzgerald.

On O'Connor and evil, see K. Feeley, *Flannery O'Connor: Voice of the Peacock*, 2d ed. (New York, 1982); S. Fitzgerald, "Rooms with a View," *Flannery O'Connor Bulletin*, 10 (1981), 5–22; P. Nisly, "The Mystery of Evil: Flannery O'Connor's Gothic Powers," *Flannery O'Connor Bulletin*, 11 (1982), 25–35.

47. *Mystery and Manners*, p. 118.

longing that we should return to God. Rather than standing judgmentally over her characters, O'Connor invites herself and her readers to recognize in them the absurdity of our own materialism, complacency, banality, and self-satisfaction. The rind of complacency is particularly thick in the twentieth century, when people are not only unbelievers but praise unbelief as a virtue: "If you live today, you breathe in nihilism."[48] Yet with enough violence, grace can break through.

The assault of grace on the absurd defenses we raise against it is comic and often grotesque as well as violent. The grotesque shakes us out of the banal illusion of what we call normality. Today, when most people do not even believe in sin, active sin is less a threat to the world than dull torpor. An active sinner may at least have a sense of uneasiness about his or her life, but the mediocre can wrap themselves in a complacency out of which they must be exploded. The comic, the grotesque, and the violent are the arsenal of grace against smugness and self-satisfaction: the heads of O'Connor's characters and of twentieth-century humanity are "so hard that almost nothing else will do the work."[49] Some of the characters need enormous and repeated shocks before their shell is broken; others hide under their apparent smugness a deep insecurity rooted in fear and anxiety. It is a paradox that the same fear and anxiety that prod us to build our defenses against reality also produce doubts about the defenses and so provide the opening for grace, which can take many forms: sudden awareness of the presence of God; sudden sensitizing to mystery; recognition of a moment of real choice between good and evil; a flood of perception of one's own character and one's dependence upon God. Grace is God offering himself to us in a variety of ways; our response to grace is faith—or the refusal to have faith. Sometimes in the stories grace is irresistible and knocks down the character's defenses against his will; sometimes grace is freely accepted; sometimes, though rarely, grace is refused and the character's soul is lost. In a world as dulled to reality as ours, O'Connor said, "I don't know if anybody can be converted without seeing themselves in a kind of blasting annihilating light, a blast that will last a lifetime."[50]

O'Connor draws some of her most powerful characters from the context of southern Protestant fundamentalism, because fundamentalism, like her own Catholicism, takes the Bible, God, and the Devil

48. *Habit of Being*, p. 97.
49. *Mystery and Manners*, p. 112.
50. *Habit of Being*, p. 427.

seriously. Fundamentalist characters such as Old Tarwater in *The Violent Bear It Away* are intended to seem comically grotesque in order to increase our shock when we become aware that the author intends us to realize that every word they utter is true.

O'Connor believed that the conflict between good and evil was a literary as well as theological necessity. "The Devil's moral sense coincides at all points with his dramatic sense," she observed, and "the writer's moral sense must coincide with his dramatic sense."[51] In other words, literature must center on the war between good and evil and do so in a morally coherent way. Unlike the Romantics, O'Connor was determined to contrast good and evil sharply and without ambiguity. "Literature, like virtue, does not thrive in an atmosphere where the devil is not recognized as existing both in himself and as a dramatic necessity for the writer."[52]

O'Connor recognized that the modern materialist finds it hard to believe that she is taking the Devil seriously, because the materialist puts "little stock either in grace or the devil." But she takes repeated pains to make it clear that she believes in the Devil as an external, personal entity: "Our salvation is a drama played out with the devil, a devil who is not simply generalized evil, but an evil intelligence determined on its own supremacy."[53] "I want to be certain that the Devil gets identified as the Devil and not simply taken for this or that psychological tendency," she said, and her Satan is rooted in traditional theology: he is the angel Lucifer who fell because of pride, who inspired original sin, and who roams the world seeking to thwart God's plan of redemption.[54] But for O'Connor, it is always the thwarter who is thwarted, the deceiver who is deceived; evil is ultimately and always overcome by good. "More than in the Devil," she wrote, "I am interested in the indication of Grace."[55]

The Devil is a comic figure in spite of his ability to cause real suffering, because God turns his every effort into an occasion of good so that he is "always accomplishing ends other than his own."[56] When Manley Pointer, the demonic Bible salesman in "Good Country People," de-

51. *Habit of Being*, pp. 124, 147.

52. *Mystery and Manners*, p. 117.

53. *Mystery and Manners*, pp. 118, 168.

54. *Habit of Being*, pp. 360, 456. O'Connor called herself a "hillbilly Thomist": p. 81.

55. *Habit of Being*, p. 367.

56. *Habit of Being*, p. 367. O'Connor was familiar with the words of the medieval hymn *Pange lingua*, in which God opposes to the serpent "schemes yet deeper than his own."

prives the haughty crippled girl of the wooden leg that represents the dead woodenness of her nihilist philosophy, God works through the salesman's twisted purposes to provide the victim with a salutary blast of grace that shocks her into reality. When the Devil assaults and shatters a character for his own ends, God uses the breach opened in the character's defenses to pour in his own grace and love: "The Devil teaches most of the lessons that lead to self-knowledge."[57] In "The Partridge Festival," the violent and obscene behavior of the psychotic killer Singleton toward the fledgling writers who come to interview him breaks down both their illusions about him and their delusions about themselves. O'Connor later said that she was "all for Singleton in this, devil though [he is]. He's one of those devils who go about piercing pretensions."[58] Demonic assault is always an occasion of grace, but whether destruction or salvation comes of it is always up to the individual. Mr. Head in "The Artificial Nigger" accepts grace; Mr. Fortune in "A View of the Woods" rejects it.

In "The Lame Shall Enter First," the mother of the child Norton has died, and her death has plunged the child into a dull, stupid misery. The father, Sheppard, is a dry, intellectual social worker who is pleased with himself and his good works, and who thinks that effort and determination can set the world right. Angry and ashamed at his son's dull despair, he decides to teach the boy to care about others by bringing home a juvenile delinquent, Rufus Johnson, to live with them. Rufus's club foot is a symbol of his demonic nature, which he takes no trouble to hide. His clear understanding that he is on the Devil's business contrasts with Sheppard's liberal illusions about human goodness and about his own ability to reform the criminal. Sheppard offers banal explanations of the delinquent's behavior: "Maybe I can explain your Devil to you," he says patronizingly. But Rufus knows better. "I already know why I do what I do. . . . Satan has me in his power. . . . When I die I'm going to hell. . . . Nobody can save me but Jesus." Rufus is clear about Sheppard's spiritual state as well as his own: "Satan has you in his power. . . . Not only me. You too." The delinquent speaks with O'Connor's voice in denouncing Sheppard's self-satisfaction.[59] The bad shepherd neglects his own son in his efforts to justify and glorify himself by socializing Rufus Johnson.

Meanwhile, he is absurdly oblivious to the fact that Johnson's person-

57. *Habit of Being*, p. 439.
58. *Habit of Being*, p. 443.
59. *Habit of Being*, p. 464: "In this one, I'll admit that the Devil's voice is my own."

ality and fundamentalist ideas have begun to dominate Norton. When the child craves his father's reassurance that his mother exists somewhere and still loves him, Sheppard offers his son not bread but the stony comfort that his mother lives on only in his memory—but Johnson says the mother is alive in heaven with the stars, and Norton readily believes him. Not until Sheppard finally realizes that he has sacrificed his son for his own pride do horror at his disloyalty and the love for Norton that wells up in him belatedly strip the scale of self-delusion from his eyes. He understands that he has "stuffed his own emptiness with good works like a glutton. . . . ignored his own child to feed this vision of himself. He saw the clear-eyed Devil, the sounder of hearts, leering at him from the eyes of Johnson." But it is too late. In the attic room where Sheppard has installed a telescope to teach Rufus astronomy, Norton hangs dead from the beam from which he had launched himself to find his mother in the stars.[60]

O'Connor's last completed novel, *The Violent Bear It Away*, is a powerful story in which the struggle between the Devil and grace explicitly transcends the merely human. Four characters are epiphanies of Satan himself: the "stranger" whose voice Young Tarwater hears in his head and whose shadowy figure accompanies him; Meeks, the copper-flue salesman who gives him a ride; the gray man in the city park; and the homosexual rapist who molests Tarwater. O'Connor was impatient with critics who failed to understand who it was that appeared in these characters. "If the modern reader is so far de-Christianized that he doesn't recognize the Devil when he sees him, I fear for the reception of the book," she commented ruefully.[61]

Young Tarwater is an adolescent who has been brought up on a

60. Other demonic figures in O'Connor's stories include the yellow bulldozer and the storekeeper Tillman in "A View of the Woods," Mr. Paradise in "The River," Mary Grace in "Revelation," the spirit of Thomas' father and Sarah Ham in "The Comforts of Home," Mr. Shiftlet in "The Life You Save May Be Your Own," and the Misfit in "A Good Man Is Hard to Find."

61. *The Habit of Being*, pp. 361, 367: Meeks is "of the Devil because nothing in him resists the Devil. There's not much use to distinguish between them." Tarwater visualizes the face of the stranger as "sharp and friendly and wise, shadowed under a stiff broadbrimmed panama hat that obscured the color of his eyes" (*The Violent Bear It Away*, p. 35). Meeks and the rapist also wear panama hats and are called "the stranger" (pp. 51, 227–229). When the color of the stranger's eyes appears, it is violet, like the lavender handkerchief, shirt, and car of the rapist (pp. 214–215). Violet is also associated with the penitential season of Lent, with tornadoes, with dryness and aridity (as in T. S. Eliot's *Wasteland*), and, verbally, with violence itself. For O'Connor's views on discernment, see *Habit of Being*, p. 410.

remote farm by his great-uncle, a prophetic old evangelical who cuts a grotesque figure to most readers but whose every word is truth as O'Connor understood it. The old man has taught the boy to believe that he too is called to be a prophet. Old Tarwater also has an older nephew, Rayber, a bloodless intellectual schoolteacher whose hearing aid symbolizes his deafness to reality. Young Tarwater and Rayber are doublets—both nephews of the prophet, both having had loose mothers and foolish fathers, both with the seed of prophecy planted in them by the old man, both torn between grace and the Devil.

Rayber resists the call of grace heroically, convinced that if he lets down his guard he will go mad like his uncle. He speaks with the voice of commonsense materialism: he is almost always reasonable and almost always wrong. In an earlier draft O'Connor portrayed Rayber as more demonic, and some traces of the earlier sketch remain: "It was as if the schoolteacher, like the devil, could take on any look that suited him" (p. 55); Rayber is "full of nothing" (p. 56); he resembles both Meeks, the diabolical salesman, and the sinister internal "stranger" (pp. 83, 173). But Rayber has one vulnerable chink in his armor: his love for his idiot son Bishop. He has convinced himself rationally that the child would be better off dead and has tried to drown him, only to be stopped by a surge of uncontrollable pity. Occasionally a flood of love for the child pours over him, but he blocks it frantically, knowing that if he opens himself to love for one, he will be vulnerable to a love that embraces all. His fight against love seems won when Young Tarwater does drown Bishop. At the child's last, terrified bellow, Rayber turns off his hearing aid. Hearing nothing, feeling nothing, he gives himself to emptiness and death. O'Connor planned a sequel in which Rayber might have had another opportunity, but in the context of the finished novel he resists grace to the end.[62]

The heart of the novel is the psychomachy between grace and the Devil within Young Tarwater. Soon after his great-uncle's death, the boy hears in his mind a stranger's voice that uses every wile to persuade him to abandon his prophetic calling. The voice is Tarwater's unconscious shadow, everything within him that resists the painful life to which the old man has assured him he has been called. It is also the voice of Satan himself. The desert fathers pointed out how the Devil rushes in through every opening that weakness leaves in our souls, and

---

62. On the struggle within Rayber, see *The Violent Bear It Away*, pp. 64–68, 73, 114–115, 182, 192; on the emptiness of Rayber, see pp. 7, 55–56, 76, 114–115, 169, 200.

to the extent that Satan lives and works in us we become part of the mystical body of the Devil. The voice becomes gradually more familiar to Young Tarwater until "only every now and then it sounded like a stranger's voice to him; he began to feel that he was only just now meeting himself" (p. 35). Eventually, the stranger becomes so familiar that he is now "his friend—no longer a stranger" (p. 161). At this point, when the Devil has become a friend, Christ becomes the outsider.

As every word Old Tarwater speaks is true, every word the stranger's voice speaks is a lie. When it says that the old prophet was crazy, we know that he must have been sanity itself (pp. 37–39). When it denies grace, resurrection, and hell; when it ridicules Adam, the Old Testament prophets, and Jesus, we know that they must be the very stuff of reality (pp. 39–46). Young Tarwater's Satan, like Ivan's and Adrian's, denies his own existence: "There ain't no such thing as a devil," the stranger scoffs. "I can tell you that from my own self-experience. I know that for a fact. It ain't Jesus or the devil. It's Jesus or *you*" (p. 39). The ironies in this statement are multiple. Since everything the Devil intends is a falsehood, his statement that he does not exist is a lie. However, the Devil is always forced to reveal the truth whether he chooses to or not, and his slip of the tongue betrays him when he says that he knows the Devil doesn't exist—not from experience, but from *self-experience*. When he says, "there ain't no such thing," he unintentionally reveals the truth that evil is ultimately only a negation of reality. He lets slip his own ultimate unimportance in admitting that the fundamental choice is not between Jesus and the Devil but between Jesus and our own self-will. Finally, the passage underscores the moral identity between Satan and Tarwater's own sinful will.[63]

The stranger and the flesh-and-blood manifestations of Satan attack the boy in similar ways. Old Tarwater early warned his great-nephew, "You are the kind of boy that the devil is always going to be offering to assist, to give you a smoke or a drink or a ride, and to ask you your bidnis" (p. 58). The prophecy is fulfilled. Both the stranger and the rapist offer the boy a smoke, both Meeks and the rapist offer him a ride, and the liquor-laced drug that the rapist gives him recalls the liquor that the stranger urges him to take from his great uncle's still (pp. 36–37, 44–46, 228–230). Tarwater accepts three rides. The first is from Meeks, who is on his way to Mobile, signifying rootless mobility. Meeks's life is

63. For other debates between Tarwater and the stranger, see pp. 11–13, 35–37, 45 (cf. 228–229), 51–58, 93, 161–167, 237.

based upon cynical exploitation of people for money, and he boasts that "I've never been turned around in my life," an inadvertent admission that he has never been converted. The last ride is with the rapist. Between the two, he rides in a truck which itself symbolizes Satan, even though its driver is not demonic. The truck swallows Tarwater up as the whale swallowed Jonah; in its interior he confesses, to his own horror, that he has baptized Bishop even as he drowned him, and, as if nauseated by grace, the monster vehicle vomits him out onto the side of the road (pp. 216–217).

When the internal stranger, now his "friend," persuades Tarwater to drown Bishop, the Devil considers his victory over the young prophet secured. But a new "stranger" dwells in Tarwater's unconscious now. Satan had once been the stranger, but the boy had so conformed his will to the Devil's that he is now a "friend." The new "stranger," tempting Tarwater to good, is Christ, and at the very moment of killing the child for his new friend, the new stranger prompts him to say the words of baptism.[64] The new stranger converts the act of violence into an occasion of grace, and the boy hears the "horrible sibilant oaths of his friend fading away on the darkness" (p. 216). A final violent action allows grace to complete its work.[65] Satan, seeing Tarwater beginning to slip out of his grasp, perpetrates a last assault on him in the form of the man with the lavender car. When the man offers him drugged liquor, he accepts it with the cry, "It is better than the Bread of Life" (p. 230). The driver takes the drugged boy into a clearing in the woods and rapes him. When Tarwater awakens and realizes what has happened, he sets fire to the polluted site. He is shattered and transformed, his eyes burnt clean. "His scorched eyes no longer looked hollow or as if they were meant only to guide him forward. They looked as if, touched with coal like the eyes of the prophet, they would never be used for ordinary sights again" (p. 233). The Devil intended to use the rape to snatch Tarwater back from the brink of salvation, but God uses it to seize him from the lips of hell.

The title of the novel is drawn from the ambiguous passage in Matt. 11:12: "From the days of John the Baptist until now, the Kingdom of Heaven suffers violence, and the violent bear it away." Among other difficulties, the original Greek is unclear. The word *biazetai* is in the middle or passive voice and can be variously translated as "does vio-

---

64. Christ is his new adversary: p. 93.
65. *Habit of Being*, p. 368.

lence," "undergoes violence," or "uses force." Perhaps the best translation is something like the following: "The kingdom of heaven forces its
way along, and the forceful seize it." O'Connor, using the translation
"suffer," seems to have assumed that it signified "permitting" violence,
a meaning disallowed by the Greek but encouraged by the ambiguity of
the English word "suffer," which used to mean "permit." That she saw
at least two dimensions of the problem seems clear from her statement:
"Violence is a force which can be used for good or evil, and among other
things taken by it is the kingdom of heaven."[66]

O'Connor uses violence ambivalently herself. The very name of Old
Tarwater's farm, Powderhead—with its associations of gunpowder and
thunderhead—sets the tone of violence from the beginning. The rape
burns Young Tarwater's eyes clean so that he sees the truth. The
drowning of Bishop also baptizes him. The Devil urges the rape and the
drowning for his own reasons, but God turns each act of violence into a
powerful occasion of grace.[67] With this ambivalence O'Connor pene-
trates to the core of evil. On one level, evil is genuine evil, and God wills
us to struggle against it with all our might. On another level, all that
happens is by God's will. On yet another, God's will turns all to good.
Central to Christianity is that God turns the greatest possible evil, the
crucifixion of his Son, into the greatest possible good, the redemption of
the world.

Outraged and dazed by the rape, Tarwater is almost ready to fall into
the hands of grace, but he is still determined to mount a rearguard
action. He sets off down the road to Powderhead, and when he arrives,
the Devil is still clinging to him, "a warm, sweet body of air encircling
him, a violet shadow hanging around his shoulders" (p. 237). But he
"shook himself free" (p. 238). Earlier he had tried to burn the farm with
the old man's body in it so as to destroy the spirit of prophecy; now he
tries again, but this time to consign Satan to the flames. He makes "a
rising wall of fire between him and the grinning presence. . . . His
spirits rose as he saw that his adversary would soon be consumed in a
roaring blaze" (p. 238). The Devil, who has moved in Tarwater's mind
from stranger to friend to adversary, is now vanquished. His eyes burnt
clean, the boy receives the prophetic calling: "GO WARN THE CHILDREN
OF GOD OF THE TERRIBLE SPEED OF MERCY." The old prophet had been
called to the city many years before; now the young prophet turns his

66. *Mystery and Manners*, p. 113.
67. On the need for violence, see pp. 200–202, 220; for the ambivalence of fire, see
pp. 5–6, 15, 20, 23–25, 41, 50–51, 76, 91, 134–135, 162, 232, 238, 242–243.

own "singed eyes, black in their deep sockets" in that direction and "moves steadily on, his face set toward the dark city, where the children of God lay sleeping" (pp. 242–243).

The work of Bernanos, Mann, and O'Connor may be seen as a lifeline connecting us to a meaningful world, something to cling to while tossed on the choppy seas of late twentieth-century cultural despair. Since the world wars we have been fearing that the lifeline would not hold, that we would find nothing at the other end, that we would either perish in nuclear war or fade forever into meaninglessness. But a new hope is rising as a new world view begins to emerge at the end of the twentieth century.

The traditional world view that dominated Western civilization through the seventeenth century was a unified, coherent cosmos in which meaning, value, and truth were inherent and integrated. This view was replaced during the eighteenth and nineteenth centuries by a materialist, mechanistic view created by philosophers relying upon natural science's proper restriction of its scope to the material world to create a philosophy of scientism or postivism—the view that the only reality is material. But this materialist view could not be a cosmos, a coherent whole, for it ignored mind, spirit, consciousness, affect, and esthetic, or else made them mere epiphenomena of matter. The living cosmos became a dead universe whose separate parts could be isolated and intensively analyzed, but without reference to the whole.

Philosophy, not science, created materialism, and it is not up to science to create a new world view now. But by removing its support from materialism, science will permit the formation of a new, coherent world view in which science, theology, philosophy, history, depth psychology, and the arts may all come together in a coherent whole deeper and more sophisticated and more charitable than any we have had before. Quantum physics has now removed the prop of an ultimate material reality from the mechanistic view, making it possible gradually to create a new cosmology in which the cosmos is seen as integrated, coherent, and alive, and in which meaning, value, and truth are again part of a unified whole.[68] What this new cosmology will ultimately be is

---

68. See, for example, O. Barfield, *Saving the Appearances* (New York, 1965); R. Bellah, "The Triumph of Secularism: The Return of Religion," *Religion and Intellectual Life*, 1:2 (1984), 13–73; D. Bohm, *Wholeness and the Implicate Order* (London, 1980); F. Ferre, *Shaping the Future: Resources for the Postmodern World* (New York, 1976); F. Ferre, "Religious World Modeling and Postmodern Science," *Journal of Religion*, 62 (1982), 261–271; D. R. Griffin, ed., *Physics and the Ultimate Significance of Time* (New York, 1985); J.

as yet difficult to discern, but it will certainly include a sense of radical good and evil. Radical evil—under whatever name or metaphor—is a reality, and for this reason the concept of the Devil will always be relevant.

W. Hayward, *Perceiving Magic: Science and Intuitive Wisdom* (Boulder, 1984); K. Hübner, *Critique of Scientific Reason* (Chicago, 1983); R. Jones, *Physics as Metaphor* (Minneapolis, 1982); C. Musès, *Destiny and Control in Human Systems* (Dordrecht, 1985); R. Sheldrake, *A New Science of Life: The Hypothesis of Formative Causation* (London, 1981); S. Toulmin, *The Return to Cosmology: Postmodern Science and the Theology of Nature* (Berkeley, 1982); F. Turner, "Escape from Modernism," *Harper's Magazine* (November 1984), 47–55; K. Wilber, ed., *The Holographic Paradigm and Other Paradoxes: Exploring the Leading Edge of Science* (Boulder, 1982). An indication of the kind of new thinking about Lucifer that the new world view can engender is the suggestion of Jack Vizzard (in a work in preparation, dealing with the connection between theology and modern science) that we, the cosmos, and the fallen angel are ultimately one and that the entire cosmos is working its way toward fulfillment, even salvation.

8 *God and Devil*

Whether it is meaningful to believe that the Devil exists depends upon one's world view. It is clearly meaningful in a Christian world view, and just as clearly meaningless in a materialist one. But the question must be put in the context of the larger question of whether any spiritual entity exists. God is as unscientific a concept as the Devil. Owing to the prevailing "commonsense" materialism of the twentieth century, the assumption of most educated people is that on the whole the weight of the evidence is against the existence of any spiritual entities.

In fact, however, materialist science can by definition offer no evidence either for or against them, so the evidence must be considered in the light of other world views, which are far from ruling out such entities. Further, as shown in the discussion of Hume in Chapter 4, a cosmos in which spiritual entities act is at least as likely as one in which they do not.

What indications are there that the Devil—a spiritual personality devoted to evil—may really exist? The question has to be broken into two modes: first, what the indications are without reference to religion; second, what the indications are within a religious context. The first may be called "natural diabology"; the second, "revealed diabology."

The first indication of natural diabology is that we do not in fact experience a morally neutral world. Psychology confirms that we begin to experience things as good and evil at a very early age, though with maturity we learn the refinements of ambivalence. The experience of good and evil applies to both what is done to us and what we do to others, and in normal people it is inherent unless eradicated by society. We experience good and evil in ourselves and in other human beings. But we also experience good and evil beyond the human race. We regard cancer, meningitis, and other natural evils as a blot upon the cosmos. We also extrapolate evil to putative other intelligent beings. Whenever we imagine extraterrestrials as real "persons" having coherent intellect and will, we imagine them as capable of good and evil, capable of suffering and of inflicting suffering. There is no reason to assume that the active evil in the universe is limited to humanity.

Nor is there reason to assume that the cause of human evil lies in human nature alone. We are making preparations for a nuclear war that at the least would bring absolute suffering to thousands of millions of people, each of whom would suffer as did the child whose parents locked her in the oven to roast to death. The argument that the arms race is actually reducing the chance of nuclear war is often heard from propagandists; it is demolished by the simple fact that the world grows yearly more dangerous. The argument that probably no one is deliberately planning to launch a nuclear war neglects the fact that the danger of an accidental nuclear war is increasing with incredible rapidity, and that the stockpiling and deployment of the weapons capable of destroying the planet is a deliberate choice that humans have made and humans can reverse.

The demonic quality of the arms race becomes clearer when we ask, to whose good are these preparations for holocaust? No individual, no nation, no ideology—nothing human will profit from a nuclear war. What is the force, then, that is leading us to prepare for a destruction exactly of the magnitude that we are capable of: the ruin of human life on this planet? If military bases are established in space, on the moon, on Mars, or anywhere in the solar system, our plans for destruction will be extended to include them. No one can doubt that we would extend the threat through the galaxy or to the entire universe if we had the power. But what is the nature of the force that can contemplate the destruction of the entire universe?

Many assume that this unlimited destructiveness is an extension of individual human destructiveness. It is true that there is evil in each of us, but adding together even large numbers of individual evils does not explain an Auschwitz, let alone the destruction of the planet. Evil on this scale seems to be qualitatively as well as quantitatively different. It is no longer a personal but perhaps a transpersonal evil, arising from some kind of collective unconscious. It is also possible that it is beyond the transpersonal and is truly transcendent, an entity outside as well as inside the human mind, an entity that would exist even if there were no human race to imagine it.

Such a transcendent Devil is difficult to defend philosophically. It would have to be a person who was not only absolutely evil but also had such enormous knowledge and power that he could extend his operations over the entire universe, or at least wherever intelligent and morally free life forms exist. He would have to oppose God's work always and everywhere. But could any created mind, however angelically powerful, have anything like the knowledge required? The universe is incredibly more complex than we had any idea of even a century ago, so complex as to render the existence of any being cosmically opposing God extremely improbable. If God can observe, in the eternal moment, the action of every subatomic particle in a universe of a hundred thousand million galaxies each containing a hundred thousand million stars, and see each particle in every moment of time in a universe already twenty thousand million years old, and moreover see all the infinity of potential universes that arise each time a particle makes a random motion, the idea of any creature having enough intelligence to offer opposition to God seems fantastic.[1]

Natural diabology is suggestive but inconclusive. Revealed diabology is much firmer. From within Christianity and Islam, arguments for the Devil are very strong. (In keeping with the scope of this series of books and for the sake of simplicity, I will put the argument in Christian terms, but similar arguments will apply to Islam.) Christian epistemology is based upon scripture, tradition, reason, and experience. Any statement about the world in a Christian context is made with reference to one or more of these bases of understanding, and the two central pillars are scripture and tradition. Both clearly affirm the existence of the Devil. It is true that belief in the Devil's existence is not part of the core of Christianity; no major Christian tradition insists upon it as a matter of dogma. At the same time, it makes little sense to call oneself a Christian while affirming a view contrary to scripture and tradition.

Theologians using historical criticism to affirm that the New Testament and church councils did not mean what they said seem to base their views less on the open search for historical truth than upon the assumptions of current materialism. Few are ready to face the logical

---

1. Another argument is that evil, being radically absurd and incoherent by definition, could have no focused intelligent source.

consequences of their denial of the Devil. If Satan does not exist, God must be responsible for evil, at least natural evil. If we admit that God creates cancer and meningitis, or at least creates a world in which cancer and meningitis exist, then God must not be entirely good in our sense of the world. But if God has a shadow, what is this shadow but the Devil by another name?

Skeptics also suggest that the idea of the Devil is socially destructive, that to believe in the Devil is to grant evil too much power. Certainly it is spiritually unhealthy to dwell upon the idea of the Devil in any way that lessens one's attention to grace. But in the late twentieth century the Devil seems to be receiving too little attention rather than too much. Skeptics also object that the idea of the Devil promotes demonization of enemies, but systems such as Soviet communism that deny the Devil are equally prone to demonize their enemies. The skeptics claim that belief in the Devil erodes human responsibility, but Christianity has always insisted that the Devil has no power to coerce or compel the human will. It may actually be that by recognizing radical evil and naming it we may gain the tools with which to fight against it. An understanding of radical evil would help us to get past palliative measures (such as arms control or prison reform) to the heart of the matter. Further, if it were better understood that a perceived spiritual voice may come from a power of evil, dangerous cult figures who argue that they speak with the voice of God might win fewer followers.

The idea of the Devil ultimately does little to solve the problem of *why* there is evil in the cosmos. At the center of the problem is the question of why God should freely choose to create a cosmos in which the Devil and other evil beings produce such immeasurable suffering. How can God, freely choosing this cosmos, not be responsible for it? And if God is responsible, why do we need the idea of the Devil?

The relation of evil to God has in the century of Auschwitz and Hiroshima once again become a center of philosophical and theological discussion. The problem of evil can be stated simply: God is omnipotent; God is perfectly good; such a God would not permit evil to exist; but we observe that evil exists; therefore God does not exist. Variations on this theme are nearly infinite. The problem is not only abstract and philosophical, of course; it is also personal and immediate. Believers tend to forget that their God takes away everything that one cares about: possessions, comforts, success, profession or craft, knowledge, friends, family, and life. What kind of God is this? Any decent religion must face this question squarely, and no answer is credible that cannot be given in the presence of dying children. Yet believers know from the depths of their experience that the cosmos is alive with the presence of God.

How can these things be reconciled? I can only offer suggestions. In one dimension, the Devil must be seen as an aspect of the cosmos that God has created and therefore a product of God's will. God could have created a different cosmos, or none at all. But in another dimension, the dimension of space and time in which we all live, the Devil and evil are the antithesis of God, and God wishes us to strive against them with every strength we have.

The concept of the Devil arises in part from the anguish of believers confronting this dilemma.

If the Devil does exist, what is he? If the concept has any meaning, the Devil is the traditional Devil. He is a mighty person with intelligence and will whose energies are bent on the destruction of the cosmos and on the misery of its creatures. The Devil puts the child in the oven and the nuclear weapons in their silos. We must strive against this evil with every syllable of our sanity. Evil can never be fought with more evil, negation with more negation, nuclear missiles with more nuclear missiles. The process of negation must be reversed. Only affirmation can overcome negation; only good can overcome evil; only love can overcome hatred. My books have been somber; I have tried to face the problem of evil without flinching. I am, I think, permitted to end on a note of optimism. In spite of our miserable record in the past, we have the ability to use our freedom to embrace new modes of thinking, to find a way to transcend and integrate evil and to turn its immense force toward the good. And I think that the cosmos is alive with a power that encourages us and aids us to do so. If we make the decision now, before nuclear war blights every hope, the world will be changed.

I look tonight from my winter window and name the stars, Procyon, Sirius and Mirzam, Aldebaran, and here in the warm south Canopus in Carina, low on the rim of the sea. I name them, but I know them not by naming but only by loving, for love is the stuff of their being and mine, O blue blazing Rigel, O long twins with burning heads, O stars grape-clustered in the vineyards of the night. For knowledge pauses when the blood stops beating to the brain, but love never ceases, because it is the true stuff of reality that moves the sun and the other stars. *Che move il sole e l'altre stelle*. And that is why the Devil, the subject of these four books, in whatever way he exists, is negation negated, denial denied, meaninglessness exploded into galaxies of meaning blooming bright in the darkness with the light of love.

Bibliography

This bibliography of material relating directly to the Devil includes the most important secondary works before 1890 and all works of book length (as well as important articles) after 1890. Additional sources relevant to thinkers discussed in the text are cited in the footnotes.

Adam, Alfred. "Die Herkunft des Lutherwortes vom menschlichen Willen als Reittier Gottes." *Luther-Jahrbuch*, 29 (1962), 25–33.
——. "Der Teufel als Gottes Affe: Vorgeschichte eines Lutherwortes." *Luther-Jahrbuch*, 28 (1961), 104–109.
Adler, Manfred, ed. *Tod und Teufel in Klingenberg*. Aschaffenburg, 1977.
Alemany, José J. "A vueltas con el diablo." *Hechos y dichos* (1974), 41–44.
——. "Fe en el diablo? Teología actual y satanisma." *Razón y fe*, 191 (1975), 239–250.
Alexander, Brooks. "The Disappearance of the Devil." *Spiritual Counterfeits Newsletter*, 10:4 (1984), 6–7.
Alexander, Marc. *To Anger the Devil: An Account of the Work of the Exorcist Extraordinary The Reverend Dr. Donald Omand*. Sudbury, Suffolk, 1978.
Allen, E. L. "The Devil's Property in the United States." *Outlook*, 127 (1920), 246–247.
Amades, J. "El diable." *Zephryus*, 4 (1953), 375–389.
Andreas-Salomé, Lou. *Der Teufel und seine Grossmutter*. Jena, 1922.
Andreev, Leonid. *Satan's Diary*. New York, 1920.
Anshen, Ruth Nanda. *The Reality of the Devil: Evil in Man*. New York, 1972.
Anstice, Robert H. *The "Satan" of Milton*. Folcroft, Pa., 1969.
Aparicio López, Teófilo. "Satán y el pecado en la novelística contemporánea." *Religion y cultura*, n.s. 21 (1975), 505–537.
Armstrong, Herbert W. *Did God Create a Devil?* n.p., 1978.
Ashton, John. *The Devil in Britain and America*. London, 1896.
Atfield, Henry. "Can One Sell One's Soul (The Faust Legend)." In Robert M.

MacIver, ed., *Great Moral Dilemmas in Literature, Past and Present.* New York, 1956. Pp. 83–97.

Aylesworth, Thomas G. *Servants of the Devil.* Reading, Mass., 1970.

Bachmann, Franz. *Lucifer: Drama in vier Aufzügen.* Dresden, 1903.

Bainbridge, William Sims. *Satan's Power: A Deviant Psychotherapy Cult.* Berkeley, 1979.

Bak, Felix. "La chiesa di Satana negli Stati Uniti." *Rassegna di teologia,* 16 (1975), 342–353.

Baker, Roger. *Binding the Devil: Exorcism Past and Present.* London, 1974.

Balducci, Corrado. *Gli indemoniati.* Rome, 1959.

Balthasar, Hans Urs von. "Vorverständnis des Dämonischen." *Internationale katholische Zeitschrift,* 8 (1979), 238–242.

Bamberger, Bernard J. *Fallen Angels.* Philadelphia, 1952.

Barbeau, Anne T. "Satan's Envy of the Son and the Third Day of the War." *Papers on Language and Literature,* 13 (1977), 362–371.

Barth, Hans-Martin. *Der Teufel und Jesus Christus in der Theologie Martin Luthers.* Göttingen, 1967.

———. "Zur inneren Entwicklung von Luthers Teufelsglauben." *Kerygma und Dogma,* 13 (1967), 201–211.

Barth, Hans-Martin, Heinz Flügel, and Richard Riess. *Der emanzipierte Teufel: Literarisches, Psychologisches, Theologisches zur Deutung des Bösen.* Munich, 1974.

Baskin, Wade. *Dictionary of Satanism.* New York, 1971.

Bass, Clarence. "Satan and Demonology in Eschatologic Perspective." In John W. Montgomery, ed., *Demon Possession.* Minneapolis, 1976. Pp. 364–371.

Bataille, Georges. *Literature and Evil.* London, 1973.

Bausani, Alessandro. "Satana nell'opera filosofico-poetica di Muhammad Iqbal (1873–1938)." *Rivista degli studi orientali,* 30 (1955), 55–102.

Baxter, James K. *The Devil and Mr. Mulcahy.* Auckland, 1971.

Bazin, Germain. "The Devil in Art." In Bruno de Jésus-Marie, ed., *Satan.* New York, 1952. Pp. 351–367.

Beard, John R. *Autobiography of Satan.* London, 1872.

Béguin, Albert. "Balzac and the 'End of Satan.'" In Bruno de Jésus-Marie, ed., *Satan.* New York, 1952. Pp. 394–404.

Bekker, Hugo. "The Lucifer Motif in the German and Dutch Drama of the Sixteenth and Seventeenth Centuries." Ph.D. diss., University of Michigan, 1958.

———. "The Lucifer Motif in the German Drama of the Sixteenth Century." *Monatshefte für deutsche Sprache und Literatur,* 51 (1959), 237–247.

Belloc, Marie. "Satanism, Ancient and Modern: M. Jules Bois—Some of His Views." *Humanitarian,* 11 (1897), 80–87.

Bender, Hans. "Teufelskreis der Besessenheit." In M. Adler, ed., *Tod und Teufel in Klingenberg.* Aschaffenburg, 1977. Pp. 130–139.

Bennett, Joan S. "God, Satan, and King Charles: Milton's Royal Portraits." *Publications of the Modern Language Association,* 92 (1977), 441–457.

Bernanos, Georges. *Sous le soleil de Satan.* Paris, 1926.

Bernhart, Joseph. *Chaos und Dämonie: Von den göttlichen Schatten der Schöpfung.* Munich, 1950.

Bernus, Alexander von. *Gesang an Luzifer.* 3d ed. Nürnberg, 1961.

Birrell, T. A. "The Figure of Satan in Milton and Blake." In Bruno de Jésus-Marie, ed., *Satan*. New York, 1952. Pp. 379–393.

Bizouard, Joseph. *Des rapports de l'homme avec le démon: Essai historique et philosophique*. 6 vols. Paris, 1863–1864.

Blatty, William Peter. *The Exorcist*. New York, 1971.

———. *Legion*. New York, 1983.

Blisset, William. "Caesar and Satan." *Journal of the History of Ideas*, 18 (1957), 221–232.

Bloch, Ernst. "Aufklärung und Teufelsglaube." In Oskar Schatz, ed., *Hat die Religion Zukunft?* Graz, 1971. Pp. 120–134.

Blomster, W. V. "The Demonic in History: Thomas Mann and Günther Grass." *Contemporary Literature*, 10 (1969), 75–84.

Bloom, Harold. *The Flight to Lucifer: A Gnostic Fantasy*. New York, 1979.

Blunt, Wilfrid. *Satan Absolved: A Victorian Mystery*. London, 1899.

Böhm, Anton. *Epoche des Teufels: Ein Versuch*. Stuttgart, 1955.

Bois, Jules. *Les noces de Satan: Drame esotérique*. Paris, 1892.

———. *Le satanisme et la magie*. Paris, 1895.

Boltwood, Robert M. "Turnus and Satan as Epic 'Villains.'" *Classical Journal*, 47 (1952), 183–186.

Boucher, Ghislaine. *Dieu et Satan dans la vie de Catherine de Saint-Augustin 1632–1668*. Tournai, 1979.

Bounds, Edward M. *Satan: His Personality, Power, and Overthrow*. New York, 1922.

Bouvet, Alphonse. "Rimbaud, Satan et 'Voyelles.'" *Studi francesi*, 21 (1963), 499–504.

Brandon, Samuel G. F. "The Devil in Faith and History." *History Today* (1963), 468–478.

Breig, James. "Who in the Hell Is Satan?" *U.S. Catholic*, 48:2 (1983), 7–11.

Bricaud, Joanny. *J.-K. Huysmans et le satanisme: D'après des douments inédits*. Paris, 1913.

Brik, Hans Theodor. *Gibt es noch Engel und Teufel?* Stein am Rhein, 1975.

Brincourt, André. *Satan et la poésie*. Paris, 1946.

Brouette, Emile. "The Sixteenth Century and Satanism." In Bruno de Jésus-Marie, ed., *Satan*. New York, 1952. Pp. 310–350.

Browning, Preston M. "Flannery O'Connor and the Demonic." *Modern Fiction Stories*, 19 (1973), 29–41.

———. "Flannery O'Connor's Devil Revisited." *Southern Humanities Review*, 10 (1976), 325–333.

Bruffee, Kenneth A. "Satan and the Sublime: The Meaning of the Romantic Hero." Ph.D. diss., Northwestern University, 1964.

Bruno de Jésus-Marie, ed. *Satan*. New York, 1952.

Bruns, J. Edgar. "Toward a New Understanding of the Demonic." *Ecumenist*, 4 (1966), 29–31.

Buchrucker, Armin-Ernst. "Die Bedeutung des Teufels für die Theologie Luthers: 'Nullus diabolus—nullus Redemptor.'" *Theologische Zeitschrift*, 29 (1973), 385–399.

Cabell, James Branch. *The Devil's Own Dear Son: A Comedy of the Fatted Calf*. New York, 1949.

Čajkanović, Veselinus. "De daemonibus quibusdam neohellenicae et serbicae superstitioni communibus." In *Atti del V congresso internazionale di studi bizantini.* Róme, 1939. Pp. 416–426.

Caldwell, Taylor. *Dialogues with the Devil.* New York, 1967.

Camerlynck, Elaine. "Fémininité et sorcellerie chez les théoriciens de la démonologie à la fin du Moyen Age: Etudes du *Malleus maleficarum.*" *Renaissance and Reformation,* 19 (1983), 13–25.

Carducci, Giosuè. *Satana e polemiche sataniche.* 13th ed. Bologna, 1879.

Carlsson, Anni. *Teufel, Tod, und Tiermensch: Phantastischer Realismus als Geschichtschreibung der Epoche.* Kronberg, 1978.

Carsch, Henry. "The Role of the Devil in Grimms' Tales: An Exploration of the Content and Function of Popular Tales." *Social Research,* 35 (1968), 466–499.

Carus, Paul. *The History of the Devil and the Idea of Evil, from the Earliest Times to the Present Day.* Chicago, 1900.

Cavendish, Richard. *The Powers of Evil in Western Religion, Magic and Folk Belief.* London, 1975.

Černý, Vaclav. *Dostoevsky and His Devils.* Ann Arbor, 1975.

"Ces merveilleux démons du cinéma." *Relations,* 34 (1974), 178–179.

Chafer, Lewis S. *Satan and the Satanic System: An Exhaustive Examination of the Scripture Teaching from Genesis to Revelation.* Glasgow, n.d.

——. *Satan: His Motive and Methods.* 2d ed. Philadelphia, 1919.

Chambers, Whittaker. "The Devil." *Life,* February 2, 1948, pp. 77–84.

Charcot, Jean-Martin, and P. Richer. *Les démoniaques dans l'art.* Paris, 1887.

Checca, Peter Anthony. "The Role of the Devil in Golden Age Drama." Ph.D. diss., Pennsylvania State University, 1976.

"Christian Faith and Demonology: A Document Commissioned by the Sacred Congregation of the Faith." *The Pope Speaks,* 20:1 (1975), 209–233.

Cilveti, Angel L. *El demonio en el teatro de Calderón.* Valencia, 1977.

Clavel, Maurice. *Deux siècles chez Lucifer.* Paris, 1978.

Cocchiara, Giuseppe. *Il diavolo nella tradizione popolare italiana.* Palermo, 1945.

Coe, Charles N. *Demi-Devils: The Character of Shakespeare's Villains.* New York, 1963.

Colleye, Hubert. *Histoire du diable.* Brussels, 1946.

Collier, J. *Defy the Foul Fiend.* London, 1934.

Collins, Gary. "Psychological Observations in Demonism." In John W. Montgomery, ed., *Demon Possession.* Minneapolis, 1976. Pp. 237–251.

Coomaraswamy, Ananda. "Who Is Satan and Where Is Hell." *Review of Religion,* 12 (1947), 36–47.

Corelli, Marie. *The Sorrows of Satan; or, The Strange Experience of One Geoffrey Tempest, Millionaire.* London, 1895.

Corte, Nicolas [L. Cristiani]. *Who is the Devil?* New York, 1958.

Cortés, Juan B., and F. M. Gatti. *The Case against Possessions and Exorcisms: A Historical, Biblical, and Psychological Analysis of Demons, Devils, and Demoniacs.* New York, 1975.

Craig, Terry Ann. "Witchcraft and Demonology in Shakespeare's Comedies." Master's thesis, Duquesne University, 1974.

Cristiani, Leon. *Présence de Satan dans le monde moderne.* Paris, 1959.

——. *Satan in the Modern World.* London, 1961.

——. *Satan, l'adversaire.* Paris, 1956.

Cullen, Patrick. *Infernal Triad: The Flesh, the World, and the Devil in Spenser and Milton*. Princeton, 1974.

Curto, Girolamo. *Die Figur des Mephisto im Goethe'schen Faust*. Turin, 1890.

Cushman, Lysander. W. *The Devil and the Vice in the English Dramatic Literature before Shakespeare*. Halle, 1900.

Dahiyat, Eid A. "Harapha and Baal-zebub/Ashtaroth in Milton's 'Samson Agonistes.'" *Milton Quarterly*, 16 (1982), 60–62.

Daniels, Edgar F. "The Seventeenth-Century Conception of Satan with Relation to the Satan of *Paradise Lost*." Ph.D. diss., Stanford University, 1952.

Dansereau, Michel. "Le diable et la psychanalyse." *Relations*, 34 (1979), 168–172.

Daur, Albert. *Faust und der Teufel*. Heidelberg, 1950.

Davenport, Basil, ed. *Deals with the Devil: An Anthology*. New York, 1958.

Davidson, Gustav. *A Dictionary of the Angels, Including the Fallen Angels*. New York, 1967.

Davison, R. M. "*The Devils*: The Role of Stavrogin." In Malcolm V. Jones and G. M. Terry, eds., *New Essays on Dostoevsky*. Cambridge, 1983. Pp. 95–114.

De Bruyn, Lucy. *Woman and the Devil in Sixteenth-Century Literature*. Tisbury, Wilts., 1979.

De Haan, Richard W. *Satan, Satanism, and Witchcraft*. Grand Rapids, Mich., 1972.

Dehmel, Richard. *Lucifer: Ein Tanz- und Glanzspiel*. Berlin, 1899.

Delaporte, Albert. *Le diable, existe-t-il et que fait-il?* 2d ed. Paris, 1864.

Delpech, Henri. *Satan: Epopée*. 2 vols. Paris, 1859.

———. *Satan: Poème*. Bordeaux, 1856.

Delumeau, Jean. "Attentes eschatologiques et peur de Satan au début des temps modernes." *Ricerche di storia sociale e religiosa*, 12 (1977), 141–161.

Demos, John. *Entertaining Satan: Witchcraft and the Culture of Early New England*. New York, 1982.

Devine, Philip E. "The Perfect Island, the Devil, and Existent Unicorns." *American Philosophical Quarterly*, 12 (1975), 255–260.

Le diable dans le folklore de Wallonie. Brussels, 1980.

Didier, Raymond. "Satan: Quelques réflexions théologiques." *Lumière et vie*, 78 (1966), 77–98.

Dieckhoff, John S. "Eve, the Devil, and *Areopagitica*." *Modern Language Quarterly*, 5 (1944), 429–434.

Dilthey, Wilhelm. "Satan in der christlichen Poesie." In Dilthey, *Die grosse Phantasiedichtung*. Göttingen, 1954. Pp. 109–131.

Doderer, Heimito von. *The Demons*. New York, 1961.

Doinel, Jules. *Lucifer démasqué*. Paris, 1895.

Dragon, Antonio. *Mephistophélès et le problème du mal dans le drame de Faust*. Paris, 1907.

Dreher, Diane E. "Diabolical Order in Hell: An Emblematic Inversion in *Paradise Lost*." *Studia mystica*, 8 (1985), 13–18.

Dubal, Rosette. *La psychanalyse du diable*. Paris, 1953.

Duhr, Bernhard. "Teufelsmystik in Deutschland in der Zeit nach dem dreissigjährigen Kriege." *Görresgesellschaft Vereinschrift*, 3 (1918), 5–20.

Duncan, Ronald. *The Death of Satan*. In *Satan, Socialites, and Solly Gold: Three New Plays from England*. New York, 1954. Pp. 11–110.

Duquoc, Christian. "Symbole ou réalité?" *Lumière et vie*, 78 (1966), 99–105.

Dustoor, P. E. "Legends of Lucifer in Early English and in Milton." *Anglia*, 54 (1930), 213–268.

Ebon, Martin. *The Devil's Bride: Exorcism Past and Present*. New York, 1974.

Eliade, Mircea. *The Two and the One*. London, 1965.

Elliot, Gil. *Lucifer*. London, 1978.

Elliot, Robert, and M. Smith. "Descartes, God, and the Evil Spirit." *Sophia*, 17:3 (1978), 33–36.

Elwood, Roger. *Prince of Darkness*. Norwalk, Conn., 1974.

_____. *Strange Things Are Happening: Satanism, Witchcraft, and God*. Elgin, Ill., 1973.

Emmanuel, Pierre. *Baudelaire: The Paradox of Redemptive Satanism*. University, Ala., 1970.

Epstein, Jean. *Le cinéma du diable*. Paris, 1947.

Ernst, Cecile. *Teufelaustreibungen: Die Praxis der katholischen Kirche im 16. und 17. Jahrhundert*. Bern, 1972.

Evans, John M. *Paradise Lost and the Genesis Tradition*. Oxford, 1968.

Evil, ed. C. G. Jung Institute. Evanston, 1967.

Fahrenkrog, Ludwig. *Lucifer: Dichtung in Bild und Wort*. Stuttgart, 1917.

Fallon, Stephen M. "Satan's Return to Hell: Milton's Concealed Dialogue with Homer and Virgil." *Milton Quarterly*, 19 (1985), 78–81.

Farrell, Walter, B. Leeming, and F. Catherinet, eds. *The Devil*. New York, 1957.

Fehr, Hans von. "Gottesurteil und Folter: Eine Studie zur Dämonologie des Mittelalters und der neueren Zeit." In *Festgabe für Rudolf Stammler*. Berlin, 1926. Pp. 231–254.

Feuchtwanger, Lion. *Wahn: Oder der Teufel in Boston*. Los Angeles, 1948.

Fishwick, Marshall W. *A Brief History of the Devil*. Roanoke, Va., 1962.

_____. *Faust Revisited: Some Thoughts on Satan*. New York, 1963.

Flannagan, Roy. "Belial and 'Effeminate Slackness' in *Paradise Lost* and *Paradise Regained*." *Milton Quarterly*, 19 (1985), 9–11.

Flatter, Richard. "Mephistopheles und die Handlungsfreiheit." *Chronik des Weiner Goethe-Vereins*, 60 (1965), 37–40.

Flecniakoska, Jean-Louis. "Les rôles de Satan dans les 'Autos' de Lope de Vega." *Bulletin hispanique*, 66 (1964), 30–44.

Flick, Maurizio. "Riflessioni su Satana, oggi." *Rassegna di teologia*, 20 (1979), 58–65.

Flores Arroyuelo, Francisco. *El diablo y los Españoles*. Murcia, 1976.

Florescu, Radu. "The Devil in Romanian Literature and Folklore." In A. Olson, ed., *Disguises of the Demonic*. New York, 1975. Pp. 69–86.

Forsyth, Neil. *The Old Enemy: Satan as Adversary, Rebel, Tyrant, and Heretic*. Princeton, 1986.

France, Anatole. *La révolte des anges*. Paris, 1913.

Franz, Erich. *Mensch und Dämon*. Tübingen, 1953.

Freeman, James A. "Satan, Bentley, and 'The Din of War.'" *Milton Quarterly*, 7 (1973), 1–4.

French, Robert W. "Satan's Sonnet." *Milton Quarterly*, 11 (1977), 113–114.

Freud, Sigmund. *Eine Teufelsneurose im siebzehnten Jahrhundert*. Leipzig, 1924.

Frey, Dagobert. "Uomo, demone, e Dio." In E. Castelli, ed., *Filosofia dell'arte*. Milan, 1953. Pp. 115–126.

Freytag, Gustav. "Der deutsche Teufel im sechzehnten Jahrhundert." In Freytag, *Gesammelte Werke*. Berlin, 1920. Ser. 2, vol. 5, pp. 346–384.

Frick, Karl R. H. *Das Reich Satans: Luzifer/Satan/Teufel und die Mond-und Liebesgöttin-nen in ihrer lichten und dunklen Aspekten*. Graz, 1982.

Frossard, André. *Les 36 preuves de l'existence du diable*. Paris, 1978.

Frye, Roland M. *God, Man, and Satan: Patterns of Christian Thought and Life in Paradise Lost, Pilgrim's Progress, and the Great Theologians*. Princeton, 1960.

Fuchs, Albert. "Mephistophélès." *Etudes germaniques*, 20 (1965), 233–242.

Gabriel-Robinet, Louis. *Le diable: Sa vie, son oeuvre*. Paris, 1944.

Gagen, Jean. "Adam, the Serpent, and Satan: Recognition and Restoration." *Milton Quarterly*, 17 (1983), 116–121.

Gardner, Helen. "Milton's 'Satan' and the Theme of Damnation in Elizabethan Tragedy." *English Studies*, n.s. 1 (1948), 46–66.

Gasparro, Giulia Sfameni. "I miti cosmologici degli Yezidi." *Numen*, 21 (1974), 197–227, and 22 (1975), 24–41.

Gattiglia, Anna, and Maurizio Rossi. "Saint Bernard de Menthon et le diable dans les croyances populaires." *Histoire et archéologie: Les dossiers*, 79 (1983–1984), 60–69.

Gellner, Ernest. *The Devil in Modern Philosophy*. London, 1974.

Gilbert, Allan H. "The Theological Basis of Satan's Rebellion and the Function of Abdiel in *Paradise Lost*." *Modern Philology*, 40 (1942), 19–42.

Gildea, Peter. "Demoniacal Possession." *Irish Theological Quarterly*, 41 (1974), 289–311.

Ginzburg, Carlo. "Présomptions sur le sabbat." *Annales*, 39 (1984), 341–354.

Gloger, Bruno, and W. Zollner. *Teufelsglaube und Hexenwahn*. Leipzig, 1983.

Goebel, Julius. "Mephistopheles und das Problem des Bösen in Goethes Faust." *Internationale Wochenschrift für Kunst und Technik*, 5 (1911), 995–1008.

Goldston, Robert. *Satan's Disciples*. New York, 1962.

Goll, Iwan. *Lucifer vieillissant*. Paris, 1933.

Gombocz, Wolfgang. "St. Anselm's Disproof of the Devil's Existence in the Pros-logion: A Counter Argument against Haight and Richman." *Ratio*, 15 (1973), 334–337.

———. "St. Anselm's Two Devils but One God." *Ratio*, 20 (1978), 142–146.

Gómez Valderrama, Pedro. *Muestras del diablo*. Bogotá, 1958.

González, Gonzálo. "Dios y el diablo: Superación cristiana del dualismo." *Ciencia tomista*, 104 (1972), 279–301.

Gorecki, John. "Milton's Similitudes for Satan and the Traditional Implications of Their Imagery." *Milton Quarterly*, 10 (1976), 101–108.

Grant, C. K. "A Marlovian Precedent for Satan's Astronomical Journey in 'Paradise Lost' IX 63–67." *Milton Quarterly*, 17 (1983), 45–47.

———. "The Ontological Disproof of the Devil." *Analysis*, 17 (1957), 71–72.

Greef, A. "Byron's Lucifer." *Englische Studien*, 36 (1906), 64–74.

Greeley, Andrew. *The Devil, You Say! Man and His Personal Devils and Angels*. Garden City, N.Y., 1974.

Griffin, Robert. "The Devil and Panurge." *Studi francesi*, 47/48 (1972), 329–336.

Grillet, Claudius, *Le diable dans la littérature au XIXe siècle*. Lyon, 1935.

Grimm, Heinrich. "Die deutschen 'Teufelbücher' des 16. Jahrhunderts." *Archiv für Geschichte des Buchwesens*, 2 (1960), 513–570.

Griswold, Wendy. "The Devil's Techniques: Cultural Legitimation and Social Change." *American Sociological Review*, 48 (1983), 668–680.

Gross, Seymour. "The Devil in Samburan: Jones and Ricardo in *Victory.*" *Nineteenth-Century Fiction*, 16 (1961), 81–85.

Grossmann, Rudolf. "Vom Teufel in der lateinamerikanischen Literatur." In *Studia Iberica* in honor of Hans Flasche. Munich, 1973. Pp. 197–213.

Guilfoyle, Cheryl. "Adamantine and Serpentine: Milton's Use of Two Conventions of Satan in *Paradise Lost.*" *Milton Quarterly*, 13 (1979), 129–133.

Günther, P. Bonifatius. *Maria: Die Gegenspielerin Satans.* Aschaffenburg, 1972.

———. *Satan: Der Widersacher Gottes.* Aschaffenburg, 1972.

Guthrie, Ellis G. "Satan: Real or Fictitious?" *Brethren Life and Thought*, 14 (1969), 160–167.

Haack, Friedrich-Wilhelm. *Satan-Teufel-Lucifer.* Munich, 1975.

Haag, Herbert. *Abschied vom Teufel.* Einsiedeln, 1969.

———. "Ein fragwürdiges römisches Studiendokument zum Thema Teufel." *Theologische Quartalschrift*, 156 (1976), 28–34.

———. "Der Teufel in der Bibel." In M. Adler, ed., *Tod und Teufel in Klingenberg.* Aschaffenburg, 1977. Pp. 66–83.

———. *Teufelsglaube.* Tübingen, 1974.

Hagen, Martin. *Der Teufel im Lichte der Glaubensquellen.* Freiburg, 1899.

Haight, David, and Marjorie Haight. "An Ontological Argument for the Devil." *Monist*, 54 (1970), 218–220.

Haining, Peter, ed. *The Satanists.* New York, 1970.

Hall, Frederic T. *The Pedigree of the Devil.* London, 1883.

Hallie, Philip P. "Satan, Evil, and Good in History." In S. M. Stanage, ed., *Reason and Violence.* Totowa, N.J., 1975. Pp. 53–69.

Hamilton, George R. *Hero or Fool? A Study of Milton's Satan.* London, 1944.

Hammers, A. J., and U. Rosin. "Fragen über den Teufel." In E. Baur, ed., *Psi und Psyche.* Stuttgart, 1974. Pp. 61–73.

Hargrave, Anne. "'Lucifer Prince of the East' and the Fall of Marlowe's Dr. Faustus." *Neuphilologische Mitteilungen*, 84 (1983), 206–213.

Hawkes, John. "Flannery O'Connor's Devil." *Sewanee Review*, 70 (1962), 395–407.

Hélot, Charles. *Le diable dans l'hypnotisme.* Paris, 1899.

———. *Névroses et possessions diaboliques.* 2d ed. Paris, 1898.

Henning, Hans. "Mephistos Vorausschau." *Faust-Blätter*, n.s. 6 (1969), 232–234.

Henry, Caleb S. *Satan as a Moral Philosopher.* New York, 1877.

Hirsch, Emanuel. "Das Wörtlein, das den Teufel fällen kann." In Hirsch, *Lutherstudien*, 2 vols. Gütersloh, 1954. Vol. 2, pp. 93–98.

Hohlfeld, Alexander, R. "Pact and Wager in Goethe's Faust." *Modern Philology*, 18 (1920–1921), 513–536.

Holl, Adolf. *Death and the Devil.* New York, 1976.

Holquist, James M. "The Devil in Mufti: The Märchenwelt in Gogol's Short Stories." *Publications of the Modern Language Association*, 82 (1967), 352–362.

Huckabay, Calvin. "The Satanist Controversies of the Nineteenth Century." In Waldo F. McNeir, ed., *Studies in English Renaissance Literature.* Baton Rouge, La., 1962. Pp. 197–210.

Hunter, William B., Jr. "Belial's Presence in *Paradise Lost.*" *Milton Quarterly*, 19 (1985), 7–9.

———. "Eve's Demonic Dream." *ELH: A Journal of English Literary History*, 13 (1946), 255–265.

Huxley, Aldous. *The Devils of Loudun.* New York, 1952.

Huysmans, Joris-Karl. *Là-bas.* Paris, 1891.

Iersel, Bastiaan, ed. *Engelen en Duivels.* Hilversum, 1968.

Jackson, Basil. "Reflections on the Demonic: A Psychiatric Perspective." In J. W. Montgomery, ed., *Demon Possession.* Minneapolis, 1976. Pp. 256–267.

Jacobi, Jolande. "Dream Demons." In F. J. Sheed, ed., *Soundings in Satanism.* New York, 1972. Pp. 36–45.

Jamison, Mary T. "The Twentieth Century Critics of Milton and the Problem of Satan in Paradise Lost." Ph.D. diss., Catholic University, 1952.

Jewett, Edward H. *Diabology: The Person and Kingdom of Satan.* New York, 1889.

Jones, Ernest. *Nightmare, Witches, and Devils.* New York, 1931.

Joseph, Isya. *Devil Worship: The Sacred Books and Traditions of the Yezidis.* Boston, 1919.

Journet, Charles, Jacques Maritain, and Philippe de la Trinité. *Le péché de l'ange: Peccabilité, nature, et surnature.* Paris, 1960.

Jung, Carl G. *Answer to Job.* New York, 1954.

_____. "The Fight with the Shadow." In Jung, *Collected Works.* Princeton, 1970. Vol. 10, pp. 218–226.

_____. "Psychology and Religion: The Definition of Demonism." In Jung, *Collected Works.* Princeton, 1976. Vol. 18, p. 648.

_____. "Septem sermones ad mortuos." In Jung, *Memories, Dreams, Reflections.* New York, 1961. Pp. 378–380.

_____. "The Shadow." In Jung, *Collected Works.* Princeton, 1968. Vol. 9:2, pp. 3–7.

Jurt, Joseph. *Bernanos et Jouve: Sous le soleil de Satan et Paulina 1880.* Paris, 1978.

Kahler, Erich. "Die Säkulisierung des Teufels." In Kahler, *Verantwortung des Geistes.* Frankfurt, 1952. Pp. 143–162.

Kaiser, Gerhard. "Doktor Faust, sind Sie des Teufels?" *Euphorion,* 78 (1984), 188–197.

Kallas, James. *Jesus and the Power of Satan.* Philadelphia, 1968.

_____. *The Real Satan: From Biblical Times to the Present.* Minneapolis, 1975.

_____. *The Satanward View: A Study in Pauline Theology.* Philadelphia, 1966.

Kasper, Walter, and K. Lehman, eds., *Teufel-Dämonen-Besessenheit.* Mainz, 1978.

Kastor, Frank S. "In His Own Shape: The Stature of Satan in *Paradise Lost.*" *English Language Notes,* 5 (1968), 264–269.

_____. "Lucifer, Satan, and the Devil: A Genesis of Apparent Inconsistencies in *Paradise Lost.*" Ph.D. diss., University of California, Berkeley, 1965.

_____. *Milton and the Literary Satan.* Amsterdam, 1974.

Kehl, D. G. "The Cosmocrats: Diabolism in Modern Literature." In J. W. Montgomery, ed., *Demon Possession.* Minneapolis, 1976. Pp. 107–140.

Kelly, Henry Ansgar. "Demonology and Diabolical Temptation." *Thought,* 35 (1965), 165–194.

_____. *The Devil at Baptism.* Ithaca, 1985.

_____. *The Devil, Demonology, and Witchcraft.* 2d ed. Garden City, N.Y., 1974.

_____. "The Devil in the Desert." *Catholic Biblical Quarterly,* 26 (1964), 190–220.

_____. *Le diable et ses démons: La démonologie chrétienne hier et aujourd'hui.* Paris, 1977 (English text of 1974, with additions).

Kemp, Marie Ann. *Manifestations of Satan in Two Novels of Georges Bernanos.* Hemel Hempstead, Herts., 1976.

Kerényi, Karl. "Thomas Mann und der Teufel in Palestrina." *Neue Rundschau,* 73 (1962), 328–346.

Kerssemakers, A. "De Daemon." *Ons Geloof,* 30 (1948), 435–453.

Key, D. M. "The Life and Death of the Devil." *Religion in Life,* 21:1 (1951), 73–82.

Kiessling, Nicholas. *The Incubus in English Literature: Provenance and Progeny.* Pullman, Wash., 1977.

King, Albion R. "The Christian Devil." *Religion in Life,* 20:1 (1950), 61–71.

Kirchschläger, Walter. "Engel, Teufel, Dämonen: Eine biblische Skizze." *Bibel und Liturgie,* 54 (1981), 98–102.

Kirsten, Hans. *Die Taufabsage.* Berlin, 1959.

Klaits, Joseph. *Servants of Satan: The Age of the Witch Hunts.* Bloomington, Ind., 1985.

Kohák, Erazim. "Speaking of the Devil: A Modest Methodological Proposal." In A. Olson, *Disguises of the Demonic.* New York, 1975. Pp. 48–56.

Kolakowski, Leszek. "Can the Devil be Saved? A Marxist Answer." *Encounter,* 43 (1974), 7–13.

——. *The Devil and Scripture.* London, 1973.

——. *Gespräche mit dem Teufel: Acht Diskurse über das Böse und zwei Stücke.* Munich, 1968.

——. *Religion, If There Is No God: On God, the Devil, Sin, and Other Worries of the So-Called Philosophy of Religion.* New York, 1982.

Kolin, Philip C. "Milton's Use of Clouds for Satanic Parody in *Paradise Lost.*" *Essays on Literature,* 5 (1978), 153–162.

Kretzenbacher, Leopold. *Teufelsbündner und Faustgestalten im Abendlande.* Klagenfurt, 1968.

Krüger, Horst. "Das Teufelsmotiv im modernen Roman." *Welt und Wort,* 8 (1953), 334–335.

Kubis, Patricia. "The Archetype of the Devil in Twentieth-Century Literature." Ph.D. diss., University of California, Riverside, 1976.

La Bigne de Villeneuve, Marcel de. *Satan dans la cité: Conversations entre un sociologue et un théologien sur le diabolisme politique et social.* Paris, 1951.

La Charité, Raymond. "Devildom and Rabelais's Pantagruel." *French Review,* 49 (1975), 42–50.

Lampe, Hans-Sirks. *Die Darstellung des Teufels in den geistlichen Spielen Deutschlands von den Anfängen bis zum Ende des 16. Jahrhunderts.* Munich, 1963.

Lancelin, Charles. *Histoire mythique de Shatan; De la légende au dogme; Origines de l'idée démoniaque, ses transformations à travers les âges . . .* Paris, 1903.

Lange, Ursula. *Untersuchungen zu Bodins Demonomanie.* Frankfurt, 1970.

Langgässer, Elisabeth. *Triptychon des Teufels.* Dresden, 1932.

Langton, Edward. *Satan, a Portrait: A Study of the Character of Satan through All the Ages.* London, 1945.

——. *Supernatural: The Doctrine of Spirits, Angels, and Demons, from the Middle Ages until the Present Time.* London, 1934.

Lattimore, Richmond. "Why the Devil Is the Devil." *Proceedings of the American Philosophical Society,* 106 (1962), 427–429.

Laurance, Theodor. *Satan, Sorcery, and Sex.* West Nyack, N.Y., 1974.

LaVey, Anton Szandor. *The Satanic Bible.* New York, 1969.

——. *The Satanic Rituals.* Secaucus, N.J., 1972.

Lecanu, Auguste-F. *Histoire de Satan: Sa chute, son culte, ses manifestations, ses oeuvres, la guerre qu'il fait à Dieu et aux hommes.* Paris, 1861.

LeCompte, E. S. "Milton's Infernal Council and Mantuan." *Publications of the Modern Language Society of America*, 69 (1954), 979–983.

Lee, Vernon [Violet Paget]. *Satan, the Waster.* London, 1920.

———. "Satan's Epilogue to the War." *English Review*, 20 (1915), 199–221.

———. "Satan's Prologue to the War." *English Review*, 29 (1919), 129–140.

Leendertz, P. "Zur Dämonologie des Faustbuchs." *Zeitschrift für Bücherfreunde*, n.s. 15 (1923), 99–106.

Legge, F. "Devil-Worship and Freemasonry." *Contemporary Review*, 70 (1896), 468–483.

Lehmann, Karl. "Der Teufel—ein personales Wesen?" In W. Kasper and K. Lehmann, eds., *Teufel—Dämonen—Besessenheit.* 2d ed. Mainz, 1978. Pp. 71–98.

Lehner, Ernst, and Johanna Lehner. *Devils, Demons, Death, and Damnation.* New York, 1971.

Lenz, Joseph. "Die Kennzeichen der dämonischen Besessenheit und das Rituale Romanum." *Trierer theologische Zeitschrift*, 62 (1953), 129–143.

Leonhard, Kurt. "Der Geist und der Teufel." *Neue Rundschau*, 61 (1950), 588–602.

Lépée, Marcel. "St. Teresa of Jesus and the Devil." In Bruno de Jésus-Marie, ed., *Satan.* New York, 1952. Pp. 97–102.

Leppe, Suzanne. "The Devil's Music: A Literary Study of Evil and Music." Ph.D. diss., University of California, Riverside, 1978.

Leven, Jeremy. *Satan: His Psychotherapy and Cure by the Unfortunate Dr. Kassler, J.S.P.S.* New York, 1982.

Lewis, Clive S. *Perelandra.* London, 1944.

———. *The Screwtape Letters; and, Screwtape Proposes a Toast.* London, 1943.

———. *That Hideous Strength.* London, 1946.

Lewis, Edwin. *The Creator and the Adversary.* New York, 1948.

Lhermitte, Jean. "Pseudo-Possession." In Bruno de Jésus-Marie, ed., *Satan.* New York, 1952. Pp. 280–299.

Lieb, Michael. "Further Thoughts on Satan's Journey through Chaos." *Milton Quarterly*, 12 (1978), 126–133.

Lillie, Arthur. *The Worship of Satan in Modern France.* London, 1896.

Lindberg, Carter. "Mask of God and Prince of Lies: Luther's Theology of the Demonic." In A. Olson, ed., *Disguises of the Demonic.* New York, 1975. Pp. 87–103.

Lindsey, Hal, and C. C. Carlson. *Satan Is Alive and Well on Planet Earth.* Grand Rapids, Mich., 1972.

Liou, Kin-ling. *Etude sur l'art de Victor Hugo dans "La fin de Satan."* Paris, 1939.

Longford, Elizabeth. "Byron and Satanism." *Illustrated London News*, 265, no. 6951 (October 1977), 67–70.

Lucien-Marie de Saint-Joseph, P. "The Devil in the Writings of St. John of the Cross." In Bruno de Jésus-Marie, ed., *Satan.* New York, 1952. Pp. 84–96.

Lussier, Ernest. "Satan." *Chicago Studies*, 13 (1974), 3–19.

Madariaga, Salvador de. *Satanael.* Buenos Aires, 1966.

Madaule, Jacques. "The Devil in Gogol and Dostoievski." In Bruno de Jésus-Marie, ed., *Satan.* New York, 1952. Pp. 414–431.

Mader, Ludwig. "Zum Pakt in Goethes Faust." *Zeitschrift für Deutschkunde*, 37 (1923), 188–191.

Mager, Aloïs. "Satan in Our Day." In Bruno de Jésus-Marie, ed., *Satan*. New York, 1952. Pp. 497–506.

Magny, Claude-Edmond. "The Devil in Contemporary Literature." In Bruno de Jésus-Marie, ed., *Satan*. New York, 1952. Pp. 432–468.

Mahal, Günther. *Mephistos Metamorphosen: Fausts Partner als Repräsentant literarischer Teufelsgestaltung*. Göppingen, 1972.

Maior, Mário Souto. *Território da danação: O diabo na cultura popolar do nordeste*. Rio de Janeiro, 1975.

Mallet, Raymond. *Les obsédés*. Paris, 1928.

Mallow, Vernon R. *The Demonic: A Selected Theological Study*. Lanham, Md., 1983.

Mann, Alfred. "The Riddle of Mephistopheles." *Germanic Review*, 24 (1949), 265–268.

Mann, Thomas. *Doktor Faustus*. Frankfurt, 1947.

Maple, Eric. *The Domain of Devils*. London, 1966.

Maquart, Francis X. "Exorcism and Diabolical Manifestation." In Bruno de Jésus-Marie, ed., *Satan*. New York, 1952. Pp. 178–203.

Marion, Jean-Luc. "Das Böse in Person." *Internationale katholische Zeitschrift*, 8 (1979), 143–250.

Marranzini, Alfredo. "Si può credere ancora nel diavolo?" *Civiltà cattolica*, 128 (April–June 1977), 15–30.

Martin, Malachi. *Hostage to the Devil: The Possession and Exorcism of Five Living Americans*. New York, 1976.

Martins Terra, J. E. *Existe o diabo? Respondem os teólogos*. São Paulo, 1975.

Marty, Martin. "The Devil You Say; The Demonic Say I." In Richard Woods, ed., *Heterodoxy, Mystical Experience, Religious Dissent and the Occult*. Chicago, 1975. Pp. 101–104.

Mason, Eudo C. "Faust and Mephistopheles." In Cyrus Hamlin, ed., *Johann Wolfgang von Goethe—Faust: A Tragedy*. New York, 1976. Pp. 484–504.

———. "Die Gestalt des Teufels in der deutschen Literatur." In W. Kohlschmidt and H. Meyer, eds., *Tradition und Ursprunglichkeit*. Bern, 1966. Pp. 113–125.

———. "The Paths and Powers of Mephistopheles." In *German Studies Presented to Walter Horace Bruford*. London, 1962. Pp. 81–110.

Massignon, Louis. "The Yezidis of Mount Sindjar." In Bruno de Jésus-Marie, ed., *Satan*. New York, 1952. Pp. 158–162.

Massin, Jean. *Baudelaire "entre Dieu et Satan."* Paris, 1946.

Masson, David. *The Three Devils: Luther's, Milton's, and Goethe's*. London, 1874.

Masters, Anthony. *The Devil's Dominion: The Complete Story of Hell and Satanism in the Modern World*. New York, 1978.

Matuszewski, Ignacy. *Duabel w poezyi, historya i psychologia postaci uosabiających zlo w literaturze pięknej wszystkick narodów i weików: Studyum literackoporównawcze*. 2d ed. Warsaw, 1899.

Maurice, René. "De Lucifer à Balthasar: En suivant Robert Bresson." *Lumière et vie*, 78 (1966), 31–53.

May, John R. "American Literary Variations on the Demonic." In A. Olson, ed., *Disguises of the Demonic*. New York, 1975. Pp. 31–47.

McCaffrey, Phillip. "*Paradise Regained:* The Style of Satan's Athens." *Milton Quarterly*, 5 (1971), 7–14.

McDermott, Timothy. "The Devil and His Angels." *New Blackfriars*, 48 (1966), 16–25.

Mellinkoff, Ruth. "Demonic Winged Headgear." *Viator*, 16 (1985), 367–381.

Meyer, C. "Doctrina del magisterio sobre ángeles y demónios." *Concilium: Internationale Zeitschrift für Theologie*, 103 (1975), 391–400.

Meyer, Charles R. "Speak of the Devil." *Chicago Studies*, 14 (1975), 7–18.

Milner, Max. *Le diable dans la littérature française: De Cazotte à Baudelaire 1772–1861*. 2 vols. Paris, 1960.

Minon, A. "La doctrine catholique sur les anges et les demons." *Revue ecclésiastique de Liège*, 38 (1951), 205–210.

Mischo, Johannes. "Dämonische Besessenheit." In W. Kasper and K. Lehmann, eds., *Teufel—Dämonen—Besessenheit*. 2d ed. Mainz, 1978. Pp. 99–146.

Modras, Ronald. "The Devil, Demons, and Dogmatism." *Commonweal*, February 4, 1977, pp. 71–75.

Moeller, C. "Reflexions en marge du 'Satan' des *Etudes Carmélitaines*." *Collectanea Mechliniensia*, 34 (1949), 191–203.

Mohr, Wolfgang. "Mephistopheles und Loki." *Deutsche Vierteljahrsschrift*, 18 (1940), 173–210.

Montgomery, John W., ed. *Demon Possession: A Medical, Historical, Anthropological, and Theological Symposium*. Minneapolis, 1976.

Moore, Olin H. "The Infernal Council." *Modern Philology*, 16 (1918–1919), 169–193, and 19 (1921–1922), 47–64.

Morel, Auguste. *Histoire générale du diable pendant la mission de Jésus-Christ*. Paris, 1861.

Morris, Max. "Mephistopheles." *Goethe-Jahrbuch*, 22 (1901), 150–191, and 23 (1902), 139–176.

Mountford, W. M. "The Devil in English Literature from the Middle Ages to 1700." Ph.D. diss., University of London, 1931.

Muldrow, George M. "Satan's Last Words: 'Full Bliss.'" *Milton Quarterly*, 14 (1980), 98–100.

Müller, Ursula. *Die Gestalt Lucifers in der Dichtung vom Barock bis zur Romantik*. Berlin, 1940.

Murphy, John V. *The Dark Angel: Gothic Elements in Shelley's Works*. Lewisburg, Pa., 1975.

Muschg, Walter. "Goethes Glaube an das Dämonische." *Deutsche Vierteljahrsschrift*, 32 (1958), 321–343.

Musgrove, S. "Is the Devil an Ass?" *Review of English Studies*, 21 (1945), 302–315.

Myre, André. "Satan . . . dans la Bible" [*sic*]. *Relations*, 34 (1979), 173–177.

Nauman, St. Elmo. *Exorcism through the Ages*. New York, 1974.

Neil-Smith, Christopher. *The Exorcist and the Possessed*. St. Ives, Cornwall, 1974.

Newport, John P. *Demons, Demons, Demons: A Christian Guide through the Murky Maze of the Occult*. Nashville, 1972.

———. "Satan and Demons: A Theological Perspective." In J. W. Montgomery, ed., *Demon Possession*. Minneapolis, 1976. Pp. 325–345.

Nicoletti, Gianni. "Sull'origine giacobina del Satana romantico in Francia." *Convivium*, 30 (1962), 416–431.

Niven, Larry, and Jerry Pournelle. *Inferno*. New York, 1976.

North, Sterling, and C. B. Boutell, eds. *Speak of the Devil*. Garden City, N.Y., 1945.

Nugent, Christopher. *Masks of Satan*. London, 1983.

Numbers, Ronald C. "'Sciences of Satanic Origin': Adventist Attitudes toward Evolutionary Biology and Geology." *Spectrum*, 9 (1979), 17–28.

Nunn, Clyde Z. "The Rising Credibility of the Devil in America." *Listening*, 9 (1974), 84–98.

Nyquist, Mary. "The Father's Word / Satan's Wrath." *Publications of the Modern Language Association*, 100 (1983), 187–202.

Obendiek, Harmannus. *Der alt böse Feind: Das biblisch-reformatorische Zeugnis von der Macht Satans*. Neukirchen, 1930.

——. *Satanismus und Dämonie in Geschichte und Gegenwart*. Berlin, 1928.

——. *Der Teufel bei Martin Luther*. Berlin, 1931.

Oberman, Heiko. *Luther: Mensch zwischen Gott und Teufel*. 2d ed. Berlin, 1983.

O'Briant, Walter H. "Is Descartes' Evil Spirit Finite or Infinite?" *Sophia*, 18:2 (1979), 28–32.

O'Connor, Flannery. *The Violent Bear It Away*. New York, 1960.

Oehlke, A. "Zum Namen Mephistophiles." *Goethejahrbuch*, 34 (1913), 198–199.

Oesterreich, Traugott K. *Possession: Demoniacal and Other among Primitive Races, in Antiquity, the Middle Ages, and Modern Times*. London, 1930.

Ohse, Bernard. *Die Teufelliteratur zwischen Brant und Luther*. Berlin, 1961.

Okubo, Kenji. "Mephistopheles in Goethe's Faust." *Doitsu Bungaku*, 31 (1963), 34–43 (in Japanese with German summary).

Olson, Alan M., ed. *Disguises of the Demonic: Contemporary Perspectives on the Power of Evil*. New York, 1975.

——. "The Mythic Language of the Demonic." In Alan M. Olson, ed., *Disguises of the Demonic*. New York, 1975. Pp. 9–16.

Orr, John. "The Demonic Tendency: Politics and Society in Dostoevsky's *The Devils*." *Sociology of Literature*, 26 (1978), 271–283.

——. "Dostoevsky: The Demonic Tendenz." In Orr, *Tragic Realism and Modern Society*. New York, 1977. Pp. 73–86.

Osborn, Max. *Die Teufelliteratur des XVI Jahrhunderts*. Berlin, 1893.

Osterkamp, Ernst. "Darstellungsformen des Bösen: Das Beispiel Luzifer." *Sprachkunst*, 5 (1974), 117–195.

——. *Lucifer: Stationen eines Motivs*. Berlin, 1979.

Oswald, Erich. *Die Darstellung des Teufels in der christlichen Kunst*. Berlin, 1931.

Paine, Lauran. *The Hierarchy of Hell*. New York, 1972.

Palms, Roger C. "Demonology Today." In J. W. Montgomery, ed., *Demon Possession*. Minneapolis, 1976. Pp. 311–319.

Panichas, George A. "Dostoevski and Satanism." *Journal of Religion*, 45 (1965), 12–29.

Panikkar, Raimundo, et al., *Liberarci dal male: Male e vie di liberazione nelle religioni*. Bologna, 1983.

Papini, Giovanni. *Il demonio mi disse* and *Il demonio tentato*. In Papini, *Il tragico quotidiano*. Florence, 1906. Pp. 39–51.

——. *The Devil*. London, 1955.

——. *Un uomo finito*. Florence, 1912.

Parker, Alexander. *The Theology of the Devil in the Drama of Calderón*. London, 1958.

Parry, Michel, ed. *The Devil's Children: Tales of Demons and Exorcists*. New York, 1975.

Parsons, Coleman O. "The Devil and Samuel Clemens." In E. D. Tuckey, ed.,

Mark Twain's Mysterious Stranger and the Critics. Belmont, Calif., 1968. Pp. 155–167.

———. *Witchcraft and Demonology in Scott's Fiction*. Edinburgh, 1964.

Pastiaux, Jean. "Satan, singe de Dieu: Notes sur un aspect de la pensée politique de Georges Bernanos." *Revue des lettres modernes*, 57 (1960), 75–105.

Patrides, C. A. "Renaissance and Modern Views on Hell." *Harvard Theological Review*, 57 (1964), 217–236.

———. "The Salvation of Satan." *Journal of the History of Ideas*, 28 (1967), 467–478.

Paul VI [Giovanni Battista Montini]. "Confronting the Devil's Power." *The Pope Speaks*, 17 (1973), 315–319. Translation of the pope's address "Liberarci del male," *Osservatore romano*, November 15, 1972.

Pearl, Jonathan L. "French Catholic Demonologists and Their Enemies in the Late Sixteenth and Early Seventeenth Centuries." *Church History*, 52 (1983), 457–467.

———. "Humanism and Satanism: Jean Bodin's Contribution to the Witchcraft Crisis." *Canadian Review of Sociology and Anthropology*, 19 (1982), 541–548.

Pelton, Robert. *The Devil and Karen Kingston*. Tuscaloosa, 1976.

———. *In My Name Shall They Cast Out Devils*. South Brunswick, 1976.

Pentecost, J. Dwight. *Your Adversary, the Devil*. Grand Rapids, Mich., 1969.

Perez y González. *El diablo cojuelo: Notas y commentarios*. Madrid, 1903.

Petersdorff, Egon von. *Dämonologie*. 2 vols. Munich, 1956–1957.

———. "De daemonibus in liturgia memoratis." *Angelicum*, 19 (1942), 324–339.

Petit, Jacques, ed. "Barbey d'Aurevilly: L'histoire des *Diaboliques*." *Revue des lettres modernes*, 403–408 (1974), 1–174.

Pezet, Charles. *Contribution à l'étude de la démonomanie*. Montpellier, 1909.

Pfaff, Lucie. *The Devil in Thomas Mann's "Doktor Faustus" and Paul Valéry's "Mon Faust."* Frankfurt, 1976.

Pimentel, Altimar. *O diabo e outras entitades míticas do conto popolar, Paraíba*. Brasilia, 1969.

Praz, Mario. *The Romantic Agony*. 2d ed. London, 1970.

Prévost, Jean-Laurent. *Satan et le romancier*. Paris, 1954.

Puech, Henri-Charles. "The Prince of Darkness in His Kingdom." In Bruno de Jésus-Marie, ed., *Satan*. New York, 1952. Pp. 127–157.

Quinlan, John. "Engelen en duivels." *Tijdschrift voor Theologie*, 7 (1967), 43–62.

Rade, Paul Martin. *Zum Teufelsglauben Luthers*. Gotha, 1931.

Rahner, Karl. "Besessenheit und Exorzismus." In M. Adler, ed., *Tod und Teufel in Klingenberg*. Aschaffenburg, 1977. Pp. 44–46.

———. "Dämonologie." *Lexikon für Theologie und Kirche*. Freiburg, 1959. Vol. 3, pp. 145–147.

Ratzinger, Joseph. "Der Stärkerer und der Starke." In M. Adler, ed., *Tod und Teufel in Klingenberg*. Aschaffenburg, 1977. Pp. 84–101.

Read, Hollis. *The Footprints of Satan; or, the Devil in History*. New York, 1884.

Reaske, Christopher. "The Devil and Jonathan Edwards." *Journal of the History of Ideas*, 33 (1972), 122–138.

Recker, Robert. "Satan: In Power or Dethroned?" *Calvin Theological Journal*, 6 (1971), 133–155.

Reisner, Erwin. *Der Dämon und sein Bild*. Berlin, 1947.

Resch, Andreas. "Wissenschaft und Teufel." In M. Adler, ed., *Tod und Teufel in Klingenberg*. Aschaffenburg, 1977. Pp. 102–107.

Revard, Stella P. "Milton's Gunpowder Poems and Satan's Conspiracy." *Milton Studies*, 4 (1972), 63–77.

———. "Satan's Envy of the Kingship of the Son of God." *Modern Philology*, 70 (1973), 190–198.

———. *The War in Heaven: Paradise Lost and the Tradition of Satan's Rebellion*. Ithaca, 1980.

———. "The Warring Saints and the Dragon." *Philological Quarterly*, 53 (1974), 181–194.

Rhodes, Henry T. F. *The Satanic Mass: A Sociological and Criminological Study*. London, 1954.

Richards, John. *But Deliver Us from Evil: An Introduction to the Demonic Dimension of Pastoral Care*. New York, 1974.

Richman, Robert J. "The Devil and Dr. Waldman." *Philosophical Studies*, 11 (1960), 78–80.

———. "The Ontological Proof of the Devil." *Philosophical Studies*, 9 (1958), 63–64.

Richter, Julius. "Der Character des Mephistopheles im Urfaust." *Neue Jahrbücher für das klassische Altertum, Geschichte, und deutsche Literatur*, 21 (1918), 204–224.

Ricks, Christopher. "Doctor Faustus and Hell on Earth." *Essays in Criticism*, 35 (1985), 101–120.

Ricoeur, Paul. *The Symbolism of Evil*. New York, 1967.

Robinson, William. *The Devil and God*. London, 1945.

Robles, Laureano. "Datos históricos para una revisión de la teologia del diablo." *Studium*, 4 (1964), 433–461.

Rocca, Annette di. *Uber den Teufel und sein Wirken: Beweise seiner Existenz mit Anhang "Teuflische Geschichten."* Munich, 1966.

Rodari, Florian. "Où le diable est légion." *Musées de Génève*, 18 (1977), 22–26.

Rodewyk, Adolf. "Die Beurteilung der Besessenheit: Ein geschichtlicher Uberblick." *Zeitschrift für katholische Theologie*, 72 (1950), 460–480.

———. *Die dämonische Besessenheit in der Sicht des Rituale Romanum*. Aschaffenburg, 1963.

Roets, A. "De duivel en de kristenen." *Collationes brugenses et gandavenses*, 2 (1956), 300–321.

———. "De duivel en de stichting van het Godsrijk." *Collationes brugenses et gandavenses*, 2 (1956), 145–162.

Romi [sic]. *Métamorphoses du diable*. Paris, 1968.

Roos, Keith. "The Devil-Books of the Sixteenth Century: Their Sources and Their Significance during the Second Half of the Century." Ph.D. diss., Rice University, 1968.

———. *The Devil in 16th Century German Literature: The Teufelsbücher*. Frankfurt, 1972.

Roskoff, Gustav. *Geschichte des Teufels*. 2 vols. Leipzig, 1869.

Rougemont, Denis de. *La part du diable*. Paris, 1942.

Rowell, Geoffrey. *Hell and the Victorians: A Study of the Nineteenth-Century Theological Controversies concerning Eternal Punishment and the Future Life*. Oxford, 1974.

Rudat, Wolfgang. "Godhead and Milton's Satan: Classical Myth and Augustinian Theology in *Paradise Lost*." *Milton Quarterly*, 14 (1980), 17–21.

———. "Milton's Satan and Virgil's Juno: The 'Perverseness' of Disobedience in *Paradise Lost*." *Renaissance and Reformation*, 15 (1979), 77–82.

_____. "'Thy Beauty's Heav'nly Ray': Milton's Satan and the Circean Eve." *Milton Quarterly*, 19 (1985), 17–19.

Rudwin, Maximilian. "Béranger's 'Bon Dieu' and 'Bon Diable.'" *Open Court*, 38 (1924), 170–177.

_____. *The Devil in Legend and Literature*. Chicago, 1931.

_____. *Devil Stories: An Anthology*. New York, 1921.

_____. *Les écrivains diaboliques de France*. Paris, 1937.

_____. "Flaubert and the Devil." *Open Court*, 42 (1928), 659–666.

_____. "The Francian Fiend." *Open Court*, 37 (1923), 268–293.

_____. *Romantisme et satanisme*. Paris, 1927.

_____. "Satan and Spiritism in Gautier." *Open Court*, 27 (1923), 385–395.

_____. *Satan et le satanisme dans l'oeuvre de Victor Hugo*. Paris, 1926.

_____. "Satanism in French Romanticism." *Open Court*, 37 (1923), 129–142.

_____. "The Satanism of Barbey d'Aurevilly." *Open Court*, 35 (1921), 83–90.

_____. "The Satanism of Huysmans." *Open Court*, 34 (1920), 240–251.

_____. "Supernaturalism and Satanism in Chateaubriand." *Open Court*, 36 (1922), 257–271, 357–375, 437–448.

_____. "Der Teufel bei Hebbel." *Modern Philology*, 15 (1917–1918), 45–58.

_____. *Der Teufel in den deutschen geistlichen Spielen des Mittelalters und der Reformationszeit*. Göttingen, 1915.

_____. "Des Teufels Schöpferrolle bei Goethe und Hebbel." *Neophilologus*, 4 (1918), 319–322.

Rupp, G. "Luther against 'the Turk, the Pope and the Devil.'" In P. N. Brooke, ed., *Seven-Headed Luther*. Oxford, 1983. Pp. 255–273.

Russell, Bertrand. *Satan in the Suburbs, and Other Stories*. New York, 1953.

Russell, Jeffrey B. *The Devil: Perceptions of Evil from Antiquity to Primitive Christianity*. Ithaca, 1977.

_____. *A History of Witchcraft: Sorcerers, Heretics, Pagans*. London, 1980.

_____. *Lucifer: The Devil in the Middle Ages*. Ithaca, 1984.

_____. *Satan: The Early Christian Tradition*. Ithaca, 1981.

Russell, Ray. *The Case against Satan*. New York, 1962.

Samuel, Irene. "Satan and the 'Diminisht Stars.'" *Modern Philology*, 59 (1962), 239–247.

Santayana, George. *Lucifer*. 2d ed. Cambridge, Mass., 1924.

Sartre, Jean-Paul. *Le diable et le bon Dieu*. Paris, 1951.

Sasek, Lawrence. "Satan and the Epic Hero: Classical and Christian Tradition in 'Paradise Lost.'" Ph.D. diss., Harvard University, 1953.

Sauer, Karl Adolf, ed. *Wächter zwischen Gott und Satan: Priestergestalten aus der Dichtung unserer Zeit*. Rottenburg, 1952.

Sayers, Dorothy. *The Devil to Pay*. London, 1939.

_____. "The Faust-Legend and the Idea of the Devil." *Publications of the English Goethe Society*, n.s. 15 (1945), 1–20.

Schaible, Marlene. "Darstellungen des teuflischen, untersucht an Darstellungen des Engelsturzes vom Ausgang des Mittelalters bis zu Rubens." Ph.D. diss., Tübingen University, 1970.

Scheffczyk, Leo. "Christlicher Glaube und Dämonenlehre." *Münchener theologische Zeitschrift*, 16 (1975), 387–395.

Schirmbeck, Heinrich. "Die Wiederkehr des Teufels." In Hermann Friedmann and O. Mann, eds., *Christliche Dichter der Gegenwart*. Heidelberg, 1955. Pp. 445–463.

Schmücker, Alois. "Gestalt und Wirken des Teufels in der russischen Literatur von ihren Anfängen bis ins 17. Jahrhundert." Ph.D. diss., University of Bonn, 1964.

Schneider, Marcel. *La littérature fantastique en France*. Paris, 1964.

Schöne, Albrecht. *Götterzeichen, Liebeszauber, Satanskult: Neue Einblicke in alte Goethetexte*. Munich, 1982.

Schwab, Günther. *Der Tanz mit dem Teufel: Ein abenteuerliches Interview*. Hannover, 1958.

Schwaeblé, René. *Chez Satan: Roman de moeurs de satanistes contemporains*. Paris, 1913.

——. *Le satanisme flagellé: Satanistes contemporains, incubat, succubat, sadisme, et satanisme*. Paris, 1912.

Schwager, Raymund. "Der Sieg Christi über den Teufel." *Zeitschrift für katholische Theologie*, 103 (1981), 156–177.

Scott, Walter. *Letters on Demonology and Witchcraft*. London, 1830.

Scouten, Kenneth. "The Schoolteacher as Devil in *The Violent Bear It Away*." *Flannery O'Connor Bulletin*, 12 (1983), 35–46.

Sedlmayr, Hans. "Art du démoniaque et démonie de l'art." In Enrico Castelli, ed., *Filosofia dell'arte*. Rome, 1953. Pp. 99–114.

Seiferth, Wolfgang S. "The Concept of the Devil and the Myth of the Pact in Literature Prior to Goethe." *Monatshefte für deutscher Unterricht, deutsche Sprache und Literatur*, 44 (1952), 271–389.

Seignolle, Claude. *Le diable dans la tradition populaire*. Paris, 1959.

——. *Les évangiles du diable selon la croyance populaire*. Paris, 1954.

Semmelroth, Otto. "Abschied vom Teufel? Mächte und Gewalten im Glauben der Kirche." *Theologische Akademie*, 8 (1971), 48–69.

Seth, Ronald. *In the Name of the Devil*. London, 1969.

Sheed, Francis J., ed. *Soundings in Satanism*. New York, 1972.

——. "Variations on a Theme." In Sheed, ed., *Soundings in Satanism*. New York, 1972. Pp. 231–236.

Sielmann, C. "The Devil Within: A Study of the Role of the Devil in Goethe's *Faust*, Dostoevski's *The Brothers Karamazov*, and Mann's *Doktor Faustus*." Master's thesis, Cornell University, 1951.

Sola, Sabino. *El diablo y lo diabólico en las letras americanas (1580–1750)*. Bilbao, 1973.

Sontag, Frederick. *The God of Evil: An Argument from the Existence of the Devil*. New York, 1970.

Souviron, José Maria. *El príncipe de este siglo: La literatura moderna y el demónio*. 2d ed. Madrid, 1967.

Spanos, Nicholas, P., and J. Gottlieb. "Demonic Possession, Mesmerism, and Hysteria: A Social Psychological Perspective on Their Historical Interrelations." *Journal of Abnormal Psychology*, 88 (1979), 527–546.

Spatz, Irmingard. "Die französische Teufeldarstellung von der Romantik bis zur Gegenwart." Ph.D. diss., Munich University, 1960.

Spivack, Charlotte K. "The Journey to Hell: Satan, the Shadow, and the Self." *Centennial Review*, 9 (1965), 420–437.

Stambaugh, Ria. *Teufelsbücher in Auswahl*. 5 vols. Berlin, 1970–1980.

Starkey, Marion L. "The Devil and Cotton Mather." In F. J. Sheed, ed., *Soundings in Satanism*. New York, 1972. Pp. 55–71.

_____. *The Devil in Massachusetts*. New York, 1949.

Staroste, Wolfgang. "Mephistos Verwandlungen." *Germanische-Romanische Monatschrift*, n.s. 11 (1961), 184–197.

Stavrou, Constantine N. "Milton, Byron, and the Devil." *University of Kansas City Review*, 21 (1955), 153–159.

Steadman, John M. "Archangel to Devil": The Background of Satan's Metamorphosis." *Modern Language Quarterly*, 21 (1960), 321–355.

_____. "Eve's Dream and the Conventions of Witchcraft." *Journal of the History of Ideas*, 26 (1965), 567–574.

_____. "Satan's Metamorphoses and the Heroic Convention of the Ignoble Disguise." *Modern Language Review*, 52 (1957), 81–85.

Stein, William B. *Hawthorne's Faust: A Study of the Devil Archetype*. Gainesville, Fla., 1953.

Stock, Robert D. *The Holy and the Daemonic from Sir Thomas Browne to William Blake*. Princeton, 1982.

Stoll, Elmer E. "Belial as an Example." *Modern Language Review*, 48 (1933), 419–427.

_____. "Give the Devil His Due: A Reply to Mr. Lewis." *Review of English Studies*, 20 (1944), 108–124.

Summers, Montague. *The History of Witchcraft and Demonology*. London, 1926.

Sutter, Paul. *Lucifer: Or, the True Story of the Famous Possession in Alsace*. London, 1922.

Ten Broeke, Patricia. "The Shadow of Satan: A Study of the Devil Archetype in Selected American Novels from Hawthorne to the Present Day." Ph.D. diss., University of Texas, 1971.

Teyssèdre, Bernard. *Le diable et l'enfer au temps de Jésus*. Paris, 1984.

_____. *Naissance du diable: De Babylonie aux grottes de la Mer Morte*. Paris, 1984.

Thomas, Keith. *Religion and the Decline of Magic*. New York, 1971.

Thompson, Richard L. *The History of the Devil, the Horned God of the West*. London, 1929.

Tillich, Paul. "Das Dämonische." In Tillich, *Gesammelte Werke*. Stuttgart, 1963. Vol. 6, pp. 42–61.

Tisch, J. H. "Von Satan bis Mephistophelis: Milton und die deutsche Klassik." *Proceedings of the Australian Goethe Society* (1966–1967), 90–118.

Tonquédec, Joseph de. *Les maladies nerveuses ou mentales et les manifestations diaboliques*. 2d ed. Paris, 1938.

Townshend, Luther Tracy. *Satan and Demons*. New York, 1902.

Trachtenberg, Joshua. *The Devil and the Jews*. New Haven, 1943.

Trimpi, Helen P. "Melville's Use of Demonology and Witchcraft in Moby-Dick." *Journal of the History of Ideas*, 30 (1969), 543–562.

Turmel, Joseph. *Histoire du diable*. Paris, 1931.

Twain, Mark [Samuel Clemens]. *No. 44: The Mysterious Stranger*. Berkeley, 1982.

Ulanov, Ann B. "The Psychological Reality of the Demonic." In A. Olson, ed., *Disguises of the Demonic*. New York, 1975. Pp. 134–149.

Unger, Merrill F. *Biblical Demonology: A Study of the Spiritual Forces Behind the Present World Unrest*. Wheaton, Ill., 1967.

_____. *Demons in the World Today: A Study of Occultism in the Light of God's Word*. Wheaton, Ill., 1971.

Urgan, Mîna. "Satan and His Critics." *Istanbul University: Ingiliz Filolojsi Subesi*, 2 (1951), 61–81.

Urrutia, Udalrico. *El diablo: su naturaleza, su poder, y su intervención en el mundo.* 2d ed. Mexico City, 1950.

Urtubey, Luisa de. *Freud et le diable.* Paris, 1983.

Van den Heuvel, Albert. *These Rebellious Powers.* London, 1966.

Van der Hart, Rob. *The Theology of Angels and Devils.* Notre Dame, 1972.

Van Nuffel, Herman. "Le pacte avec le diable dans la littérature." *Anciens pays et assemblées d'états*, 36 (1966), 27–43.

Vatter, Hannes. *The Devil in English Literature.* Bern, 1978.

Veber, Pierre. *L'homme qui vendit son âme au diable.* Paris, 1918.

Verdun, Paul. *Le diable dans la vie des saints.* 2 vols. Paris, 1896.

——. *Le diable dans les missions.* 2 vols. Paris, 1893–1895.

Villeneuve, Roland. *La beauté du diable.* Paris, 1983.

Vinchon, Jean, and Bruno de Jésus-Marie. "The Confession of Boullan." In Bruno de Jésus-Marie, ed., *Satan.* New York, 1952. Pp. 262–267.

Vlad, Roman. "Demonicità e dodecafonia." In Enrico Castelli, ed., *Filosofia dell'arte.* Milan, 1953. Pp. 115–126.

Vogel, Karl. *Begone Satan! A Soul-Stirring Account of Diabolical Possession in Iowa.* New Haven, 1935.

Wagenfeld, Karl. *Luzifer.* Warendorf, 1921.

Waite, Arthur E. *Devil Worship in France; or, The Question of Lucifer.* London, 1896.

Waldman, Theodore. "A Comment on the Ontological Proof of the Devil." *Philosophical Studies*, 10 (1959), 49–50.

Walker, Daniel P. *The Decline of Hell: Seventeenth-Century Discussions of Eternal Torment.* London, 1964.

——. *Spiritual and Demonic Magic: From Ficino to Campanella.* London, 1958.

——. *Unclean Spirits: Possession and Exorcism in France and England in the Late Sixteenth and Early Seventeenth Centuries.* Philadelphia, 1981.

Wallerstein, James, S. *The Demon's Mirror.* 2d ed. New York, 1951.

Walsh, Thomas F. "The Devils of Hawthorne and Flannery O'Connor." *Xavier University Studies*, 5 (1966), 117–122.

Walter, E. V. "Demons and Disenchantment." In A. Olson, ed., *Disguises of the Demonic.* New York, 1975. Pp. 17–30.

Warnke, Mike. *The Satan-Seller.* Plainfield, N.J., 1972.

Wedeck, Harry E. *The Triumph of Satan.* New Hyde Park, N.Y., 1970.

Welbourn, F. B. "Exorcism." *Theology*, 75 (1972), 593–596.

Wenzel, G. "Miltons und Byrons Satan." *Archiv für das Studium der neueren Sprachen und Literaturen*, 83 (1889), 67–90.

Werblowsky, Raphael J. Zwi. *Lucifer and Prometheus: A Study of Milton's Satan.* London, 1952.

West, Muriel. *The Devil and John Webster.* Salzburg, 1974.

Wheatley, Dennis. *The Devil and All His Works.* New York, 1971.

——. *The Devil Rides Out.* London, 1934.

——. *To the Devil—a Daughter.* London, 1953.

White, John. "Problems and Procedures in Exorcism." In J. W. Montgomery, ed., *Demon Possession.* Minneapolis, 1976. Pp. 281–299.

White, John Wesley. *The Devil: What the Scriptures Teach about Him*. Wheaton, Ill., 1977.

White, Lynn, Jr. "Death and the Devil." In Robert Kinsman, ed., *The Darker Vision of the Renaissance*. Berkeley, 1974. Pp. 25–46.

Wigler, Stephen. "The Poet and Satan before the Light: A Suggestion about Book III and the Opening of Book IV of *Paradise Lost*." *Milton Quarterly*, 12 (1978), 51–58.

Willers, Hermann. "Le diable boiteux (Lesage)—el diablo cojuelo (Guevara)." *Romanische Forschungen*, 49 (1935), 215–316.

Williams, Arnold. "The Motivation of Satan's Rebellion in *Paradise Lost*." *Studies in Philology*, 42 (1945), 253–268.

Wills, Garry. "Beelzebub in the Seventies." *Esquire*, 80 (December 1973), 222–224.

Wilson, William P. "Hysteria and Demons, Depression and Oppression, Good and Evil." In J. W. Montgomery, ed., *Demon Possession*. Minneapolis, 1976, Pp. 223–231.

Winklhofer, Alois. *Traktat über den Teufel*. Frankfurt, 1961.

Wolfe, Burton H. *The Devil and Dr. Noxin*. San Francisco, 1973.

Woodman, Ross. "Milton's Satan in Wordsworth's 'Vale of Soul-making.'" *Studies in Romanticism*, 23 (1984), 3–30.

Woods, Richard. *The Devil*. Chicago, 1973.

———. "Satanism Today." In F. J. Sheed, ed., *Soundings in Satanism*. New York, 1972. Pp. 92–104.

Woodward, Kenneth, and D. Gates. "Giving the Devil His Due." *Newsweek*, August 30, 1982, pp. 72–74.

Wooten, John. "Satan, Satire, and Burlesque Fables in *Paradise Lost*." *Milton Quarterly*, 12 (1978), 51–58.

Wurtele, Douglas. "Milton, Satan, and the Sophists." *Renaissance and Reformation*, 15 (1979), 189–200.

Zacharias, Gerhard. *Das Böse*. Munich, 1972.

———. "Satan in Kult und Kunst." In Zacharias, ed., *Das Böse*. Munich, 1972. Pp. 33–40.

———. *The Satanic Cult*. London, 1980.

———. *Satanskult und Schwarze Messe: Ein Beitrag zur Phänomenologie der Religion*. 2d ed. Wiesbaden, 1970.

Zenger, Erich. "Kein Bedarf für den Teufel?" *Herder-Korrespondenz*, 27 (1973), 128–131.

Zumthor, Paul. *Victor Hugo, poète de Satan*. Paris, 1946.

Zweig, Stephan. *Der Kampf mit dem Dämon: Hölderlin, Kleist, Nietzsche*. Leipzig, 1925.

Index

Library of Congress Cataloging-in-Publication Data

Russell, Jeffrey Burton.
  Mephistopheles : the Devil in the modern world.

  Bibliography: p.
  Includes index.
    1. Devil—History of doctrines.   I. Title.
BT981.R865 1986   235'.4'0903   86-47648
ISBN 0-8014-1808-9 (alk. paper)